Strategy and process
in marketing

To the considerate ones:
Jane, Niall, Niamh, Rita and Sinead

Strategy and process in marketing

JOHN A. MURRAY AND AIDAN O'DRISCOLL

Prentice Hall

LONDON NEW YORK TORONTO SYDNEY TOKYO
SINGAPORE MADRID MEXICO CITY MUNICH

First published 1996 by
Prentice Hall Europe
Campus 400, Maylands Avenue
Hemel Hempstead
Hertfordshire, HP2 7EZ
A division of
Simon & Schuster International Group

Typeset in 10/12.5pt Meridien
by Photoprint, Torquay, Devon

Printed and bound in Great Britain by
Hartnolls Limited, Bodmin, Cornwall

Library of Congress Cataloging-in-Publication Data

Murray, John A., Ph. D.
  Strategy and process in marketing / by John A. Murray
and Aidan O'Driscoll.
    p. cm.
  Includes bibliographical references and index.
  ISBN 0-13-182163-6
  1. Marketing–Management.   2. Marketing.
  I. O'Driscoll, Aidan.
  II. Title.
  HF5415.13.M883   1996   95-38852
  658.8'02–dc20   CIP

British Library Cataloguing in Publication Data

A catalogue record for this book is available from
the British Library

ISBN 0-13-182163-6

---

  2 3 4 5   00 99 98 97

Contents

Preface

Strategy and Process in Marketing is written for students on advanced under-graduate, MBA, post-experience and executive development courses on marketing strategy and marketing management. The book explores these topics in a way that reflects the current paradigm shift away from the traditional view of marketing and its predominant emphasis on the immediate consumer, the marketing mix, and the functional form of organization. It embraces a wider network approach with relational marketing, order fulfilment and service as key. Business systems, core processes and re-engineering are incorporated into a reconceptualization of how marketing is managed.

We are struck by the extent to which market realities, organizational innovation and change in marketing practice are all challenging managers in new ways. Leading firms transact their business and manage their marketing in a manner that is very different to that of a decade ago. The serious students and practitioners of marketing are embracing new approaches and fresh perspectives to understanding, learning, organizing and managing in this problematic environment.

One such perspective is process. As the boundaries between traditional departments and functions in organizations, and those between the firm itself and its market environment, blur, a process orientation provides an essential insight. It offers an understanding of how marketing activity and tasks transcend conventional 'functional' organization and of how the firm operates in a business system where networks and partnerships are valuable commercial assets. We see it as opportune to add a process orientation to the more traditional approaches towards the management of marketing.

The discipline of marketing is confronting a dual challenge. First, it must deepen its own competence in functional terms. Technology, different customer requirements and new media all dictate the need for new and evolving expertise. Second, marketing must learn how to integrate better with other departments and functions in the enterprise. This is particularly so in the management of effective marketing strategy, new product and service development and in the achievement of long-term customer satisfaction through dedicated order generation, fulfilment and service activities. The exhortation that everyone in the firm must be marketing oriented must be mapped with clarity and given an organizational foundation and consistency.

The organization of the text

Part I elaborates on the concepts and contexts which effectively form the building blocks of the book. The nature of market focus, the governance of market transactions, as well as sustainable competitive advantage are explored. Markets and customers are perceived as part of a wider business system or chain of value-adding activities which brings products and services from 'mind to market'. The interconnection between consumer, business-to-business, and service markets is highlighted. The firm itself is viewed as a microcosm of this industry business system, key tasks are identified and four core marketing processes are proffered. Finally the job of the marketing manager is examined from his or her perspective.

Part II (which may be addressed more cursorily by those with a knowledge of marketing principles) focuses on the information and intelligence needs required to underpin effective marketing strategy and marketing management. Emphasis is placed on the systematic understanding of customers and customer behaviour; market measurement and marketing research; competitors, their strengths and weaknesses and likely behaviour; industry structure and market forces affecting competitive behaviour; and company resources and competences. It concludes with a discussion on pan-Europeanism and issues of convergence and divergence.

Part III describes how marketing works along with top management at the corporate level in conceptualizing and developing overall company objectives, mission and strategy. The marketing strategy process itself determines the choice of market in which the firm intends to compete. It involves scrutiny of customer need, understanding the firm's competences in the light of market need, assessment of marketing assets and liabilities, and the development of marketing objectives and a broad strategy to serve the chosen market, all within the wider context of the firm's strategic management. Issues of organizing for marketing and balancing the roles of specialists and integrators arise.

Part IV brings us to the traditional heartland of marketing. The marketing management process addresses the competitive positioning of the product or service within its chosen market and involves product choice, pricing, communication and selling, distribution, as well as the development of performance management systems and measures to monitor and adapt execution. Particular attention is placed on the order generation, fulfilment and service (OGFS) process which ultimately operationalizes marketing management. It involves a series of steps from an order being won from a customer to a point, subsequent to any aftersales sales service or query, where the customer may be deemed to be satisfied with the exchange. It thus brings marketing activity through a full circle and closes the loop between strategic intent and final customer satisfaction.

Part V examines the new product development process. Marketing has a leading role to play here. But again it is a role which must be shared with other functions within the organization; the 'rugby'-style simultaneity and speed-to-market now required for NPD success necessitate a high level of organizational teamwork. Further, the marketing manager must have a full understanding of the interrelationship of marketing and design, and appreciate the contribution of first-rate design to superior strategy.

Part VI considers how to sustain market focus over time. Why do excellent companies fail? How do firms renew themselves? How might imaginative marketing re-engineer the business system and change the rule-of-the-game in the industry to the firm's advantage? The successful marketing manager must continually and persistently align and re-align the needs and opportunities of the market with the core competences and consequent product and service offerings of the firm – the key to market focus.

In addition, some 30 marketing in action cases are interspersed throughout the text. These illustrate different aspects of marketing in action across a number of European countries and North America. We hope you enjoy them.

John A. Murray and Aidan O'Driscoll

Part I ■ *Marketing: concepts and contexts*

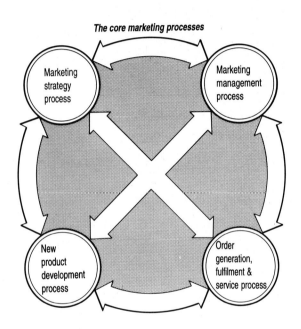

The core marketing processes

Marketing strategy process

Marketing management process

New product development process

Order generation, fulfilment & service process

CHAPTER 1

Market focus

- ▶ Marketing, exchange and transactions
- ▶ Defining marketing
- ▶ Marketing's evolving role in the firm
- ▶ Market focus
- ▶ Managing marketing

Marketing in action case
Swedish Match goes shopping

ABOUT THIS CHAPTER

Because both markets and organizations have been evolving very rapidly, the nature of marketing, which connects markets and organizations, has itself been evolving rapidly. It is suggested that, at this stage of evolution, it is productive to add a strongly process-based view of marketing to more traditional perspectives.

Traditional definitions of marketing abound, but a brief review reveals that the many variations share important common themes. In an evolutionary sense, it is possible to view professional marketing practice as evolving through a number of phases: from production orientation, through sales and marketing orientation to, most recently, market focus. This is seen as a cumulative process with the knowledge and experience of each phase accumulating as part of the bedrock from which each subsequent phase rises.

The concept of market focus is key. It involves the continuing and persistent alignment of a firm's resources and unique competences to changing needs and opportunities in the marketplace in order to create profitable and often durable relationships. In the changing marketing landscape of the late 1990s, market focus is best realized by four core marketing processes.

Marketing's domain

Marketing affects our lives in a most pervasive manner. The clothes we wear, the food we eat, the entertainment we enjoy, the cars, buses, bicycles or trains that bring us to and from work, the houses we live in, the financial services we depend on, the media through which we stay in touch with our world – all are the products of a marketing process which is fundamental to modern societies. Firms as well as public and non-profit organizations are the active elements of the process, and managers are the people who organize the process. The readers of this book will find it difficult to envisage their daily lives without marketing activity.

Despite this pervasiveness of organized market activity the *discipline* of marketing is still far from well elaborated as a science. In common with many disciplines based on professional practice (engineering, medicine, architecture, for example) marketing developed for many years on the basis of the codification of best professional practice. The essence of marketing knowledge lay in the description of marketing activities.

This has changed enormously, and especially in the 1970s and 1980s the discipline moved beyond description to a general focus on analysis and theory building. This is not a matter to be dismissed as relevant only to the academician and researcher. Apart from being fuelled by the researcher's curiosity and search for appropriate theory, the development of marketing has been driven above all by the demand from business for analytical, well-grounded and robust theory to help guide decision-making. The complexity of markets and market transactions has grown rapidly. In parallel, the stakes involved in marketing decision-making have also grown. As a result, traditional 'best practice' is seldom enough to guarantee competitive success. The best companies reach beyond conventional approaches in making decisions. Only a theoretically well-grounded approach to marketing will respond adequately to these managerial imperatives. The need for good analytical technology and for robust theory is a pressing professional need. For the marketing manager there can be nothing more practical than a good theory!

Marketing, exchange and transactions

Marketing is a management process. Its goal is to make exchange take place in a competitive marketplace in a manner that creates mutual profit for particular buyers and sellers. When a seller understands what a buyer needs and has been able to mobilize the resources and activities required to respond with an offering that has an appropriate balance of valued features at an acceptable cost, an exchange can take place. The exchange is profitable for buyers if the offering satisfies their needs, solves their problems – and creates value for them that exceeds the price that they have paid. It is profitable to the seller if the cost of mobilizing resources and undertaking the activities involved in getting to market is less than the price buyers are willing to pay – the seller has created more value than the accumulated cost. The professional practice of marketing deals with organizing profitable exchanges of this nature.

At the centre of the market lies the transaction – the single act of exchange. A transaction involves two parties exchanging value – most typically money for a good or service. A transaction happens once. However, an exchange relationship may be created within which a series of transactions is conducted according to some set of mutual expectations. A transaction is driven on the one hand by a 'customer' who wants a product or service, and on the other, by a 'producer' who has the capability to provide a product or service at a price. The customer's ideal transaction is one in which the product satisfies all relevant needs and costs nothing. The producer's challenge is to provide a product which embodies some acceptable offering for the customer in terms of value content – how well it satisfies the customer's need – and the price that must be charged to cover the cost of producing the product and provide for a return on the investment that has been made in order to complete the production. Producers continuously balance the 'value-for-money' offer that they make in the market – in a sense, find a compromise – by adding or subtracting value content (more or fewer features for the product or service) and increasing or decreasing price in consequence of their decisions about features and as a result of their learning about how to produce more efficiently. Each producer does this in a competitive context and competition is assumed to drive the efficiency of the market. Competition and the customer's freedom to choose then determine which producer's decisions with regard to value and price are most preferred.

What does it take to make a transaction happen? Customers must have needs that can be interpreted and some resources that they can trade in return for a product or service. A producer must have the ability to understand the customers' needs and the capability to create and deliver a product or service that satisfies that need. Marketing is defined by these requirements. Managing marketing is seen as a challenge to the producer to respond to customers' needs, and competition between producers is based on their success in understanding and fulfilling those customers' needs. If we consider such activity in detail, we can quickly begin to envisage the complexity of marketing processes which must be managed creatively and efficiently.

Defining marketing

Definitions of marketing abound, but a quick review will reveal that the many variations share some common themes. McCarthy simply notes that marketing 'provides needed direction for production and helps make sure that the right products are produced and find their way to consumers'.[1] He claims that, together with the production or operations function in business, marketing provides the four basic economic utilities:

1 *Form utility*: the tangible embodiment of the product or service that people actually want, remembering that there can be no utility if no need is satisfied.
2 *Time utility*: having the product or service available when it is needed.
3 *Place utility*: having the product or service available where it is needed.
4 *Possession utility*: obtaining the product or service and having the right to use or consume it, usually in return for money or something else of value, as in barter.

This rather formal statement of the utility created by marketing reflects the familiar cliché that marketing is all about ensuring that consumers get the right product at the right time in the right place and at the right price. The notion of utility and its specific dimensions is helpful when we turn to the task of specifying the goals of marketing activity – the four utilities are precisely those which must be created and delivered to the customer and the exact nature of which the manager must decide.

Drucker's often quoted definition places special emphasis on customer understanding: 'The aim of marketing is to make selling superfluous. The aim is to know and understand the customer so well that the product or service fits him and sells itself.'[2] This definition was well in tune with the 1970s' emphasis on 'customer-as-king' and the popularization of what we now refer to as the 'marketing concept'. The marketing concept stresses customer orientation as a fundamental business philosophy. It emphasizes that customer-oriented firms are more likely successfully to integrate the various activities of production, selling, financing, and human resource management in a profitable manner in the service of chosen customers. The development and popularization of concepts of business process re-engineering by Hammer and Champey in the 1990s have refocused attention once again on this necessity in many companies and provided tools and methodology to tackle the design challenge in a fresh manner.[3]

Kotler and Armstrong, whose work remains seminal to the managerial school of marketing theory, have evolved a tight but quite complex definition: 'Marketing is human activity directed at satisfying needs and wants through exchange processes.'[4] These authors view the core concepts of marketing as: needs, wants, demands, products, exchange, transactions and markets.

Needs

A human need is a state of felt deprivation in a person, ranging from the physical to the psychological, and is intrinsic to the human state rather than created by the world of advertising or social comparison.

Wants

Wants are the forms and manifestations that human needs take when shaped by culture and individual personality and result in the expression of needs in many and varied ways around the world and between individuals. As economies develop so too do the range of wants of citizens. However, Kotler and Armstrong counsel that marketers are well advised to remember the distinction between needs and wants. Needs are basic and unchanging. Wants are changing and often ephemeral. For example, demand for clothing springs from basic needs for shelter (from cold or heat) and from needs for belonging (being in fashion) and for display. The wants associated with these needs are myriad and constantly changing, as can be established by comparing what you will see on any one day in different clothing stores, and day by day and season by season as the stocks in these same stores change in response to what customers buy or refuse to buy. The company that focuses on wants and forgets underlying needs is on the road to failure, leading to that famous comment that 'a manufacturer of drill bits may think that the customer needs a drill bit but what the customer really needs is a hole'.[5] The need for the hole in the do-it-yourself market is, of course, driven by the rather basic need for shelter and home-making, which is then expressed in all the many aspects of demand for construction and home improvement products and services.

Demands

Wants become demands when realized through the allocation of limited buying power to the products that customers judge will provide most satisfaction for their money.

Products

A product is anything that can be offered to a market for attention, acquisition, use or consumption in the satisfaction of a want or need, including not just those things we traditionally view as products or services but also people (for example, politicians), places (for example, tourist destinations), organizations (for example, Amnesty International), activities (for example, ecological responsibility) and ideas (for example, equal opportunity employment). Essentially, we are concerned with things that have some value in the sense that they may become the subject of exchange. What is exchanged for them most typically is money, but may also be political support in an election for a politician's agenda, or time to visit an art gallery to gain some aesthetic pleasure, or national legislative change to join a common economic market.

Exchange

Exchange is central to any concept of marketing and is embodied in the act of obtaining a desired product by offering something of value in return.

Transactions

A transaction involves a trade of values between two parties and is marketing's basic unit of measurement. The transaction may be money-based, may be arranged as a barter or may involve the exchange of psychological commitment.

Markets

A market in the Kotler and Armstrong framework is the set of actual and potential buyers of a product who may deal directly with suppliers or may acquire the products they need through various intermediaries and market mechanisms as markets grow and develop.

Marketing's evolving role in the firm

The nature and role of marketing have evolved considerably and will continue to change. The fact that it is only during the last fifty years that marketing as a word or description has come to enjoy an everyday currency does not mean that marketing activity has not taken place since the start of commercial exchange. The period from the industrial revolution to the 1920s has often been characterized as a *production-oriented* era. The opportunity was to produce goods in large, standardized quantities and get them to large, waiting markets for the first time. If it could be made, it could be sold was often a guiding principle. In any economy, organizations can still be found that claim to produce a good product and that assume the world will somehow turn up to purchase it. This viewpoint often characterizes companies built on a strong but narrow technical or craft tradition. Working to an order backlog and having customers approach the company for its products can reinforce this attitude.

In the short term such organizations will often survive and may even prosper. In the long run their viability is not sustainable, as they have no means to track market changes, new opportunities and competitive threats. By failing to stay in touch with customers the company may also fail to produce the standards of quality demanded by the market. Shoddy products or services reflecting a very parochial concept of quality often lie at the heart of failure, especially in international markets. The central problem with this production orientation is, however, the fact that the product or service is defined in the producer's terms. The result is usually one or a number of the following:

▶ shoddy products or services, where the producer's standards are below those of the market;
▶ over-designed, over-engineered and over-priced products, where the producer uses some technically defined standard of excellence rather than the customers' standard of usefulness in application;
▶ technically well-designed, well-produced and reasonably priced products that just do not fit customers' needs as readily as competitors' offerings, which have been based on a clearly researched approach to serving the user's needs.

It is often suggested that during the 1930s and post-war years the developed economies of Western Europe and North America were characterized by a *sales-oriented* philosophy. This arose from the emergence of an abundance of productive capability and a shift towards a buyer's market, which placed emphasis on competitive rivalry between suppliers. A guiding principle of the sales and marketing functions in companies was often characterized by a commitment to 'moving the product' – the factory made it, the task was for someone else to sell it. Many companies can still be found where sales maximization is considered the role of marketing and the measure of its success. Quite apart from the threat to business viability which this approach ultimately represents, it also embodies the greatest danger of unethical behaviour in marketing. It is characteristic of some ventures created solely to take advantage of customers who are ill-informed and open to the influence of high pressure sales and promotional techniques.

Many companies exhibit a sales orientation temporarily when sales are falling short of budgeted targets. A company not meeting year-end targets will often react by discounting prices, selling and promoting its offering in a particularly aggressive manner to bring actual sales back in line with budget. While such a strategy may pay off in the short run and give the appearance of success, it often represents no more than a transfer of demand from a later period to an earlier one. Stock is often transferred under such circumstances from producers to the distribution or retail trade or indeed to final customers whose future purchases then decline sharply as they gradually run down their heavy stock position. Sales become very difficult to achieve in the new budget period and relationships with trade members and final customers may be damaged by the perception of the supplier as unstable or as a ready target for pressure to reduce prices in any future period.

The emergence of a *marketing orientation* is often dated to sometime in the 1950s in more developed economies and more sophisticated companies. This marked the realization that the core market-related task was not to make products or to sell what factories could produce, but rather to understand market demand well enough to specify what should be produced and to see that this 'right' product could be brought to the 'right customer' at the 'right price' and at the 'right' time and place. It was from this perspective that the marketing concept emerged as a guiding, company-wide philosophy: profits and competitive success derive from seeing customer needs as the guiding principle in strategy and in coordinating company activities to serve them profitably. Out of this phase of evolution emerged the marketing department as a commonplace element of any organization, headed up by a marketing manager. The marketing concept emphasized that a customer orientation led to long-term profitability. Profit, not sales maximization, was stressed as the objective of marketing activity, but profitability was seen as the outcome of dedication to serving market needs.

The marketing concept also saw as essential that all the activities of the business should be coordinated, with profit through customer satisfaction as the common unifying objective. This implied that not only should marketing and sales activities be dedicated to the objective of satisfying customer needs, but all activities, including manufacturing, R&D, finance and human resource management, should be imbued with the same dedication to customer service. Such integration should ensure a common, clear and market-directed orientation in the entire company. This emphasis on integration is of considerable organizational importance and marked a transition in the development of thinking about marketing from one of viewing it as a relatively independent business function to one of seeing it as an integrative force, which should therefore have effective interfaces with all other business functions. This development laid the groundwork for the development of a sub-field within marketing that came to be called strategic marketing and strategic market planning.[6, 7, 8, 9] The more strategic aspects of marketing could now be seen as an essential part of the work of general management – coordinating all the company's activities to focus on delivering customer satisfaction at a profit.

It could now be claimed with considerable weight that no general manager could perform effectively without applying a marketing approach to the management of the business, and no business strategy could be complete without a foundation in identified customer needs and a commitment to mobilizing the company's resources to serve these needs. However, it takes the application of a process view of organizations to harness these evolving perspectives effectively to the role of marketing. As we shall see in the next chapter, such a process view recognizes the flatter and less layered nature of today's organization structure. The need to respond quickly and effectively to changing market and customer requirements necessitates management focusing increasingly on tasks which cut across traditional company boundaries and functions. The 'boundary-less' firm of the future suggests seamless multi-functional activity where the emphasis is on managing a process to fulfil key customer and market-focused tasks.

As long as the view is just of marketing as a function, the issues of integration in strategy and of organizational coordination around customer orientation all too easily slip into the hopelessness of exhortation across organizational walls – the marketing function encouraging, cajoling, harassing others to be customer-oriented and integrated in their decision-making. Hierarchy and functional organization have to be joined by heterarchy and process organization before this begins to work effectively. A transition towards this is now in progress.

Of the business functions, marketing remains unique in its outward-looking nature. Because it is committed to the market and the customer it is fundamentally concerned with the external environment of the firm. This feature also gives it a vital role in the formulation of business strategy since its role is so central to the identification and choice of the markets the company will serve and therefore of the competitive arenas in which it must prove superior. This is the very essence of the basic business decision concerning the answer to the perennial question 'What business are we in?'

Market focus

A more recent phase has seen the development of the market-focused company. The concept of market focus and the importance of core competences have helped to expand our earlier notion of the marketing concept.[10, 11] These additions to our perspective on marketing are strategic in nature and are based on assumptions about the vital interdependence of business strategy, organizational capability, company performance, market and competitive realities, and marketing action. The importance of the core competences or capabilities of any company to its ability to survive and prosper has always been acknowledged, but the aggressive market and competitive orientation of management in Western companies sometimes caused them to pay too little attention to the fundamental resource base of the organization. The resurgence of attention to identifying, nurturing and managing core competences has been driven by a world market in which product lifecycles have become much shorter than the life of the key competences that produce those products. Thus the relationship between organizations and their markets must be guided not only by looking out creatively and analytically into those markets, but also by looking deeply inward to the company's competences in order to understand what it is truly superior to competition in doing.

This new emphasis might be captured by the image of marketing as scissors-like: one blade represents real market understanding and market orientation and the other represents the organization's competence to do certain things very well. When the two blades are present and coordinated, one has an effective scissors. With only one blade, however, little is likely to result. The emphasis is, therefore, on an effective marriage of market need and company competence. This differs significantly from the marketing orientation of the 1970s which was often interpreted, especially by marketing professionals, to mean that marketing should lead and coordinate the other aspects of a business. The emphasis of the 1990s is on interdependence and a more integrated approach to management, represented in marketing by the notion of *market focus* – aligning in a very focused manner the unique competences of any one organization with chosen needs and opportunities in the marketplace. The challenge is therefore to develop ways of analyzing and designing company processes that couple precisely with distribution and consumption processes. As we shall see in Chapter 3, these company processes may be thought of as carefully constructed and integrated value-adding activities, which underpin profitable exchange for both the customer and the company.

Along with this development of market focus has come a need to reappraise the past concentration of marketing on short-term market transactions and to deal with the nature of the *relationship-based* markets, which began to attract great attention in the 1980s. Kotler suggests that marketing is characterized by 'a movement away from a focus on exchange – in the narrow sense of transaction – and toward a focus on building value-laden relationships and marketing networks'.[12] Marketing is increasingly a matter of managing networks and relationships within which transactions take place. This does not necessarily imply that we should move away from a transaction focus as suggested by Kotler, but rather that we must develop the ability to understand and manage systems and structures in which multiple transactions take place in a relatively stable and predictable manner. It is the governance and management of multiple transactions over time, and in a more or less stable set of understandings between exchange partners, that call for new theoretical understanding and managerial skills. The interest in relationship-based markets reflects the major shift in many business-to-business as well as consumer markets towards buyer–supplier partnerships, especially as pioneered by Japanese manufacturing industry. There are good economic reasons for the concern. It has been noted that in mature markets it may cost five times as much to attract a new customer as to maintain the goodwill of an existing customer.[13] Under such circumstances, sound established relationships are of great value. It can be said that we are moving towards a definition of marketing which emphasizes mutual profitability for the two parties involved in a market relationship.

This perspective on marketing, while differing from the various previous views of its role, is not a substitute for them. It rather represents a further stage of evolution in the managerial interpretation and professional practice of marketing. This is represented in Figure 1.1 by the successive layering of approaches to marketing, suggesting that the approaches of the 1990s both build on previous traditions and practice and extend these in new ways. And just as we see the management of marketing as creatively combining market needs with the unique competences of the organization, so too our evolving conceptualization of marketing reflects both the demands of a changing competitive marketplace for better ways of thinking about marketing and the developing ability or competence of the marketing discipline to analyze and explain markets.

It is interesting to note that one may still find individual companies, and even economies, at various stages of development along the continuum suggested. There are many firms still firmly rooted in a production orienta-

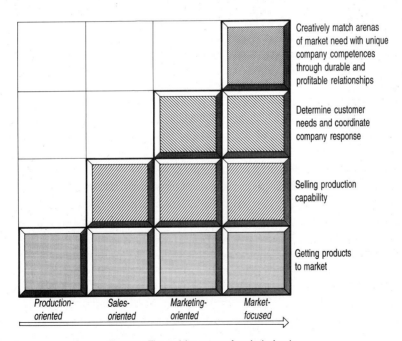

Figure 1.1 The evolving nature of marketing's role

tion just as there are managerial pioneers winning market focus by matching corporate capability to market need. Equally, many firms have evolved
along this continuum (see Exhibit 1.1). Being 'stuck' at either a production
or sales-oriented phase of development will in general have unpleasant
consequences in the competitive markets of today, while an acceptance of
the marketing orientation of the 1970s and 1980s will prove insufficient to
meet the challenge of world-class competition in the 1990s.

Exhibit 1.1	*Marketing in action case*

Swedish Match goes shopping

Swedish Match, a world leader in matches and lighters, is part of the
Scandinavian-owned Branded Consumer Products AB, a consortium of businesses
ranging from beer and mineral water to food and tobacco. Branded Consumer
Products established its global postion by acquisition of firms in the matches and
lights business and, with the fall-off of cigarette smoking in Europe, by
imaginative diversification into consumer branded products.

One of its more interesting acquisitions in the early 1980s was a small, Irish fast-
moving consumer goods (FMCG) distributor whose own experience over the
previous decade very much mirrored that of Swedish Match itself. Maguire and
Paterson was founded in 1882 to manufacture matches in Dublin and flourished to
become the sole manufacturer of matches in Ireland and the dominant supplier to
the market. The hallmark of Maguire and Paterson was efficiency in the
manufacture of a high quality match, comparable to any produced in the world.
The company laid great emphasis on continuity and enjoyed excellent industrial
relations with its 160 employees, although its management style was conservative
and production-oriented.

However, by the mid-1970s it was becoming clear that a storm cloud, in the form
of a change in consumer behaviour, was threatening Maguire and Paterson's
profitability. Put simply, people were beginning to smoke less – and some 70 per
cent of matches were used to light cigarettes, the rest for domestic purposes. To
aggravate matters further, the growing sales of imported disposable lighters in
Ireland were beginning to make noticeable inroads into the demand for matches.

Management at Maguire and Paterson had to adapt or die. Yet what were the
options? Its skill in match-making represented very little synergistic possibility to
manufacture any other type of product. The answer lay in the company's
distribution network. Here the company had an expertise and experience built
literally over generations. Could it identify products which had similar consumer
characteristics as matches, i.e. intensive/wide distribution, small purchase
decision, national brand advertising supported by point-of-sale merchandising,
and so on, and push them through this network? It would not have to manufacture
such products but market them on an agency basis.

In 1977 Maguire and Paterson acquired the agency for Wilkinson Sword shaving products and Foster Grant sunglasses in Ireland. Over subsequent years brands like Dart disposable lighters, Marigold rubber housegloves, Newey hair care products and Revlon shampoo products were added to the list. By the end of 1980 annual turnover at Maguire and Paterson stood at £5.1million with £2.1million coming from its personal care and household range of products.

The diversification programme obviously involved a very substantial reorientation on the part of Maguire and Paterson. Its management approach and capability had to be regenerated. A marketing director was appointed and under him an effective marketing function with skills in branding and product development was nurtured. Sales representation was increased and the distribution network deepened. By 1980 the number of employees had increased to 190. As Maguire and Paterson moved into the 1980s it had come to see itself increasingly as a marketing and distribution company of FMCG goods through a network of supermarket, retail, grocery, chemist and hardware outlets.[14]

Managing marketing

Marketing's changing landscape

In a number of regards the competitive landscape of the 1990s is significantly different from that of previous decades. Important new modes of manufacturing and service, e.g., total quality management (TQM), have taken widespread root in Western firms. The nature of organizations has changed; the possibilities and demands of new technology, real-time communication and innovative products and services have necessitated flatter structures and a consequently greater staff empowerment at lower levels. Marketing is increasingly characterized by the pressures of intense competition, fragmented and deregulated markets, more sophisticated customers requiring more segmented and targeted approaches, multi-media technology, and powerful distributor/retailer networks. Table 1.1 summarizes the key features of this changing landscape under a number of headings.

Markets

Following the Second World War, industrial output in Western economies grew at an unprecedented level until being slowed by the oil crises of the 1970s. Most markets exhibited high growth, stable behaviour and concentrated structures. By contrast, as the millennium approaches, markets show more modest levels of growth and new forms of competition. Western governments have adopted *laissez-faire* economic polices, which have involved considerable deregulation in many spheres. Further, fragmentation in market structures is to be observed to a greater extent.

Table 1.1 Marketing's changing landscape

	1960s 1970s 1980s	1990 towards 2000
Markets	High growth	Modest growth
	Concentrated	Fragmented
	Regulation	Deregulation
Customers	Accepting/trusting	Sophisticated/demanding
	Homogeneous	Micro segmented
Marketing Modes and	Mass marketing	Niche/highly targeted
Responses	Advertising-led	Databased/multi-media technology
	'Plan–do' time gap	Speed of response
Channels of Distribution	Traditional structures	New powerful players

Customers
The era of the trusting, easily defined, homogeneous consumer has also faded. The customer to whom the marketer is now appealing has become increasingly sophisticated, sceptical, demanding and literate – basically harder to persuade. This is particularly true of younger consumers for whom consumption is often an act of self-expression and empowerment. The propensity of marketers to segment into smaller 'micro' categories and to develop databases, allied to the increasing array of communication modes, has both produced and responded to audience fragmentation and decreased effectiveness in traditional mass marketing appeals.

Marketing modes and responses
Technology, greater leisure time availability and changing socio-economic and demographic factors have resulted in a fractionalism in advertising media, particularly TV and print. New magazines and newspaper titles, extra national, regional and even global television channels, the development of the 'super highway', the Internet and multimedia instruments have all conspired to make the marketer's job of communicating with the target audience more difficult. This complexity is further compounded by the increasing heterogeneity and segmentation in customer profiles. The need for speed-of-response in the context of shortening product lifecycles is a further hurdle for the marketer.

Channels of distribution
An important feature of the last decade has been the increasing sophistication, abetted by new technology, in channels of product and service distribution. Just-in-time delivery modes, automated teller machines

(ATMs) and electronic point-of-sale (EPOS) systems are all widely used. There has been the rise of new powerful players along the distribution chain. In the food and clothing industries, for example, retailing structures have become very concentrated, with a smaller number of retailers controlling a greater share of the market than was previously the case. One result has of this been the rise of so-called distributor own brands (DOBs).

Process in marketing

Such an altered landscape requires that traditional approaches to marketing practice be strengthened by others. In particular, marketing is benefiting from a process view of its activity and tasks. Many subdisciplines in business studies have embraced a process perspective to assist in understanding how organizations might work better and enterprises be managed more effectively in the challenging circumstances of the late 1990s. Concepts like core business processes and re-engineering reflect a belief that traditional functional organization has limitations, and benefits from a process approach. To reiterate, it is worthwhile to overlay function and hierarchy with task and heterarchy.

A process perspective encourages the manager to reassess existing modes of doing business. It assumes that firms are likely to be underperforming if they adhere only to conventional beliefs about what each function should do and how work should be organized. Instead, it suggests a focus on the key tasks and activities involved in bringing products and services to market in a way that ensures satisfied customers and firm profitability. Starting with the customer, it 'unbundles' performance in order to reconfigure it more effectively. The relentless customer focus that a process orientation must take makes it particularly important for marketing to embrace such an approach.

Core marketing processes

Marketing activity is best managed in terms of four core processes – a marketing strategy process, a marketing management process, an order generation, fulfilment and service process, and a new product development process (see Figure 1.2). As a process approach challenges conventional notions about hierarchical/functional 'ownership' of task, a first important point to be made about these four marketing processes is that only one – marketing management – is owned and managed exclusively by the marketing department. Marketing has a driving role in the other three, but they must be shared and co-managed with many other functions and departments in the firm:

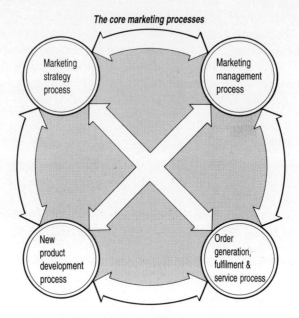

Figure 1.2 The core marketing processes

1 *The marketing strategy process* determines the choice of market in which the firm intends to compete. It involves scrutiny of customer need, understanding the firm's competences in the light of market need, assessment of marketing assets and liabilities, and the development of marketing objectives and a broad strategy to serve the chosen market, all within the wider context of the firm's strategic management. Issues of organizing for marketing and balancing specialists and integrators arise. Managing performance and programming action lead to the next process.

2 *The marketing management process* addresses the competitive positioning of the product or service within its chosen market, whom precisely to serve and what particular benefits to propose to the customer. It involves product choice, pricing, communication and selling, distribution, as well as the development of performance management systems and measures to monitor and adapt execution. This is very much the heartland of marketing.

3 *The order generation, fulfilment and service (OGFS) process* operationalizes the day-to-day business of achieving customer satisfaction in a manner that is profitable to the firm. It involves generating orders and managing these orders 'through' the organization. It includes activities, often multidisciplinary, such as costing, order entry and prioritization, scheduling, delivery, invoicing, installation, service and aftersales support.

4   *The new product development (NPD) process* concerns itself with renewing the firm's portfolio of goods and services. While rooted in the firm's overall strategy, it encompasses activities such as idea generation, concept screening and development, product development and launch.

These four processes, while forming the basis for marketing practice, might best be thought of as the 'technology' of marketing. The technology is the servant of a set of values and assumptions which governs the success of marketing activity. At the heart of these values and assumptions lie the notions of market focus along with concepts about the nature and governance of transactions, the role of the marketing manager, and the nature of the competitive marketplace, as we shall see in the next chapter.

Market focus – *the continuing and persistent alignment of a firm's resources and unique competences to changing needs and opportunities in the marketplace in order to create profitable and often durable relationships* – is best realized by these four core marketing processes. The marketing strategy process enables customers to be identified in a 'ballpark' context – where they are in the market and what their characteristics and requirements are. The marketing management process sets the agenda for delivering to those customers – the type of product, its broad price level, promotion and feasible distribution outlets. The order generation, fulfilment and service process actually 'connects' with the customers. It enables strategic intent to be successfully fulfilled. The new product development process looks to the future to ensure a continuing application of the firm's competence to market need in order to sustain market focus.

REVIEW QUESTIONS

1.1   Consider some definitions of marketing and examine what common themes run through them.

1.2   Assess the view that it is possible to observe marketing activity in the firm evolving through a number of phases. Can you recognize companies known to you in each of the phases?

1.3   What is meant by the concept of market focus?

1.4   In what ways is the marketing landscape of the 1990s significantly different from that of previous decades?

1.5   Why is it productive to add a strongly process-based view of marketing to more traditional perspectives?

CHAPTER 2

Marketing contexts

▶ Transactions
▶ Marketing processes
▶ The marketing manager
▶ The competitive marketplace
▶ International marketing

Marketing in action case
The organization of tomorrow

ABOUT THIS CHAPTER

The conventional managerial presentation of marketing activity centres on the 4Ps of product, place, price and promotion. The emphasis is on short-term transaction and gain, and on the formulation and subsequent implementation of decisions and plans based on these 4Ps. In this book, *marketing processes* are seen as the pivotal concept and four core marketing processes are proffered – the marketing strategy process, the marketing management process, the order generation, fulfilment and service process, and the new product development process. Marketing is uniquely responsible for the marketing management process (in the conventional functional or disciplinary sense) and must be the co-owner and co-manager of the other three processes.

In order to understand more fully how these processes work, it is necessary to re-examine the ways in which transactions are governed – whether by open markets, by managed arrangements or by hybrid forms of both, such as partnerships and alliances. It is also useful to revisit the role of the marketing manager as the critical actor and to consider dimensions of today's competitive marketplace as the context for action.

Understanding the key concepts

This book treats of several aspects of marketing which demand some further discussion at this early stage. It focuses on the *transaction*, on the linked activities that constitute what we propose are the *core marketing processes*, on the *marketing manager* as the critical actor, and on the *competitive marketplace* as the context for action. This is different from the more conventional treatment of marketing and its management in the textbooks that have dominated the field since McCarthy's and Kotler's early work. These latter authors built their treatment of the subject around the concept of there being four elementary decision areas in marketing management – the so-called 4Ps of product, price, promotion and place (distribution). They established a tradition of studying marketing by looking at the analysis necessary to these decision areas and the organizational necessities for implementing decisions. In this book, the marketing processes are taken as the pivotal concept and marketing activity is perceived as best managed through these four processes – the marketing strategy, marketing management, order generation, fulfilment and service, and new product development processes.

The transaction is used as the basic unit of analysis and the four core processes as the organizational means of making transactions possible and profitable. Examining the ways in which transactions are governed – whether by open markets, by managed arrangements or by hybrid forms of both – helps to explain the manner in which marketing's managerial work varies in different contexts and to provide some reasons for the structure and dynamics of markets in different industries.

Transactions

A transaction involves a trade of values between a buyer and seller. It may also be seen as a form of contracting – a promise of a want satisfied in return for a promise of consideration to be paid. The particular character of a transaction will lead to different ways of organizing the execution of the transaction. For example, a 'simple' transaction might be seen as one for which the 'product' may be produced without any great investment or the commitment of very special purpose assets, where there is little uncertainty about the outcome and consequences of the transaction and which is repeated frequently. In such cases one would generally expect an open and competitive market transaction to be the most efficient resolution of how to conduct and complete the transaction.

In contrast, visualize a transaction whose execution requires investment in special purpose assets which may not be readily deployed to produce other products or services in other ways (e.g. a pulp mill for making paper pulp or an airline reservation system), where there is considerable uncertainty about the outcome and consequences, and which is repeated infrequently. In such instances the open competitive market transaction may provide a less satisfactory and less efficient resolution. Transaction cost theory would predict that under the latter circumstances the transaction will tend to be managed, or governed, by other ways of organizing – by relationship marketing (which may be viewed as a form of bilateral trading), by hybrid forms of organization such as alliances, networks, joint ventures and franchising, or ultimately by so-called vertical integration under unified ownership.[1,2]

In the case of vertical integration – that is where one organization owns several, or all, of the stages of production and distribution in an industry – the managerial hierarchy and its rules and procedures replace the classical open market contract. Marketing, in such circumstances, turns its attention to 'internal' or 'organizational' marketing in order to preserve the purpose and enhance the efficiency of the 'internalized' transactions. In the case of the market for paper pulp, the answer is often to absorb the market into a vertically integrated system where the pulp-maker and the paper-maker customer exist under unified ownership. The market is frequently internalized – that is, brought inside the organization – because of the size of investment involved, the specialized nature of the pulp mill (it cannot make anything else – and not even all types of pulp!), the uncertainties of over- and undercapacity in the industry and the fact that the mill will have a 10–15-year life. In the case of the airline reservation system, the answer has typically been to manage the market for its services through an alliance of several airlines. Here, a number of airlines have joined together to fund the investment in the development of the system and then retained exclusive rights for themselves to the services produced.

Considering the manner in which transactions are organized, therefore, allows us to understand many of the basic concerns of managing marketing and gives us insight into the demands placed on marketing managers under the different circumstances represented by forms of transaction, ranging from classical 'open' market contracting to relationships, networks, alliances and joint ventures, franchising or vertical integration, such as suggested in Figure 2.1. It can be observed that as one moves along this spectrum towards the 'managed market' end, the nature of the exchange and transaction involves relationships and supporting structures which become deeper, more long term and more codified. Each of these alternative ways of organizing the individual transaction, and its extension into exchange relationships, reflect a struggle for the most efficient solution to the complex problem of managing exchange activity by minimizing the transaction costs involved.

Marketing processes

The focus on the linked activities that constitute marketing processes helps to identify and understand the systemic aspects of marketing and its

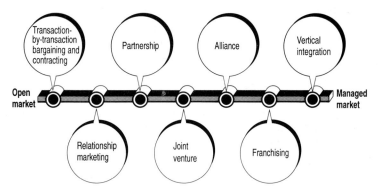

Figure 2.1 Alternative ways of managing transactions

management, and in particular to draw attention to the challenge faced in managing processes that span internal organizational boundaries. The fundamental order generation, fulfilment and service provision process is one that 'crosses' almost every hierarchical departmental frontier within an organization. A traditional platform of the marketing concept – orienting the company in a unified manner towards the satisfaction of its customers – emerged from the struggles of early marketing departments with organizational problems in delivering promises to customers. The development and popularizing of business process re-engineering and redesign tools and techniques provide marketing with improved methods of diagnosing problems in serving markets adequately and in creating integrated processes to focus on value creation for both customer and supplier. In their research among companies that led to the publication of their influential book, *Reengineering the Corporation*, Hammer and Champey note that they 'found that many tasks that employees performed had nothing at all to do with meeting customer needs. . . many tasks were done simply to satisfy the internal demands of the company's own organization'.[3] Furthermore, they claim that:

> in most companies today, no one is in charge of the processes. In fact, hardly anyone is aware of them. Does any company have a vice president in charge of order fulfillment, of getting products to customers? Probably not. Who is in *charge* of developing new products? Everyone – R&D, marketing, finance, manufacturing, and so on – is involved, but no one is in charge. . . People involved in a process look *inward* toward their department and *upward* toward their boss, but no one looks *outward* toward the customer. [4] (emphasis added)

As can be seen from Figure 1.2 (p. 18), our particular concern is with four core marketing processes: the marketing strategy process, the marketing management process, the order generation, fulfilment and service process, and the new product development process. It is contended that marketing must be *uniquely responsible* for the marketing management process (in the conventional functional or disciplinary sense), and must be the *co-owner* and *co-manager* of the other three processes.

A process map of an organization may look very different from our traditional map of hierarchical relationships – the traditional organigram. The organigram maps hierarchy; the process map documents heterarchy. Heterarchy describes interconnected nodes, without any necessary implication concerning a permanent or single node that has dominant position, power or authority. Marketing has been familiarly positioned in the hierarchy of the organigram as a 'function' with a reporting line and accountability upward to general and top management and authority downward to sub-areas such as product management, sales, marketing research, advertising and promotion. But when we examine how organizations actually function and malfunction, the hierarchy is often most revealing of the origins of malfunction. Marketing strategy, for example, is rooted in the general practice and theory of strategic management, in which considerations of markets are of the essence and in which marketing decisions are concerned with market choice. There are few more fundamental decisions for the organization than its choice of market. This establishes its domain and the competitive arena in which it must then succeed in outperforming competitors. These are matters of corporate and business strategy that deal with *market-based* issues. They are not the preserve of the marketing function, but they do demand the knowledge that specialist marketing practice, theory and education should provide. They demand that the role of senior manager as marketer and marketer as senior manager be played.

Between strategy and the transaction lie the processes of order fulfilment and new product development. What is an order fulfilment process and how should it be designed and managed? The process begins in abstraction in the context of market arenas in which demand may be realized by the resources at the command of the organization; potential exchanges must be sought out and confirmed – the order generation process. The continuing process must next run through myriad activities, which include such elements as order entry, credit checking, prioritization and scheduling of order, assembly and manufacturing – whether of product or service, shipment, receipt, payment, installation, consumption, and support and service provision. Whose process is this? Not marketing's the hierarchy tells us! It is a multidisciplinary, multi-functional process involving people from many parts of the organization – a story best told in terms of heterarchy and a process map.

The tradition in much of marketing has been to see the marketing department as 'owning' some of the activities and exhorting everyone else in the organization to be 'customer-oriented'. We see marketing as part of the team that manages the process – a team whose members encompass knowledge about all relevant process activities. Marketing as part of a core process team must be expert in the specialized knowledge of marketing *and* in the integration of that competence with that of other disciplines. In the hierarchy of the organization, marketing is 'home' to this competence – a place where the intellectual capital of marketing is nurtured and its competitive distinctiveness enhanced. But marketing action is in the heterarchy of the organization – in the process and the team. The same argument may be made with regard to the new product development process. It is only when we look at the marketing management process that we find a more unifunctional, unidisciplinary process for which marketing experts must be held solely responsible and accountable. The marketing management process is the heartland of the professional discipline, dealing with the acquisition, deployment and enhancement of specialist marketing knowledge and contributing through its interaction with the other core processes of marketing strategy, order generation, fulfilment and service, and new product development, to the successful management of the market relationships of the firm.

These four key marketing processes and those involved are visualized in Figures 2.2–2.5. As is suggested, the marketing strategy process is managed in a manner that fully integrates with the wider strategic management of the firm – it is a vital part of overall business strategy. It must take business strategy fundamentals as part of its parameters, while at the same time informing and shaping business strategy through its deep insights into the market and competition. The marketing management process is marketing's 'home ground'. It is fully responsible for the expertise and competences required to conduct this work in a manner that contributes directly to the firm's overall competitive advantage and to the sustaining of this advantage. Skill in marketing management should therefore be regarded and managed as an intangible asset of the firm. The marketing manager's role is to manage this asset as a distinctive competence – one that embodies knowledge, skills and attitudes that set it apart from competitors – and in doing so to give the company a basis for outperforming competition on marketing-related issues. We argue that marketing must become the co-owner, as in the strategic marketing process, of both the vital processes of order generation, fulfilment and service and of new product development. It cannot be the sole owner, as tasks and activities cross functional and disciplinary lines and are completely dependent for their success on multi-disciplinary cooperation. Process management is the work of teams and marketing must therefore learn the skills of team work. Exhibit 2.1 conveys some of the characteristics and dynamics of this process approach.

| Exhibit 2.1 | *Marketing in action case* |

The organization of tomorrow

Today's middle managers have the life expectancy of flies in October. Managers at all levels will need to abandon the notion that their jobs are primarily concerned with direction and control. The twenty-first-century manager will be an adviser, a communicator and a facilitator. Self-managed teams of employees will replace today's hierarchical organization.

As one of the advocates of employee self-management and empowerment notes, 'In the future executive positions will not be defined in terms of collections of people, like head of the sales department, but in terms of process, like senior-VP-of-getting-stuff-to-customers, which is sales, shipping, billing. You'll no longer have a box on an organization chart. You'll own part of a process map.'

There are three powerful forces driving this fundamental restructuring of the way we work. The first of these is the 'high-involvement' workplace where operations are conducted by self-managing work teams. Employees are empowered to make decisions rather than constantly having to refer to supervisors and managers for direction. This results in spectacular increases in productivity, quality and morale.

The second driving force is a new emphasis on managing what is termed 'business processes'. Business processes form the link between high-performance work teams and the organization at large. They break up the fratricidal fighting between the traditional functional departments of the organization which results in sub-optimal performance. Organising around business processes involves getting employees from differing functional backgrounds working together for the benefit of the firm's customers, rather than pursuing the often conflicting interests of the various functional departments. In a financial institution, lending officers, title searchers and credit checkers work together, not sequentially.

The third driving force concerns information. In the traditional hierarchical organization communication is indirect and filtered by the structure. Decision-making takes longer. In the new organization, if you have a problem with people upstream from you, you deal with them directly, rather than going through the hierarchy. The result is phenomenal increases in productivity and reaction times.

McKinsey & Co. claim that companies applying the new principles of organization can cut their cost base by a third or more. This claim is based on results achieved by organizations that have already transformed their structures: an industrial goods manufacturer which cut costs and raised productivity more than 50 per cent; a financial services company where costs fell by 34 per cent. These results do not stem from small incremental changes in organization structure. Rather, to create the organization of the twenty-first century what is required is dramatic and radical restructuring.

McKinsey & Co. give a blueprint for achieving the organization of tomorrow. Organize primarily around process, not just function. Base performance objectives on customer needs. Identify the processes that meet those needs. These processes, not departments, become the company's main components. Link performance objectives and evaluation of all activities to customer satisfaction. Make teams, not individuals, the focus of organization performance. Individuals acting alone do not have the capacity to improve workflows continuously. Combine managerial and non-managerial activities as often as possible. Let workers' teams take on hiring, evaluating and scheduling. Emphasize that each employee should develop several competences. You need only a few specialists. Inform and train people on a just-in-time, need to perform basis. These are the 'keys' to the post-hierarchial organization.[5]

The marketing manager

To consider the marketing manager as the critical actor simply reflects the managerial intent of the book – to elucidate the bases on which managerial action may be taken and to support the decision-making responsibilities of a marketing professional. The associated and critical assumption is, of course, that managers make a difference! If managers cannot and do not make a difference, then this book, like most work written in the managerial tradition, is largely irrelevant. The intention is to help managers to make better decisions in the conviction that better managerial decisions produce superior performance for the firm. While such an assumption may seem beyond question to many, there is good reason to draw attention to it and to advance some support for its validity.

The debate concerning whether managers matter is often cast as the debate between environmental determinism and managerial choice. Environmental determinism suggests that a form of natural selection is at work in the world of organizations, driven by competition as the engine of selection. Put at its crudest, the environmental determinism hypothesis suggests that firms make choices concerning their markets (environment) and their resources or capabilities. Competition selects in favour of those which have made the most efficient combinations of resources to serve the market's needs. At the extreme, the choices that firms make can be seen as comparable to the random mutations that nature generates in biological systems – managers are no more in control of their firm's evolutionary destiny than are 'Darwin's finches' in control of the attributes of their beaks

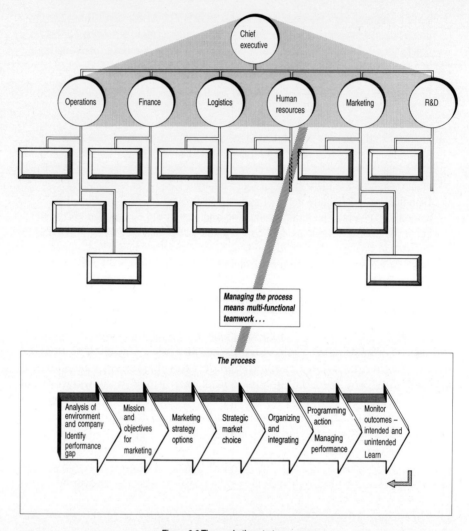

Figure 2.2 The marketing strategy process

which have been demonstrated to have such a profound impact on their survival or disappearance.[6]

Most economic theory attributes little or no importance to the manager. In the field of organization theory, organizational ecology is often regarded as ascribing no important role to managerial discretion on the grounds that it is environmentally deterministic – the environment selects among organizations.[7] When the environment and the organization's form 'match', selection is positive and reinforcing and survival is enhanced. When a mismatch occurs, selection is negative and survival probabilities decline.

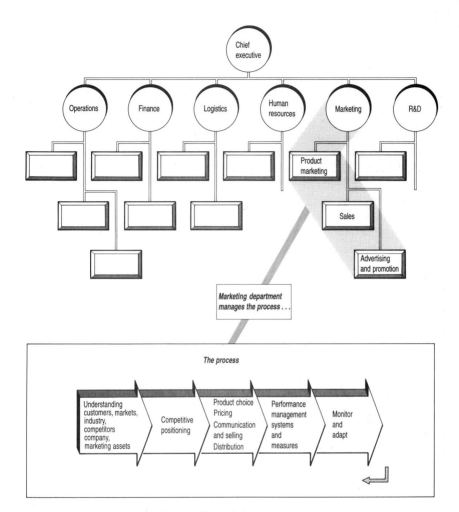

Figure 2.3 The marketing management process

Furthermore, it is argued that organizations have limited abilities for change so that change in populations of organizations come about through the death of 'old' and the entry of new firms. While this rather Darwinian explanation may be unsettling to managers who would like to see themselves as prime movers in corporate success – especially those who see themselves cast in the role of Tom Wolfe's caricature 'masters of the universe' – it must be accepted that the explanation has considerable power. It must further be conceded that aspects of its assumptions are deeply engrained in some influential threads of the management literature

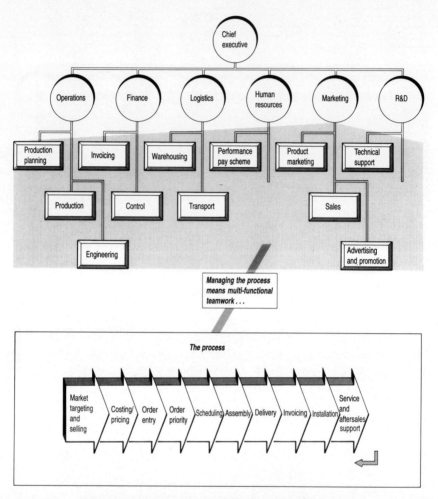

Figure 2.4 The order generation, fulfilment and service (OGFS) process

which have shaped current managerial practice. Porter's work on industry and competition, for example, reflects the traditional assumptions of the industrial organization school of thought – industry structure shapes the conduct of industry participants which in turn shapes firm performance.[8] Much of the mainstream work on strategy during the 1980s reflects the assumption that managers must understand their industry, market and competitive environment well enough to 'fit' their company to the forces at work in that environment. The message might be paraphrased as 'fit in or be selected out'.

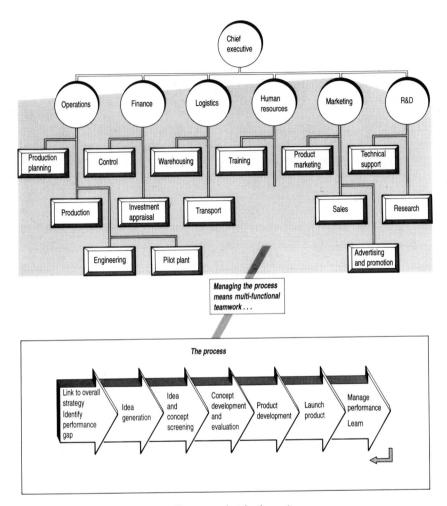

Figure 2.5 The new product development process

The managerial choice hypothesis has swung back into high profile in the 1990s with increasing interest in resource-based explanations of competitive success and with the wide impact of writers such as Hamel and Prahalad, the subtitle of whose book tells of their message – 'Breakthrough strategies for *seizing control* of your industry and *creating* the markets of tomorrow' (emphases added).[9] It is little wonder that their approach is so popular with practising managers! Those who argue for the predominance of managerial choice point out the undeniable fact that people make decisions, that decisions count and that organizations can change within reasonably limited periods of time. If organizations can adjust to changing environmental conditions in a timely manner, or even more powerfully, influence their environments in a manner that suits them, then they are not 'trapped' by forces of selection. If organizational inertia is sufficiently contained to escape this trap, then the manager has a central role in directing the process of adaptation. Managerial choice is then indeed pivotal to the performance of the firm. The debate between these two opposing positions often provides an entertaining and dramatic basis for rhetoric but the reality of most of the debate and associated research suggests that both explanations are partial – environments, through the competitive mechanism do select, but managers also make better and worse choices and their choices influence performance deeply. We shall take this position and try to demonstrate how both forces work – how the quality of managerial decisions makes a difference and how the power of environmental selection through the engine of competition must never be ignored.

The competitive marketplace

The emphasis on the *competitive marketplace* as the context for action signals both an assumption and a context for application. Command economies typical of Eastern Europe in the post-war years until 1990 were built on centralized decision-making with regard to what and how much should be produced and distributed to whom, by whom, how and at what price. Market-based economies are founded on the philosophy that the system optimizes its performance if all the many producers and consumers make their independent decisions freely in an open market. The *assumption* is that competitive markets, grounded in the principle of free choice, represent the most efficient mechanism for ordering economic activity – superior to the command economy of state centralism or the publicly managed markets of socialism. The assumption does not stretch as far as assuming that so-called free markets must be completely unfettered.

The drawbacks of 'purely' capitalist market structures are reasonably well understood and documented.[10] If competition weakens or becomes technically or institutionally infeasible, monopoly will normally result, bringing inefficiency and abuse of power. Because efficiency depends on the myriad individual decisions of sellers and buyers there is no guarantee of short-term optimization of the whole market system – there may well be unpredictable short-run disturbances. The distribution of wealth is unlikely to be even, so that some members of a society find themselves economically marginalized. The nature of individual transactions and economic contracting between parties in exchange is likely to generate side-effects (externalities in the language of economics) that carry a cost for others – such as when air is polluted, silence is destroyed or natural beauty is disfigured – but the cost is carried by society in general rather than the parties to the exchange which creates the cost. A market system, therefore, requires that the state should overlay the dynamics of free enterprise with safeguards that promote competitive markets and that carefully regulate necessary monopoly, that stabilize short-run economic volatility, that protect and support the underprivileged and economically marginalized, and that impose regulations that deal with externalities.

In this context, marketing, as a discipline, is concerned with enhancing the efficiency of markets by creating, capturing and developing a knowledge base concerning the exchange process and the efficient management of transactions. Marketing knowledge plays the key role in identifying and interpreting market wants and needs – whether explicit or implicit, in designing product and service responses, and in putting in place effective and efficient routes to market for those products and services. Without marketing's specialist knowledge assets, the potential for successful transactions in a complex and free market becomes fraught with randomness – consumers and producers separated by a void of ignorance about what the one wants and needs and what the other can make and deliver profitably.

Emphasizing the competitive marketplace as a *context* also serves to remind us that competition is the key force or engine of selection, deciding between the strategies that managers in different companies implement. Buyers enter the marketplace to be served. Competing sellers enter with their alternative solutions to buyers' needs and problems. In the competition between the buyers, winners and losers emerge. Winning and losing signals to the effective manager which decisions are more and less successful and if learning is fast and accurate enough, the manager can amplify success and repress failure. In such a way the manager becomes a partner with market forces in an adaptive mode.

It is productive at this introductory stage to note that the various definitions and aspects of marketing reviewed so far raise issues that go far beyond the normal ambit of the individual firm or marketing manager. This is because marketing is essentially societal in scope, although many of the activities involved are performed by individuals and individual organizations. The term macro marketing is used to describe this larger social dimension 'that directs an economy's flow of goods and services from producers to consumers in a way that effectively matches supply and demand and accomplishes the objectives of society'.[11] The concern is with the whole marketing system at national or regional level. Thus we are concerned as citizens and consumers with the effectiveness of the marketing system. Through the 1990s we are all participants in an historic experiment to create a new European marketing system based on a single unified market spanning the nations of Europe.

All economies need marketing systems but vary in the social and political choices they make about the form of these systems. However, even those marketing systems based on strong adherence to free market principles require some intervention by government and regulatory agencies and legal systems to mediate the conflicts that can result and to express the social and political preferences of the citizen. Hence regulation is always part and parcel of free market structures, if only to preserve freedom of competition and to avoid the abuse of market and economic power. Thus most free market systems will, for example, also have monopolies commissions or anti-trust agencies and laws to regulate the workings of the market so as to protect the citizens' rights and interests.

International marketing

The societal aspect of marketing is not the focus of this book. The concern is with marketing at the firm level, but it is important to remember that this is significantly influenced by the social context in which it operates. This becomes especially visible when issues in international marketing are considered. Many of the challenges faced by marketers as they move services and products internationally derive from inherently different social, cultural and institutional circumstances. The degree of regulation in financial services markets varies considerably across the world as a reflection of differences in legal structures and the power and role of central banks or their equivalents. Those competing in financial services markets must understand and cope with this reality if they are to succeed on an international scale. Distribution systems still vary greatly from one country to another and lead to major differences in how companies can bring products and services to market. In Europe, for example, there has been a long-term trend towards concentration in most forms of retailing – that is, fewer and fewer multiple retailers selling more and more of what is purchased by consumers. This leads to a significant shift in market power away from producers and towards the retailers, bringing with it growth in retailer brands and a major redistribution of profits in the affected industries. This development is supported by consumers, who associate lower prices and high service levels with the move to retail concentration.

In Japan, by contrast, retailing has remained very fragmented and small in scale, with a high proportion of family-run businesses. This different structure has been supported by legal constraints on the floorspace of retail food stores and by a general adherence to retail price maintenance. It has been difficult, until very recently, to buy deeply discounted products anywhere in Japan. This pattern of retailing had an important social consequence since its fragmented structure employed many people and could act as a buffer-zone for variations in employment in the manufacturing sector of the economy. What would be seen as economically inefficient in Europe, leading to higher than necessary consumer prices, was partly institutionalized in Japan and led to significant local employment creation. In one system the consumer bought products relatively cheaply and paid taxes to deal with problems of unemployment. In the other the consumer paid relatively high consumer prices but paid little to support social policies to deal with unemployment. The international marketer soon realizes that there are few 'right' answers for such issues and that different societies create and evolve macro-marketing systems to reflect their traditional and emerging social and political choices. Understanding this reality is often central to effective marketing strategy.

In general, it might be argued that all marketing is international marketing. So-called domestic markets almost always turn out to have important regional differences in the structure of distribution systems, in the availability of promotional media, and most especially in the nature of buyer behaviour. North and south Holland are seen by their residents as different cultures. France is often seen as Paris and 'the rest'. Marketing between Bavaria and North Rhine-Westphalia may be more complicated than between the latter region and Alsace. The evolution of the European Community's unified market will, in some ways, make European marketing all 'domestic' marketing. But the social, cultural, trade and infrastructural idiosyncrasies of Europe will never disappear. Alongside the forces for economic unification run other forces of regionalization and nationalism that are politically and culturally deep-rooted and profound. Marketing as a complex, segmented, differentiated activity would appear to be the most realistic picture of the future and distinctions between 'domestic' and 'international' less productive unless subsumed within a framework for dealing with intrinsic market heterogeneity. This topic is addressed in more depth in Chapter 10.

REVIEW QUESTIONS

2.1 What is the difference between hierarchy and heterarchy? How does the distinction help in understanding the four core marketing processes?

2.2 Consider the alternative ways of managing 'transactions' and give examples of firm-specific situations with which you are familiar.

2.3 In the debate between environmental determinism and managerial choice, what is meant by the phrase 'fit in or be selected out'?

2.4 A market system, therefore, requires that the state should overlay the dynamics of free enterprise with safeguards that promote competitive markets. What role does marketing play in this context?

2.5 Japanese and European retailing systems are very different. What does this tell us about managing marketing?

CHAPTER 3

The business system

- The macro business system
- Organization of markets in a business system
- From upstream to downstream marketing
- Firm's micro business system
- Identifying key process activities
- Linking micro and macro business systems

Marketing in action case
National Panasonic's human bicycle

ABOUT THIS CHAPTER

Marketing is concerned with a range of activities of which consumer products represent only the very tip of the iceberg. One way of viewing this complexity is to envisage markets and industries as 'business systems'. A macro business system is the chain of value-adding activities that is undertaken in order to bring a product or service from raw material stage to the provision of final customer service and support.

The type of market – whether open, managed or hybrid – varies along this chain. So does the nature of marketing activity evolve along it. In general, as value is added along the business system and one moves downstream, the product will evolve from standardized commodity form generating low margins towards more differentiated, heterogeneous and higher margin form.

The individual firm or organization may be viewed as a microcosm of the industry business system within which it lives. Thus the firm's micro business system may be visualized similarly as an organized chain or series of activities. This understanding of macro and micro business systems represents the basic building block of market focus.

Concrete blocks to soap powders

Initial impressions of the nature of marketing are commonly formed by the very visible aspects of consumer marketing: the products of daily life and their presentation in retail outlets and their promotion through advertising. Yet marketing is concerned with a wide range of activities – an iceberg of which consumer products represent only the very tip. Markets and marketing also involve industrial products such as machine tools, building materials, electronic components or food ingredients which are sold from one organization to another and services such as engineering consultancy, air travel or holidays which are provided to both organizations and individual consumers. But the impression remains that many perceive marketing mainly in terms of consumer goods and indeed that the marketing of soap powder represents in some way the epitome of the discipline. This approach is not only simplistic, but it fails to appreciate the need to understand markets and marketing in the totality necessary to win and sustain competitive advantage over the long term.

The macro business system

One way of viewing this complexity is to envisage markets and industries as 'business systems'. A business system is the chain of value-adding activities that is undertaken in order to bring a product or service from raw material to the provision of final customer service and support. Figure 3.1 represents such a general business system – it may also be referred to as a macro business system, as it encompasses a whole industry. Figure 3.2 illustrates a simplified and general business system for paper products. One can see that it starts with forests and their cultivation and the market for timber. Timber is marketed to pulp and papermills which produce paper pulp and then paper and paperboard products. One possible route from here is for the mills to market their paperboard to packaging companies. These companies will buy the paperboard and 'convert' it into packages – for example, the package in which you buy your breakfast cereal. The packaging companies have the task of marketing their package-making ability to companies which wish to use packages and cartons to transport, protect and promote their products (whether a breakfast cereal or the pouch into which an airline ticket is inserted). Once the packagers have purchased the package they will insert their product into it and perhaps ship it onward to a retailer. The retailer's decision to stock the particular product is partly influenced by the quality and performance of the packaging, as is your decision to take the product from the shelf and pay some of your discretionary income for it.

In the case of paper products there may be one more market: that for recycled paper, if there is an effective market for such material. In this way the business system becomes a partial loop as some of the raw materials are drawn not just from the forests but from the used final product of the

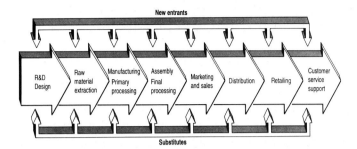

Figure 3.1 A macro business system

system. In a world increasingly concerned with environmental issues more and more business systems are becoming partially closed loops in order to protect the environment from unwanted and dangerous waste. Closing the loop involves the processes of de-manufacturing and recycling. De-manufacturing involves disassembling final products into component elements so that they can be sorted and readily recycled. A used package may, for example, have to be disassembled into its paper, paperboard, plastic and perhaps metallic foil elements.

Industrial markets, business-to-business markets, consumer markets, products and services are all interconnected within any business system. What may be viewed initially as a product in a consumer market (say, an automobile) is in fact the outcome of many business-to-business (or industrial) markets in automotive components supplied by firms such as Bosch of Germany (engine management systems) or by Ericsson of Sweden (mobile telephones). The ability to create and manufacture the car will have depended on many service inputs such as those provided by design studios like Pinninfarina of Milan, engineering design specialists like International Automotive Design of England and certain manufacturing management consultancies. Once the car is sold on the consumer market, final satisfac-

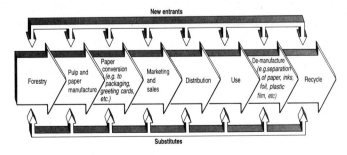

Figure 3.2 A macro business system for paper products

tion with the product will be experienced only if service and support are provided through the car manufacturer's dealerships and spare parts service system.

Organization of markets in a business system

As one inspects the macro business system of any industry, it becomes quickly visible that *an industry consists of a series of markets* with the product or service offering of each one becoming an input or raw material to the next. Each 'step' in the business system involves an economic and techno-logical transformation – inputs are transformed into a new output with the objective of adding value in the process. Each transformation undertaken within an industry demands a market from which to source inputs and a market in which to sell outputs, as suggested in Figure 3.3. As described in the previous chapter, these markets may be open, classically competitive markets on occasion, or 'in house' managed markets if the transforming activity has been vertically integrated. Between these two opposites in terms of market organization lies a variety of increasingly common 'hybrid' forms. Some of the alternative ways of organizing the markets in a business system are visualized in Figure 3.4. For example, alliances, supply partner-ships, joint ventures, franchised relationships and the interactions involved in relationship marketing arrangements are all partly free market structures and partly managed market structures.

Managed markets operate with agreed administrative rules which attempt to reduce the risk that one or both parties take in entering into exchange, usually by extending the predictability of exchange activity from one to many transactions. In doing this, the cost of the transactions is reduced as there is less need for special vigilance and monitoring under the umbrella of some form of longer-term agreement. Managed markets may also increase the likelihood of mutual and planned adaptation between supplier and buyer; each party is agreeable to modify supply and demand requirements to allow for mutual adjustment, each may share plans and technology, quality requirements and upgrading may be negotiated into practice. By contrast, open markets can only rely on contracting and legal

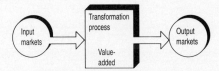

Figure 3.3 A transformation step

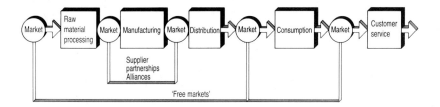

(i) A series of managed markets based on supply partnerships at manufacturing and distribution stages, with 'free' markets at raw material sourcing stages and at downstream stages

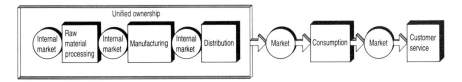

(ii) A series of markets in an industry in which there is almost complete vertical integration such as may be found in the petrochemical industry

Figure 3.4 Hybrid forms of market organization

court ordering or reordering of contracts. In instances where it is difficult to write a complete contract – where the future is uncertain and the contract for a transaction has to leave some open-endedness to account for this – a 'managed' market may be much less costly and risky for both parties.

Open markets carry the cost of eternal vigilance in purchasing (embodied in the traditional legal warning about contract, caveat emptor – let the buyer beware!) and selling and the cost of resort to the law in the case of dispute. Managed markets carry the cost of administering and monitoring the relationship in some bilateral structure. Whether markets will be organized as 'free', vertically integrated under unified ownership, or as some intermediate hybrid form will reflect the relative costs of the transactions under one or other arrangement.[1] In the international arena it is also possible to speculate as to whether there are cultural influences on the manner in which we choose to govern market transactions. Japanese business has been associated with extensive networks of partnerships and alliances as opposed to some European and especially North American practice which favours 'free market' contracting and the use of the law to mediate dispute. In the Japanese case there are powerful social forces at work that 'enforce' good faith and mutual adjustment without resort to law or other forms of governance that carry direct monetary cost. It might be argued that the cultural norms of some societies may, on average, generate lower transaction costs than others.

From upstream to downstream marketing

Understanding an industry as a series of markets in a business system highlights the manner in which marketing activity alters as the business system moves from raw material markets to the markets for service and support and on to the newer markets for de-manufacturing and recycling. The marketing of 1 tonne of 3 mm rolled paper will be rather different from the marketing of the airline ticket made from this raw material, and different again from the marketing of recycled paper containing the discarded ticket.

In general, as value is added along the business system, the product will evolve from standardized commodity form generating low margins towards more differentiated, heterogeneous and higher margin form (see Figure 3.5). The early stages are usually typified by the production of commodity or standardized products, often produced to externally arbitrated standards. For example, a concrete block may be made to BSO 49 (British Standards Organization) specification or a length of rebar steel to the BSO 106 standard. Further along the system, offerings tend to be more heterogeneous. They become differentiated on the basis of quality, performance characteristics, service back-up, brand identity and other factors. As a result, the nature and tasks of marketing activity change considerably as one moves from 'upstream' companies to 'downstream' companies.

Upstream markets and companies – those involved in the early stages of raw material production and primary manufacture and fabrication are most likely to have to develop marketing strategies and practices that emphasize product standardization, low cost structure to underpin aggressive price competition in volume-driven, low margin businesses. Companies marketing basic building products and materials will tend to become excellent at such aspects of business if they are to survive and prosper. Price is increasingly joined in such markets by the importance of high quality supplier–buyer relationships, leading us to emphasize the growing importance of marketing as relationship bonding as well as the traditional focus on it as a series of one-off market transactions. Many of the most successful marketers of commodity type products now win and defend business on the basis of excellence in managing long-term relationships which effectively become partnerships between supplier and buyer.

As already noted, Japanese industry has done much to demonstrate just how effective an approach to marketing this can be and the extent to which it can lead to significant increased profitability for both partners. The deepening of such upstream market relationships is usually based on adding service features to the physical product flow. Thus, service features such as customer problem-solving, guaranteed reliability, full delivery and just-in-

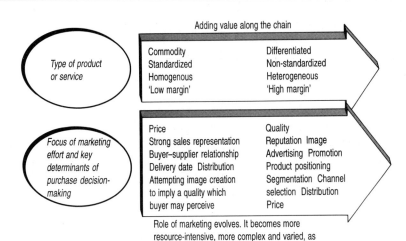

Figure 3.5 Marketing and the macro business system

time delivery become critical elements of marketing. A potato supplier who adds value by ensuring consistency of potato breed, by grading, washing and packing potatoes in factory-ready quantities and then delivering them as needed to a potato processing plant is much more likely to build a sustainable relationship with a buyer than one that offers to supply potatoes without such added services. Suppliers of potatoes to McDonalds for conversion to french fries, to the major producers of oven ready-chipped potatoes, or to the multinational marketers of potato waffles have to respond to these necessities or fail.

As one moves to the downstream end of any industry, marketing activities become dominated by aspects familiar to us all in our role as consumers. Downstream markets and companies gain competitive advantage increasingly from detailed segmentation of markets and tailoring of products and services to the special needs of each segment. Higher margins may be created in this way and proprietary positions in the market established and defended through investment in brands and specialized distribution channels. Frozen potato waffles may therefore take their position in supermarket freezers as strongly branded items tailored for exactly defined customer segments such as households needing quick-preparation food products where both parents work and children may be categorized in the language of market researchers as 'latch-key kids'. In this instance marketing is all about detailed market research, careful brand development, strong advertising to create market awareness and brand loyalty and elaborate distribution and logistic systems to ensure full shelves in the supermarket. It can readily be seen that the task of marketing for a potato producer supplying a food processing company is significantly different from that of the branded food manufacturer supplying the final consumer market through the supermarket.

In the middle sections of any industry chain or macro business system these rather dramatic contrasts in marketing tasks and practices blur and companies have to deal with the necessity to respond to their markets with a blend of upstream and downstream practice. Interestingly, this progression is less likely to be observed in services markets along the business system. The nature of services required at raw material extraction stage (e.g.,veterinary medicine for beef production) are likely to be high margin just as are the services required to cook and prepare beef for the table in a restaurant at the end of the beef business system.

As one moves through a business system and its markets from upstream to downstream stages it will generally be the case that variety will increase – more products and/or services for more groups of customers. In general, this is driven by the nature of the technologies and economic commitments required at the different stages. Upstream activities required to transform inputs to outputs in a value-adding manner usually (but not always!) require technologies and plants that respond sensitively to scale so there is a pressure for large plant producing long runs of single products in order to drive down costs and guarantee quality and consistency. As the major raw materials for the industry flow downstream further stages work with technologies and investments that demand less scale and allow greater flexibility. In the clothing industry, for example, the production and spinning of yarn and the manufacture of textiles are dominated by technologies and investments that militate against great variety. However, by the time fabric reaches a small clothing company where cloth is cut, sewn and trimmed with accessories the amount of variety that can be economically handled is vastly greater.

New manufacturing methods and new technologies continuously strive to break this pressure to limit variety for as long as possible in the business system – and where success is achieved the structure of the industry and the nature of its intermediate and final markets can be radically changed. The possibilities for 'mass customization', for example, may well radically change many industries and markets. Mass customization involves supplying the mass market with products that are made – and not just assembled from standard modules – to meet the individual requirements of a customer at prices and lead-times comparable to those of a mass production (i.e. no customization) system. The promise of mass customization is an individually tailored product at a mass-produced price. Some global companies, ranging from Toyota to Dow Jones, are struggling with the potential of mass customization in the hope that it will become the next basis for competitive supremacy.[2] Westbrook and Williamson tell the interesting and illustrative story of National Panasonic Bicycle, as summarized in Exhibit 3.1.

Exhibit 3.1   *Marketing in action case*

National Panasonic's human bicycle

National Panasonic Bicycle (NPB), part of Matsushita Electronics Industries, faced a bleak prospect from the start of the 1980s in an industry with falling sales, dropping prices, cheaper imports from newly industrializing countries and consumers fragmenting into ever smaller segments. NPB had not adapted well to the sports bike market nor to the mountain bike market.

In 1987 the company set itself new targets to turn the situation around. These were to create demand for high value-added products that met diverse needs; to differentiate themselves clearly; to avoid any unsold or obsolete stock; and to prevent retail price-cutting. Their marketing strategy to achieve these objectives became the 'Panasonic Order System' (POS) and combined with a new pilot plant in their Osaka factory it became their mass customization initiative.

When a customer enters any bike shop in Japan or the United States that displays the 'POS' sign, they are measured so that the frame for their bicycle will be individually custom-built, piece by piece. The customer may then choose from a variety of design options for type of bike (18), handle extensions (6), handlebar widths (3), colour patterns (199), pedal types (2), toeclip types (3), tyre types (2), as well as six styles of typeface in which the customer's name can be painted on the frame and two different positions for the name! The customized bike will be in the hands of the customer within two weeks in Japan, or three weeks if shipped to the United States.

How is the order fulfilled so quickly? When it arrives at the factory in Osaka by fax, minutes after the customer has left the store, there is no basic frame in stock, no pre-cut components, only 20 ft lengths of metal tube. The customer's requirements are entered into the computer system which converts the specifications into a set of manufacturing instructions for each stage of frame manufacture. Then, when a section of tube arrives at the first process, it has a bar code attached which identifies it as that of a particular customer. The operator need only swipe his bar code reader across this label and the computer-controlled tube cutting machine can, drawing on individual measurement data, automatically adjust the end stop of the cutting machine to suit and cut a tube of precise length. The operator is free to deal with the ancillary processes grouped around him in his production cell. The company has developed new skills in CAD/CAM, the use of bar coding, and 'production cell' organization.

On introduction in 1988, there were 11,655 custom combinations available. By 1993 there were over 11 million. The apparent complexity of this is controlled and managed so that many mass production techniques are still viable while NPB learns the new technology of individualization at low cost and fast response. Their 'POS' bicycles are priced at the top of the standard bike price range – about 15 per cent above the cost of the best mass-produced product, but many customers happily trade up in order to have their tailored bicycle. The strategy regenerated the company's image and boosted sales of its standard products and switched retailers to selling differentiation rather than price.[3]

It is important to remember that the underlying principles of marketing and the theories on which they are based must be acted on managerially in a situational manner. The manager must be aware of the need to manage marketing in a manner that reflects the business system context. The lessons of fast-moving consumer goods marketing cannot be applied without modification to the marketing challenges of upstream companies and vice versa. The practice of marketing is therefore fundamentally contingent or situational in nature.

Firm's micro business system

The individual firm or organization may be viewed as a microcosm of the industry business system within which it lives. Each organization necessarily sources raw materials and other inputs such as labour and capital from its input markets. It then converts these inputs into products or services and sells them in its output market in the hope that customers will pay more than the combined cost of all the inputs, thus generating a margin of profitability and a return on investment. The organization may therefore be visualized as an organized chain or series of activities in the same way that an industry may be viewed as a long chain of production and distribution. The micro business system maps the input–transformation–output process at the firm, that is the micro, level of analysis. A generic micro business system is illustrated in Figure 3.6.

Porter, in his 1985 work, called this micro business system a value chain and popularized the technique of value chain analysis (see Figure 3.7).[4] It is useful at this juncture to describe briefly the structure of a micro business system using the Porterian approach to mapping, while Figure 3.8 sets it in the context of a printing company. There is no one ideal way of mapping the micro business system; as is seen below, different writers have suggested different key processes or tasks, but the tools and techniques of process design and redesign which are drawn upon here are usually best applied to the type of progressive activity flow of Figure 3.6.

A micro business system disaggregates a firm into its strategically relevant tasks and activities in order to understand better their structure

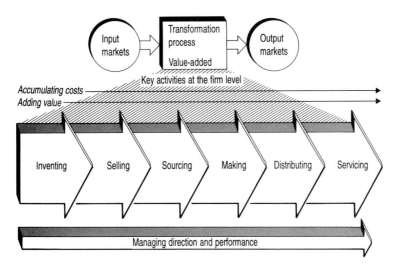

Figure 3.6 A generic micro business system

and interrelationships, the behaviour of costs, and existing and potential sources of competitive advantage. It does so by identifying the key value-adding activities that the firm carries out. Porter's approach focuses on five activities which he describes as *primary* and four which he categorizes as *support*. These in fact correspond, not so much to defensible primary–secondary groupings but rather to an identification of *physical flows* as primary and *managerial flows* as secondary. He suggests that primary activities are those that are involved in the *physical creation* of the product or service, its distribution to the buyer and any after-sales service. These

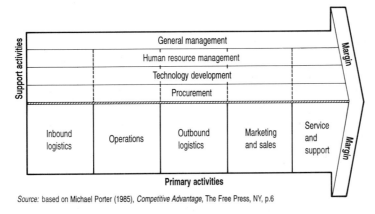

Source: based on Michael Porter (1985), *Competitive Advantage*, The Free Press, NY, p.6

Figure 3.7 A firm's micro business system

primary activities are in turn divided by him into the following categories:

1 *Inbound logistics*. Activities associated with the receipt, storing and dissemination of inputs to the product (includes warehousing, inventory control, vehicle scheduling).
2 *Operations*. Activities associated with transforming inputs into the final product (machining, packing, assembly, testing, equipment maintenance).
3 *Outbound logistics*. Collecting, storing and distributing the product to buyers.
4 *Marketing and sales*. Activities associated with providing a means by which buyers can purchase the product, and persuading them to do so (advertising, selling, channel selection, pricing, promotion).
5 *Service*. Providing a service to maintain or enhance the value of the product (installation, training, parts supply, technical advice and maintenance).

Support activities can be divided into four categories:

1 *Procurement*. This is the function of purchasing inputs. It includes all the procedures for dealing with suppliers. Procurement activity goes on across the whole firm; it is not just limited to the purchasing department. Although the costs of procurement activity themselves form only a small proportion of overhead costs, the impact of poor procurement can be dramatic, leading to higher costs and/or poor quality.
2 *Technology management*. This encompasses not just machines and processes, but 'know-how', procedures, systems and learning curve benefits. In some industries (like paper manufacturing) process technology can be a key source of advantage.
3 *Human resource management*. This includes all the activities involved in the recruitment, training, development and remuneration of staff. Firms that are successful continuously tend to be those that are highly selective in their recruitment policies and invest heavily in training and development of personnel.
4 *General management*. Ultimately, all the primary and support activities depend on a focused general management perspective. General management activities like directing finance resources, planning, information systems, suitable organization structure, quality assurance, and so on all provide the necessary infrastructure and integration to enable all other activities. Thus, general management supports the whole micro business system or value chain.

A firm may have a distinctive competence or expertise in any or each of these primary and support activities. Analyzing the micro business system enables the firm to understand its cost structure, identify where it differentiates itself from competitors and appreciate how the various activities must be linked together optimally if market focus is to be achieved.

Using this framework, marketing is seen as one of the five primary activities that must be carried out by any organization, supported by the four generic support activities which are needed to manage and organize the primary activities. Marketing itself may then be further analyzed as a series of specialized activities, such as marketing management, advertising, salesforce administration, promotion, and so on. Analysis of the micro business system should lead to:

▷ the identification of the activities in the firm that are critical to its cost structure and to an understanding of how these costs are influenced;
▷ the identification of the activities that are central to the creation of customer value and the factors that influence value creation positively or negatively;
▷ the identification of critical interdependencies between activities since these interactions are often important drivers of both cost and customer value.

Identifying key process activities

The Porterian value chain framework is useful in suggesting the character of basic organizational processes. The distinction between primary and secondary activities has an uncomfortable feel of old measurement and accounting conventions of categorizing direct and indirect costs separately. Newer approaches to accounting measurement have changed many of these conventions with the introduction of activity-based accounting which, in the spirit of business system analysis, seeks to define and fully cost each activity undertaken in an organization. The result of this is to shrink the attribution of costs to and from 'overhead' and to associate costs of all kind directly with individual activities. The 'support' activities of Porter's framework are ones which are involved in many or all primary activities. It would, therefore, seem worthwhile to dispense with this category and focus on defining the central input, conversion and throughput activity of the organization. The organization in total is an input–conversion–output process. In order helpfully to define and analyze an organization from a business systems or business process viewpoint, however, one must go beyond this obvious statement. None the less, taking a process view of business in some ways demands a revolutionary change in managerial perspective – 'it amounts to turning the organization on its head, or at least on its side'.[5] A process view brings a strong emphasis on how work is done, on how value is added and on how costs and time are consumed.

Identifying the key processes in an organization is not readily done using standardized categories. Those working on business process design and redesign issues variously propose anything from 2 to over 100 processes. Shapiro, Sviokla and Rangan propose two: managing the product line and managing the order cycle.[6] Rockart and Short suggest three: developing new products, delivering products to customers and managing

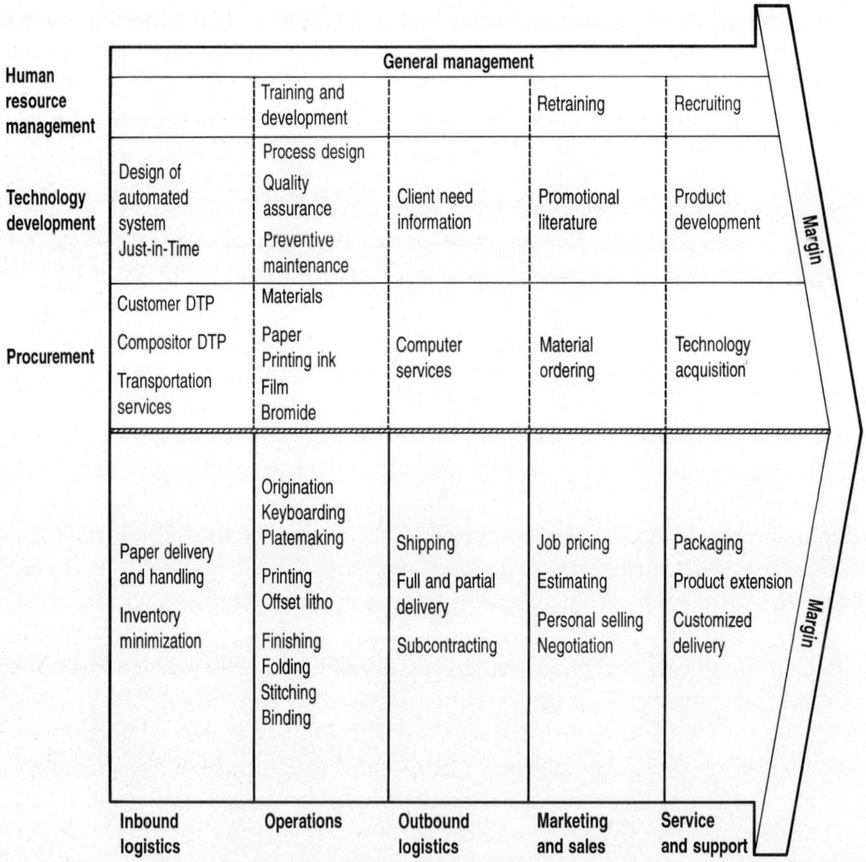

		General management			
Human resource management		Training and development		Retraining	Recruiting
Technology development	Design of automated system Just-in-Time	Process design Quality assurance Preventive maintenance	Client need information	Promotional literature	Product development
Procurement	Customer DTP Compositor DTP Transportation services	Materials Paper Printing ink Film Bromide	Computer services	Material ordering	Technology acquisition
	Paper delivery and handling Inventory minimization	Origination Keyboarding Platemaking Printing Offset litho Finishing Folding Stitching Binding	Shipping Full and partial delivery Subcontracting	Job pricing Estimating Personal selling Negotiation	Packaging Product extension Customized delivery
	Inbound logistics	**Operations**	**Outbound logistics**	**Marketing and sales**	**Service and support**

Figure 3.8 The micro business system of a printing company

customer relationships.[7] Xerox has identified 14 key processes but focuses its change efforts on a smaller number; IBM worked in 1993 with 18 key processes while British Telecom was focusing on 15.[8] In the latter case, it might be suggested from Figure 3.9 that there are, in fact, three main underlying processes – strategic management processes, managing operations processes and management service processes.

Kaplan and Murdock approach the problem by defining a core process as one that is focused on one or more of the business objectives that determine competitive success. Based on their experience in working with the consultancy clients of McKinsey & Company, they suggest that there are no more than four or five core processes. They note that 'a computer manufacturer's core processes might be new product development, order generation and fulfillment, and integrated logistics. A consumer goods company, on the other hand, might have the following three core processes: new product development, brand development and trade management, and integrated logistics.'[9]

The most appropriate approach therefore appears to be to map the core processes that are evident at the micro level in any one organization, acknowledging that these processes will differ from firm to firm, and indeed, that in these differences may lie much of the explanation for superior or inferior competitive performance by the company. If a radical approach to design or redesign of the business is at stake, broad definitions of key processes seem to serve the purpose best by exposing the underlying logic of the firm's value-adding activity and the conflicts and inadequacies which may inhere in existing, incrementally evolved activities and structures.

From a marketing perspective some generalizations are appropriate. Above all, taking a process approach demands the adoption of a customer (whether internal or external) viewpoint. The objective of all processes is to produce value for customers and to do so by accumulating the minimum of cost and time. This is a design principle that is completely consistent with the notions of market orientation and market focus articulated in Chapter 1. Detailed definition of marketing-related processes – '*customer facing processes*', as Davenport calls them – usually focuses on marketing processes designed to initiate a transaction; on sales processes designed to enable purchase, receipt and payment; and on customer service processes that deal with post-purchase involvement with customers.[10] In this book we view these three processes as elements of the order generation, fulfilment and service (OGFS) process, which we in turn see as one of the four core marketing processes (the other three being the strategic marketing process, the marketing management process and the new product development process).

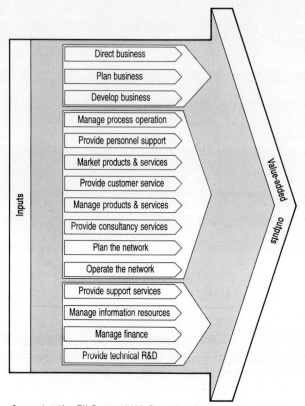

Direct business

Plan business

Develop business

Manage process operation

Provide personnel support

Market products & services

Provide customer service

Manage products & services

Provide consultancy services

Plan the network

Operate the network

Provide support services

Manage information resources

Manage finance

Provide technical R&D

Source: adapted from T.H. Davenport (1993), *Process Innovation*, Harvard Business School Press, Cambridge, Mass., p.29.

Figure 3.9 Key business processes in British Telecom

Process analysis of the firm – the micro business system – helps to establish the role of marketing in the individual organization and to isolate the leverage which marketing activity has on overall company performance. It is vital to establishing the interdependence between marketing and other company activities and therefore in ensuring integrated planning and action – one of the central concerns of the market-focused company.

Linking micro and macro business systems

The analysis of the micro business system should be set firmly in the industry business system context. Doing this ensures that the manager is alerted to the challenges faced not only by his own organization but also by the organization's customers and the customers' customers. On the upstream side it has become increasingly vital that the manager should also

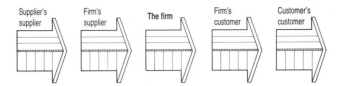

Figure 3.10 A chain of micro business systems

understand the issues faced by suppliers and suppliers' suppliers. This is the kind of framework within which we may build an approach to marketing that places appropriate stress on relationships and networks.

Figure 3.10 illustrates this perspective. Here a chain of micro business systems is observed which, of course, ultimately makes up an overall macro business system. Based on such analysis the challenge to the marketer is to understand and solve customers' problems by understanding their business and their competitive challenges in serving their customer base. A producer of DIY home care products must therefore develop a sophisticated appreciation of the competitive necessities faced by a DIY retailer who competes for the patronage of householders. If the manufacturer is to produce and supply DIY products of quality and cost appropriate to the DIY retailer's needs, he must also understand, and identify with, the needs of his own suppliers. Excellent supplier relationships are needed to guarantee the procurement of the necessary components and raw materials, just as much as first-rate downstream relationships that allow an understanding and nurturing of the customer base.

REVIEW QUESTIONS

3.1 Explain what is meant by a macro business system and indicate how marketing activity might differ or evolve along this system.

3.2 Different types of market organization, whether open, managed or hybrid, have differing types of costs and contractual obligation associated with them. Discuss.

3.3 What is meant by 'mass customization'?

3.4 What are the salient features of the firm's micro business system or value chain? Relate these ideas to a company or organization with which you are familiar.

3.5 Different writers suggest different key process tasks or activities in a firm. Is there a common thread running through these? Can you identify the key processes in the National Panasonic Bicycle Company?

CHAPTER 4

Strategy and process

▶ Sustainable competitive advantage
▶ Strategic management and strategic marketing
▶ Strategic frameworks
▶ Strategy and process
▶ Consumer, business-to-business, services marketing
▶ Theory and practice: the need for integration

Marketing in action case
Svenska Kullager Fabriken's (SKF) competitive advantage in bearings

ABOUT THIS CHAPTER

The nature of sustainable competitive advantage (SCA) is explored, with its three key dimensions of high perceived value (HPV), low delivered cost (LDC) and scope. Achieving SCA is a company-wide or corporate activity into which marketing is a key input. Strategic marketing is enveloped in, and derives from, the overall strategic management of the firm. This relationship is illustrated succinctly in the case of two classic techniques deployed in strategic management – Ansoff's growth matrix and the Boston Consulting Group's growth-share matrix.

The high level of cross-functional interaction and teamwork required to undertake strategic marketing successfully emphasizes again the process approach to business organization. An important benefit of this approach is that it enables the real-time implementation of strategic intent. Process overlays strategy. Strategy represents the choice of direction, while process is the force which implicitly or explicitly propels the organization in that direction.

While the link between strategy and process constitutes a theme in this book, so also does the interconnection between consumer, business-to-business and services markets. The marketing strategy process depends significantly on integrating consumer goods marketing, services marketing and business-to-business marketing with other key firm activities.

Competitive superiority in the business system

The understanding of macro and micro business systems represents the basic building block underpinning market focus. The analysis of the business system leads to decisions about how to compete effectively or, put in the language of the business strategist, how to establish and sustain a competitive advantage. The notion of competitive advantage stresses that commercial success flows from having an advantage over competitors in the marketplace which allows the firm to serve customers more effectively and at a profit. The idea of sustaining this advantage is just as important since competitive advantage that cannot be sustained over any appreciable time is of little value. Just as the operations manager is charged with creating advantage based on the operations or manufacturing activities, the aim of the marketer is to create advantage over competing organizations in the marketplace in such a manner that at least some element of temporary monopoly is generated – a marketing advantage that cannot readily be imitated. This idea is usually encapsulated in the phrase 'sustainable competitive advantage' (SCA).

Sustainable competitive advantage

Sustainable competitive advantage can be created in many ways, but the work of business strategy writers such as Porter, Gilbert and Strebel, and others has drawn attention to the reality that competitive advantage, in its fundamental form, has only a few basic roots.[1, 2, 3] These roots are generally regarded as inherent in 'generic competitive strategies'. Generic competitive strategies may be seen as based on choices that have to be made along three dimensions of competitive strategy (see Figure 4.1).

High perceived value (HPV)

This is the extent to which the company will compete on the relative differentiation of its products or services (their uniqueness and valued 'differentness' from competitive offerings) and hence the perceived value of the product or service to customers. Organizations that decide to invest in differentiation – and succeed in convincing their customers of the worth of this differentiation – are seen to pursue high perceived value (HPV) strategies. Customers perceive their offerings on the market as providing greater value in use than competitors. Examples of this approach include many widely known branded products from Porsche in cars to Chanel in cosmetics and fashion.

The use of the word perceived is not casual in this context. It is used to emphasize the fact that only value perceived by the customer bestows a competitive advantage. High value as perceived by the producer is irrelevant competitively unless matched by customer appreciation of that value.

Low delivered cost (LDC)

This is the extent to which the company will compete on the relative cost-in-use of its products or services, i.e. the delivered cost-in-use to the customer. Such firms must be driven by a desire to minimize costs at every stage of production and delivery – but not, it must be stressed, at the cost of quality. Organizations that decide to invest in such low-cost competitiveness are seen to pursue low delivered cost (LDC) strategies. In the grocery trade, the German discount chain Aldi has been successfully offering low-priced value-for-money products since the early 1950s. Every aspect of the Aldi formula exudes a passion for cost reduction, thereby constantly reinforcing the credibility of the low-price claims promoted loudly in the popular press. This approach has been pursued by Aldi in other European countries and by the early 1990s more than a third of its stores were outside Germany.

Just as value is competitively effective only when perceived by the customer, so too low cost is only effective when it is experienced directly by the user. A supplier with the lowest factory cost and ex-factory price in the industry has no competitive advantage necessarily unless its products are also lowest cost-in-use. Expensive peripherals and high service costs can negate a relatively low purchase price. Full cost-in-use is the critical measure of advantage. A large part of the success of Japanese small cars in Europe is explained by the fact that, while their initial purchase price is not lower than competitive offerings, reliability and low service costs mean that cost-in-use is.

Scope

This is the extent to which the company chooses to define the scope of its business as encompassing all the various markets and market segments of the industry or to confine its activity to serving one or several selected market segments. Organizations may, therefore, choose to invest in a strategy that involves broad industry scope or alternatively to focus on a segment. The Dutch company Philips serves a very wide variety of market segments from light bulbs to semi-conductors, whereas the Hungarian firm Tungsram specializes in light bulbs.

Narrow scope may confer advantage through depth of specialization and intensive market coverage. Part of the Danish company Lego's competitive advantage in the toy industry depends on its intensive focus on the building toy segment, on the one material – moulded plastic – on children from pre-school to early adolescence in age, and on parents oriented towards educational toys. This narrow scope allows great specialization in market understanding, design, manufacturing, merchandising and database marketing to established customers. This depth of concentration continues to generate significant perceived value for parents and children, but also, and critically, makes Lego one of the few toy producers in the world that can maintain its manufacturing facilities in Europe while holding to a competitive pricing policy.

Broad scope may bestow benefit through winning economies of scope across all the shared activities, investments and organizational infrastructure of the firm. Philips achieves such economies from its investment in the parent brand, the benefit which is enjoyed by all its businesses and products at a lower unit cost than could be realized if each had to build a global brand identity separately.

When these three dimensions of competitive choice are brought together as in Figure 4.1, the basic options open to the company and the marketer in developing strategies for competitive advantage become clear. A company can choose to focus on one dimension as in most of the examples set out above, or it may opt to compete across two or more dimensions. Black and Decker, for example, competes across all three, simultaneously pursuing a strategy of high perceived value, low delivered cost and a broad scope. The strategy typically followed by a small specialist sub-supplier in the electronics industry focuses on both HPV and LDC but over a very limited scope.

Of course, the pursuit of competitive positional superiority across any of these dimensions may have to change over time in response to changes in the macro business system. Apple Computer in developing its personal computer products followed a high perceived value approach with corresponding high prices. However, in the early 1990s, the maturing of this market saw Apple adding a more standardized low delivered cost strategy with lower prices to its traditional value-based strengths. Toyota won its market dominance through an LDC policy with its small and medium-sized cars; in the 1990s it added on an HPV approach with its luxury Lexus car range, which now competes with Mercedes on both value and cost.

Thus, the successful, market-focused company must understand fully its macro and micro business systems, make choices along the three dimensions of generic competitive strategy, and win and sustain competitive advantage in the marketplace. Svenska Kullager Fabriken (SKF), the famous Swedish engineering company and the world market leader in bearings, rebuilt itself during the 1970s and 1980s to add both cost competitiveness and service value to its products. In doing so it continues to

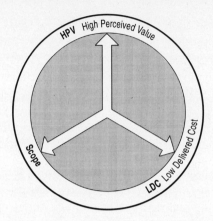

Figure 4.1 Three dimensions of competitive advantage

compete on the basis of wide scope in the bearings industry but has added a deep defence against low-cost competitors and significant value-based advantage for its customers (see Exhibit 4.1).

Exhibit 4.1   *Marketing in action case*

Svenska Kullager Fabriken's (SKF) competitive advantage in bearings

Svenska Kullager Fabriken (SKF) was created in Sweden in 1907 to exploit a new bearing design developed by Sven Wingquist, a young maintenance engineer, and soon became world leader in its product area. From their postwar strength in Asia, Japanese competitors such as Nippon Seiko began to attack world markets in the 1970s. Their competitive strategy was based on aggressive pricing. SKF responded by cutting its costs and expanding beyond its traditional and predominantly European and Latin American markets. The company cut manufacturing costs, reduced staff numbers and invested in new manufacturing modes. These initiatives increased cost competitiveness and underpinned SKF's defence of its number 1 position in the world market (20 per cent share versus 10 per cent for Nippon Seiko, the industry number 2).

In 1985 Mauritz Sahlin became the new chief executive of SKF and encountered further economic and competitive pressure in 1986 and 1987. Demand became weaker and profit margins declined. He responded by looking in a fresh manner at market segmentation, and by reorganizing the company around the three key markets of:

▶ standard bearings for all customers, managed by the Bearing Industries division;

▶ replacement bearings for the industrial and automobile segments, run by the Bearing Services division;

▶ bearings for specialty applications that need highly specialized technical, scientific and engineering skills, run by the Specialty Bearings division.

This restructuring around different markets reconfigured a traditionally centralized and product-led company, and had as its central thrust depth of market understanding and quality of customer service. A good illustration of this new emphasis on moving further out on both the high perceived value axis and the low delivered cost axis was seen in the strategy of Goran Malm, the new head of the Bearing Services division. He defined his business as delivering 'trouble-free operations' to customers in the belief that many companies can produce and sell bearings, but few can produce solutions to the problems that bearing users encounter. Malm's objective became that of helping customers to operate more profitably by using SKF bearings.

For example, in the replacement market for automobile bearings, Goran found that the main user problems were finding the correct bearing, figuring out how to install it and how to get the accessories necessary to install the bearings. His response was to develop ready-made kits containing the necessary bearings – including competitive brands if needed! – and installation accessories and instructions. Kits were developed for all the main applications (wheels, gearboxes, differentials, etc.) and the main car models. These kits were supplied to the 46 SKF companies worldwide and through them to automobile distributors and dealers. The result was high perceived value for customers – a problem solved in one kit – but also lower delivered cost since most of the traditional cost of search and acquisition of materials and information was removed by the pre-designed kit.

The implementation of such market-focused strategies throughout the company allowed SKF to move out along both value and cost axes while retaining its wide industry scope. By 1989 SKF profits had doubled; share price increased 50 per cent in June 1990 when the 1989 results were announced. According to Goran Malm, customer surveys showed that price had become the fourth most important buying criterion versus second in 1981; price had been passed out by reliability and speed of delivery, while quality remained the primary consideration.[4]

Strategic management and strategic marketing

Winning and sustaining competitive advantage are in reality no easy matter. Obviously not all companies in an industry can be competitively superior. What distinguishes those that are? Such firms have a deep understanding of the macro business system and within it of the configuration of their own micro business system, and make clear choices about generic competitive strategy. These are fundamental marketing activities, of a primarily strategic nature, which enable the achievement of market focus. But they are not exclusively marketing activities. Other expertise and resources of the firm – operations, finance, logistics, and R&D – must be involved if there is to be effective strategic analysis and good strategic choice. The roots of generic competitive advantage permeate the whole organization. To believe that the marketing manager and the marketing team can achieve all this on their own is naive and fails to appreciate the nature of the strategic management of the firm.

Strategic management is a subdiscipline of management and addresses, both as an academic discipline as and a managerial practice, the problems of directing a firm from a general manager's or *chief executive's perspective*. The chief executive is responsible to the board of the company for its long-term commercial viability. He or she must concern himself about the expectations of shareholders and other stakeholders in the organization. He or she must orchestrate in an optimal way the work of and resource allocation between R&D, marketing, operations, logistics, finance and human resources; he or she must do this at both a strategic and more short-term operational level. Fundamentally, the task of the chief executive finds expression in a corporate strategy or plan for the firm. This indicates the chosen future direction for the company and contains objectives and mission statements, as well as detailed strategies for various component activities, including marketing. Strategic marketing is enveloped in, and derives from, the overall strategic management of the firm.

The marketing manager and team must work closely with the chief executive and the rest of the senior management team in the development of the firm's corporate strategy. This involves not only analysis and choice, but also lengthy discussion, lobbying of functional interest, special plea bargaining, compromise and ultimately a resolution and agreement that all managers 'buy into'. Marketing is often a catalyst here in ensuring that the company maintains an outward perspective on markets, needs and customers. Too often there is a tendency for firms, and their general managers, to internalize their problems, to become preoccupied with issues like cost cutting, inventory reduction, short-term return on investment, product rationalization, and so on, without any concomitant focus on market impact and market opportunity. Figure 4.2 suggests that achieving long-term profitability in corporate strategic terms is achieved through a balance of inward and outward perspective, through strategies of LDC and HPV, and through efficiency and innovation.

Strategy in marketing deals with the identification and understanding of market opportunities and company capabilities, leading to the choice of markets in which to compete and the manner in which to compete, with a view to satisfying corporate goals. The strategic marketing process is both a premiss for the other three core marketing processes while also related intrinsically, both as driver and derivative, to the firm's corporate strategy. This relationship is illustrated succinctly in the case of two classic tech-

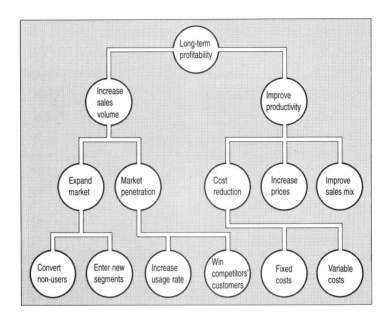

Figure 4.2 Corporate strategy and long-term profitability

niques or frameworks used in strategic management – the Ansoffian growth matrix and the Boston Consulting Group's growth-share matrix.

Strategic frameworks

Ansoff's matrix dates from 1965, an era which had seen two decades of the greatest growth in economic output in history. How to cope with and manage this rate of growth was a dilemma for managers. The matrix was an aid to assessing strategic options for companies in their pursuit of growth objectives. Its early use both managerially and theoretically was related to the planning of corporate growth and development – businesses could grow through market penetration, market development, product development or diversification, and the relative opportunities, merits and risks of these options could be identified and carefully weighted (see Figure 4.3).

Within the marketing literature the same framework came to be widely used in considering product policy – posing the same options and choices but at a very micro level of analysis. What is sometimes forgotten within the marketing debate is that product policy choices of this nature must find their context in broader corporate strategy and company-wide priorities. It is both futile and dangerous for such a debate to occur within the marketing team, unless it derives from growth directions set at the corporate level or unless the marketing team plans to communicate carefully the result of its

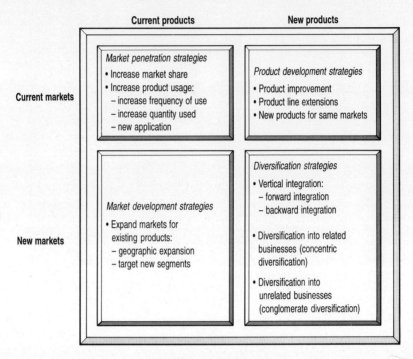

Figure 4.3 Ansoff's growth matrix

deliberations to the top management team with a view to influencing – but not pre-empting – future company direction.

Portfolio analysis

Much the same must be said concerning the use of the BCG matrix. By the early 1970s firms had grown not only in size but in the range of product markets or industries in which each operated. Top management of large diversified companies found itself trying to coordinate businesses and divisions – or what became known as strategic business units (SBUs) – across many different markets and industries, sometimes with little marketing or manufacturing synergy between each business or SBU. The Boston Consulting Group's growth-share matrix was a response to the problem of managing this diversity. In particular, it helped in allocating scarce cash between businesses which top management could not hope to understand in all their complexity.

The matrix views the business world along two dimensions – market attractiveness, for which it uses market growth rate as a proxy, and company capability or competitive strength, for which it uses relative market share as a proxy. Market share dominance is used as the second dimension because of the evidence that market share is strongly and positively correlated with profitability and with net cashflow.[5] Share dominance is used to indicate not absolute market share but a business's market share relative to that of the largest competitor. This acknowledges that there is a vast difference between having a 30 per cent share when the next largest competitor is 20 per cent, compared with when the largest competitor has 50 per cent of the market. Market growth rate is used as a dimension because of the implications for cash management and strategic direction. In a period of rapid growth market share can be captured relatively easily, but at the expense of considerable investments of cash to fund the growth necessary to win this share. In maturity, however, the structure of the market hardens and market share is expanded with great difficulty, but maintenance of a strong position should by the same token be quite achievable and should generate a cash surplus on trading.

This categorization of businesses or SBUs in terms of their relative market share (and therefore their assumed cost position relative to competitors and their ability to generate cash) and the rate of growth in their market (and therefore their assumed requirement for cash investment) provides an elegant if simple framework for assessing the cashflow characteristics of each SBU, for allocating cash, and deciding strategy at both a corporate level and at business/SBU level strategy. Figure 4.4 plots the positions of a company's businesses into one of four cells, each of which has broad policy implications:

1 *Cash Cows.* The lower left quadrant consists of SBUs with high market shares operating in low growth markets. Because they enjoy high

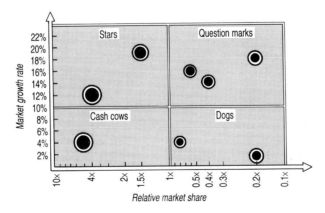

Figure 4.4 The Boston Consulting Group's growth-share matrix

market share, profitability will be good and because investment requirements will be low, considering the maturity of the market, the need for cash investment will be small. Cash cows, today's 'breadwinners', generate the resources to fund the company's development in other high growth markets.

2 *Stars*. A star is a market leader in a high growth market. Profitability is likely to be high, but investment requirements to maintain the SBU's position will be high also. Such stars should be the company's top priority for resourcing. In the future, as the market matures, these become the firm's cash cows.

3 *Question Marks*. These are low market share businesses in high growth markets. They have high cash requirements because of their weak positions in resource-rapacious markets. The company faces a 'double or quit' situation. The decision to invest aggressively to overtake the leading players and become a star depends on a number of considerations. Has the firm the resources? Is the business really destined to achieve star status? What is likely to be competitor reaction should it attempt to do so? If a question mark's position cannot be improved, it will continue to absorb cash. As the market matures, its fortunes will decline even further to that of a dog.

4 *Dogs*. These have low market shares in low growth markets. Usually, they are unprofitable and, if they require investment to keep their position, they become cash users. Dogs can consume more management time than they are worth. The best strategy is to harvest – milk for short-term profits if possible without any investment – and then divest them.

The original BCG matrix uses the two dimensions of relative share and market growth. Many elaborations of this approach followed BCG's innovation. These mostly revolved around generalizing from market share to *competitive position/capability* and from market growth to *market attractiveness*. An extensive range of factors and considerations is used to identify and assess the firm's strength in different businesses and the attractiveness of the markets and businesses themselves. The most widely used techniques include the business portfolio popularized by General Electric with McKinsey & Co., A. D. Little Inc.'s product-market evolution portfolio, and Royal Dutch Shell's directional policy matrix. A composite of matrices from several sources is presented in Figure 4.5 where each of the nine cells contains strategic recommendation.

Such a portfolio approach has attractions to the marketer as well as to the general manager. George Day, in a seminal 1977 article, applied the framework to the product policy decision and to marketing strategy by changing the unit of analysis to product and naming the resultant framework the product portfolio.[6] Portfolio analysis then became viable as a hierarchical tool – a business portfolio used at corporate management level, a product portfolio used at SBU level, and even a product line portfolio used at a marketing or product management level. The portfolio tool, in all its various forms postdating BCG's initial innovation, must be viewed in this hierarchical manner. The levels of analysis are nested within each other and deeply interconnected. When a marketing team uses the tool it must be conscious of the nature of, and set of policies attaching to, the corporate portfolio; of its own role in configuring the product portfolio; and of its direct responsibility for the balancing and rebalancing of the product line portfolio.

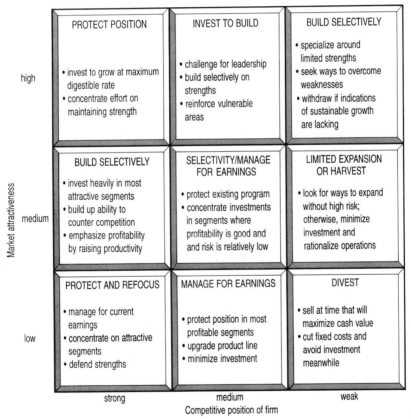

Source: G.S. Day, (1984), *Strategic Market Planning: The Pursuit of Competitive Advantage*, West Publishing Co. St. Paul, Minnesota, p.121.

Figure 4.5 A market attractiveness/company capability portfolio matrix

Strategy and process

The high level of cross-functional interaction and teamwork required to undertake strategic marketing emphasizes again the process approach to business organization adopted in this book. The 1990s began with a widespread concern in industry about the tradition of organizational specialization around functions and an acute awareness of the competitive damage that can be done when such specialization is taken to an extreme. The Ford Motor Company began to talk of the dangers of 'chimney stack' management; Hewlett Packard spoke of the damage caused by 'silo management'. The images were intended to suggest the organizational problem of managers who felt as if they worked at the bottom of a silo or chimney and could only communicate to their colleagues in other functions if they climbed right to the top of the organization and then back down the adjacent chimney. Under such circumstances, timely and effective horizontal communication becomes a virtual impossibility. Both companies and researchers became alarmed at the extent to which organizational fortresses could be built in companies that made communication and coordination across functional boundaries difficult or impossible, and began to search for more fluid organizational mechanisms to break down such barriers or to prevent their occurrence.

The design of 'flat' rather than 'tall' organizations is one result. The emphasis on cross-functional taskforces and temporary special groupings is another. Figure 4.6 maps this horizontal organizational focus and signals the move from hierarchy to heterarchy, from function to process. The marketer has a special need for sensitivity to these interfacing challenges since marketing sits at the interface between an organization and its market environment. Marketing action can only be effective if it can communicate market realities to all parts of the organization and if it can mobilize all parts of the organization to invent, design, produce, deliver and support a service or product for the market. This is the essence of market focus – focus on the market on the one hand, and market focusing of the whole organization on the other.

Managing the core marketing processes requires skill and expertise in interfacing and in teamwork. The importance of interfaces at the top of the organization – to manage the marketing strategy process within the wider context of the strategic management of the firm – has already been stressed. The marketing manager is of necessity a member of the strategic management team just as all members of this team must be marketers in viewpoint and persuasion. Equally, the order generation, fulfilment and service process is one which penetrates all parts of a business, including a majority over which marketing managers typically have no direct control (e.g. credit

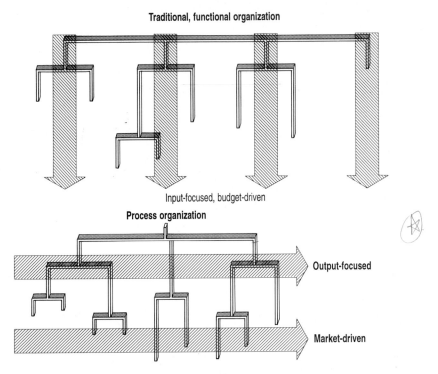

Figure 4.6 From hierarchy to heterarchy

approval, production scheduling, procurement, production, quality management, testing, dispatch, logistics, parts supply, maintenance contracting,
just to mention a few!). The new product development process which
guarantees the future of the business is also a fundamentally interdisciplinary and interfunctional one, requiring the integration and alignment of
activities from market research through R&D, engineering, pilot production, testing, financing, and commercialization to sales.

Real-time implementation of strategy

An important benefit of the process approach is that it enables a real-time
implementation of strategic intent. The traditional approach to managing
strategy has been to categorize it into two sequential parts – formulation
and implementation. A manager drew up a strategy, and then set about
putting it in place at a later, often unclearly specified occasion. A process
orientation offers greater simultaneity of intent and operation, of plan and
implementation. It does so because as a manager conceives a plan or
strategy, he or she must almost simultaneously consider its execution –

Strategy is choice of direction . . .

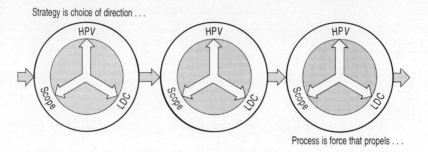

Process is force that propels . . .

Figure 4.7 Linking strategy and process

what are the structures and systems, skills and resources, style and shared values necessary to implement the strategy? So, conception is quickly followed by delivery of product or service. Process overlays strategy. Strategy represents the choice of direction, while process is the force which implicitly or explicitly propels the organization in that direction. This real-time interaction is suggested in Figure 4.7.

A real-time view of strategy and process is more in accord with what actually happens in the day-to-day management of enterprises. Managers plan while they act and act while they plan. Research shows that the time managers spend in drawing up plans formally only accounts for a very small amount of their work time. Mintzberg's notion of 'emergent' strategy – strategy that emerges from everyday operations as revealed in a consistent pattern of decisions – is redolent of the process approach to business organization.[7] This approach also highlights the irony that most traditional business strategy and planning textbooks spend, in a Pareto-like fashion, 80 per cent of their content on formulation and the remaining 20 per cent on issues and problems of implementation – quite the reverse of what managers actually do!

Consumer, business-to-business, services marketing

While the link between strategy and process constitutes a theme in this book, so also does the interconnection between consumer, business-to-business and services marketing. The concept of the business system helps to illustrate the fact that all consumer products are usually the outcome of many business-to-business marketing activities and that both consumer and business-to-business markets usually depend on services markets if business is to take place. The potato producer cited in the previous chapter will probably depend on the technical advisory service of a chemical company such as Ciba Geigy or Monsanto, that supplies the farm with fertilizer, with herbicides and with potato disease preventatives. Equally, the multinational brander of frozen potato waffles will depend very vitally for success on the quality of the services purchased from market research suppliers and advertising agencies. Industrial markets, business-to-business markets, consumer markets, products and services are all interconnected within any business system.

Marketing does differ, as we have seen, as one moves from consumer to business-to-business and on to services marketing, but the differences are in matters of degree rather than fundamental principle. The same turns out to be true when we turn our attention to marketing for not-for-profit organizations. The same concerns, challenges, theories and principles of good practice apply to the marketing of safe driving behaviour, dental hygiene, the activities of an arts centre or the promotion of a wildlife trust as apply to other forms of marketing. In managing the four core processess, and in particular the marketing strategy process, the marketing team must be able to integrate and synthesize these various viewpoints. Indeed, having to do so should be taken as a signal to the subdisciplines within marketing to pay special attention to developing integrating frameworks and concepts rather than unduly divergent ones.

Theory and practice: the need for integration

Within the discipline of marketing, important subdisciplines, such as services marketing, business-to-business marketing and not-for-profit marketing, have established themselves. Each subdiscipline has provided an important contribution to explaining how its world works and has built a useful body of scholarly knowledge. Yet as each subdiscipline seeks to understand more fully the characteristics of its domain and establish its ascendancy, there is a danger of a 'blinkering' of vision and of myopia.[8] Kuhn, in his book *The Structure of Scientific Revolutions*, argues that the full acceptance of a paradigm (put simply, a model or framework of how a particular set of phenomena interacts) is unavoidably accompanied by drastically reduced vision.[9] This can lead to a failure to grasp the whole picture and to see marketing activity in a narrow disjointed and divergent manner, rather than as a series of integrated and often simultaneous, customer-focused activities.

There are, in effect, limitations to the ability of the various subdisciplines to explain this wider picture. There can be over-emphasis on convergence within the subdisciplines at the expense of studying trends and interdependencies *between* the subdisciplines. Indeed, even within the subdisciplines, divergence increasingly expresses itself. For instance, services marketing theory is built around four main constructs of intangibility, inseparability, heterogeneity and perishability. Yet on the inseparability dimension we witness an increasing decoupling of consumption and production, e.g. banks' use of ATMs to reduce customer/personnel contact while expanding business hours for basic services. Electronic publishing and video rental stores provide sophisticated inventory and distribution facilities which minimize the notion of perishability of services.

So too, there is evidence that in the goods/services and consumer/industrial dichotomy, the difference between the subdisciplines is exaggerated. Both practice and scholarship benefit from attempting to find similarities between services and other marketing activities, in an integrated rather than a dual path of theory development. Indeed companies in both the manufacturing and service sectors have started to look beyond their own traditional reference points for more effective ways of meeting customers' needs. The 'service factory' concept, described by Chase and Garvin, shows how manufacturers can involve customers before, during and after the production process.[10] General Motor (GM) Company's approach to marketing its Saturn line illustrates the service company. GM has worked hard to create a competitive advantage by incorporating services marketing concepts into both the production and sales of its cars. Saturns are designed and manufactured by cross-functional teams. After the sale, the firm maintains a relationship with its customers by contacting them frequently for feedback, inviting them to barbecues with other Saturn customers, and providing each customer with his or her own Saturn representative to contact if problems arise with the car. Ford has recently had to follow suit with its 'service advisers', who liaise between the dealer's service shop and the customer whose car is being serviced.

Achieving and sustaining market focus are not just about one of consumer goods marketing, business-to-business marketing or services marketing. They are about integrating consumer goods marketing and services marketing and business-to-business marketing with other key firm activities through the four core marketing processes. The central implication is that marketing shares a common set of concerns and is based on a common set of theories and principles of good practice no matter what kind of market relationships and processes we study or have to manage. It is also true, and vital to understand, that the practice of marketing is essentially situational – the market and business system context must determine the way in which theory and principle are applied. By pursuing this approach both managers and scholars stand to benefit by constructing a *contingency* theory of marketing which integrates the contribution of its subdiscipline in a meaningful and cumulative manner.

REVIEW QUESTIONS

4.1   Elaborate on the three key dimensions of generic competitive advantage. How are they illustrated in the case of SKF Bearings?

4.2   The marketing strategy process is both a premiss for the other three core marketing processes while also related intrinsically, both as driver and derivative, to the firm's corporate strategy. Discuss.

4.3   Explain the historical context of portfolio analysis and consider how the framework is used at different strategic levels within a firm.

4.4   What links do you perceive between the concepts of strategy and process?

4.5   Why is it important to take an integrated view of consumer marketing, business-to-business marketing and services marketing in managing the marketing strategy process?

CHAPTER 5

The job of the marketing manager

- ▶ Managing the core marketing processes
- ▶ Competences in marketing
- ▶ Managing marketing interfaces
- ▶ Tasks of the marketing manager
- ▶ The international marketing manager

Marketing in action cases
Computer manufacturer redesigns its core processes
Kindle Software's 'shoe leather' marketing

ABOUT THIS CHAPTER

The job of the marketing manager is examined from his or her perspective. In essence, this job is to ensure that the firm or organization wins and sustains market focus throught the adroit management of the four core marketing processes in the context of the relevant macro and micro business systems.

The marketing manager is an expert in the specialized knowledge of marketing *and* in the integration of that competence with that of other disciplines. In the hierarchy of the organization, marketing is 'home' to this competence – a place where the intellectual capital of marketing is nurtured and its competitive distinctiveness enhanced.

The tasks and skill requirements of the marketer in managing and co-managing the core processes are described. (This also provides an effective 'guidemap' through the rest of the book.) The nature of marketing competence, as well as the benefits and problems of managing marketing interfaces and redesigning core processes, are addressed. Finally, the international context of the marketing manager's work is highlighted.

Marketing and market focus

Put simply, the marketing manager manages the marketing function in an organization and co-manages the processes that create customer value. In

72

the first case, the manager has sole responsibility for the organization's competence in marketing and for deploying that competence to good effect as well as for nurturing it as a strategic asset. In the second case, the marketing manager can only have co-responsibility since virtually all processes that create customer value are dependent on the involvement of other aspects of any business – whether operations management, finance, logistics or R&D. Here the marketing manager must be a team player focusing on task outputs and the activities that have to be designed and coordinated to achieve the required results.

In the first three chapters we have looked at how marketing involves achieving and keeping market focus through the skilful management of the four core marketing processes in the context of the relevant macro and micro business systems. Marketing is pivotal to matching customer needs with company competences in a manner that creates valued relationships which are competitively unique and profitable to both parties to any exchange. This matching of market needs and company competences takes place in a dynamic manner – both needs and competences are continuously changing. The marketing manager and marketing team must keep pace with this ever-changing intersection of needs and capability in a market-place where competitors are also continuously changing, bringing new offerings to the market and acquiring new competencies that may render those of other companies less unique or outmoded.

Managing the core marketing processes

The result of the effective conduct of this work is the provision to markets of products and services needed by customers, available to them where and when needed, priced at an acceptable level, profitable to the supplier and with all the relevant information about the product or service persuasively communicated to the customer. This is conventionally known as managing the marketing mix – the 4 Ps of product, price, promotion and place (distribution). But such a successful outcome must be seen in a much broader perspective than merely managing the marketing mix. Getting the 4 Ps 'right' is a crucial part of marketing activity. This is dependent, however, on the 'right' management of the core marketing processes that comprise marketing's task and its contribution to competitive effectiveness.

As described earlier *the marketing strategy process* determines the choice of market in which the firm intends to compete. It involves scrutiny of customer need, assessment of marketing assets and liabilities, and the development of marketing objectives and a broad strategy to serve the chosen market, all within the wider context of the firm's strategic management. *The marketing management process* addresses the competitive positioning of the product or service within its chosen market and involves product choice, pricing, communication and selling, distribution, as well as the development of performance management systems and measures to monitor and adapt execution.

The order generation, fulfilment and service (OGFS) process operationalizes the day-to-day business of achieving customer satisfaction in a manner profitable to the firm. It involves generating orders and managing these orders 'through' the organization. It includes activities, often multidisciplinary, such as costing, order entry and prioritization, scheduling, delivery, invoicing, installation, service and aftersales query. *The new product development (NPD) process* concerns itself with renewing the firm's portfolio of goods and services.

These four processes, while forming the basis for marketing practice, might best be thought of as the 'technology' of marketing. The marketing manager has a role in both the architecture and task management of this technology. Parts of it he or she owns and 'drives' exclusively; this is essentially the marketing management process. In others parts he or she shares ownership and must integrate his or her competence with that of others and other departments in the firm; this is in the case of the other three marketing processes. Figure 5.1 illustrates this activity.

The marketing strategy process is part of the overall strategic management of the firm. It is impossible to manage effectively if it is not enveloped in the broader strategic direction of the whole enterprise. Strategic marketing both derives from, and is a crucial driver of, strategic management. The top management team, irrespective of functional or disciplinary allegiance, all participate. The order generation, fulfilment and service process involves the specific activities of generating orders, bringing these orders into the organization, 'assembling' the required product or service, delivering it to the customer, providing such support and service as is required and dealing with any associated recovery and recycling necessities after consumption. Thus these activities penetrate all parts of a business, including a majority over which the marketing department conventionally has no direct control. The new product development process is also a fundamentally inter-disciplinary and inter-functional one, requiring the integration and alignment of activities from market research through R&D, engineering, pilot production, testing, financing and business strategy development as well as marketing. Teamwork both within and across functions and disciplines is crucial.

Marketing is usually presented as one of the central managerial functions, along with financial management, operations management and

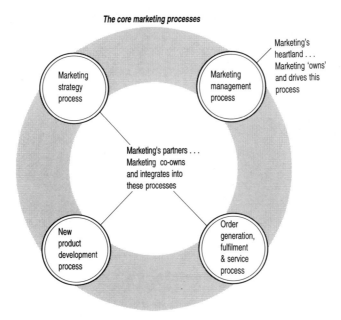

Figure 5.1 Managing and co-managing marketing

human resource management, as well as possibly logistics/transport and R&D. In the small venture it is often carried out by the owner-manager, or general manager, and will normally emerge as a specialist function managed by a marketing manager only as the firm grows. With the growth of a company, the marketing function may encompass all the subsidiary tasks and managerial positions associated with sales management, advertising, distribution, delivery logistics, selling, promotion, merchandising, public relations and product management. However, whether there is a person called a marketing manager or not, marketing activity and tasks must be performed in all businesses.

Indeed, part of the evolving emphasis in marketing discussed in Chapters 1 and 2 points towards the sharing of parts of marketing activity among the top management team, including the general manager or the chief executive and other relevant senior managers. In some ways this might be seen as an attempt to recreate the central and integrated role of marketing in business management that is typically found in new and small ventures – ones that might be characterized as being entrepreneurial-spirited. This integration is all too easily lost as organizations grow and necessarily specialize their management functions. A process view encourages marketing to develop and respect its specialized technical, disciplinary competence but never to lose sight of the reality that this competence is meaningful only when integrated fully with the work of other functions and the strategic management of the whole enterprise.

Competences in marketing

It is only when we look at the marketing management process itself that we find a more unifunctional, unidisciplinary process for which marketing experts must be held solely responsible and accountable. The marketing management process is the heartland of the professional discipline, dealing with the acquisition, deployment and enhancement of specialist marketing knowledge and contributing through its interaction with the other core processes to the successful management of the market relationships of the firm. In so far as this is done particularly well, those in the function can build a distinctive competence for the organization. The marketing discipline in any one company may therefore represent:

1 A core competence which helps the company to compete but which provides it with no distinctive and competitively valuable advantage – the marketing discipline represents a level of competence that allows the company to participate in the competitive game but does not give it a winning edge.

2 A core and distinctive competence which not only allows the company to participate in the competitive game but gives it a positive marketing advantage over competitors – marketing and all its knowledge resources and skills become a vital strategic asset for the company.

3 A competence that is not core to the company and that is poorly developed and that represents a competitive disadvantage actually or potentially debarring it from participation in the competitive game – a weak marketing department can destroy competitiveness.

Marketing activity requires thoughtful and, at times, complex management. Those in the discipline have sole ownership of and responsibility for, a core competence that may also become a distinctive competence. The competence must, at a minimum, be maintained at a level that qualifies the company to compete effectively. More importantly, it is the task of marketing to seek ways to build the competence of the discipline into a source of competitive advantage by deepening and extending its knowledge resources and its skills. As well as this sole, direct responsibility, marketing then has further responsibility to co-manage the key processes over which it has only partial authority.

Managing marketing interfaces

This emphasis on the necessity for the manager to manage and co-manage marketing's mission, to think and plan strategically, to nurture the philosophy of market focus in the company points to the inescapable necessity for effective integration of marketing tasks and activities with those of other functions in the business and with the general management of the enterprise. Success in doing this will reflect the manager's understanding of the interfaces between marketing and other aspects of the organization and his or her ability to handle these interfaces successfully. It requires a mindset which can seamlessly overlay departmental activity with cross-functional task.

In the area of new product development, for example, it has become increasingly clear that R&D, marketing, operations and logistics cannot and must not be kept apart. For much of the post-war period this was unfortunately standard practice with new product development arranged in the manner of a relay race with each functional specialization involved for its brief period after which it passed the embryonic product onto the next specialist in line. Starting in the 1960s and 1970s Japanese companies in particular began to use a 'rugby style' in which interfunctional teams take responsibility for the entire process from concept to market launch. This allows problems of 'manufacturability' to be anticipated and solved right from the product concept stage. It allows the financial expert to assess and reassess financial feasibility continuously as variations and options for development are suggested and as costings change. It allows marketing to influence all stages and to interpret market needs continuously for the benefit of designers, production engineers and pricing analysts. Thus the marketing manager must develop a deep knowledge of his firm's micro business system, its dynamics and interrelationships.

Core process redesign

The last decade has been characterized by an enormous increase in the depth and importance of the interface between operations management and marketing. Total quality management (TQM) and world class manufacturing (WCM) have become an important part of the vernacular of management. Such 'lean production' competences, initially developed at Toyota in the late 1950s and known as the Toyoda system, led Japanese business down a route of development which gave it unprecedented market flexibility and low cost but high quality products, which Western companies scramble to imitate. This approach to manufacturing and operations methods has enormous implications for marketing, particularly in the area of new product development, as it so often confers simultaneously inherent cost and production flexibility advantages which companies that organize production in the Western mass production tradition cannot match. This is clearly evidenced in the car manufacturing industry. In the early 1990s US and European car makers were still taking up to five years to develop a new car, whereas the Japanese manufacturers had a three-year development (see Exhibit 20.2, p.419). Moving towards the twenty-first century, the speed with which new products or services can be launched – speed-to-market or 'turbomarketing' – is a critical dimension of market focus.

For existing products and services a firm can achieve significant increases in competitiveness by reshaping the core activities which link manufacturing and delivery to ultimate customer satisfaction. This involves scrutinizing its micro business system for inefficiencies and shortcomings and being attentive to the key value-adding tasks, systems and structures. Thus there is considerable value in spending time and effort in defining the core processes. While such activities may share broad generic similarities, their precise configuration in one firm in one industry is likely to be different from that of its competitors. The intention should be to define these key tasks and activities such that they drive the competitiveness of the firm for years to come. Exhibit 5.1 provides an interesting example of a computer manufacturer that redesigned its core marketing processes and IT systems. In doing so it achieved sizeable cost savings, slashed order-cycle times, improved customer satisfaction and increased sales through better use of information about customers.

Exhibit 5.1 *Marketing in action case*

Computer manufacturer redesigns its core processes

A large European computer manufacturer recently redesigned its core marketing processes and IT systems to overcome competitive shortcomings. Comparisons with leading competitors indicated that sales and order administration costs had reached uncompetitive levels, and surveys showed that customers wanted faster response times to inquiries and more reliable on-time delivery performance.

In order to keep customers satisfied, sales representatives were spending inordinate amounts of their time correcting problems introduced by inefficient workflows and systems. Errors and rework were as high as 100 per cent of orders for some product groups. Changes in orders (whether due to customer changes, factory requirements or the discovery of errors) would result in an administrative nightmare as the saleforce and factory, as well as the customer's purchasing agent and end user, had to coordinate rescheduling manually. Further, information systems 'blind spots' hindered order tracking.

The order administration department tried to reduce errors and minimize turnaround time, but its efforts were frustrated by the fact that the bulk of the company's rework arose because of errors or changes generated outside its department. A large percentage of rework could be traced to incorrect configurations of the customers' computer systems and poor information from manufacturing on actual lead-times – both of which had apparently nothing to do with administering orders!

Only when the company adopted a core process approach was it able to focus attention on the errors made early in the order generation and fulfilment process that caused rework later in the chain. By widening both the problem and solution sets, it was able to see that minor errors made in the initial configuration of a computer system could delay installation of the system for days or weeks.

One part of the solution, therefore, was to develop an expert system that could help sales representatives configure complicated computer systems. As an added benefit, the expert systems not only reduced rework but also improved response time to customer inquiries. In addition to time spent correcting errors, routine customer inquiries were found to take up a large part of the saleforce's time. Saleforce costs were reduced considerably – first, by making additional order status information available on-line to the sales offices; second, by off-loading routine customer inquiries to a lower cost customer contact representative; and later, by developing an automated order entry and intelligent inquiry system available to the customer.

This facilitated greater integration between quotation and order entry processes and between sales office and factory. Through this core process redesign, the computer manufacturer identified savings in excess of the 30 per cent required to be competitive, while simultaneously slashing order-cycle times, improving customer satisfaction, and increasing sales through better use of information about customers.[1]

Thus the management of interfaces within the micro business system is a very special and urgent priority for the marketing manager. He must learn to understand how to manage with others as well as to manage within the marketing area itself. The ability to obtain information, to analyze and to conceptualize must be matched with skills in decision-making and interpersonal relations. The reward is substantial in terms of company effectiveness as well as in terms of personal development. Equally, the manager who manages marketing as an isolated fiefdom is now a danger of potentially lethal proportion to companies in both local and international markets.

Tasks of the marketing manager

The work of the marketing manager has many dimensions. He or she takes charge of creating and maintaining the reality of a market-focused organi-

zation. This involves the management of the four core marketing processes
– tasks that demand both an appreciation of the evolving role and nature of
marketing activity and the organizational, political and interpersonal skills
to communicate well with the rest of a management team. In particular, the
manager must provide leadership and direction to the marketing team.

The marketing manager is responsible for the creative, insightful and
disciplined analysis of customers, markets, competitors and their interrelated dynamics. Thus he or she must have analytical skills. In Part II of this
book special emphasis is placed on the development of ability to understand
systematically:

▶ customers and customer behaviour;
▶ market structures, size and trends;
▶ the need for marketing research and the structuring of such research;
▶ competitors, their strengths and weaknesses and likely behaviour;
▶ industry structure and market forces affecting competitive behaviour;
▶ company resources and competences, strengths and weaknesses.

This information underpins and provides the crucial raw material for 'The
Marketing Strategy Process' described in Part III. The marketing manager
works with the chief executive and other top managers at the corporate
level in conceptualizing and developing overall company objectives, mission and strategy. The marketing strategy process itself determines the
choice of market in which the firm intends to compete. It involves scrutiny
of customer need, understanding the firm's competences in the light of
market need, assessment of marketing assets and liabilities, and the development of marketing objectives and a broad strategy to serve the chosen
market, all within the wider context of the firm's strategic management.
Issues of organizing for marketing and balancing specialists and integrators
arise. He or she must, in effect, overlay strategy with process. Equally
importantly, he or she must provide leadership, empower the key players
and help towards nurturing a supportive company culture, sometimes
referred to as internal marketing.

The ultimate shape of this marketing strategy and its successful expedi-
tion will involve 'The Marketing Management Process and the Order
Generation, Fulfilment and Service Process'. These processes are the subject
of Part IV. Marketing management addresses the competitive positioning of
the product or service within its chosen market and involves product
choice, pricing, communication and selling, distribution, as well as the
development of performance management systems and measures to monitor and adapt execution, e.g.:

▶ decisions about competitive positioning of a firm's product or service –
exactly whom to serve in the chosen market and what particular

benefits – or 'bundles' of benefits – might be proposed to that customer;

▶ decisions about product or service choice – exactly what offering(s)
with what attributes and characteristics will the company bring to the
market;

▶ decisions about pricing policy – exactly what price will be paid for the
company's offerings at each stage in the business system through to
final consumption;

▶ decisions about communication policy – exactly what information will
be provided to the market on the company and its offerings so that
potential customers, influencers and members of the business system
are appropriately informed and persuaded to do business with the
company;

▶ decisions about distribution policy – exactly how will the company's
products or services be brought to the final consumer, involving
choice of and commitments to other members of the business system
who must handle the products or services, the design and implementation of logistical systems whether physical (trucking, shipping,
warehousing, etc.), electronic (as in ATM for banks or financial information via a teletext system) or other, to move the company's offerings to where they are needed.

Executing the strategy involves 'actioning' decisions in terms of developing
programmes, action plans, annual budgets and the design of performance
management systems and criteria. This enables the execution of decisions
and their consequences to be monitored, corrective action to be taken
where necessary and ensures that effective learning takes place.

Order generation, fulfilment and service (OGFS) ultimately operationalizes marketing management. It involve a series of steps from an order being
won from a customer to a point, subsequent to any aftersales service or
query, where the customer may be deemed to be satisfied with the
exchange. It thus brings marketing activity full circle and closes the loop
between strategic intent and final customer satisfaction. This OGFS process
of necessity involves much cross-functional activity and teamwork beyond
the marketing department.

Part V examines the work of the marketing manager in the context of
'The New Product Development Process'. The firm's portfolio of goods and
services is constantly evolving. As existing offerings are wound down and
eventually deleted, new ones must take their place. Marketing has a leading
role to play here. But again it is a role which must be shared with other
functions within the organization; the rugby-style simultaneity and speed-
to-market now required for NPD success require a high level of organiza-

tional teamwork. Further, the marketing manager must have a full understanding of the interrelationship of marketing and design, and appreciate the role of first-rate design in superior strategy.

The only certainty about marketing activity is change – and learning how to cope with it. A marketing performance which is currently excellent may well falter over time and need to be reshaped and renewed. A key concern or requirement for the marketing manager is not only to achieve but to sustain market focus over time. This is examined in Part VI. Why do excellent companies fail? How do firms renew themselves? How might imaginative marketing re-engineer the business system and change the rule-of-the-game in the industry to the firm's advantage? The successful marketing manager must continually and persistently align and realign the needs and opportunities of the market with the core competences and consequent product and service offerings of the firm – the key to market focus.

The international marketing manager

The international marketing manager has the special role of displaying all the abilities and expertise discussed above and then, in addition, of dealing with the tasks of managing marketing across international boundaries. There are special challenges in entering export markets from an initial domestic base, and then helping to develop a truly international marketing orientation as the company grows from exporting to having an established international presence. Companies pursue international marketing strategies as a fundamental platform for their growth strategy. This is especially true for companies based in smaller countries or more peripheral economies where the domestic market is seldom of adequate size to support even modestly ambitious growth plans. The international marketing manager is, therefore, at the centre of the growth path in such firms.

Business needs international marketers who can identify overseas market opportunities accurately. It needs marketers who can develop a deep understanding of how customers purchase and use products in these different markets and who can guide product and service adaption and new product development to suit the needs of markets that do not conform to the domestic pattern of marketing. As is explored in more detail in Chapter 10, the international marketing manager is faced with a Europe very much in transition. The structures of the European Union should lead to more common marketing practices across Europe, yet forces of regionalization and quasi-nationalism mean that the manager will have to think in an international context even within regions and countries that ostensibly seem geographically defined or cohesive.

International marketers must be able to assess the merits of the various ways in which a company can enter overseas markets – through export relationships, through joint ventures or through direct investment in sales, distribution, logistics and service facilities, and, in due course, in manufacturing facilities. In the case of the small firm, it will often be the case that international marketing activity in its initial stages will be characterized by a managing director who travels intensively and takes on the role of export salesperson – what might be termed 'shoe leather' marketing (see Exhibit 5.2). The international marketer manages the market entry mode, and later the market development avenue as well as the planning, coordinating and controlling of the company's marketing activity across different countries and cultures. He or she works as part of a team with world-class standards of performance in manufacturing or service operations and with strategically-oriented general management.

| Exhibit 5.2 | *Marketing in action case* |

Kindle Software's 'shoe leather' marketing

Kindle Software is a small European software company specializing in the financial service sector with sales of some £20 million, employing 250 people at its Dublin headquarters. Kindle was established in 1979 by Tony Kilduff, its founder and driving force. Yet Kilduff himself has never written or designed a commercial software program.

After getting his business degree, Kilduff had joined the UK textile conglomerate Coates Viyella. He spent eight years with the company travelling extensively from the United Kingdom to the Far East and Australia. While his background was rooted in financial management, Kilduff became heavily involved in the use of information technology. It was this experience that prompted a move into consultancy and the establishment of Kindle.

Despite early contract work and the development of software packages for the distribution and retail sectors, Kindle's success was to be built on the phenomenal sales growth of its Bankmaster product. Kilduff's strength in developing Kindle was his ability to define and focus on market niches. The single product strategy was to prove a huge success. Kindle has sold in excess of $100 million worth of Bankmaster packages. The product has been installed in more than 200 financial institutions in 1,000 locations worldwide and is among the most successful financial services software products ever developed.

The Bankmaster market, principally wholesale and mid-sized retail banks, is truly international. 'Banking is pretty much the same around the world; it's a homogeneous market,' Kilduff said in a recent interview. In the early years, Kilduff was the company's only salesman. 'At that time Kindle was a very small company and we couldn't afford the cost of a dedicated salesperson. Most spare resources had to be ploughed into research and development.'

For the best part of five years, Kilduff was his company's international marketer in the Far and Middle East, Africa and Eastern Europe. Bankmaster found sales in 80 countries worldwide. 'We worked very hard at marketing Bankmaster in lots of places. We succeeded because we were willing to go anywhere in the world where there was a bank. We deliberately stayed away from areas where our competitors were strong and concentrated on our own niche,' adds Kilduff.[2]

These tasks demand special skills which are still very scarce in business. At a very specific level they demand language skills and an associated appreciation of how other cultures conduct business relationships and of the economic institutions and procedures characteristic of different countries. The need for the pan-European marketer has become especially evident – a need for professional managers capable of conducting business in several languages; familiar with many cultures; at home in negotiations with German, French, Italian, Belgian or many other counterparts; and willing to see Europe as their natural market and not as a series of 'foreign' export markets. To take on world markets, companies increasingly take on the characteristics of global corporation. Unilever, perhaps one of the most successful of all of Europe's international companies, takes these competences so seriously that its board includes members from six different countries, and virtually every one of its country operating companies contains expatriate managers as well as locals. In 1992, it had an Italian managing its company in Brazil, a Dutchman in Taiwan, an Englishman in Malaysia, and an American in Mexico.[3] Smaller national European companies that grow through step-by-step internationalization will find it necessary to evolve towards a truly international style of management too, and will provide many opportunities for marketing professionals to build exciting international careers.

REVIEW QUESTIONS

5.1 The job of the marketing manager is basically to take charge of creating and maintaining the reality of a market-focused organization. Discuss.

5.2 Marketing managers have to be effective managers as well as experts in marketing. In the light of this statement what are the competences, skills and abilities that an effective marketing manager should possess?

5.3 What do you perceive to be the difference between the marketing mix with its 4 Ps and the four core marketing processes?

5.4 What do you understand by a core process redesign? Indicate what benefits it might confer on a company.

5.5 All marketing is international marketing. Consider this view.

Part II *Informing marketing activity*

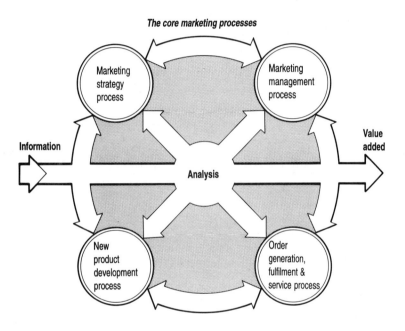

The core marketing processes

Marketing strategy process

Marketing management process

Information

Value added

Analysis

New product development process

Order generation, fulfilment & service process

CHAPTER 6

Understanding the customer

- Concepts of customer behaviour
- Need recognition
- Search for alternatives
- Evaluation of alternatives
- Choice
- Usage: post-purchase behaviour

Marketing in action cases
ICI's Eclat – plastic packaging to customer need
Ladona Teja Construcción's tiles on TV

ABOUT THIS CHAPTER

Understanding customers, and why they make a decision to purchase a product or service, is best approached in a systematic way. A general framework for doing this normally contains five crucial steps: need recognition; the search for alternatives; their evaluation; the final choice; and post-purchase appraisal. Each step is considered in detail and concepts such as high- and low-involvement, evaluative criteria and decision-making units (DMUs) are examined.

Knowledge of customer behaviour is fundamental to informing marketing activity because of its implications for segmentation – whether on the basis of class, life-style or gerontographics – for the choice of target markets, the positioning of the product or service relative to competition, and for the design and management of all subsequent marketing action.

To buy or not to buy?

The domain of customer analysis focuses on understanding people and organizations and their needs for services or products. It is concerned with understanding *who* they are, *what* exactly their need is and with *why, where, when* and *how* they wish to acquire and consume. At least a basic understanding of all these factors is necessary if good marketing decisions are to be made.

The approach to understanding the customer documented in this chapter is a relatively simple and general one, which none the less demands that the manager confront the critical questions outlined above. It has the advantage of being readily applied to both business-to-business customer relationships and to final customer/consumer purchase. The approach may be applied at a judgemental level – by the manager or student using their experience of a market to supply the required information – or it may be used as a basis for identifying the questions which should be explored in a detailed and formal marketing research study.

Concepts of customer behaviour

The 1960s and 1970s saw enormous growth in the development of theory about the behaviour of consumers in the marketplace and about the nature of buying behaviour between organizations. Most of the work followed from the rapid diffusion into marketing of knowledge from areas such as psychology, social psychology, sociology and cultural anthropology.

The results, therefore, rested significantly on intellectual borrowing from these disciplines. Not only concepts but also research techniques and approaches to the measurement of behaviour were borrowed and applied. Marketing and its research base gained greatly from this activity. However, by the end of the 1970s the limitations of many of the more general models and constructs that had been developed became clear. Managers in particular had become somewhat sceptical of the immediate value of the general models in explaining and predicting the behaviour of the customers with whom they dealt on a daily basis.

The classical 'general' models in consumer behaviour[1, 2, 3] and in organizational buying behaviour[4, 5, 6] are all based on an assumption of a rational and very involved customer who acquires and uses information carefully. The criticisms of these models during the 1980s revolved about the lack of evidence in reality for such a degree of rationality and for all but a relatively few purchase situations being characterized by very high customer involvement. The result has been the recognition of a much wider variety of consumer and organizational decision-making modes and the development of more context-bound explanations – the implication being that it is important to understand the particular circumstances and type of purchase situations involved if we are to explain behaviour successfully.

This context-bound dimension is highlighted by studying the business sytem and ascertaining the key value-adding steps both within the firm and its immediate customers *and* in the overall industry. This enables the identification of who are the key players in terms of existing and potential needs and wants. Exhibit 6.1 describes how a business team at ICI found, understood and exploited a new product opportunity in the cosmetics packaging industry. Exhibit 14.2 (p.284) outlines similarly how a broadened understanding of customer wants in a consumer product – men's fashion clothing – allowed the Italian company, Hugo Boss, to reposition itself.

Exhibit 6.1	*Marketing in action case*

ICI's Eclat – plastic packaging to customer need

At ICI plc, the business team for Melinar faced a challenge to grow the business profitably. Melinar is an ICI plastic brand used to make the ubiquitous PET bottles for carbonated soft drinks and mineral water. The customer needs of this business require a company to respond with high-volume production, low costs and strong, large containers. In order to develop its business further and improve profitability the Melinar business team had to find customer needs that required non-seasonal, small-scale, added-value polymer products that would broaden ICI's business base in this area without major investment in new plant.

The team identified cosmetics packaging as the perfect match for the business's competences and strategic needs. Research among cosmetics brand owners showed dissatisfaction with both the materials available and the technical support offered by existing competitors. 'We felt that despite their experience in the marketplace, it should be possible to outclass them by creating a better performing product and supporting it with superior customer service,' noted Chris Blanc, technical service representative. 'Melinar is easily mouldable and shatterproof. and we knew that if the complex moulding and high quality appearance requirements of the cosmetic business could be matched, Melinar's inherent strength would also offer brand owners, retailers and consumers an important safety advantage.'

A small new product team from two ICI sites – Wilton in the United Kingdom and Rozenburg in The Netherlands – was formed in 1990. As a result of discussions with potential customers, the team set out to develop a new product with the following customer-specified characteristics for premium quality packaging:

▶ high clarity and sparkle;
▶ design flexibility at point of manufacture;
▶ shatterproof strength combined with light weight;
▶ ability to match the quality and luxury image of glass;
▶ at a competitive price.

Customer support service was designed as part of the product 'bundle' to enable the new product, branded Eclat, to be tailored precisely to the customer's needs. Each sample of Eclat was put on trial with a member of the new product team present to ensure that customers used the polymer optimally. 'The result of this collaboration not only enabled us to meet customers' high standards of quality but gave us a greater understanding of the cosmetics packaging business – a very definite two-way benefit,' said Chris Blanc. 'The ICI team felt we were delighting the customer with speed, quality and product awareness.'

Following rigorous trials with major cosmetics packaging manufacturers, brand owners such as Lancôme, Ungaro and Givenchy began to use the new product. At the end of 1990 the company had a 20 per cent share of polymer cosmetics packaging. By 1992 share had increased to 35 per cent and they were the number 2 PET brand in the market. The target was to build this to 50 per cent and brand leadership.[7]

A framework for buyer behaviour

A central theme in almost all the general models of both consumer and organizational buying behaviour is the belief that customers proceed through some series of steps in arriving at a decision to purchase and use a product or service. For purposes of exposition such a framework for customer decision-making is now outlined, while reminding the reader that decision modes will vary greatly in their nature depending on the person, organization and business system involved. It must also be remembered that the way in which purchase decisions are made is fundamentally influenced by the inherent characteristics of the people involved, their experience and the social, organizational and marketing context within which decisions take place.

Customer behaviour may be interpreted as a number of decision-making steps which start with the recognition of a consumption need and end with the learning involved in consuming the product or service purchased to satisfy that need. This sequence is visualized in Figure 6.1. and the next sections of this chapter will discuss the stages in turn.

Need recognition

Two important issues are raised by attempting to understand how customers come to recognize a need. The first brings us back in a very practical way to the definitional distinction made between needs and wants in Chapter 1. The second focuses attention on the setting or context of this stage in the buying sequence.

An important distinction was made between needs and wants on the basis that needs are underlying and relatively unchanging factors, whereas wants are the manifestations of those underlying needs and are shaped by culture, the personality of the individual and the fashion of the day and by many other factors which ensure that wants are in continuous flux. In understanding how a need is recognized a marketing team is well advised to consider both these factors. For example, the underlying and persisting human need for entertainment leads to endless fluctuation in the way in which this is expressed in the form of specific wants. Through most of the 1970s and 1980s cinemas declined radically as a form of entertainment service as individuals expressed their wants in the form of television viewing and later in video rental. However, one of the very elemental aspects of the need for entertainment of this form – leaving the home for a 'night out' – was never addressed by television and video. By the 1980s a new generation of cinema services had begun to develop which not only delivered satisfaction in terms of 'an evening out' but had also incorporated many other relevant benefits missing in the old cinema – wide choice of programmes under one roof in multi-screen complexes, greater locational and parking convenience for a mobile population, higher standards of physical comfort as well as the enhanced technical quality of film, projection and sound. Marketers who focus too narrowly on wants are likely to

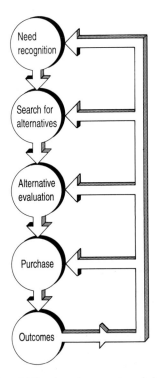

Figure 6.1 Steps in customer purchase decision

suffer inevitable decline in their businesses as the market continues with its unceasing reinterpretation and re-expression of its basic needs. Identifying and understanding the underlying need are therefore the first critical step in analysis.

The manager must also identify the circumstances under which a need for his or her type of product or service is recognized. A manufacturer of office chairs will find that exploring this issue generates several alternative buyer 'scenarios' with far-reaching influences on marketing strategy. The need for office chairs may arise when:

1 an owner/tenant moves into new office space;
2 a user expands and needs additional chairs;
3 old furniture has to be replaced.

The specific need recognized will vary depending on the use to which the chairs will be put; for example, in most office buildings one will find: (1) workstation chairs; (2) chairs for use by those working at desks; (3) chairs unique to senior management offices; (4) chairs in the boardroom; (5) chairs in a reception/visitors' area. Taking just these two sets of variables, we can visualize a simple matrix of need-recognition scenarios as shown in Table 6.1. In the case of the 'new office occasion' the customer is likely to want chairs of all types and will probably find it most satisfactory to deal with a supplier carrying a full range rather than with many individual specialist suppliers. On the other two occasions the specialist supplier may be more relevant to the need recognized.

However, this only probes the surface in understanding need recognition. The nature of the potential buyer will also affect the perception of the need, as will the specific persons involved in the decision to buy. We can therefore take any one cell in Table 6.1 and explode it using these two additional sets of variables as shown in Figure 6.2. It is immediately obvious

Table 6.1 Analyzing need recognition

| | Occasion of need | | |
Type of chair	New office	Expansion	Replacement
Workstation			
General desk use			
Senior management			
Boardroom			
Visitors'			

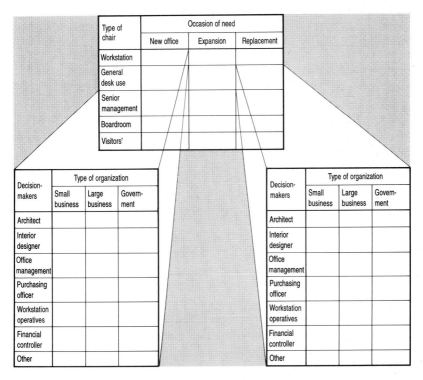

Figure 6.2 Analyzing needs in detail

that the customer purchase behaviour will be quite different for the two 'exploded' areas of need. In the case of the workstation chairs, the need will normally arise as part of a complete package of seating needs, and the customer is most likely to be interested in a package solution that includes such chairs. Indeed, the small business customer may not distinguish between workstation and general purpose chairs and may simply identify a need for as many standard chairs as there are people to be seated. Large businesses and government buyers may recognize the need for special support, flexibility and mobility in workstation chairs and consequently specify a specialist chair.

Who will be involved in recognizing the need is also of primary importance to the marketer. In the case of the new office building, architects and interior designers may well be involved in specifying an aesthetic dimension of need – certain kinds of materials, fabrics, colours, or perhaps a need to have all furniture coordinated on those dimensions. In the replacement case, such people are unlikely to be involved, and the immediate user of the chair may have much more influence, subject to budget constraints set by financial management and experience with the product to be replaced.

Generalizing from this illustration, it may be stated that need recognition arises when the customer's perception of the actual state of affairs diverges sufficiently from his ideal state to motivate action. Action is therefore triggered either by changing concepts of what is ideal or by dissatisfaction with actual circumstances. In a traditional Maslovian hierarchy, the ideals we seek in consuming products and services range from those driven by the very basic motivations to avoid hunger and thirst and to be safe and loved to those driven by our needs for respect, status and self-actualization. Marketing action can trigger these motivations and the consequent recognition of a need in many ways, varying from the smell of freshly brewed coffee escaping onto Vienna's city centre streets from its many *Kaffeehäuser* to an advertisement for yoga classes on Copenhagen's Studiestraede, containing promises of greater self-awareness and inner peace.

Implications

Understanding how customers recognize consumption needs and wants allows the marketing team to identify:

1 The critical difference between the underlying need which is likely to create a demand for economic goods and services over the very long run and the want which may be no more than a temporary expression of that need. The strategically focused business addresses this underlying need and responds to changing wants with the introduction and deletion of individual services and products.
2 When, where and how the need arises.
3 Who recognizes the need.

Knowledge of these factors is fundamental to marketing because of its implications for segmentation and the choice of target markets, the positioning of the product or service relative to competition, for the design and management of all subsequent marketing activity. Customer segmentation is the primary building block of successful marketing practice. Such segmentation may be on the basis of occupational status, as above, or on any of a wide range of variables from class, to income, to demographics, to gerontographics (characteristics particular to the grey or senior market).[8]

Search for alternatives

Depending on the nature of the need recognized, search may or may not occur, or may be extended or very limited in duration and scope. In many brand-loyal, low-involvement and routine purchases, search behaviour is minimal. However, as one considers larger-scale, high-involvement and less frequent purchases the benefits to the customer of searching for alternatives and for information rapidly outweigh the costs.

It is therefore important to recognize that there is a continuum of purchase situations. At one extreme we find the slow, careful approach to a major, infrequent and risky purchase, e.g. a car. At the other extreme we find the virtually instantaneous, non-analytical decision about a routine, low-risk, incidental purchase, e.g. a bag of potatoes. This continuum is suggested in Figure 6.3.

Search activity has immense importance for the marketer because if his or her product is not included in the list of alternatives that results from search, and if appropriate information about it is not available to the searching consumer, then there is no opportunity to compete actively for the potential business.

Take, for example, the problem of marketing fish products for human consumption. Fish is one of several food alternatives that may be considered by someone preparing a meal or ordering food in a restaurant. One of the challenges in expanding the demand for fish is that it is not considered often enough in the search for alternatives by consumers. This arises because of a traditional reluctance on the part of some categories of customer to consume fish, concerns about freshness of product and a lack of knowledge about its cooking. Other sources of protein, especially various meats, more usually constitute the list resulting from the search for alternatives. Thus the company selling fresh fish must attempt to promote and position the product to overcome such resistance; this might include in-store sampling and cooking advice. Or the company may decide to move further along the value-added to chain and process the fish into a ready to

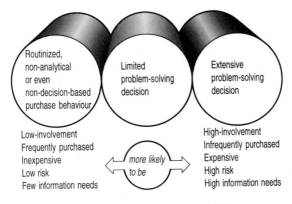

Figure 6.3 A continuum of purchase possibilities

be cooked format. This convenience dimension may make it more likely to be added the consumer's list of alternatives for consideration. Understanding these factors helps to appreciate the nature of the barriers to increasing demand. It provides the framework to identify mechanisms that might be employed in influencing search behaviour so that such products and relevant information about them at least enter the menu or meal-preparation decision sequence. It also illustrates how search behaviour and marketing communication evolve as one moves through the business system.

The extent of search behaviour undertaken reflects a trade-off between the costs of searching for alternatives, and information about them, and the benefits of doing this. Benefits will be substantial if:

1 there is little past experience of the consumption problem (e.g. buying a house; buying new technology);
2 memory of previous experience is poor;
3 perceived risk is high (i.e. the cost of making a wrong decision is high for the customer, as is typically the case when the product is expensive relative to income or when it is 'socially visible' and could be regarded by others whom the buyer respects as ugly, inappropriate, gauche, etc.);
4 confidence in one's ability to make a good decision is low.

One might expect search to increase confidence by lowering risk and generating more information. However, for some customers search results in information overload and reduced confidence. In consumer markets this can lead to a rejection of search activity and to a choice of brand leader products as the easiest way to allay lack of confidence. Equally, the highly confident consumer will often search extensively, happy in the knowledge that he or she can handle all the information and even derive some intrinsic satisfaction from search activity itself.

The costs of search are equally straightforward, although not always remembered by the marketer who provides too much, or inappropriate, information for the potential customer. Search will cost time and therefore forgone consumption. It may cost money through travel, telephone or mail inquiry. It may entail psychological discomforts because of frustration and tension generated through inadequate supplier response, poor handling of inquiries, travel and waiting for responses that turn out to be inadequate. It will often result in information overload because many companies insist on providing potential customers with information that is interesting to the company rather than information that is relevant to the customer's need – relevance means conciseness and focus on the very specific issues a customer needs at this stage in making the decision.

The marketing manager must also understand who it is that does the searching. This knowledge defines a critical target audience for any communication strategy. In the case of marketing decorative paint to the home DIY market (accounting for 25 per cent of all the paint sold in the world), the woman in a household is central to both search and purchase decisions. To quote John Thompson, ICI Paints planning manager, 'We have done market research in Turkey, Italy, and Colombus, Ohio, and the same overall pattern emerges: the woman in a household determines when a surface is to be painted and she determines the colour. The husband selects the brand, usually on the basis of price and technique, although women are increasingly also making this decision. In terms of paint application, it is about evenly split between husbands and wives.'[9]

If the information requirements and the person or group involved in search at this stage are known, then one may proceed to analyze the sources of information (1) to which they are exposed, (2) which they find credible, and (3) which are persuasive. Many, if not most, of the important sources judged on these three criteria are not marketer-controlled in any direct sense and can only be affected by the marketer through satisfied customers who create favourable word-of-mouth recommendation for the product.

The many potential sources of information also vary in their importance or effectiveness depending on the reason for search. Thus it is generally the case that awareness of a new product – its inclusion in a list of alternatives for the first time – is best created by media advertising. Search for information about such products, and data on which to base evaluations, are, however, much more likely to be influenced by personal sources often beyond the direct influence of the marketer.

Implications

The power of brand loyalty and habitual purchasing activity is illustrated by understanding search behaviour in a market. For the newcomer to a market, or for a low market share competitor, it is a major challenge to find a way to become considered as an alternative, especially if it demands that the consumer engage in search activity which he or she would prefer to avoid.

Search clearly responds to perceived risk; and for products that are expensive or that have significant implications in use for the buyer, risk reduction strategies (e.g. allowing the customer to sample or try out the product before purchase or allowing the organizational buyer to visit a demonstration site where new technology is already being used by another company) are a key to effective marketing. Market-focused companies always seem to appreciate the cost of search for the customer and have the knack of providing just as much information as is needed and in the consumer's own language (e.g. in the energy market telling the customer how much it costs to run an appliance such as a cooker rather than the cost of the energy input per kilowatt hour or per therm).

Evaluation of alternatives

When a potential customer has all the information considered necessary on alternatives, the next problem faced is how to evaluate them in order to make a choice. The evaluation is best understood theoretically from the perspective of information processing theory. An overwhelming feature of such research is the evidence of its selectivity. Because of the almost infinite range and variety of information in the environment, the individual can only cope by being very selective in what is addressed, taken into account and used in decision-making. Identifying accurately, and influencing the nature of, the criteria a customer uses to evaluate and choose between alternatives is therefore of great importance, but by the same token quite difficult.

Thinking about criteria brings us back to one of the starting points for thinking about marketing discussed in Part I. Evaluative criteria are usually best conceived of as *benefits* sought by customers from competing products or services. Customers do not buy replacement car tyres so much as they buy safety, conformity with the law, economy, quick fitting, a reputable brand, etc. The identification of such criteria which consumers will use in making their evaluations not only allows us to understand their decision-making but also makes it possible to segment the market in terms of customers requiring similar 'bundles' of benefits and to develop products that incorporate the identified 'bundles'.

Before considering the analytical procedures required to identify the customer's evaluative criteria, it is important to note that the marketer deals with a single decision-maker in only a minority of instances. It is much more usual for purchase decisions to be the outcome of joint decision-making by a group of people generally referred to as a decision-making unit (DMU). In the case of a great many household purchases, it is a DMU that makes the decision, not the housewife. The housewife may act out the role of purchasing agent and therefore become the only member of the DMU to show up in a retail outlet. The unwary marketer will accept this as evidence that the purchaser is the decision-maker and will accordingly develop product design, distribution, pricing and communication strategies targeted at the housewife. The purchase of many brands of breakfast cereal or coffee, for example, are however fundamentally determined by the preferences and influence of family members who do not accompany the housewife on her supermarket shopping trip. The great danger of targeting industrial selling on the purchasing officer of a client firm is equally widely recognized by successful industrial marketers who know the reality of complex DMU structures in buying organizations that formulate a need, specify it, search out suppliers, evaluate their products or tenders, and make final decisions on placing orders. Exhibit 6.2 shows how marketing activity by a Catalan roof tile company handles this complexity.

Exhibit 6.2	*Marketing in action case*

Ladona Teja Construcción's tiles on TV

Ladona Teja Construcción is a roof tile manufacturer in the environs of Barcelona, the capital of Catalonia, a region where building construction has been flourishing since the decision to host the 1992 Olympic Games. Its roof tiles are used on houses, apartments and certain types of institutional building. But similar competitive offerings are also available. How and why are Ladona tiles chosen? In the final decision to purchase a Ladona roof tile any one, or a combination, of the following are responsible, with varying degrees of influence:
- *The specifier* – included professional specifiers like architects, and semi-professionals like technical school instructors who acted as part-time or informal designers.
- *The builder* – included contract builders of public housing developments, large speculative builders of private apartments and estates, and small builders of single or 'one-off' houses or villas.
- *The tile contractor* – companies which provided an overall 'supply and fix' service on a subcontract basis to larger builders.
- *The merchant* – both builders' providers and small hauliers.
- *The householder* – mainly of custom-built one-off private houses; but increasingly larger speculative builders were selling potential homeowners the attractions of certain roof tiles.

Further, at a more specific level, sales eventually materialized from one of three types of specification:
- *The formal specification* – this tended to be either for public sector housing projects or for the architect-designed luxury end of the 'one-off' market. With a formal specification the order was as good as placed when the house was at the drawing-board stage.
- *A loose specification* – here the architect or designer still played an important role, but the final decision was made after consultation with the builder and others.

▶ **An open specification** – the choice of roof tile was left to the builder or client; the only part the architect played was in the original decision to design the roof suitable for the use of concrete roof tiles.

The company approached its marketing mindful of these various influences on the final decision. Technical representatives called on architects and designers, while less specialized salespeople canvassed builders and merchants. This was complemented by merchandising, trade exhibition attendance and trade press advertising. Recently, Ladona had advertised its tiles on television – it believed potential homeowners were assuming a greater role in selecting a roofing product, and TV provided a suitable medium to appeal to this diverse segment. Although expensive, the company was pleased with initial responses to this advertising.

It is therefore important in analyzing the evaluation stage to consider a two-dimensional framework such as that shown here for the purchase of a child's jeans (see Table 6.2). The research that is typically undertaken to identify and measure evaluative criteria is based on two assumptions. First, customers' evaluations are made on the basis of multiple criteria, not just one, such as price or quality. Second, customers often allow poor performance by a product on one criterion to be compensated for by strong performance on another.

A customer's evaluation of the product alternatives open to him or her may therefore be visualized as based on (1) several criteria, (2) evaluations of the alternative products on each criterion, and (3) a final evaluation of a 'best' or 'worst' choice which reflects an adding up and comparison of the several evaluations per product.

A graphic representation of this approach to measurement helps to communicate its impact. The evaluative map shown in Figure 6.4 reflects housewives' evaluations of four competing food items. Information of this nature is of considerable value in understanding how purchase decisions are made and in developing a suitable positioning strategy.

Table 6.2 Analyzing evaluative criteria

		Evaluation criteria for a child's jeans				
DMU membership	*Colour*	*Length of life*	*Style*	*Brand reputation*	*Fabric*	*Country of origin*
Mother						
Father						
Teenager(s)						
Pre-teen child(ren)						

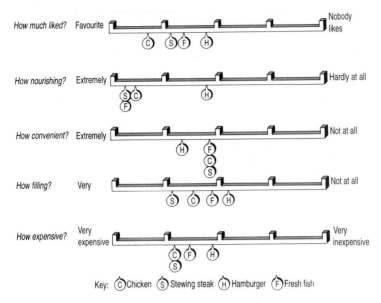

Key: (C) Chicken (S) Stewing steak (H) Hamburger (F) Fresh fish

Figure 6.4 Evaluating four competing food alternatives

Changing evaluations

Considerable marketing effort is devoted to changing customer evaluations of products and services. For example, many tourism service operators wished to change the evaluation of Spain as a mass market holiday location with just sun and sand attractions on the Mediterranean coast. This image had become self-limiting for the Spanish industry by the late 1980s, leading to overcrowding of traditional beach destinations and great difficulty in attracting customers from premium segments of the tourism market that seek cultural and historical attractions and sophistication in accommodation and services, while having the spending power to pay premium prices. The result was the creation of an international advertising and promotion campaign which played on the likelihood of customers in the target segment being surprised by the various attractions of Spain's historic cities, its castles and vast interior. Historic and culturally interesting sites and the country's luxury Parador hotels in ancient buildings became the physical symbols of the appeal to the discerning tourist (see Exhibit 15.1)

Reflecting on this experience it might be noted that the first action of the marketing team must be to 'fix' the product if a problem exists and only then to address the task of communicating the change to potential customers. If a negative evaluation is based on misconception of the product's characteristics, then there is a legitimate communication task for the marketer to perform. However, such a task may be very difficult and lengthy if evaluations have been learned over a period of time or if customers do not have sufficient interest in the product category to rethink their evaluations. Faced with this challenge, many consumer goods companies will choose to relaunch a product rather than attempt to change attitudes towards its existing form.

Implications

A clear understanding of the evaluative criteria used by customers in choosing between the alternative products on offer to them is fundamental to effective marketing. Knowing the criteria, the customers' preferences and competitors' strengths and weaknesses on the criteria is a key to good marketing. Changing customer evaluations is a difficult but not impossible task provided that it is based on real product characteristics and performance rather than an attempt to disguise or misrepresent these. Strategies of change may focus on:

1 changing the evaluations by means of better communication of the product's characteristics;
2 changing the importance (weighting) customers attach to individual evaluative criteria – as, for example, when a tyre manufacturer shifts customer emphasis from purchase cost to life of tyre and therefore to cost in use, under which criterion a high quality, well-designed tyre will far outperform a lesser quality own brand type;
3 changing the criteria themselves – as, for example, with the introduction of speed of service, convenience, standardized product and assured quality by major fast-food outlets into the eating-out decision.

Choice

The choice stage in customer decision-making is of interest because it demands the examination of issues such as:

▶ unplanned and impulse purchases;
▶ place of final choice and especially the importance of the retailing or selling environment.

Intentions versus unplanned outcomes

Even if we understand the customer decision sequence through the stage at which evaluations have been made, one can never be quite sure of predicting with complete accuracy the actual purchase that will be made.

Why is this? The uncertainty arises from several sources. The customer may not be engaged in a high commitment type of purchase, and therefore the decision mode prior to moment of purchase will have been very short, cursory and unlikely to have resulted in strong preferences. Walking into a shop to buy sweets may reflect such a situation. The availability of individual products on the shelf and their presentation may well overturn any low commitment intention to purchase a given brand of chocolate bar. Equally, the evaluation stage may result only in an intention to purchase a certain class of product – as, for example, where a customer intends to purchase a skirt rather than a dress and decides in-store which kind of skirt to buy. Finally, even with a well-formed intention to purchase, the context in which purchasing takes place and the social pressure to behave one way rather than another may cause a contrary decision. So, for example, the approval or otherwise expressed by a salesperson concerning a choice, or ideas of how choice might be regarded by those whose opinion the customer values, may precipitate a change in intention. The marketer is well advised to understand not only the evaluations that are made concerning his or her product relative to competitors but also customers' intentions to purchase and how their intentions are affected by the retail and selling environment.

For low commitment purchases – typically, low-cost consumables – it is also clear that the place of purchase, the availability, presentation, packaging and promotion of the product may be overwhelmingly important determinants of a sale; distribution and merchandising are the key marketing factors. Impulse purchases are an important component of consumer demand, and the marketer of consumer products must consider how much of his or her business comes from such behaviour and adapt practice accordingly. In addition, the creative marketer will search for the opportunity to expand demand for a product category by providing an innovative version of the product in a distribution channel that allows for impulse buying. This happened when watches and calculators were introduced to non-traditional outlets such as variety stores and discount stores.

The place of purchase

Choice of retail outlet and in-store presentation and merchandising is vital to the success of consumer products. Consideration of this factor demands that the firm appreciate where the customer wishes to shop and purchase. The preferred context, presentation, merchandising, sales assistance and payment/delivery conditions of the customer must be explored and how these can be designed to yield a competitive advantage at point, and time, of sale.

Typically the consumer's place of purchase is seen as a retail outlet. Yet information technology makes in-home shopping a viable option for many consumers through systems that allow for video demonstration of products, and enable purchase, funds transfer and delivery arrangements to be made from uncomplicated consoles. The information superhighway is facilitating shopping in virtual reality. As this trend in shopping behaviour evolves, innovative companies will grasp it as an opportunity, while others will cling to traditional and declining retail channels, as has happened in previous retailing revolutions.

Implications

The context of final customer purchase must be understood to enable the market-focused firm to:

▶ ensure that customers who plan to choose its product actually do so;
▶ maximize the number of unplanned purchases in its favour, and away from planned competitor purchases;
▶ maximize share of impulse buying.

These objectives are achieved through careful and creative choice of distribution channels and superiority in product presentation, merchandising, physical distribution and trade service.

Usage: post-purchase behaviour

A universal feature of market-focused companies that build their long-term development on responsiveness and service to customers is that the making of a sale is no more than a way-station on the long shared journey of customer and supplier. To the superior company, what happens after the sale – how the customer receives the product, how it is used, its defects, the customer's suggestions for improvement – is at least as important as what happens up to and at the time of purchase.

It is during usage that customer satisfaction is realized or not, and that brand or supplier loyalty is built. Customer satisfaction-in-use, and the servicing of his or her usage-related needs, are the keys to repeat purchases and to unsolicited recommendations to potential customers. These in turn are fundamental to long-term business survival and growth. In addition, many studies of successful innovation indicate that customers may be the most fruitful source of new product ideas developed through their usage of, and improvements on, currently available products. The careful management of the relationship between firm and customer, supplier and buyer, is vital to both product innovation and to long-term customer retention.

In consumer products, it is imperative to monitor satisfaction-in-use through consumer research and through discussion with members of the distribution channel. Advertising, promotional and public relations activity have a significant role in reassuring customers of the appropriateness of their decisions and in providing information on use and care of products.

In consumer durables, liaison in regard to product guarantee and after-sales service is critical to ensure satisfaction-in-use. Firms embracing the concept of relationship marketing are increasingly using such contacts with customers to build a database about them. Such a database can be employed in further commercial exchange and in direct marketing.

In industrial products, the post-purchase stage, with its emphasis on customer service and customer problem-solving, is the key battleground between successful competitors. A small sub-supplier of specialist components can often succeed in competition against major multinational suppliers on the basis of a competitive advantage built around its closeness to its customers, on-site servicing and assistance, short delivery time and reliability. Equally, many large companies owe their success primarily to working with the customer, seeing their role as one of customer problem-solving, and developing many of their best new products from placing prototypes with customers for testing and evaluation in use. Exhibit 6.1 illustrated earlier how an ICI business team developed a new cosmetics packaging product, Eclat, in just this way.

Implications

Companies which manage their marketing well know how their product is used by customers and innovate by improving performance-in-use or developing with the customer new ways of performing a required product function. Marketing never ends with the conclusion of a sale – in many significant ways it only begins then. The post-purchase period is studied to understand how to build customer loyalty, how to gain the support of opinion leaders and how to encourage favourable word-of-mouth communication between prospective buyers. It is also a time when the marketing team should attend to reducing any second thoughts or doubts in the customer's mind.

In conclusion, the sequence through which a customer passes from recognition of an economic need through to the consumption or use of the product or service chosen to satisfy this need is an integrative and insightful framework within which to comprehend customer behaviour. Such a study demands answers to fundamental questions about the determinants of demand and competitive effectiveness. If well conducted, such information will provide clear answers to these questions, ensuring that the market-focused firm has much of the basic knowledge required to make marketing decisions that are both relevant to the consumer and competitively superior.

REVIEW QUESTIONS

6.1 What implications does the distinction between needs and wants have for the marketing manager attempting to understand his or her customers?

6.2 Differentiate between low- and high-involvement products and services. How does such a distinction help in explaining search behaviour?

6.3 Why is it important for the marketer to understand the criteria that are used by customers in evaluating the product alternatives open to them before they make a purchase?

6.4 Marketing never ends with the conclusion of a sale; in many significant ways it only begins then. Discuss.

6.5 Select any product you have purchased recently and analyze your own behaviour in terms of each of the five decision steps discussed in this chapter.

CHAPTER 7

Measuring the market

Marketing in action case
AmEx goes database marketing

ABOUT THIS CHAPTER

Without the basic measures of market size, trend and share it is impossible to make properly judged marketing decisions. The need for such data is identified, and the meaning and role of these key measures discussed. Market segment feasibility is explored, as are the problems encountered in even sometimes defining a market. The importance of and the bases on which forecasts are built are reviewed, as is the role of sensitivity analysis and scenario planning.

As understanding the customer was approached in a systematic way, so also must be the gathering of information about the market. The mechanism for undertaking this activity is the company's marketing information system (MIS) which, even at a very informal level, must operate in any effective business. The elements of this system are explored – the types of data, the way in which they are collected, how they are analyzed, stored and communicated.

Setting a boundary to the market

The question of *who* buys *what, when, where, how* and *why* was addressed in the last chapter. This fundamental step in informing marketing activity indicates what it is that the market needs. In this chapter the questions of *how many?*, *how often?* and *for how long*? are examined, as also is the manner in which answers to all these questions should be sought if good information and good decisions are to ensue. Information is the key resource used by a marketer, and decisions can only be as good as the information used.

How many? How often? For how long? These are questions that must be answered by measuring the current state of the market and by forecasting its future dimensions. Doing this draws on the analysis of customers and of the markets, industries and the competitive situations in which they are found. Needs must be quantified to indicate the current and future size of a market so that decisions can be made about whether it is commercially feasible to serve it, and to understand whether the size of market and the size of a company's resources are compatible. Matching need to competence must be carried out in the context of defining the market, its relevant constituent segments, and its boundaries.

Why measure the market?

Market measurement is vitally necessary to understand how many customers there may be for a product or service, and how much and how often they consume, both at present and in the future. A knowledge of these facts is an essential basis for any economic analysis of market feasibility, production requirements and the strategic fit between market demand and company resources. Research or experienced intuition may well indicate that there is a window of opportunity or 'gap' in a particular market or segment. But is there a market – in a commercially viable sense – in the gap?

Many needs exist which are experienced by too few consumers, or too infrequently, to support an economically viable enterprise. Many new ventures fail for just this reason. An entrepreneur, obsessed by an innovation, assumes there will be a market to buy it, and buy it in sufficiently large quantity to support the investment and operating overheads necessary to go into business. But conviction that there must be many customers just waiting for an entrepreneur's new brainchild is not enough: the reality of a viable number of customers willing to purchase the innovation must be verified before rational investment can take place.

Such measurement also indicates to a company something about the strategic fit between its competences and its resource size and the magnitude of the market. Small and medium-sized firms can seldom successfully address the needs of a large national or international market for a standardized product. Their resources are so limited that they can neither satisfy customers on quality and consistency of supply nor compete with large marketers on costs. More typically, they can compete very effectively in speciality or niche markets, small markets and custom-built product markets. A measure of the market, therefore, also gives a sense of strategic compatibility between customer needs and company resources.

Knowledge of market size, when related to company sales, yields one of the simplest but most important measures of marketing performance – market share. This measure is vital to any understanding of competitive performance. Indeed, without it, firms frequently reach quite dangerously misleading conclusions about their marketing performance. For example, a marketer of a laxative medicine whose sales were declining over the long run assumed that this reflected a decline in market demand. This assumption was rationalized on the grounds that improved diet and a more educated population made laxatives less necessary. A check on market size and trend, however, showed that the market was growing and that the company's brand was losing market share steadily. Here is one of the greatest traps into which a marketing manager can walk. If total market size and trend are unknown, there is no way of knowing whether an increase in sales represents good performance or not! An increase in sales less than the rate of increase in market size represents competitive loss and a threat to the company's future in the market. Yet how many companies regard an increase in sales as a cause for celebration while remaining quite ignorant of the total market situation? A simple growth-gain matrix such as that shown in Figure 7.1 is a useful mechanism for tracking this relationship.

One of the great weaknesses of sales-oriented companies is that they typically ignore total market and therefore market share measures. Increases or decreases in company sales are therefore largely beyond interpretation. Does a sales gain reflect greater or perhaps lesser competitive

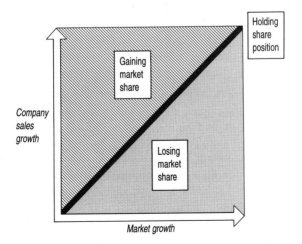

Figure 7.1 Growth-gain matrix

effectiveness? Does a sales decline represent a loss of competitiveness or perhaps an increased share of a market that is contracting faster than the company's sales? Without a good estimate of market size and trend, a marketing team is flying blind.

Key measures

Markets can be measured in many ways and with great sophistication. Nevertheless, a relatively few basic measures provide the manager with most of the required information. The *size* of the market in value and volume terms is the most fundamental measurement requirement. Generally, volume measures are the most useful ones, as they are unaffected by inflation or pricing and discounting variations. Great care must be exercised in using value measures because they are typically distorted by these same inflationary and pricing factors. When using value measures to track a market over time, it is therefore necessary as a minimum precaution to adjust them for inflation so that real growth or decline can be identified.

The *trend* in market size is the second essential measure as it tells whether a market is growing, declining, stable or cyclical. Which of these four kinds of market represents the firm's environment has enormous implications. It tells us about the stage in the lifecycle of the product market and therefore about the kind of competitive conditions and customer behaviour we might expect, as well as suggesting strategies that are appropriate for the varying market conditions. The historical trend in the market also provides one basis for developing forecasts of future market size, although care must be exercised in a changing world in assuming that the future will reflect the past.

Market share has already been discussed and is the third basic and essential market-related measure. As noted, this provides one of the most vital indicators of marketing effectiveness: 'Am I outperforming the competition or losing to them? How many customers prefer my product to my competitors?' Market share has additional strategic significance because, in many markets, share and profitability are directly linked: the bigger a company's share, the greater its return on investment. The work of the PIMS (Profit Impact of Market Strategy) Programme working with over 1,000 companies and as many as 5,000 business units since the early 1970s has produced consistent evidence of a strong relationship between market share and profitability.[1] The research indicates that companies ranking first in market share earn rates of return that are three times greater than businesses with a market share ranking of fifth place or less. It is noteworthy that research in the United States on the Federal Trade Commission's line-of-business database also supports the argument for a strong

Table 7.1 A segmentation framework

Application segments	Customer segments		
	Residential	Commercial	Industrial
Space heating			
Process heating			
Cooking			
Central heating			
Water heating			

positive relationship between pre-tax return on sales and absolute market share.[2] The reasons for a strong relationship between share and profitability are not proven. Indeed, the direction of causality is open to debate – are profitable companies more likely to grow share or are high share companies more profitable? However, the general explanations usually advanced for a relationship between share and profitability focus on the cost advantages of larger scale and greater experience compared to rival companies, and on the market power that large share often confers. Market power may be exercised in matters ranging from negotiating the price of raw materials to the imposition of terms and pricing guidelines among one's channels of distribution. Market share is not just important, therefore, to an understanding of competitive superiority, but is also vital to strategic direction and the setting of objectives.

These three vital and necessary market measurements must be subject to one overall qualification: measures of size, trend and share at total market level are seldom adequate. What is necessary is these measures by *market segment*. A market segment is a subdivision of any total market where customers, while buying the same type of general product as any other customers in the total market, nevertheless buy it in a particular form or place or manner and use it in a particular way.

The market for natural gas in Holland may be used as an illustration. Natural gas from the North Sea is distributed through town gas companies to many customers. They all purchase and consume natural gas, but the houseowner who makes a decision to install a natural gas cooker in her new house near Amsterdam behaves very differently and buys very different product benefits than does a large glassmaking factory that uses the same gas in a local industrial estate to fuel its furnaces. The houseowner market for natural gas for cooking and the industrial process-heating customer belong in two different market segments. One can readily appreciate how relatively meaningless it is for a gas marketing manager to know the size and trend of the market for gas – or, even more so, for energy – and the share that natural gas holds. Managerially he or she can only understand his or her market, and develop his or her strategy, when he or she has these measures for the main segments of demand. In marketing natural gas it is, therefore, necessary to measure the main segments of the market by principal energy applications as shown in Table 7.1. For each cell in this matrix, measures of size, trend and share provide valuable data. Careful identification and choice of segments allow the company to address the underlying basis of demand. By doing so it has the opportunity to:

1   build competitive advantage by serving one or more segments with products and marketing strategies uniquely attuned to their specific needs;
2   build a partial monopoly position in such segments and therefore hope, at least temporarily, to earn profits above the industry average;
3   disaggregate demand and therefore understand the basis of trends and behaviour in the total market and business system with accuracy and insight;
4   identify opportunities for marketing innovation as old segments decline and new ones emerge.

Evaluating feasibility of market segments

Approaches to market segmentation are explored further in Chapter 11, which addresses in a broader strategic context how the marketing manager chooses a market in which to compete. Identifying market segments can proceed until each potential customer is represented as a unique segment. Some industrial markets do conform to this limiting situation – for example, major public works contracts for hospitals, power stations, airports, etc. For most markets, however, the manager must limit the number of segments to what is realistic and worthwhile to service in terms of economic and strategic criteria. Evaluating the feasibility of a segment is best done with reference to the following criteria:

1   *Measurability*: Can the size and characteristics of the segment be measured and quantified? If not, it will become virtually impossible to develop a sensible marketing strategy and programme to address the segment.
2   *Accessibility*: Can the segment be reached with a separate marketing programme? Are there communication media and distribution channels? If not, the marketer cannot effectively address the segment.
3   *Substance*: Is the segment big enough to justify a tailor-made marketing investment? While managers may identify a gap in any

market they must be careful to ask whether there is a market in the gap! Many segments are too small to support the expenditure necessary to exploit the opportunity. In small markets such as those commonly found in Europe's smaller countries (Denmark, Norway, Finland, Ireland, Luxembourg or Portugal, for example), this is a particularly important consideration.

4 *Defensibility*: Having developed a marketing programme for a segment and invested in entry to the market, can the company defend its position against existing or future competitors attracted by any success? In the car rental business in Europe the multinational companies can generally defend their international business traveller segment very successfully but are endlessly open to attack in the tourism segment where domestic companies come and go with aggressive pricing strategies as the tourist market changes from year to year.

5 *Durability*: How long will the segment persist in reasonably stable form, or is it likely to change and merge with other segments in the short to medium term? This is a particular problem in rapidly growing markets before a competitive shake-out occurs, and many new ventures enter such an industry with false expectations of a long life for a specialist segment they have identified.

6 *Competitive capability*: Does the company have the necessary resources, experience and marketing strengths to implement a marketing strategy appropriate to the segment identified? 'Can we do the necessary job?' is the difficult question that must be faced with realism and cool objectivity.

Market definition

The concept of a market is not as simple as it may appear at first glance. The importance of measuring market segments rather than total markets has already been illustrated. But how to draw a boundary on the total market and the market segments of relevance to a business can sometimes become difficult. Normally, three levels of market can be isolated, as shown in Figure 7.2.

Creative marketing insights can be generated by thinking through the implications of defining a company's market at these various levels. A brand manager for an instant coffee brand can learn a great deal about the market and competitive environment by thinking about the position of his or her brand in a generic market for convenience beverages – not just coffee – where coffee must compete with products such as soft drinks, fruit juices, tea and other traditional and innovative beverages. Recent years have

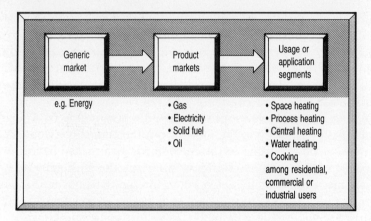

Figure 7.2 Levels of market definition

witnessed an interesting debate as to whether non-alcoholic beers such as Clausthaler from Germany or Buckler from Holland serve the beer market or a completely different market traditionally supplied by soft drinks. Market definition therefore revolves about the concept of substitutability – a market consists of a somewhat similar, substitutable array of products, services and competitors which compete for the customer's attention and patronage. Generic definitions are useful for highlighting the extent to which customer needs may be satisfied by a wide variety of goods and services, while definitions of usage, application or functionality highlight the level at which competitors vie with one another to satisfy very detailed, transitory and specific wants.

Forecasting

As all marketing decisions commit company resources for the future, it is essential that the manager should have a reasonable estimate of where the market will go in that future time. Forecasting markets and competitive outcomes is a difficult task. The key market forecasts are of the same factors discussed under market measurement: size, trends and market shares. These measures, translated into sales forecasts, become the essential basic information for all financial project appraisal activities, ultimately translated into cashflow forecasts and measures of financial payoff.

In addition to the key measures of market size, trend and share, marketing decisions generally demand forecasts concerning such important environmental factors as product technology, economic and political conditions, changes in retail structures and retail power, and so on. The market analyst therefore works towards detailed forecasts of products or service requirements by starting with broad environmental measures (economic growth, personal income, demographic forecasts, for example), then moving to industry-level forecast which focuses on total demand and competitive factors, and finally narrowing in to company market share and sales volumes.

The information on which forecasts may be developed emerges from three sources: (1) what people say; (2) what people do; and (3) what people have done.[3] The forecaster can ask people about the future: what they *say* becomes the basis of the forecast. People can be asked about the future in a variety of ways. A survey of buyer intentions collects customers' opinions about what they intend to purchase over a future period. A survey of salesforce estimates is frequently used where time is scarce and the cost of contacting final customers is substantial. Salespersons are asked to estimate how much each customer they call on is likely to buy and from what supplier over the forecast period. When these estimates are added up, and if the salesforce covers all or almost all of the buyers in the market, the resulting estimates of future market trends and market shares can be very accurate. Forecasts of this nature must be treated with some caution, of course, as there is an inherent tendency for sales personnel to be conservative about projections which may become the basis for their own sales targets and incentive payments. Expert opinion is sometimes consulted as a basis for making forecasts; when such an approach is used in an iterative manner with a number of experts it is called a Delphi method. Here experts who specialize in collecting information on a market and who continuously monitor trends are asked for their informed estimate of where the market is going and the relative success of competitors.

What people *do* may be monitored as in test market exercises to assess how the market responds to various products and services. Here closely observed behaviour in the market during a carefully designed test period is used to construct an estimate of future behaviour. The rapid development in retail markets of electronic point-of-sale (EPOS) technology is proving a major force for change in allowing companies to test products and services and to monitor virtually instantaneously their success or failure. Benetton's great success in the fashion clothing market is partly attributable to its investment in information technology which allows it to monitor sales as they take place in retail outlets across Europe and to adjust its production planning for different colours and fashions in response to emerging customer preferences. As a result, the company has a much lower incidence of unsaleable stock and sales of reduced price garments than the rest of the fashion clothing industry.

What people *have done* can provide information for both very dubious and very powerful forecasts of future market trends. What people have done, represented by historical figures for market size and market share, is most frequently translated into a vision of the future by extrapolation: for example, the average annual growth rate over the past five years becomes the projected growth rate for the next year. Extrapolation in all its more or less sophisticated forms must always be used in marketing with the appreciation than the past is often a faulty guide to the future. A more valid use of historical data is embodied in the application of a variety of methods of statistical demand analysis which seek to identify the structure, correlates and driving forces underlying market demand – for example, econometrics, regression analysis and time-series analysis. Knowing these basic determinants of demand, the manager is in a better position to allow for a changing future environment.

Sensitivity analysis and scenarios

Whether the task faced is to measure the current size of a market or to forecast its future direction, the problems of estimation and of resource constraints in collecting data are usually such that estimates rather than perfect measures are the objective. Because of this inherent difficulty in achieving exact measures, almost all market estimates and forecasts must be handled carefully. A key forecast about future market growth will often form the basis of a marketing, and indeed overall company, plan. The forecast becomes a crucial assumption in the overall corporate plan. Such pivotal assumptions should be clearly articulated and known to all managerial decision-makers in the company. The assumed view of the future may prove to be incorrect and there is thus the danger of very elegant edifices being built on shaky foundations. If key assumptions are transparent, corrective action can be quickly initiated.

One of the best and simplest ways to deal with the uncertainty about the precision of estimates is to use a range of figures from optimistic, through most likely, to pessimistic. As these figures are then used in the financial analysis of a marketing project, the market-related risk can be identified. For example, if a pessimistic forecast of market size and market share achievement yields a revenue projection 10 per cent less than the most likely figure, and this in turn results in a change from a profitable to an unprofitable outcome for the project, then one must regard the proposal as having a high-risk content. In a highly competitive and changing market a 10 per cent shortfall in sales is not a very unlikely event. Equally, if the manager finds that market estimates 10 per cent and 20 per cent less than the most likely one still yield profitable forecast outcomes, it would seem justifiable to judge the project as a relatively low-risk one in terms of demand variability.

Scenarios and scenario planning allow the manager to undertake a similar kind of sensitivity analysis, but more typically in the context of evaluating overall company options. Scenarios may be constructed about a set of alternative, but quite feasible, future states of market: its size, competitive conditions, consumer tastes, technological change, etc. Scenarios describe not only future states of a market but also the sequence of cause and effect leading to this emergence. A good test of any proposed strategy is to examine whether it is a realistic one under each of the possible future states of the market. A strategy that will only work in one future scenario is a high-risk one. A strategy that will work under many scenarios, or that can be easily adapted to them, is a flexible robust low-risk one and more likely to be preferred in a dynamic market.

Marketing information system

As understanding the customer was approached in a systematic way, so also must be the gathering of information about the market. The mechanism for undertaking this activity is the company's marketing information system (MIS) which, even at a very informal level, must operate in any effective business. An information system is analogous to the business system in that it takes an input, in this case information, and adds value to it by transforming it into an output useful for decision-making. This transformation is visualized in Figure 7.3 and in more developed forms in Figures 7.4 and 7.5.

The marketing environment consists of customers, market segments, competitors, plus broader aspects such as the technological, cultural, legal, political and governmental forces that shape market behaviour. An enormous amount of data which may be tapped by the marketer exists concerning all these elements of the environment. This material, however, has no informative content until it has been chosen, collected, ordered, analyzed

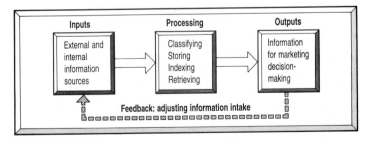

Figure 7.3 An information system

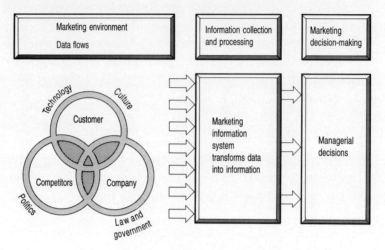

Figure 7.4 Marketing information system

and communicated by some transforming activity. This is the role of the marketing information system. This system should be able to identify:

1 what information is needed to inform the core marketing processes and for relevant decision-making;
2 what data sources can provide the required information;
3 how data can be transformed into usable information for decision-making (e.g., how the Census of Population can be made useful in estimating market size or market segments); .
4 how this information should be communicated to decision-makers.

This may seem like an elaborate activity appropriate only for large companies with sizeable marketing departments. Such companies will certainly organize their marketing information system in a relatively formal and elaborate manner. But just as marketing is a function that must be performed in any company irrespective of whether it can employ a marketing manager, so too there must exist the rudiments of an information system if any company is to survive. In small companies or in businesses at an early stage of growth the owner-manager or general manager will personally 'sift' marketing information on a daily basis. So the form of the marketing information system will vary enormously in its character and formality from company to company. What is important to remember is that the chore involved must take place. The elements of a marketing information system are now examined and their complementary roles discussed.

Elements of a marketing information system

Figure 7.5 summarizes the various elements that constitute a marketing information system. Activities such as marketing research, marketing intelligence work, use of internal accounting data, and so on are necessary in order to acquire data and initiate the transformation into useful information. These activities should only be engaged in when there is a decision-need to direct them, whether it is monitoring sales to identify a need for tactical change in, say, price discounting or a fundamental need to decide what market or market segment to serve.

Actual transformation of the information is the next step. Having collected data on, say, consumers' attitudes to a product, the manager, or the system serving the manager, must be able to analyze the data so that the important implications of consumer attitudes for the product and its future become clear. Much information has lasting value and must therefore be stored and updated. Sales records are an obvious example. This requires the design of a database – from a simple filing cabinet to a computer database with neural-network software. And finally there is the issue of who needs to know, how much do they need to know and when do they need to know it? This is not a problem in a small or new venture where the few key managers are the information system. In large companies, however, the communication problem is of significance. Poor communication can lead to duplication of research, to the routeing of information vital to one person to someone for whom it has incidental value, or to information overload where managers are so inundated by reports that they cannot distinguish the important from the trivial. Well-directed and shared communication is central to the teamwork involved in managing marketing.

Marketing research

Marketing research is the more or less formal research of any marketing-related decision issue. It is not just consumer surveys and questionnaire administration. Marketing research is as much concerned with determining distribution costs for a company's delivery trucks as with attitude surveys of housewives; as much concerned with test marketing a new product as with studying long-term technological change in the company's industry. However, any form of marketing research must be both objective and systematic. This means that doing research should observe the norms of scientific practice in moving through the following steps:[4]

1 *Problem definition*: What is the marketing problem to be solved or decision to be taken? Care and executive time must be devoted to specifying the problem clearly.

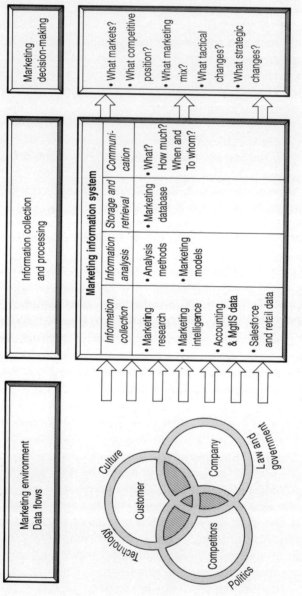

Figure 7.5 Elements of marketing information system

2   *Setting research objectives*: In order to solve the problem or make the decision, exactly what information is needed that is not already available?

3   *Choosing a research approach*: How can the required information be collected, and from whom? What is the most cost-effective method? What is the plan for data collection, analysis and reporting?

4   *Data collection*: When, how and precisely from whom are the data to be acquired, and how will collection be controlled and its objectivity ensured?

5   *Data analysis*: By what valid statistical or other methods can the data be transformed into meaningful information?

6   *Reporting*: What and how much information, in what format, must be provided for whom?

While a systematic, scientific approach of research is generally followed by companies, especially if they hire a reputable and professional marketing research agency or consultancy to do the work, it can be difficult to ensure the presence of one key component of scientific method – objectivity. Marketing research is sometimes undertaken in the hope of finding evidence to support a decision already taken. Or research results may be ignored when they are at variance with the manager's judgement. Research may also be designed in such a way that bias in the selection of sources of data, or in the questions asked, predetermines the research outcome. In all such cases the research and its cost are totally wasted. It has no validity as a basis for rational decision-making. A systematic and objective approach is therefore the *sine qua non* of marketing research.

Some of the elementary issues in choosing a research approach, or design, are outlined in Figure 7.6. The three basic design options will often be implemented in sequence. A company will first carry out exploratory research to uncover what is going on in the problem area of interest, or to check whether its own assumptions are valid. When this has been done, descriptive research may be undertaken with much greater confidence that the important issues are being studied and the correct questions asked.

Descriptive research normally results in an ability to identify associations between several factors (consumption of fresh fish and interest in dietary matters, for example). Such associations must not be confused with *causal* relationships. There are many spurious associations, such as an historical correlation that once existed between bathtub sales in Britain and the number of suicides. The manager must always be careful not to read causation into research results that document nothing more than an association of two factors.

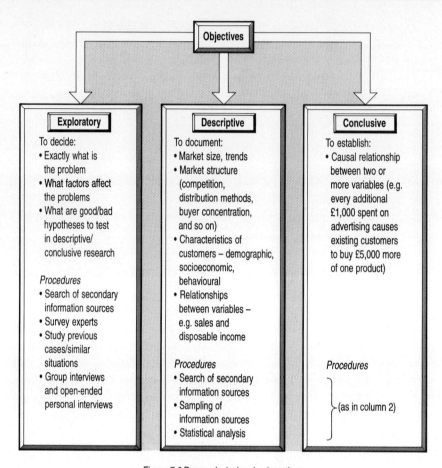

Figure 7.6 Research design: basic options

Data collection options in marketing research are also many and important to the outcome of the research. Figure 7.7 summarizes basic choices that are faced. Choice of *method* demands evaluation of the role that can be played by secondary and primary sources. Primary data are observed and recorded or collected directly from respondents. This type of data must be gathered by observing phenomena or surveying respondents. Secondary data are compiled inside or outside the firm for some purpose other than the current investigation, e.g. reports on market size and share, on customer buying behaviour and technology development. Figure 7.8 illustrates how primary and secondary sources compare.

Secondary data are often gathered as a starting point for marketing research. Such data exist in the form of reports and various databases which allow the manager to take somebody else's work of data collection and

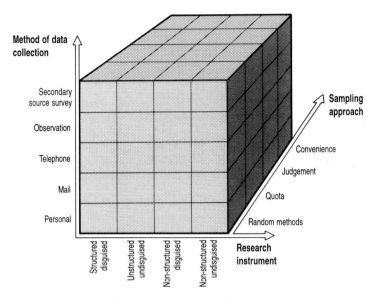

Figure 7.7 Data collection: basic options

apply it to his own needs. Government publications such as the Census of Population, the Household Budget Inquiry and Trade Statistics on imports and exports, are fundamental sources of secondary data. Equivalent data are available at EC level, and from agencies like the OECD and the United Nations. In addition to these public documents, the manager will usually find that industry associations and trade journals collect and publish market data. There is also a variety of market reports prepared by consultancy, business information and market research firms that are available on subscription. A more recent but potentially powerful innovation, especially when exploring export markets, is the variety of international computer databases which may be assessed remotely via computer terminal.

Primary data are collected at first hand from the market by or on behalf of the marketer. Visiting customers and potential customers and asking them about their needs and their current and planned purchases is something that all marketing teams must do regularly if they are to stay in touch with their market. Primary data on market size and trends may also be collected on behalf of the firm by a professional marketing research company. These may be one-off surveys designed to specific project or product needs, or they be more regular market monitoring services (e.g. retail sales month by month through grocery outlets). The options within primary data sources must be evaluated in terms of the kind of information needed, its value and the cost of obtaining it by each method. Observational methods have not been widely used in marketing except in store auditing research. However, the use of electronic check-out systems (EPOS) and standard product bar-coding has made a new form of observational research widely available. Many consumer goods and service companies use electronic check-out data from supermarkets and service counters to monitor movement of brands and to do test marketing with continuous and almost instantaneous feedback on product sales.

The choice of *research instrument* simply refers to the manner in which data are to be collected and recorded once the means of getting to the source of data has been decided. The choice can range from unstructured questioning of a small group of customers where the identity of the company doing the research is disguised, to a totally structured questionnaire with pre-specified answering alternatives (such as yes/no; some-

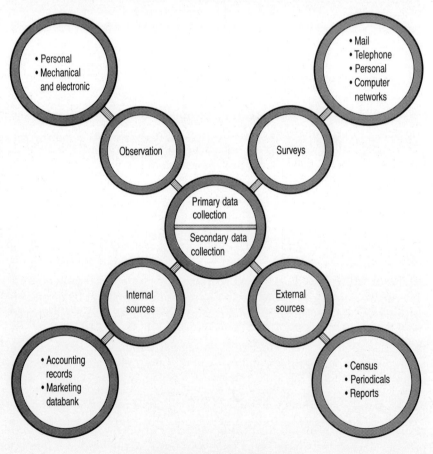

Figure 7.8 Approaches to collecting data

times/seldom/never; £0–10/£11–20/£21+) and the identity of the company openly disclosed.

A *sampling approach* is usually required in implementing research for two reasons. First, it is usually possible to guarantee, through statistical sampling methods, estimates of the feature of interest that are sufficiently accurate for most marketing decision-making purposes. Second, companies may have very limited resources available for research and can afford only limited data collection.

Sampling methods vary from a range of random sampling techniques that yield estimates which may be generalized to the total population of interest with specified margins of error, to convenience procedures which involve no scientific procedure but simply the choice of data sources that are most convenient to the researcher. While the latter approach may be cheap and quick to implement, it provides no basis for the generalization of findings.

Marketing intelligence

Marketing intelligence keeps a company informed of current events in its marketing environment, and especially about competitors' initiatives, early signals of changes in customer preferences and buying habits, and of shifts and changes in the broader technological and socio-political environment. Intelligence gathering and interpreting are usually somewhat haphazard. It can be formalized to a certain degree by ensuring that company personnel attend relevant trade and professional meetings, conferences and industry association meetings; read a broad range of business trade and general publications; and maintain regular contact with persons in touch with new trends, ideas and technologies.

Marketing intelligence typically sparks off two kinds of action: tactical adjustment to unanticipated changes, and the initiation of more formal research into issues that could have significant long-run impact on the company. In attempting to formalize the intelligence system it is important to ensure that managers have a regular opportunity to meet with a relatively unstructured agenda in order to exchange observations, check on perceptions and spot patterns in the variety of intelligence gathered.

Accounting and MgtIS data

Internal company records, and especially accounting and management information system (MgtIS) data, represent one of the least exploited sources of valuable marketing information. The regular internal records of any company contain vital marketing information such as:

▶ distribution of sales volume by customer and customer group,

▶ distribution of net contribution by customer and customer group (and often the alarming fact that 20 per cent of customers generate 80 per cent of contribution!),

▶ sales and contribution by product line or model,

▶ sales by sales region or territory or salesperson,

▶ customers who pay on or before time, and those who persistently delay payment or fail to pay,

▶ credit taken by customer groups,

▶ sales, discounts, level of returns, partial deliveries or damaged goods by customer group/area.

This kind of information should be available in all internal information systems. Extracting it requires some thought in the design of documentation for orders, invoices, statements, etc., and attention to how these are analyzed and reports extracted. As firms review and redesign their computer-based information systems there is no reasonable managerial excuse for not having such information regularly available. The process approach to business organization very much requires all internal company information sources, be they accounting, marketing or logistics, to be knitted together in a customer-focused manner.

Salesforce and retail data

Firms running a salesforce must ensure that the salesperson's call-reporting and account-reporting procedures are designed not only for the purpose of salesforce control, but also with marketing information needs in mind. The salesforce provides an excellent and low-cost mechanism for:

1 building up market estimates on a customer-by-customer basis;
2 forecasting future demand on a customer account basis;
3 monitoring competitive activity through questioning buyers on new product introductions, pricing tactics, services provided and level of customer satisfaction;
4 monitoring customer satisfaction with the company's own product or service and changes in customer needs.

Information on issues such as these should flow to management regularly from the salesforce through formal reporting systems and through regular meetings at which these topics are reviewed. Information of this nature must be treated with some caution, of course, as there is an inherent tendency for sales personnel to be conservative about estimates which may become the basis for their own sales targets and incentive payments.

Further, the major changes introduced by electronic scanning and check-out systems in retail outlets represent a rich and powerful source of data on market behaviour. Indeed, companies need to work with retailers on the specification of such systems to ensure that they can exploit their full potential as marketing information-generation mechanisms. The principal benefits of such systems should be rapid feedback of retail sales movement by very finely defined product categories, and almost real-time monitoring of special promotion, new product launches and test market activities by shop or region.

Information analysis

Data, once collected by any of the methods discussed above, are just that – raw data. Analysis will transform them into practical, usable information. Methods of analysis are many and often technically demanding, but simple methods of documenting frequency distributions, averages, ranges and cross-tabulation of two factors at a time (e.g. age of customer vs. brand purchased) still predominate. The power of various statistical methods is considerable in adding greater depth to such analyses and uncovering otherwise unseen relationships. The manager with serious research needs is well advised to discuss all the possible options on analytical methods with an expert in the area and with a professional marketing research agency.

The major advances in the application of quantitative methods to marketing problems that began some decades ago yielded the opportunity for the marketer to model many marketing problems in order to gain a better understanding of their nature and to make more efficient decisions. Well-developed models now assist decisions on warehouse and facilities location or delivery truck routeing or salesforce routeing. In marketing planning, and especially in the new product launch area, several models of new product diffusion have been developed and applied successfully. Models to assist in media choice and scheduling are also available to support advertising decisions, although these are generally used by advertising agencies on behalf of their clients.

The most widely used models are simple financial models based on computer spreadsheets which allow the marketer to evaluate a variety of 'what if . . .?' situations by varying sales forecasts, margins, product costs and credit given/taken. These are hardly models in the sense in which we spoke of models in the preceding paragraph, but they are very useful, and cheaply accessible, mechanisms to test the sensitivities of plans to changes in basic assumptions.

Marketing database

Much of the information required to make marketing decisions is used time and time again and updated regularly. For this kind of information to be maintained up-to-date and accessible for study, a computer-based database is mandatory. Indeed, computing innovations like parallel processors – capable of scanning huge volumes of data in a flash – and neural-network software – able to automatically 'learn' from large sets of data on its own – are enabling the development of an important tool for the marketer in the form of database marketing (see Exhibit 7.1).

| Exhibit 7.1 | *Marketing in action case* |

AmEx goes database marketing

Is your credit card company taking quite a friendly interest in your life these days, making you offers of purchase possibilities, like getaway weekends, and so on, which seem surprisingly well tailored to your life-style? If so, you're on the receiving end of a sophisticated high-tech twist to the marketing's art of persuasion. It goes by different names – database marketing, relationship marketing, one-to-one marketing. But it adds up to the same thing. Companies are collecting mountains of information about you, crunching it through massive parallel computers, using neural-network software, to predict how likely you are to buy a product and employing that knowledge to craft a marketing message precisely calibrated to get you to do so.

American Express has been doing just this since since March 1993. Following its introduction in Ireland, this 'relationship billing' has been rolled out through Europe, Canada, Mexico and just recently the United States. AmEx has seen an increase of 15–20 per cent in year-over-year cardmember spending in Europe and gives the new billing format much of the credit.

Kraft Foods Inc. has amassed a list of more than 30 million users of its products who have provided their names when sending in coupons or responding to some other Kraft promotion. Based on the interests they have expressed in surveys, it regularly sends them tips on such things as nutrition and exercise, as well as recipes and coupons for specific brands. The company believes that the more information consumers have about a product, the more likely they'll be to use more of it (sample tip: Use Miracle Whip instead of butter for grilling sandwiches). Kraft constantly refines its database by sending surveys to the names on the list.

In 1992 General Motors Corp. joined with Mastercard to offer the GM Card. As a result, GM now has a database of 12 million GM cardholders, and it surveys them to learn what they're driving, when they next plan to buy a car and what kind of vehicle they would like. Then, if a cardholder expresses an interest in, say, sport-utility vehicles, the card unit mails out information on its jeep line and passes the cardholder's name along to the appropriate division. Such targeted offerings garner a considerably higher response rate than the typical 2–4 per cent for normal junk mail. Point-of-sale terminals, teller machines and 1–800 telemarketing all contribute to the flood of information.

Is this all Big Brotherism or mere cybernetic intimacy? Marketers see an opportunity to close the gap that has widened between companies and their customers with the rise of mass markets, mass media and mass merchants. Database marketing can create a silicon simulacrum of the old-fashioned relationship people used to have with the corner grocer, butcher or baker. 'A database is a sort of collective memory,' says Richard G. Barlow, president of Frequency Marketing Inc., a US consulting firm. 'It deals with you in the same personalized way as mom-and-pop grocery stores, where they knew customers by name and stocked what they wanted.'[5]

Customers who send in a coupon to a firm, fill out a warranty card, enter a competition, participate in a retailer's affiliation club – all are volunteering information which is increasingly being computerized and combined with more information from public records. Using sophisticated statistical techniques, the computer merges different sets of data into a coherent, consolidated database. Then, with powerful software, the marketing manager can 'drill down' into the data to any segment or level of detail he or she requires. For instance, the computer identifies a model consumer of a chosen product based on the common characteristics of high-volume users. Next, clusters of consumers who share those characteristics – their interests, incomes, brand loyalties and so on – can be identified as targets for marketing efforts. Direct response marketing, in particular, is facilitated in this way.

These developments are permitting a greater use of direct one-to-one communication, through postal or electronic media, with the customer. At a time when many marketers are reassessing the power of mass marketing techniques and mass media, such highly targeted approaches are enabling firms to win a closer rapport with their customers. Such relationship marketing is increasingly complementing more established modes of advertising and above-the-line communication.

REVIEW QUESTIONS

7.1 There may be a gap in the market, but is there a market in the gap? Assess this comment.

7.2 Why is market share such an important measure for the marketing manager?

7.3 What is the role of sensitivity analysis in forecasting?

7.4 What are the elements of a marketing information system, and how do they link together?

7.5 What are the basic steps in designing and conducting marketing research, and what major options exist in terms of research design?

7.6 What benefits does a first-rate database bring to marketing?

CHAPTER 8

Analyzing competition and industry structure

▶ Analyzing competitors
▶ Strategic group mapping
▶ Leakage analysis
▶ Competitive structure of an industry
▶ Five driving forces model
▶ The business system and competitive analysis

Marketing in action cases
Toshiba's laptop and expeditionary marketing
Continuum's old masters change the rules

ABOUT THIS CHAPTER

As the marketing manager understands the customer and measures the market, so too he or she must analyze the competitors. How rival firms compete in the market, are likely to compete and their unique competitive strengths and weaknesses must be scrutinized. Strategic group mapping and leakage analysis are useful techniques in this regard.

Different industries have different competitive structures. In each industry setting, the nature and degree of competitive forces vary considerably. A company's industry environment therefore gives the marketer a set of competitive conditions over which very limited and, on occasion, no control can be exercised. To be effective the marketer understands these conditions and behaves in a manner consistent with the industry's rules of the game. On occasion it may be possible to reshape these rules to the firm's advantage.

Porter's five driving forces framework can be employed to analyze this competitive behaviour and industry structure. This Porterian approach can be enhanced greatly by incorporating it within the broader business system. This enables the manager to study the long linked chain of transforming activities that are combined through market mechanisms – internal and external – to provide a final product for consumption.

Rules of the game

In all markets that are not monopolized a number of suppliers compete to provide customers with what they need. It is not enough for the company to understand the customer alone. It must also understand what competitors are doing to gain customer loyalty and find a way of differentiating itself from them to win market share and long-term viability. It was noted earlier, in examining the characteristics of the competitive marketplace, that competition is the engine driving efficiency and selection. It is therefore vital to understand how this force operates and to prepare strategies both to deal with and shape it.

At a more general level, it must also be remembered that the industry in which a firm and its marketing team compete, or choose to compete in when setting up a new venture, has much to do with determining the kind of competition that will be faced and the level of profitability that may reasonably be expected. Different industries have different competitive structures. Some have many small suppliers chasing many small consumers, as in the case of the full-service restaurant industry. Some have a few large suppliers chasing many buyers as in the case of the fast-food industry or the supermarket business. In some industries many small suppliers compete for the custom of a very few large buyers, as for example in the case of engineering or electronics subsuppliers to major multinational production plants. In each industry setting the nature and degree of competition vary considerably. This industry environment, therefore, gives the marketer a set of competitive conditions over which he or she has very circumscribed and, on occasion, no control. He or she must comprehend these conditions and behave in a fashion consistent with the industry's rules of the game if he or she is to manage the marketing activity effectively.

Analyzing competitors

It is important to study competitors, their strengths, weaknesses and business direction for two reasons. Good strategy cannot be developed in a vacuum – it is essential to understand competing companies if one is to outmanoeuvre them and to predict how they may react to one's own moves or game-play. Furthermore, strategies of firms in any market are highly interdependent – what one does affects all others. To pick the optimum strategy for any company the manager must be able to assess the interaction between the available strategy options and those of the main competitors.

As illustrated in Figure 8.1, six elements of a competitor analysis can be undertaken:

Figure 8.1 Competitor analysis

▶ Who are the present and potential competitors?
▶ What is the position they have established in the market?
▶ What are their mission and objectives?
▶ What is their typical pattern of competitive behaviour?
▶ How strong is their resource base?
▶ What key competitive advantages and vulnerabilities do they possess?

If these six questions can be answered confidently by the marketer, he or she will have a very powerful grasp of the competitive challenge of winning customer loyalty. He or she will also be able to identify the opportunities that exist to differentiate his or her company and build market success.

Who are the competitors?

At first sight this seems a trivial question. Yet many go into business without any really clear knowledge of the answer. Identifying existing competitors is seldom difficult and can be quickly established by checking with customers about alternative suppliers, by consulting retailers, wholesalers and distributors, and by contacting industry groups or associations. What is much more difficult to ascertain is who the *potential* competitors are. Companies entering a market very often change the entire face of competitive behaviour. The entry of Toyota into the luxury car market with its Lexus brand in 1990 fundamentally changed the nature of competition for Mercedes Benz, BMW and Jaguar. The entry of supermarket chains into the grocery retailing business altered forever the competitive viability of the independent small grocer. The entry of IKEA from its Swedish home base into the European furniture industry changed the economics and the retailing of popular furniture beyond all recognition. With its unique combination of focus on the younger householder, simple but elegant design, low-cost structure and well-designed out-of-town retailing, IKEA left many traditional furniture companies and retailers floundering hopelessly in search of a competitive response (see Exhibit 12.2, p.236). The entry in the early 1980s of a firm with the resources and reputation of IBM changed the competitive rules of the game for all the entrepreneurial new ventures that formed the first wave of personal computer suppliers and resulted within a short few years in a reduction in the number of competitors from hundreds to tens.

The creation of the European Single Market heralded a major step on the road to free, open and international competition with all its attendant opportunities and pressures. For many firms that learned to compete in relatively protected domestic markets, the cumulative freeing of trade has marked the onset of competitive change to which they have not been able to cope. Some have not been able to adapt inefficient high-cost structures to meet new price competition. Others have not been able to adapt to new quality and customer service standards in order to retain customer loyalty.

Establishing who the potential competitors are is never an easy task, but effective marketers always look over their shoulder to check for signs of emerging competition. Firms in new industries and in technology-based industries must be especially vigilant for potential entrants with new competitive advantages or new technologies, as such industries are inherently characterized by uncertainty over which technology will ultimately dominate and become the industry standard. But neither are mature industries immune to change. The long-standing hegemony, and profits, enjoyed by UK chemists or pharmacists in developing and printing amateur photo film were suddenly challenged in the mid-1970s. Larger film processing companies used innovative mail order techniques to bypass the chemists, whose position was further eroded by high street mini-processors or one-hour photo shops, as well as by local newsagents becoming collection agents for film processors. The market for amateur film developing and printing changed profoundly with a number of traditional players, mainly chemists and inefficient film processors, losing out to new distribution practices, economies of scale and new technology.

Competitors' positioning

For each of the main competitors identified, it is important to understand what customer segments they focus on and what distinctive product or service benefits they offer. An understanding of their segment focus and strengths shows what areas of the market will be most difficult to penetrate, and also what areas are not being serviced adequately or perhaps at all. The success of Bailey's Irish Cream shows how advantage was taken of a largely unsatisfied segment of demand for a new drink, different from traditional liqueurs and brandy, and appealing especially to women.

The position that competitors have built reflects not only what customers they have chosen to serve, but also the product benefits they have developed to respond to their needs. Once again, the implications of this knowledge are two-fold. It allows the marketer to identify how the competitor serves customer needs and therefore the competitive strengths that it is foolhardy to try to attack, as well as the benefits not offered or poorly provided that represent an opportunity to steal market share with a product or service differentiated to provide the missing benefits.

Car manufacturers scrambled to offer economy-related benefits to car buyers in all segments of the market in a bid to win market share by responding to a widely expressed need through much of the 1980s. Not only was there intense competition in the small car market to provide economy benefits to buyers, but even in luxury car segments companies such as BMW and Audi built competitive advantage on the basis of fuel economy in addition to traditional benefits of comfort and performance. As we entered the 1990s, BMW made an early move to capture the advantage on being seen as environmentally friendly by launching its new 3-series as 80 per cent recyclable. Other companies responded with further attempts to be 'green' through design for recycling and the development of cleaner engines.

Competitor mission and objectives

Knowing the reasons why competitors are in business tells us a lot about how they will play the competitive game. A competitor dedicated to market share growth through low-cost manufacture and price discounting presents a type of opposition which is very different from that of a competitor whose aim is to maintain profitability and provide family shareholders with a regular dividend income. Knowing the mission and objectives that competitors have set for themselves tells the marketer what kind of behaviour he or she can expect from them, and what kind of reactions he or she may provoke by engaging various strategies. Sometimes objectives are publicly stated in annual reports, press releases or trade journal articles. Sometimes they have to be inferred from observation of past and current behaviour. Whatever the method, it is almost always possible to form a reasonably accurate estimate of the ends being pursued by any one competitor.

Patterns in competitor behaviour

Decisions about how to compete in the market very often revolve about complex judgements concerning action and reaction. 'If I lower price, will Competitor A meet my price, hold the old price, or go even lower and start a price war?' This is a common consideration facing the decision-maker. To make the difficult judgement about competitive reaction to the various decisions that could be taken, the market-focused company has to depend significantly on a sense of what is the normal or typical behaviour of the competitor. This sense of a normal response pattern is most usually built up informally by a good manager in much the same way that all of us build up over time an ability to predict the reactions of people we know well.

The marketing team should pay deliberate attention to the signals contained in competitors' behaviour that illustrate a stable tendency to respond to certain situations in predictable ways. Are certain companies price followers or price leaders? Which companies will discount price and offer promotional deals when market share is threatened, and which ones will always hold their price but perhaps respond with increased advertising or sales coverage? Which companies will innovate regularly and match any competitive new product quickly, and which will stay with their traditional product line until disaster stares them in the face? Monitoring competitors to build up judgements about questions such as these is vital if good marketing decisions are to be made that fit with current market conditions but also with the set of likely future competitive reactions. Much of the information required to do this well will reflect knowledge about the conventional wisdom used by managers in rival firms. Knowing these managers and their beliefs about the market, its behaviour and its trends is therefore important.

Competitor resource base

As in warfare, a priority for the strategist and tactician is to know the enemy's strength and competence. The considerations already documented tell much about the competitors' place in the market and their response tendency. We must also know something about the internal resources they can call on to expand or defend their competitive position. This necessitates evaluating their managerial, marketing, financial, manufacturing and technological capability. Are they resource-rich and able to outlast us in any direct market confrontation, or are they cash-starved and poorly managed and therefore unable to sustain a defence of market share? Are they weak in marketing, merchandising and innovative capability and therefore vulnerable to competition on these fronts, in the way, for instance, that many of the established national European-branded ice-creams were before the entry of Mars, with their ice-cream bars, brought to the market a new level of expertise in marketing, branding and merchandising based on pan-European resources and scope? Are they firms that display innovation in the way they transact business, often 'doing it different' from other competitors? Toshiba's staggering pace of product introduction in its laptop computer business during the late 1980s allowed it to explore almost every possible market niche, to outpace rivals like Grid, Zenith and Compaq and practically 'invent' a new mode of new product development (see Exhibit 8.1).

Key advantages and vulnerabilities

The steps in competitor analysis outlined so far provide the raw material for identifying the key competitive advantages and disadvantages, strengths and vulnerabilities, of each significant competitor. It is vital to isolate these factors, as they ultimately tell us how and where to compete for the custom of the chosen market. Normally the manager will, like a good military strategist, avoid competition in areas where competitors are at their strongest and will instead mobilize marketing forces to attack the weak points. The message from a good analysis is the essential information it provides about the competitor strengths one cannot hope to defeat and the resource weaknesses that betray a market vulnerability. Decisions about how to compete and on what issues to compete are at the heart of marketing strategy.

Exhibit 8.1 *Marketing in action case*

Toshiba's laptop and expeditionary marketing

Launching new products and exploring new markets are a risky business. For a new product or service to be successful it must combine just the right blend of functionality, price and performance to penetrate its target market quickly and deeply. In new business development, there are two ways to increase the likelihood of such success. One is to try to improve the odds on each individual bet; the other is to place many small bets in quick succession and hope that one will hit the jackpot.

Most companies, and particularly Western ones, pursue the former approach. Thorough market research, skilful analysis of market segments, competitors and industry structure, along with careful phase reviews, all take place. Yet the quality of this research and development process is no guarantee of subsequent success in the marketplace. Little is learned in the laboratory or in product development group meetings. True learning begins only when a product – imperfect though it may be – is launched.

If the goal is to accumulate learning and understanding as quickly as possible, a series of low-cost, fast-paced market incursions – expeditionary marketing – can bring the target more rapidly into view. Staking out virgin territory is a process of successive approximations. Consider an archer shooting arrows into the mist. The arrow flies at a distant and unclear target, and a shout comes back, 'right on the target' or 'a bit to the left'. More arrows are fired and more advice comes back until the cry is 'bull's eye'. What counts most is not being right the first time but the pace at which the arrows fly.

How fast can a company gather insights into the particular configuration of features, price and performance that will 'unlock' the market, and how quickly can it redesign its product offering? Speed and flexibility in doing this – reacting quickly to real-time information feedback from the marketplace – yield significant competitive advantage.

JVC's success and Sony's near-success in opening the consumer market for VCRs in the late 1970s came on the back of a whole string of product launches – many of them less than outstanding successes – over a decade. More spectacularly, Toshiba's staggering pace of product introduction in its laptop computer business during the late 1980s allowed it to explore almost every possible market niche and to outpace rivals like Grid, Zenith and Compaq. Between 1986 and 1990 Toshiba introduced no fewer than 31 new models to the market. Further, when one particular model failed, its withdrawal hardly caused a ripple in customer confidence. In fact, by 1991 Toshiba had discontinued more laptop models than some of its tardier competitors had launched.

The key to expeditionary marketing depends on minimizing the time and cost of product 'iteration'. Speed of iteration refers to the time it takes a company to develop and launch a product, accumulate insights from the marketplace, and then redesign and relaunch. Flexible manufacturing processes and low plant-tooling costs are critical in this context.[1]

Strategic group mapping

Strategic group analysis is a useful technique of competitor analysis. It helps in understanding the *positioning* of a firm in relation to the strategies of other firms. It basically asks the questions: who are the most direct competitors and on what basis is competition likely to take place? The aim is to identify clearly defined groupings of competitors so that each represents organizations with similar strategic characteristics, following similar strategies or competing on similar bases. Such groups can usually be identified using two, or perhaps three, sets of key characteristics. A typical list of such characteristics might include:

- product or service quality,
- product scope and diversity,
- extent of geographic coverage (local, regional, international),
- distribution modes,
- pricing policy,
- technological competence (including R&D expertise),

▶ level of differentiation (e.g. high perceived value in offerings),
▶ cost position (e.g. low delivered cost in offerings),
▶ marketing intensity (marketing investment as a percentage of sales),
▶ organization structure (e.g. centralized or decentralized),
▶ extent of business system ownership (e.g. degree of 'vertical' integration).

This list could be extended to include any basis on which a firm or group of firms seeks to win positional superiority. Which of the characteristics are particularly relevant in terms of a given organization or industry needs to be comprehended in terms of the history and development of that industry, studying the forces at work in the environment, the competitive activities of the firms under scrutiny, and so on. The marketing manager is trying to establish which characteristics most usefully differentiate groupings of firms from one another.

For example, Figure 8.2 shows a strategic group map of some leading retailers – in particular, it seeks to analyze important characteristics of their internationalizing policy. Two dimensions of this policy are examined: local responsiveness and flexibility; and the benefits accruing to retailers from having high levels of organizational integration and centralization between their home market interests and their foreign interests. Three groups of competitors are identified. One group, labelled global, enjoys considerable advantage from integration, but little by way of local responsiveness. The reverse holds true for the group labelled multinational. While a third group, categorized as transnational, follows a middle path and enjoys a critical mass of benefits along both dimensions. This sort of analysis is useful in a number of ways;

1 It helps to gain a better understanding of the bases of rivalry within strategic groups, and to comprehend how this is different from that within other groups.
2 It allows speculation about how likely or possible it is for an organization to move from one strategic group to another. Mobility between groups is a matter of considering the extent to which there are barriers to entry between one group and another. In Figure 8.2 it would be extremely difficult for the global category of retailers to develop high levels of local responsiveness. It would probably involve them taking on a cost structure that would make them unprofitable, or uncompetitive if they sought to pass on the added cost to customers in higher prices.
3 Strategic group mapping can also be used to predict market changes or identify strategic opportunity. Again in Figure 8.2 it is possible to speculate that an innovative retailer might succeed in bringing more

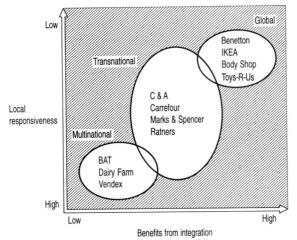

Source: Alan Treadgold (1991), 'The emerging internationalization of retailing: present status and future challenges', *Irish Marketing Review*, vol. 5, no. 2, p.26.

Figure 8.2 Strategic group map of some leading retailers' positions in international development

local flexibility *and* benefits of integation to the way it transacts business, and move downwards to the right on the diagram. To achieve this would involve changing the rules of the game, but it would confer considerable positional advantage on the mould-breaking firm.

While strategic group mapping is a worthwhile instrument of analysis, a caveat should be mentioned. Analysis normally tends to focus on direct competitors in the immediate competitive vicinity of the firm. This may lead the manager to ignore the study of competitors and competitive behaviour further along the business system, either upstream or downstream – something which can limit the competitive imagination of the manager and his or her firm!

Leakage analysis

The essence of competitive strategy is to carve out of the market a segment of loyal customers whose needs the company can serve better than any other competing supplier. Market share and, through it, revenue and profit consequences are the measures of success. Understanding how well a company competes and where and how it might search for additional market share can be gained by a relatively simple exercise known as 'leakage analysis'. The implications of this analysis are illustrated in Figure 8.3.

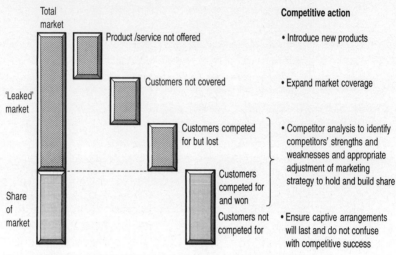

Source: Adapted from K. Ohmae, *The Mind of the Strategist: The Art of Japanese Business* (McGraw Hill, New York 1982), pp. 128–9.

Figure 8.3 Leakage analysis

This analysis helps managers to understand their marketing effectiveness. They can identify market share won as a result of their efforts rather than because of any captive customer arrangements where sales may reflect inter-company deals or a monopoly position in some segment. By applying competitor analysis to the business competed for but lost, it is possible to understand *why* the business was lost and set realistic market share gain objectives based on effective competitive differentiation of the company's product. They can also consider the magnitude and attractiveness of the opportunities that exist to compete in parts of the market that are not yet covered by the company for example, additional geographic areas, or segments where a different form of the product or service is needed to satisfy demand.

Competitive structure of an industry

What has been discussed so far takes as given the industry in which the marketer is planning to compete. However, different industries have different competitive structures which result in quite different rules of the game for competitive behaviour, and in quite different levels of profitability that are 'normal' among competitors. So-called *fragmented* industries, such as furniture manufacturing or transport, have many competitors, many customers and a considerable variety of bases on which to distinguish a company's product or service; are normally characterized by modest profit levels, considerable exit and entry of competitors; and have little scope for large growth in market share.[2]

Earlier, alternative ways of managing market transactions were examined (see Figure 2.1, p.23). Fragmented industries are likely to characterize the 'open market' end of this spectrum, whereas *concentrated* industries are likely to appear towards the 'managed market' end of this spectrum. In concentrated industries, such as car manufacturing or retail banking, a small number of competitors dominate the industry; the actions of any one player impact substantially on the industry; barriers to entry whether cost efficiency or differentiated product offerings are high; and stable behaviour and strong profit levels are a feature of the industry.

Such structural features set the nature of competitive behaviour that the marketer must accept as given in the short run. He or she must equally accept, with his or her entry into any industry, that profit targets are only partially responsive to his or her efforts: some industries, of their nature, have higher or lower 'normal' profit levels than others. In some industries, the environment very much circumscribes managerial choice and ambition. The manager must in effect 'fit in or be selected out'. The manager's objective under these circumstances is to set minimum profit targets at the 'normal' level and try to compete with sufficient effectiveness to raise his or her return on investment into the upper region of what is feasible in the industry environment.

Five driving forces model

Understanding the competitive structure of an industry and identifying the critical rules of the game set by this structure can be achieved by employing Porter's five-part analysis.[3] Porter argues that the nature and degree of competition in an industry are a function of five driving forces (see Figure 8.4):

1 the threat of new entrants;
2 the bargaining power of customers;
3 the bargaining power of suppliers;
4 the threat of substitute products or services;
5 the competitive rivalry for share among current competitors.

New entrants are an important feature of any industry that does not have high barriers to entry – for example, where a new firm does not need large economies of scale in manufacturing or marketing; where capital investment is low; where a new entrant can compete as cost-effectively as a long-established supplier; where there is easy access to distribution channels and where government does not regulate entry. Where there are low barriers many new firms will be attracted into the industry by any sign of attractive profits. They will compete hungrily to fill capacity and build market share, thus driving down overall profits of all competitors. In order to reap acceptable levels of profit and to achieve a degree of long-term security of market position, marketers will always aim to erect or maintain barriers to entry in their sector of an industry. The more successful, growth-oriented European printing firms have done this by shifting out of general printing, where there is great ease of entry, into areas such as quality magazine printing or security printing, where the investment required and the sophistication of the necessary marketing activity exclude many potential entrants and raise profit levels for the successful competitor. The creation of a strong brand name by an established player, and the consequent customer loyalty it attracts, are also a powerful deterrent to new entrants.

The development of the business format franchise is also a way of coping with the industry that has low entry barriers, many players and low capital requirements – the classic fragmented industry. Such business formats involve highly systemized procedures and operations for offering a product or service to the customer which have been developed by the franchisor. These mean that the franchisee can enjoy economies of scale in sourcing raw material and operating, as well as marketing advantages that would not otherwise be readily achieved. Examples of well-known business format franchises include McDonald's, Prontaprint and The Body Shop.

Customer power is perhaps a more readily grasped force. If the marketer is faced with few and very powerful buyers with whom he or she must deal in order to stay in business, then he or she may expect to see prices forced

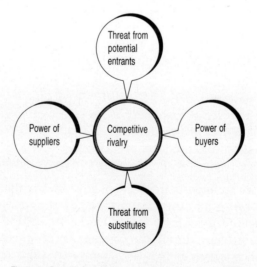

Figure 8.4 Porter's five driving forces framework of competition

down, pressure for greater quality and service, and the competing companies played off against each other. All these consequences force down industry profit levels, as has been experienced by the suppliers to the grocery trade in many countries as power has shifted into the hands of a few supermarket chains.

Supplier power is the opposite side of the coin from customer power. If a marketer depends on a few powerful suppliers of raw material or semi-finished products as input to his or her company, then he or she can be squeezed easily on prices, service and delivery. Many parts of the European agribusiness sector are affected by supplier pressures as farmers, abetted by politicians, press processors for higher input prices for milk, grain or livestock production. This, allied to problems of seasonality of supply and variation in quality, often militates against successful 'downstream' added-value activity in the sector. If suppliers are many, relatively weak and/or experiencing significant overcapacity, however, the marketer can reverse the situation by playing them off one against the other on price and service. Farmers across Europe did so for many years with the agrochemical companies as market growth for fertilizers and plant health products contracted in the face of reforms in the common agricultural policy of the EU, environmental pressure and the intensification and commercialization of farming.

Substitutes represent a force that varies by industry, depending on the extent to which it is feasible to develop new product forms or new technologies. The viability and profit expectations of many companies based on mechanical technology have been wiped out over the past fifteen years by substitute electronic solid state technology. For example, Olivetti's great strength in the European market for typewriters was translated into a weaker position in the electronic typewriter market and then into an 'also ran' position in the microcomputer-based wordprocessing market. Many industries, however, do not live under a threat of sudden radical obsolescence as a consequence of new technology. What is much more common and warrants continuous attention is the shifting balance of competitive advantage between close substitutes.

The tourism business provides an interesting example. Tourism consumption is always open to substitution by other leisure pursuits – you may choose to take a week off at home in order to pursue do-it-yourself home improvement activities or just to catch up on visiting friends and relatives rather than take a one-week break for skiing or lying on the beach. Within tourism the mode of travel is a continuous flux of substitution between cars (personal and rented), air transport, ferries, buses, trains and indeed hitch-hiking for those with only a backpack to worry about. The substitution between these modes reflects their changing economics and the levels of service – customer value – provided. The construction of the Channel

Tunnel (connecting London and Paris in 3 hours from city centre to city centre on the Eurostar train) and the building of bridges in Scandinavia precipitate substitution of car and rail for ferries – and just at a time when the technology of roll-on-roll-off ferries was being criticized on safety grounds.

The large-scale government investment in a new generation of high-speed rail technology has begun radically to alter the economics and especially the convenience value of short-haul intercity air travel. Tourists planning a holiday respond to their own economic circumstances by substituting less for more costly modes of transport when recession strikes – taking their own cars rather than flying, or travelling with a bus tour rather than independently. The traveller also responds to changes in convenience and service level introduced by substitutes. The arrival of France's TGV (trains à grande vitesse) providing a smooth 300 kph trip between French city centres changed the future of internal tourist air travel radically. Substitutes also put a ceiling on profits in good times. In the domestic central heating market the relative prices of gas, oil, solid fuel and electricity will always act as a check on the pricing freedom and therefore the profit potential of any one source of heat.

Competitive rivalry reaches its peak typically where there are many equal-sized competitors; where market growth is slow; where products or services cannot be differentiated significantly; where fixed costs and capacity are high, inviting price competition to maintain volume; where it is difficult to leave the industry because of redundancy payments or other exit barriers; and where rivals see no common set of rules of the game. Intensely competitive markets clearly drive down profit levels and competitors must accept this or else relocate themselves in a less fiercely competitive environment. Within a highly competitive market creative marketers will try, through segmentation of customers and differentiation of their products, to develop a sub-market where the intensity of competition becomes less and profit potential increases. In doing so they effectively rewrite industry boundaries and create new barriers to competition which protect service or product and its profit potential.

Analyzing these issues for the industry in which they operate is an important task for marketing managers, and one which will give them a considerable sense of confidence in knowing what is reasonable to expect and what they can and cannot hope to control through their marketing strategy. At the end of such an analysis they should be able to identify (1) how the five forces influence competition, (2) what are the rules of the game in the industry, and (3) what they need tactically or strategically to exploit or counter the forces at work. It was described above how some large UK film processors used innovative direct mail techniques to rewrite the rules of the game in the amateur film developing and printing industry with major consequences for all involved. Exhibit 8.2 illustrates how Bill Gates, founder of Microsoft, is rewriting the rules in art education, publishing and museum management by assembling a digitized inventory of the world's greatest works of art.

| Exhibit 8.2 | *Marketing in action case* |

Continuum's old masters change the rules

Bill Gates, the billionaire founder of Microsoft, recently started a new company, Continuum, to create and manage a library of the world's greatest works of art all stored on computer digitized images. It is revolutionizing the world of art education, gallery management and publishing.

Continuum has bought the licensing rights to hundreds of thousands of images, from a number of world famous museums including the National Gallery in London, the Barnes Collection in America and the State Russian Museum, as well as from scores of individual photographers, historical archives and private collections. The images are scanned into a computer and are available to those with CD-Rom drives, schools, colleges, newspapers, magazines and individuals – at a price.

The way millions of people look at art is changing, as are the speed and method of gathering related information. Continuum is also licensing the information that describes the images, and writing most of it with the help of curators and academics. This is of no small importance. For the company is making sure that this information cross-refers to other images in its inventory. The student writing an essay, or the publisher of a book, will be told that Continuum has a photograph of an artist, say Matisse, and information about the period in which he lived.

'Demand will come from CD-Rom, then on-line publishing, then home and business computers,' says Scott Sedlik, Continuum's head of corporate affairs. 'The whole publishing industry is changing to desktop publishing, creating a demand for digital images. Art magazines and newspapers are already coming to us for their images. We're building an archive for a market that doesn't really exist yet. But in five years' time it will be substantial!'

Product development is key at Continuum. It is producing themed topics for reference and entertainment. There is, for example, an Africa database, with paintings, sculpture, photographs and historical material, all digitized. It has joined forces with an audio-guide producer to devise a portable CD-Rom guide for the Seattle Art Museum. Unlike normal cassette guides, it is non-sequential and can store hundreds of hours of sound. Such developments are quickly thrusting art galleries into the age of multi-media.[4]

The business system and competitive analysis

So far we have used the Porter framework to analyze the forces at work in an industry that shape the nature of competition. A limitation of the framework is its concentration on the portion of the industry business system immediately adjacent to the link in the industry chain being studied. Indeed, one of the principal weaknesses of the framework is its adherence to the definition of industry as consisting of those firms producing near-substitutes. A business system view of the concept of an industry is different – it emphasizes the long linked chain of transforming activities that are combined through market mechanisms (internal and external) to provide a 'final' product for consumption. This view of an industry combines a series of individual competitive arenas that economists would regard as industries in their own right. Business system analysis argues for its broader scope on the grounds that all the linked arenas of competition or sub-industries are mutually interdependent in a systemic manner. In this view it is not adequate to analyze any one link in the chain – they must all be analyzed in order to understand fully the forces acting on one link (see Figure 8.5).

Take, for example, the toy industry (see Figure 8.6). An analysis of the toy manufacturing industry is very incomplete if undertaken in a narrow Porterian manner. Toy manufacturers are predominantly subcontractors which produce for toy companies, which decide which toys to bring to market and how to market them. Toy design is typically undertaken by small consultant firms that specialize in creative work. Downstream, the toy business is increasingly dominated by large retailers, a radically reduced number of specialist toy shops and the rapidly growing superstores such as Toys-R-Us. To undertake an industry and competitive analysis of the toy manufacturing sector of this industry would be meaningless without taking all these upstream and downstream activities into account. A rounded industry analysis therefore demands (1) a system-level analysis of the full

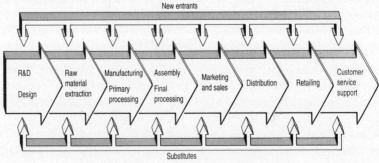

Figure 8.5 Business system analysis of industry structure

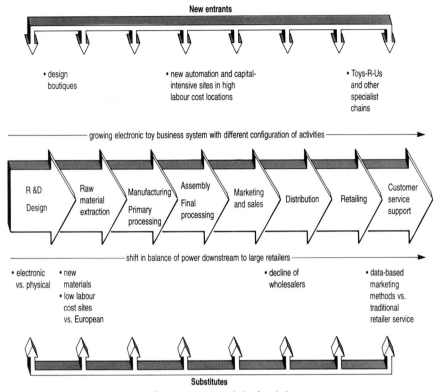

Figure 8.6 Business system analysis of toy industry

chain and the manner in which the dynamics of any one link affect all others, and (2) the conduct of a Porter-type analysis at each point of transformation in the chain.

The benefit of studying the overall business system to understand competitive behaviour is that it often enables the imaginative firm to consider how it might change the shape of the business system – and the rules of the game in its industry – to its advantage. An interesting example of a firm whose actions have had a profound effect on its industry's configuration is the Cott Corporation. In the late 1980s this firm was a low-key Nova Scotia-based company producing own-label soft drinks, especially cola, under agreement for retailers and wholesalers in eastern Canada. By the mid-1990s Cott had grown dramatically to become a global company manufacturing and canning cola under own label brands for hundreds of retailers in North America, Europe and Asia – names like President's Choice Cola in Canada, Sam's Choice for Wal Mart, K-Mart Cola and private label cola for the Southland Corporation's 7-Eleven stores, Sainsbury's Cola and

Virgin Cola in the United Kingdom, and cola for Ito Yokado and Seven-Eleven Japan.

It had teamed up with another 'also ran' US company, Royal Crown, which supplied it with a higher quality concentrate, and Cott quickly capitalized on the decade's growth in retailer power and distributor own brands (DOBs). Its success dealt a striking blow to the two players which dominated the cola industry, Coca-Cola and Pepsi Cola. The Cott Corporation changed deeply the business system of the cola industry right through from concentrate manufacture to final purchase, and provides a good example of how frame-breaking strategies derive from an understanding of the workings, relationships and value-adding steps along the whole business system.

REVIEW QUESTIONS

8.1 Explain the six general elements of a competitor analysis. Apply such an analysis to a firm of your knowledge.

8.2 How might strategic group mapping be of benefit to a marketing manager?

8.3 What is meant by 'leakage analysis'?

8.4 What are the implications for managerial choice of the existence of many different types of industry structure?

8.5 Elaborate on Porter's five driving forces framework.

8.6 Explain why the Porterian approach benefits from being incorporated into a broader business system analysis.

CHAPTER 9

Assessing company capability

- ▶ Core competences
- ▶ Resource-based advantage
- ▶ Assessing company competence
- ▶ An evaluation framework
- ▶ Matching capability to market need

Marketing in action case
Richardson's competences with knives

ABOUT THIS CHAPTER

Market focus and competitive success emerge from a well-managed marriage of core and long-lasting company competences to well-defined and equally long-lasting market needs (not just wants!). Core competences are viewed as the source of the company's core products around which it builds its business which in turn generates its changing array of product and service offerings.

Identifying core competences involves analysis and appraisal of the company's capability. A basic framework for such evaluation, from performance measurement, through performance evaluation and diagnosis, to identification of key capability strengths and weaknesses is discussed from a 'hands-on' managerial perspective. A market attractiveness/company capability matrix is used to link arenas of competence to market need and to suggest future direction for the firm.

A resource-based view of competitive advantage is espoused – a belief in the power of the firm and its managers to determine their own future, rather than being 'selected' by their environment in a Darwinian sense. Thus in cases where the market or industry appears unattractive or even hostile, it remains possible for the determined firm to exploit its competences in a superior and profitable way.

Matching the inside to the outside

'How good are we? We know what the market needs. We know how well our competitors can serve the market. Just how competent are we at serving those needs better than anyone else? How can we do it in an even more superior way?' These are questions to preoccupy the firm, the marketing manager and the marketing team. Looking inward and judging the firm's ability to 'deliver' is as challenging, if not more so, than looking outward to the industry, the market and the customer.

Managers often reach the wrong answers to these questions. Numerous case histories exist of the naive company that tried to implement ambitious marketing programmes way beyond its ability, and of the resourceful and talented company that persistently produced weak and unchallenging strategies far below its capabilities. In both cases the company lost market share; customers lost a competitive source of supply; and only the competition won! The trick, of course, is to match the right capability with the market need or opportunity. But many needs and opportunities, and hence the strategic options, will suggest themselves. The right response on the firm's part requires a clear-minded assessment of its own competences and shortcomings.

Core competences

Attempting to understand the underlying strengths and weaknesses of individual companies led managers and researchers during the 1980s to analyze the remarkable successes of Japanese global firms and the fact that relatively few Western companies achieved and sustained similar success. This work initiated a new concern for the 'core competences' of companies and the way in which these were at the root of significant market and business achievement. The work of Prahalad and Hamel in particular has led us to view market and competitive success as emerging from a well-managed marriage of core and long-lasting company competences to well-defined and equally long-lasting market needs (not just wants!).[1] Core competences are viewed as the source of the company's core products around which it builds its business, which in turn generates its changing array of product and service offerings. It is important to note that in this view individual products and services are seen as important but transitory reponses to important but equally temporary market wants.

Capturing this perspective is essential to successful marketing as it isolates the tactical and ever-moving relationship between products/services and market wants from the strategic and relatively stable relationship between competences and market needs. Understanding this distinction is an essential requirement if we are to avoid what Levitt called marketing myopia.[2] Marketing myopia leads the producer of buggy whips to continue to make them long after the horse and buggy have disappeared. Marketing myopia leads a railroad company to define itself as in the railroad business, when customers have begun to solve their transportation needs with cars and airplanes. In both instances, *products responding to wants are confused with competences responding to needs.*

It is essential therefore in undertaking internal company analysis to identify the company's core competences and the long-term market needs to which they can be deployed to serve profitably. Core competences will normally:

▶ provide potential access to a wide variety of markets,
▶ make a significant contribution to the benefits of the end product(s) as perceived by the customer,
▶ be difficult for competitors to imitate.

This latter point emphasizes that core competences – when difficult for rival firms to replicate – will also be 'distinctive' competences. For example, a pharmaceutical company may have a distinctive competence in researching and developing a particular line of respiratory drugs which competing companies would take a long time to imitate and perfect. It is this difficulty in replication which confers sustainability on competitive advantage.

Resource-based advantage

The reader of the last chapter might be forgiven for concluding that, given the complexity of industry structures, the ability of the manager to respond proactively, to influence events and initiate strategic change appears very limited. Put in the more formal language of the debate outlined in Chapter 2, environmental determinism may appear to outweigh managerial choice considerably. The perspective of this book, however, is that the firm matters. This is a resource-based view of competitive advantage.

For much of the 1980s the popular argument about the relative importance of environment and firm in determining performance outcomes (akin to the never-ending debate about 'nature and nurture' in the human sciences) swung quite strongly in favour of environment. The widespread appeal and use of Porter's industry analysis framework based on the industrial economics assumption that industry structure determines company conduct, which then determines performance, pointed towards an explanation heavily weighted towards the industry as the critical force. The 1990s have witnessed a resurgence of interest in resource-based explanations, to be seen in Hamel and Prahalad's ideas on core competences, strategic intent and in *Competing for the Future.*[3, 4] In addition to the popular swing towards a greater belief in the power of the firm and its managers to determine their own future, rather than being selected by the environment in a Darwinian sense, there has been an upsurge of theorizing on the subject of resource-based advantage in competition.[5, 6, 7] New theoretical insights have argued in favour of attributing considerable importance to the actions of the individual firm, and there has a reconsideration of some the basic premises of the 'environment is all' school of thought.

Recent research evidence does not support the view that the choice of industry is important. At best only 10 per cent of the differences in profitability between one business and another can be related to their choice of industry. By implication, nearly 90 per cent of profitability variations are not explained by the choice of industry, and at least half appear to be attributed to the choice of strategy. Put simply, the correct choice of strategy seems to be at least five times more important than the right choice of industry.[8] Attention is also drawn to the fact that economists from outside the industrial organization tradition, such as Milton Friedman, have asserted that causality flows in the opposite direction – from firm to industry – and would claim that some industries are more profitable than others because profitable firms are unevenly distributed across industries. Industries characterized by poor profitability have a preponderance of ineffective and inefficient firms, while profitable industries have the opposite.[9]

This latter argument – that firms make the industry – fits well with the resource-based view of many strategy and management theorists and with the claim that frame-breaking strategies are the real key to long-term success. If an unprofitable industry is characterized by ineffectual firms, there is a high probability that they pursue similar strategies with similar organizational forms. It is in fact this very sameness that drives down profits, makes advantage unsustainable and results in the 'commoditization' of products and services. It is the primary challenge of marketing to decommoditize the firm's goods and services by creatively differentiating its offerings and imaginatively adding value for the customer. In order to do this the firm must first look to itself and consider its strengths and weaknesses.

Assessing company competence

To undertake a basic capability audit it is most practical to start with past and current performance in the market. Relative success and failure in the market should then be traced back to the company strengths and weaknesses responsible for performance. Performance in the market is the ultimate yardstick against which company resources are evaluated. Before discussing a simple framework for evaluating company capability, it is worthwhile to reflect on two considerations.

In the first instance, it can be surprisingly difficult at a managerial level to make an objective assessment of company capability. This is normally the case for two reasons. First, the time, and on occasion cost, required to do a thorough audit of the company's resources and their quality can be an inhibiting factor. Second, personal and political stakes can become involved and influence managers to conceal, defend or even present as strengths, weak aspects of their operations. The reality of this latter consideration should not be underestimated. For these reasons, an outsider to the company's day-to-day business – such as a consultant or board member with marketing experience – is sometimes necessary to provide both objectivity and the required input of time.

In the second instance, there is always the temptation to take some convenient 'stocklist' of 'things one ought to find in a good company' and to tick off 'have' or 'have not' after each item. The reality of business is such that these general lists must be used with caution. Why? Because companies compete in different markets, in different industries, against different competitive forces, serving different kinds of customers from widely varied resource bases.

Capability must therefore be evaluated in the market context in which it is to be deployed. The same set of company resources may yield unbounded success in one market environment but dismal failure in another, a lesson which companies diversifying into new markets often learn painfully and at considerable cost. Rank Xerox, a company of very considerable resources, attempted without success to move into the mainframe computer market. Similarly, Texas Instruments failed in the microcomputer market.

In understanding the role of resources, competences and skills in the competitive arena it is important to distinguish between the quantity of resources and their appropriateness. A firm may have a narrow resource base, but if it is relevant and can be used creatively, success will often follow. Richardson, a UK knife company, had relatively few resources when it started its rejuvenation; yet within two decades it had nurtured its competences to become a world leader (see Exhibit 9.1).

Exhibit 9.1   *Marketing in action case*

Richardson's competences with knives

In the late nineteenth century, the Sheffield cutlery industry was the best in the world. It exported knives and forks to the four corners of the earth and had an enviable reputation for quality. But by the early 1970s Sheffield's fortunes had declined drastically. It was now a marginal producer on a world stage dominated by Japan, Germany, the United States and Far Eastern producers on the Pacific Rim.

UK producers blamed much of their problems on unfair competition. Steel, the principal ingredient of the production of knives, was priced more highly in the EC than elsewhere. Management at Richardson, a Sheffield-based cutlery manufacturer, decided to fight back despite considerable disadvantages stemming from high input prices. It noted that over 50 per cent of knife imports came from countries that did not always have a raw material advantage, e.g. Japan, France, Switzerland and Germany. It believed that British businesses failed to invest in the right technologies, failed to make a decent product, sell it right or present it better and, crucially, failed to innovate. 'They did not deserve to survive,' commented Richardson's MD.

Yet on the face of it, Richardson's strengths were few. It possessed a loyal workforce whose skills were in outdated technologies, a management resolute but not familiar with new manufacturing techniques, old plants, inefficient sub-suppliers, and selling though little marketing ability. Yet over the next decade, Richardson rose like a phoenix from the ruins of the UK industry.

It invested first in human and physical capital to improve the process by which the product was made. This allowed it to become one of the world's lower-cost producers of blank knives. It also invested in speed and flexibility to create a competitive advantage over its rivals in the United Kingdom and overseas. It went on to innovate new products, including the famous Laser knife.

It also innovated new marketing approaches. It worked to develop a strong brand identity and created effective distributor networks. It became a fashion leader in its business and won a reputation for high quality among its customers. By 1990 it had captured 5 per cent of the world's knife markets to be among the global leaders. Its resource base is now formidable, and most of these capabilities were built in-house.[10]

An evaluation framework

Figure 9.1 outlines a four-stage process by which company capability may be evaluated for the specific industry, market and competitive context in which any company finds itself.

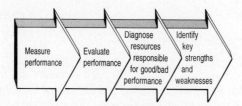

Figure 9.1 Evaluating company capability

Measuring performance

Three general measures of performance are needed:

1 the degree to which target customer needs are satisfied by the company's products or services – their relative quality, availability, performance in use and acceptability to the customer;
2 the competitive performance of the company, measured in terms of market share and whether it is moving up, down or holding position;
3 the profitability of the company and the maintenance, development or destruction of its asset base.

Precise measurement of these factors demands that the company undertake some customer research and maintain a good internal marketing information system. However, even the relatively small or unsophisticated company can make reasonable qualitative judgements of the first two factors and should not be in business if it does not know the third.

Performance evaluation

'How good is our performance?' is a question that demands an honest, objective answer from the manager. Is the company's product as good as it could be, or has the company taken shortcuts in design or manufacturing at the customer's expense? Is quality consistent and high? The market share figure is, of course, an undeniable measure of the market's verdict on the company relative to competitors. Is the share increasing or decreasing? Is it big or small? If it is small, is this because the company cannot do its job as well as the competition, or is it because it is in an industry where everyone has a small share and there is no route to large share positions?

Is the company profitable or not? How profitable does it have to be to rate a 'good' evaluation? The analysis of industry and competitive structure discussed in Chapter 8 is one way to set benchmarks of normal, high or low levels of profitability. The PIMS (Profit Impact of Marketing Strategy) programme provides such a standard of normal, or 'par', profitability to its subscribers, allowing them to make the good/bad evaluation with reference to other similar members of the programme. When these evaluations of market performance as good, bad or adequate have been discussed and debated by the marketer with the senior management team and perhaps with an outside, independent third party, the time for some detective work – or diagnosis – has arrived.

Diagnosis

The challenge at this stage of the analysis is to trace the origins of the 'goods' and the 'bads' to the areas of the company's resource base – to aspects of its capability – that are responsible for the particular performance level. An approach to doing this is visualized in the table illustrated in Figure 9.2, which may be used as a worksheet in undertaking the analysis. By way of illustration let us take the case of a sizeable company supplying a range of paint products to the market. The marketing manager in charge of one important brand, a rust treatment paint, found in evaluating its performance that:

1 The product and its quality were excellent, both in technical and customer perception terms.
2 Availability, however, was not as universal as it might be, because of concentration of selling and distribution on larger and more traditional hardware shops.
3 Market share was sizeable, but decreasing slowly because of lesser quality discount and private label brands, and new branded introductions sold as part of a competitor's wide product range to retailers.

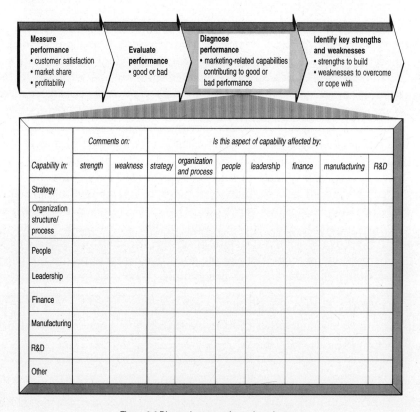

Figure 9.2 Diagnosing strengths and weaknesses

4 Profitability was good and understood to be above average for most
paint products.

Working down through the diagnosis table, the marketing manager of the
rust treatment brand considered that the only identifiable weakness in his
strategy was in the sales and distribution area, where his market coverage
was limited to the older outlets, typically in high street locations. There
were increasing numbers of new hardware stores in new housing areas,
located in suburban shopping centres and malls. He had no clear information about how many of these existed and for how much of total market
sales they accounted. His salesforce had tightly organized, efficient call
routines for established hardware shop selling, but had not traditionally
been asked to search out new shops and open accounts with them.

Thinking about his management of marketing activity and processes in
his business, he could see that the distribution weakness in his strategy was
partly created by the absence of market information flowing into him. What
were the trends in hardware retailing? Where were householders buying
their do-it-yourself supplies? He had no information system to tell him
about the market other than salesforce call reports. The strategic problem
with distribution also prompted him to evaluate why he did not have
planning procedures that looked ahead and alerted him to long-term
changes in shopping behaviour and retail location. At that time planning
involved preparing each year's sales budget: maybe there should be more to
marketing planning than that?

Looking at the people he employed and managed, he knew he was
evaluating his most important and costly resource. How well was the
salesforce performing? Was it their 'fault' – were they a 'problem resource'
– because of the inadequate distribution coverage? Not really, since they
had not been asked to do missionary selling and were tightly scheduled and
controlled in their coverage of well-established accounts. But if this were to
change, if they were asked to develop new business, would their skills,
attitudes and training be appropriate to the new task? Here was a strength
and a weakness: an excellent salesforce at its current job, but possibly a
weak one at a redefined job.

Leadership, he knew, meant self-evaluation, and here he had to confess
that he had to reach a conclusion akin to that about the salesforce. By any
standards he had been leading his team successfully and had good profits to
show. But new developments had not received much of his attention, and
he felt he had created a climate in which 'the name of the game was to do
the job we have always done and keep doing it better'. Now he began to
feel that he had unconsciously left innovation out of his leadership
approach. He had not pushed anyone to think about market changes and

required responses. He had not questioned the annual budgeting ritual and whether it contributed to longer-term marketing effectiveness or not.

Finance he had initially pencilled in as a distinct strength: he was delivering above-average profitability for the paint industry. Then, however, he began to think about from where that level of profitability was coming. He was losing a small but consistent share of the market from year to year and was not charging premium prices. So the profits were not due to the price-volume part of the profit equation. That left costs. Why should he be more cost-effective than his competitors? He ran a very tight salesforce management and control system, so maybe he was just more efficient. Then he started a new train of diagnosis. His advertising and promotion budgets had been cut back in each of the past three years by the managing director to provide money for the launch of new paint products. All his requests to increase the salesforce had been turned down for the same reason. His salespeople certainly were efficient, but could that be because they were calling on well-known retail accounts, while competitors were out opening new accounts and trying aggressively to steal retail shelf space for their products from his?

His above-average profitability, he now began to see, was a result of running down the competitive capability of his product area. While this had shown handsome profits for the past three years and left him basking in the managing director's approval, he could now see a day of reckoning drawing close. More share loss would soon leave his absolute revenue and contribution figures looking rather meagre and leave the brand with little scope to regain share against aggressive competitors who were investing marketing resources in their brands. Had he unknowingly turned a brand with a long healthy life ahead of it into a rapidly decaying one with poor life prospects?

Identification of strengths and weaknesses

It is easy to see how this line of diagnosis led this particular marketing manager to list in the worksheet shown in Figure 9.3 his product's key marketing-related pluses and minuses. Marketing strengths and weaknesses demand three kinds of response from the manager:

1 He can, and is well advised to, build on his strengths, especially if they are to some extent distinctive to his company.
2 He can attempt to turn around his weaknesses where they hinder effective performance.
3 He can plan to cope as best as possible with strengths or weaknesses over which he has little control.

	Feasible options		
Strengths	*Build*	*Turnaround*	*Cope*
• Product and brand reputation	✓		
• Satisfied customer base	✓		
• Full coverage: traditional retailers	✓		
• Competent motivated salesforce	✓		
• Personal openness to change	✓		
Weaknesses			
• Coverage of new retailers and new population areas		✓	
• Contracting marketing investment		✓	?
• Financial strategy		✓	?
• Poor market information		✓	
• Budgeting instead of planning		✓	

Figure 9.3 Key marketing strengths and weaknesses

The problem faced by the manager of the rust treatment paint brand illustrates the third point, and is the reason he put question marks in the 'cope' column opposite marketing investment level and financial strategy. He did not have the freedom to make a final decision on changing these factors. The managing director, concerned with overall company fortunes, had to face the problem of how he should allocate scarce cash across several paint brands. His decision had to be guided by analysis of which brand would return the greatest long-run profits for each pound of marketing expenditure.

Matching capability to market need

Now that the essentials of analysis have been covered it is useful to examine some relatively simple ways in which the conclusions of analysis may be synthesized and summarized. Thus syntheses are needed that:

▶ summarize the results of the analysis,
▶ identify core or distinctive competences, and
▶ suggest directions for marketing and overall company decisions.

So far, analysis of the *external* environment has addressed the customer and his likely behaviour, defined the market and possible trends therein,

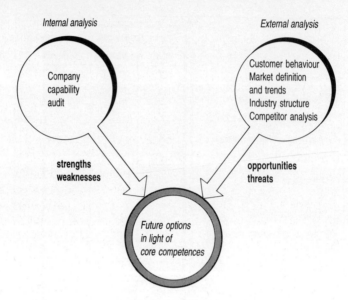

Figure 9.4 SWOT analysis

examined industry structure and profiled the competition. *Internal* analysis of the company focused on its strengths and weaknesses, particularly those in the marketing area. By assessing these pluses and minuses in the light of the various external factors, it is possible to identify key or core competences. For example our marketing manager of the rust paint brand might consider his well-trained and disciplined salesforce, along with his strong relationship with and coverage of traditional outlets, as core or distinctive competences. He has, as we can see from Figure 9.3, a number of feasible options to build on this advantage. In this way the marketing manager can 'marry' such core and long-lasting company competences to well-defined and equally long-lasting market needs – and opportunities.

Figure 9.4 presents this synthesis in a schematic framework and illustrates a particular approach to what is commonly referred to as SWOT analysis. It is so called because its outcome is a concise and insightful summary of the critical opportunities (O) and threats (T) identified by the firm and the essential strengths (S) and weaknesses (W) inherent in its resource base.

Market attractiveness and company capability

In order to advance this approach one further step towards action implications, it is useful to connect the foregoing analysis with the decision framework inherent in a market attractiveness/competitive capability matrix. Figure 9.5 represents such a simplified matrix based on approaches developed by General Electric, A.D. Little and others and described earlier in Chapter 4. By combining the conclusions of the analysis of customers, competitors and industry trends into a summary notion of 'market attractiveness' and relating it to the analysis of the company's capability, any company or product of a company can be positioned along the two dimensions. The possible options or policy implications of various positions on the matrix are indicated in summary form on the figure.

Returning to the marketing manager for the rust treatment product discussed earlier, he positioned his brand in a highly attractive market (stable market growth, relatively recession-proof DIY demand, good margins, changing but identifiable distribution patterns) with medium capability (small share losses, non-coverage of new retail outlets, excellent product compared with competitors', solid competitive brand image, ability to improve marketing). This put the product in the position shown in the figure – one normally demanding that the company defend its existing position or try to build market share by improving its capability to compete. This indeed was the essence of the difficult decision that had to be faced by the managing director of the company. Should he continue to take money from the brand in order to support new products and allow the brand to

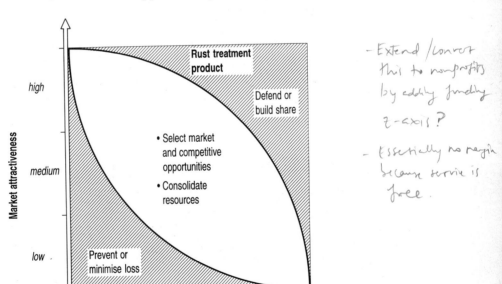

Figure 9.5 A simplified market attractiveness/company capability matrix

162 Strategy and process in marketing

lose share? The analysis illustrated here suggested that this was not appropriate. At worst, he should leave the brand with enough cash to defend its market share position. He should also consider the payoff from investing in rebuilding share and market leadership relative to the payoff from making the same investment elsewhere in the company.

This relatively simple but informative approach to putting all the analysis together belongs to a 'family' of portfolio analysis methods which will be explored in greater depth in Chapters 11 and 15.

The industry is not always to blame

The market attractiveness/company capability matrix is just that – a matrix or framework helpful in assessing market opportunity and linking it to firm competence. Care must be used in interpreting it; it suggests guidelines rather than purporting to be a predictive model. In cases where the market or industry appears unattractive or even hostile, it remains possible for the determined firm to exploit its competences in a superior and profitable way. Further, in line with thinking about resource-based advantage, the actions of such a firm may well initiate a reversal in the overall industry's fortunes.

The story of William Cook outlined in Exhibit 11.1 (p. 196) highlights the point that organizations can be successful in an industry which seems unpromising. In the early 1980s, UK industry sales of steel castings were declining; there was excess capacity; rationalization schemes had been tried and failed, and Cook itself had very limited resources. The firm showed a clear understanding of the roots of generic competitive advantage in refocusing its operations. In less than ten years, Cook moved from being a barely profitable business with only 2 per cent share of the industry, to a highly profitable business earning an excellent return with some 30 per cent industry share. Cook's performance encouraged new competitors to arrive in the market to copy and rival it. Partly on account of all the actions of the players in the industry, industry sales stopped declining, excess capacity disappeared and the industry looked more attractive. But the sequence of events was from firm action to industry improvement, not the other way around.

REVIEW QUESTIONS

9.1 What are the objectives of a capability audit, and what problems are likely to be encountered in its implementation?

9.2 Explain the steps involved in conducting an evaluation of company capability and the desired outcome of each step.

9.3 Market focus emerges from a well-managed marriage of core and long-lasting company competences to well-defined and equally long-lasting market needs. In practical terms, how does a marketing manager go about achieving such focus?

9.4 In cases where the market or industry appears unattractive or even hostile, it remains possible for the determined firm to exploit its competences in a superior and profitable way. Elaborate on this view.

CHAPTER 10

Convergence, divergence and pan-Europeanism

▶ Competitive structure
▶ A business system perspective
▶ Marketing strategy in a European context
▶ The pan-European debate

Marketing in action case
Unilever and P&G Euro-clash in detergents

ABOUT THIS CHAPTER

The competitive characteristics and structures of one of the world's three largest trading blocs are analyzed using Porter's driving forces framework. A business system perspective broadens this understanding. A number of themes emerge.

The pressure on marketers to compete simultaneously on the basis of lower price and higher quality is making a necessity of fundamental cost restructuring and innovation for quality in manufacturing, logistics, distribution and marketing on a European scale. This market imperative drives business systems towards the consolidation of upstream companies through tightly linked supplier relationships and the careful location of each element of the value chain across Europe in a manner that reflects cost, factor availability and logistical forces in different country locations. In downstream firms, the redesign of distribution and logistics, retailing structures and recycling arrangements is widespread and often radical.

On the issue of convergence versus divergence, if one isolates marketing in the business system, it is clear that its constituent elements are differentially affected – product policy is most likely to become pan-European; pricing policies are rapidly converging in response to market unification; distribution strategies are still necessarily locally configured because of the radically different national distribution structures across Europe; and sales, service and promotional strategies are most likely of all to be quite localized even where a standardized product is being brought to market.

A marketing environment in transition

Europe is in transition – as perhaps it has always been – but just now with the added pace and urgency of the Single Market programme and the associated changes in political and social values. In so far as business success relies on well-judged adaptation to a changing environment this is a decade in which environmental responsiveness will be vital. In so far as marketing is the managerial function with special responsibility for reading and interpreting the environment it is also a critical decade for European marketing practitioners.

Europe has long been a huge economic force, accounting for more than 40 per cent of world trade. However, its own market remained a complex web of internal trade barriers until the Single European Market project took shape in the mid-1980s. Industries that were built on nationally regulated frameworks such as financial services or those that lived on contracts from their own governments, such as telecommunications, have experienced enormous change. The national markets for public procurement contracts have become open competitive markets on a European scale. Companies with traditional strategies based on serving local markets protected by physical and regulatory barriers to trade have had to deal with direct international competition. Start-up companies and those with growth objectives can aim for an EU market of almost 350 million people to support marketing strategies based on low cost and world-class product quality.

European consumers increasingly view the same media, listen to the same music, respond to similar fashion trends and are ever more aware of each others' consumption behaviour. While demographic and consumer trends vary across Europe, in general terms it is an ageing market with a high disposable income wielded by increasingly smaller households in which female members are more and more likely to work outside the home. Like consumers everywhere, its population still spends most of its income on food and shelter, while paying increasing attention to leisure, health and education.

Defined in its Single Market scope, Europe is one of the three largest markets for goods and services on a global scale, bigger than the United States, and a GDP as big as the United States and nearly twice that of Japan. In simple demographic and economic terms, the Single Market is one of enormous size and importance to firms worldwide. If the seven member states of EFTA (who signed an agreement with the EU in 1991 to create the European Economic Area (EEA) as a free trade zone) are included, then 380 million people are encompassed in a step that is defining the next stage of expansion of the EU itself. Beyond this group of countries the question then arises as to whether the EEA will, in due course, expand to include

Poland, the Czech and Slovak republics and Hungary. While Europe may have been accustomed for many years, and without much justification, to seeing itself as the centre of the trading world, the realities of the 1990s signal that it is one of the three key global markets along with the United States and Japan and the other rapidly growing economies of the Pacific Rim.

Competitive structure

One of the central challenges to those managing marketing in European companies is to develop an understanding of how the political, legal and economic restructuring of the EU will affect competitive forces that dictate success or failure in local, regional and pan-European markets. The driving forces in the restructuring of the market are broadly two-fold. On the one hand, the political and regulatory agenda of the European institutions and their implementation through negotiation and legislation are driving change through the environment to the firm.

On the other hand, the strategic initiatives of European companies seeking to anticipate the new structures and to position themselves in advance of its reality with early pan-European marketing strategies are altering the nature of inter-firm competition in fundamental ways. The political and regulatory momentum gained by attempts to meet the 1992 target date was important in radically altering the pace of change in the EU. In the area of initiative-taking by firms, a long list of companies pursuing European-wide marketing strategies already exists, ranging from Nestlé in food markets, to Electrolux in household durables, to Asea Brown Boveri (ABB) in industrial and capital goods. For example, Nestlé's sales doubled between 1981 and 1993 through a series of acquisitions across Europe designed to secure its market position and to capture brands with multi-country appeal. Similarly, Electrolux set out to acquire and coordinate electrical white goods brands and distribution channels from Italy to Scandinavia, while ABB has created a European giant by combining and rationalizing the operations of two traditional Swedish and Swiss companies (see Exhibit 23.1, p. 468).

Rivalry between firms

Intermittent over-capacity, decreasing switching costs, increasing exit barriers and increased numbers of rival firms are all factors that are expected to intensify rivalry among competitors in many European markets. In industries such as steel, detergents, pharmaceuticals and banking, over-capacity is seen as a well-established reality.[1] The switching costs facing buyers in most industries inevitably decrease with the opening of borders and the harmonization of technical standards. This liberalization leads to greater price and other competitive pressure especially on nationally oriented companies. On the other hand, a harmonized market allows the achievement of greater economies in production and distribution in those firms that pursue more pan-European strategies, reducing both fixed and storage costs.[2] For example, companies such as Jacobs Suchard of Swiss chocolate fame or SKF Bearings (see Exhibit 4.1, p. 58) in the industrial products market have been consolidating production of individual products in specific European-scale plants to gain focus and scale in manufacturing; shutting down the over-capacity that was characteristic of a nationally structured European market and exploiting these changes through quality, service and price advantages in their marketing strategies.

Exit barriers are high in many industries and are unlikely to be lowered, especially where government shareholding and national pride are involved as in the case of airlines. It seems unlikely that the Single Market can support twelve national airlines and even with their reduction in number through strategic alliances and mergers, protracted competitive uncertainty seems likely to result from both over-capacity and political barriers to exit. It has been suggested that the sheer size and global strategic importance of the Single Market will attract more American and Pacific Rim competitors as well as further competitors from within Europe. In 1990 Japanese investment of US$13.3 billion in the EU accounted for almost one quarter of Japan's total direct foreign investment, with its major concentrations being in electronics, machinery, chemicals and general machinery markets.[3] A 1992 survey of 90 executives in 25 leading Japanese companies reports that 58 per cent see Europe post-1992 as an opportunity and only 2 per cent see it as a threat.[4] Furthermore, they report that the focus for their expansion in the 1990s will be 32 per cent in the United States (versus 60 per cent in the eighties), 27 per cent in Western Europe (versus 20 per cent), 10 per cent in Eastern Europe (versus 2 per cent) and 16 per cent in Asia outside Japan (versus 11 per cent).

It must be noted that Europe has been swept by consolidation, mergers, acquisitions and strategic alliances among those supplying its markets. Conflicting forces are therefore at work in determining the state of rivalry among firms competing for the markets of Europe but they might be expected, on balance, and when combined with slow economic growth, to lead to the intensification of rivalry in most markets. The pressure on marketers to compete simultaneously on the basis of lower price and higher quality is making a necessity of fundamental cost restructuring and innovation for quality in manufacturing, logistics, distribution and marketing on a European scale.

Threat of entry

High barriers to entry are generally assumed to lessen the intensity of competition and to support high profitability for incumbent companies. In European marketing, barriers often reflect past investment in local or international brand assets and the creation or exploitation of local or national niches free from the full force of international competition. The removal of entry barriers to markets within Europe has been the central objective of the harmonization process and changes the rules of the game for all nationally oriented companies. Perhaps because of its traditionally fragmented nature, the European market has not produced many global brands. Indeed, among the ten best-known brands worldwide, Nestlé is the only European brand, compared with six American brands and three Japanese. The Single European Market restructuring process is expected to encourage the emergence of more pan-European brands. This would reflect the opportunity to exploit economies of scale in both marketing and manufacturing and the manoeuvring of European competitors to build barriers to entry based on brand assets as protection against marketers from North America and Japan.

In the area of consumer products this likelihood is confounded by the growth of very large-scale retailers with significant buying power and their success in transferring customer loyalty to retail brands and away from manufacturer brands. Thus retailers such as Carrefour, Aldi or Marks & Spencer have already begun on European expansion strategies which gain leverage from their brand identities but which weaken that of traditional manufacturers. However, their sourcing strategies for own brand products increasingly stress supply partnerships with European rather than offshore companies. This reflects a new era of intense relationship marketing in business-to-business markets based on long-term partnership concepts, service as the key marketing variable, and real-time electronic exchange of marketing data to underwrite fast and flexible supplier response.

In the services sector, financial services provide an illustration of just how slowly market restructuring can proceed and how long it takes for the threat of entry across internal market boundaries to be translated into practice. Despite the fact that financial services account for an estimated 7 per cent of GDP, there has been less progress in the dismantling of national barriers than in tackling barriers to trade in goods. However, progress towards a free market in financial services is generally expected to result in significant concentration as a result of pan-European competition and in new forms of market specialization by institutions based on regional segments over the remainder of the decade. Companies and consumers will enjoy more and more freedom to 'shop around' on a regional basis for their financial services. One commentary on the process notes that by the year 2000 industry sources expect 'greater competition within each country as well as more concentration in the region as a whole. Likely "winners" in the 1990s are expected to be the leading banks in each country, with deep penetration of their home markets and large resources of capital and people.'[5]

Threat of substitution

As a force influencing structure and performance, the threat of substitute products is generally expected to reduce profitability. Substitution operates not just within narrowly defined product categories or immediate substitutes, but also between near-substitutes. Thus, in the market for energy, the individual fuel sources – gas, oil, electricity and solid fuels – represent a persistent threat of substitution to each other and create price boundaries beyond which each energy form may become a substitute for another. The development of European grids for both natural gas and electricity has already redefined the market dynamics of these sectors and the relative market shares of both. It is interesting that the logistical infrastructure to enable this now extends throughout Europe.

The harmonization of fiscal barriers can have far-reaching impact through altering the probability of substitution. For example, excise-related harmonization may dramatically reduce liquor prices in Denmark, Ireland and the United Kingdom while greatly increasing them in Italy. In the United Kingdom, price decreases for wine should be greater than for beer, suggesting the likelihood of substitution between these two classes of alcoholic beverages in a market that has already seen a consumer taste shift in favour of wines.[6]

Bargaining power of buyers

In general, it may be argued that the bargaining power of buyers is likely to increase as a result of structural shifts in European markets although the impact will vary greatly across industries.[7] This is predicted on the grounds that there will be, in general, greater concentration of buying power, and greater availability of substitutes both from within and beyond the EU. In the retail and wholesale sectors, for example, buying groups are emerging which transcend traditional national boundaries and which promise to create formidable market power. The alliance in grocery retailing between the Argyll Group (UK), the Ahold Group (Holland) and Casio (France) is an example of the creation and deployment of pan-European purchasing power, based on convergence in consumer tastes and demand, and the harmonization of trade. The traditional national structure of European markets allowed pricing policy to vary by country without undue danger of 'parallel importing' or arbitrage across national boundaries. However, with the implementation of harmonization and the concentration of retail and industrial purchasing power, pricing policies are rapidly becoming standardized as a matter of necessity across Europe. This puts an end to many traditional price discrimination policies that were used to increase overall profitability or to cross-subsidize various national marketing strategies.

Bargaining power of suppliers

The pressure for consolidation among producers in Europe and the general intensity of rivalry already noted suggest that the widespread restructuring of industry to create lower cost structures will continue unabated. This process of cost restructuring typically involves reconsideration of supply relationships and, in general, a movement away from multiple suppliers towards single supplier relationships or a very few supply linkages. For example, in the course of its drive to regain competitiveness, Philips has ceased to deal with 10,000 traditional suppliers.[8] The same process of supplier rationalization is visible in sectors as disparate as automobile components and clothing. This would seem to suggest that the forces working towards industry consolidation and concentration spell out a future of lower power for sub-supply sectors. However, the balance of power will also reflect the uniqueness of suppliers' products or services and the dependence of buyers on their differentiated inputs. In so far as a shift to single rather than multiple supplier relationships is occurring, this may reflect an underlying change in the nature of industrial and business-to-business markets as much as it reflects the forces at work in the emergence of a Single Market. Single sourcing arrangements, or supply partnerships as they are often called, also confer power on the effective sub-supplier as dependency becomes mutual between buyer and supplier.

A business system perspective

An alternative view of structural forces at work in European markets is suggested by taking a business system view. Observation of current marketing strategies in Europe suggests that many companies are exploiting or anticipating the advantages of a unified market by moving to integrate their business systems on a pan-European scale. In order to build the critical market advantages required for success and sustainability, companies must increasingly seek to compete on a combination of product quality, low delivered cost and speed to market. This market imperative drives business systems towards the consolidation of upstream companies through tightly linked single supplier relationships and the careful location of each element of the value chain across Europe in a manner that reflects cost, factor availability and logistical forces in different country locations.

Within the ambit of marketing, the redesign of distribution and logistics arrangements is widespread and often radical. For example, Ford of Europe now manages its parts distribution to dealerships across Europe in a centralized manner so as to minimize locally held and duplicate stocks while still guaranteeing rapid fulfilment of parts orders for the repairs of customers' cars. Such reconfiguration of business systems' cost structures and responsiveness is based on being able to operate in an integrated fashion through the whole system across Europe – from suppliers through manufacturing to marketing. It is also based on investment in information technology infrastructure, which allows a multi-country management of response to demand and of inventory positions – in real-time.

At the consumer end of business systems one of the most heated debates in marketing analysis and practice rages over the issue of whether consumer tastes and behaviours are converging on a pan-European basis. Increases in international communication, urbanization, disposable income, education, English language ability, similar product ownership patterns and a continuing surge in travel are all presented as reasons for a convergence in consumer behaviour in Europe. Evidence of such convergence in European teenage culture is to be found, for example, in the sheer size of the network connections of the pop music satellite channel, MTV (see Table 10.1).

Companies such as IKEA or Benetton are often advanced as exemplars of those who choose marketing strategies to exploit this process of convergence. IKEA, a Swedish furniture company, addresses a segment or niche consisting of relatively young consumers across Europe with its common marketing strategy of reasonably priced, self-assembly products retailed in combination showroom-warehouses across the continent. To the young urban couples with mid-range but rising incomes, whom they target through their marketing, IKEA is as attractive in Italy or Hungary as it is in Sweden.

The advantage of targeting such pan-European segments lies in the ability to exploit the consequential economies of scale in everything from investment in design to brand building. In integrated business systems of European scale, the key to success lies in control of the complete system – but not necessarily in ownership. IKEA, for example, makes no furniture but rather relies on over 17,000 sub-suppliers despite being the largest furniture company in Europe. Its success and profitability to date reflect its control of the important elements of the business system – especially design

and retailing – underwritten by a deep investment in information technology to provide the instantaneous information flows it takes to coordinate
the full system. Benetton's strategy reflects similar commitments. It manu-
factures almost none of the garments that bear its label, just as it owns
almost none of the shops that retail them. However, it does own its design,
information technology and distribution infrastructure, while controlling
the rest of its business system tightly without bearing the costs of ownership.

While these companies have exploited trends towards consumer convergence, there are also examples of markets in which convergence has not
occurred and which illustrate the alternative viewpoint in the consumer
convergence debate. In the area of domestic electrical appliances a study
found that attempts by manufacturers to implement standardized strategies
have failed.[9] The research contained in the study indicates that this market
has been characterized by increasing divergence since the early 1970s with
growing demand for variety *within* countries compounded by growing
differences in demand *between* countries. Electrolux attempted to pursue a
pan-European strategy with its many acquisitions but, even today, it
produces 120 basic designs and 1,500 variants. After failing in its efforts to
standardize its products and marketing strategy it now plans to standardize
when it may and to 'localize' when it must, in response to the persistence

Table 10.1 MTV Europe network

Total homes connected (at 31 July 1994):	
Austria	1,378,452
Belgium	3,611,284
Bulgaria	500
Croatia	68,000
Czech Republic	564,100
Denmark	1,247,565
Estonia	8,820
Finland	690,869
France	1,034,727
Germany	19,570,101
Greece	1,540,591
Hungary	1,094,326
Iceland	17.000
Ireland	390,530
Israel	710,943
Italy	6,424,002

Latvia	12,564
Liechtenstein	10,310
Lithuania	15,465
Luxembourg	85,110
Malta	14,208
Monaco	4,823
Montenegro	4,336
Netherlands	5,429,440
Norway	561,099
Poland	1,531,395
Portugal	102,528
Romania	148,450
Russia	133,357
Serbia	51,700
Slovak Republic	551,500
Slovenia	303,286
Spain	1,289,747
Sweden	2,159,327
Switzerland	1,774,073
Turkey	5,000,000
United Kingdom	3,453,278
European hotel rooms total	**176,070**
Total	**61,163,876**
Last month	60,799,890
Growth	363,986

Source: MTV Europe, Hawley Crescent, London NW1 8TT.

of variety in consumer demand, based on deep-seated differences in national usage habits and taste.[10]

As a consequence of the social and political concern about the physical environment, business systems are now being redesigned across Europe to recover waste and used products and to recycle them where possible or to return them to nature in a harmless manner. EU directives have been important levers on change in this area as they typically reflect the increased concern of citizens about pollution and health. For marketing strategy it has meant that 'environmental friendliness' has become one of the common criteria for product acceptability in both industrial and consumer markets. To guarantee the 'greenness' of products marketers have had to adapt product design to incorporate recyclability and to eliminate the use of certain materials such as CFCs in aerosols. But differences in regulatory requirements have caused considerable disparities in competitive ability and economic rewards across markets. In general, Germany has been the first to establish demanding environmental standards and its companies have necessarily been the first to adapt – but often to their own short-term disadvantage in competition with suppliers from less 'advanced' European nations. In the medium to long term this competitive disadvantage may be reversed as both EU and national environmental legislation and its enforcement spread, and the early mover advantages that have been gained in making, marketing, recovering and recycling environmentally friendly products pay off. The advantage to the early movers is most likely to arise from (1) positive consumer perceptions and attitudes which become attached to companies and their brands, (2) the accumulated experience of dealing with new materials, technologies and processes and, (3) the ownership of proprietary design, recovery and recycling technologies and processes.

An interesting example of how far-reaching this environmental force has been in its impact is the change that has taken place in the European paint industry. Solvents have been the traditional 'carriers' for paints. However, they present a pollution, health and safety threat in use. Between 1970 and 1992 the proportion of decorative paint that was water-based rather than solvent-based consequently grew from about 30 per cent to 70 per cent and is expected to grow to 85 per cent by the year 2000. In industrial applications, where water-based paint is less appropriate, a major change to powder paints has been experienced and continues. Car and appliance manufacturers, on the other hand, are the subject of marketing campaigns by manufacturers of steel which would like to supply them with pre-painted steel coil which the manufacturers would then stamp or fabricate without having to worry about painting or dealing with waste and effluent and worker health problems.[11]

Marketing strategy in a European context

It was argued in Chapter 4 that all strategies for competitve advantage may be reduced to three generic categories: high perceived value (HPV) – the uniqueness of a product or service and its valued 'differentness' from competitive offerings; low delivered cost (LDC) – the extent to which the company competes on the relative cost-in-use of its products or services; and scope – the extent to which the company chooses to define the scope of its business as encompassing all the various markets and market segments of the industry or to confine its activity to serving one or several selected market segments. Increasingly, marketers are also finding that speed-to-market is becoming another crucial dimension of positional advantage.

The strategic decision concerning choice of scope – whether to market to an entire industry's markets or to focus on one segment – has been lent added drama by the changes in European integration. Many traditional, nationally oriented, European companies effectively implemented strategies of regional market segmentation that were reinforced and protected by barriers to trade between the nations of the EU. This situation made focused strategies based on premium pricing, which in turn reflected the small scale and investment characteristics of local small enterprise, commonplace across the continent. With the unification of the internal market, competitors have increasingly moved to strategies of consolidating national niche markets into pan-European segments that, in aggregate, radically change the economics of design, production, distribution and marketing.

Those who have moved to take advantage of such opportunities can acquire marked improvements in cost advantage, which they can then exploit through investment in quality improvements and in marketing. The consequences for competitors who choose to remain nationally focused with a premium pricing strategy are usually disastrous. Marketing strategies that are based on low cost, product quality and sharp focus across national markets have become a distinctive feature of the decade. Guido presents evidence for the emergence of cross-national segments among young people, trend-setters and business people, each with common attitudes, behaviours and preferences.[12] Vandermerwe and L'Huillier forecast the emergence of six 'clusters' of Euro-consumers based on geographic proximity as well as cultural, demographic and economic factors.[13] They suggest that even small companies can compete effectively in the new Europe by accurately targeting the needs of narrow multi-country segments.

The pressure to compete on a combination of cost, quality and speed of response has also led to some thematic changes. The pressure for cost competitiveness to support keen pricing policies has dictated the continuing wave of restructuring in European industry and, more recently, the widespread investment in the redesign of whole business systems including basic marketing activities such as order fulfilment processes. The simultaneous pressure for improvement in product quality and environmental friendliness has emphasized the importance of integrating strategy and implementation practice in such previously diverse areas as R&D, design, manufacturing, marketing, waste management, and recovery and recycling. While responsiveness to these pressures has yielded significant advantage in certain markets for some competitors, the same forces have encouraged industry concentration where the attendant cost of change has been substantial. In the paint industry, for example, it is estimated that the investment in resin technology alone to support new environmentally friendly products may typically cost US$2.5–US$3.0 million per major research project. Given the uncertainty about success and the number of such R&D projects that are required, it is easy to appreciate the extent of financial resources needed to support strategies of product innovation. Only large companies with deep financial resources can sustain such investment levels, leading to significant consolidation in industry membership.[14]

The demand for speed of response is best seen in the intense pressure to reduce new product lead-times and to move to just-in-time arrangements in many physical distribution systems. This in turn has necessitated a new level of investment in information technology to track activities and inventories throughout organizations and logistical systems. Exhibit 20.3 recounts how Thermo King Europe stole a march on its competitors in response to changing EU transport legislation and designed, developed and dramatically launched its SMX transport temperature control unit in a rapid period of time. Satellite communications were established between Europe and the United States for the transfer of CAD drawings from the design group directly to the CAD driven manufacturing systems in Europe. This meant that as a part or component was designed in the United States, it was being built in Europe the same day.

Where a product or service has the potential to be a pan-European, or even global product, an important issue for the marketer is how quickly and with what degree of simultaneity does he or she tackle the total potential market? Getting to all market segments quickly and at the same time is an attractive proposition. But if such a project backfires the fall-out can be grievous for a company. Whatever the consequences of failing on a local or national market, few companies can sustain Europe-wide failure. Unilever launched a new detergent product, Persil Power and Omo Power, on the European market in 1994. It contained a special manganese catalyst which the company claimed dramatically improved the cleansing power of the detergent. Despite growing evidence that the special agent could bleach and damage some fabrics, Unilever persisted with the pan-European launch of its new brand and got embroiled in an acrimonious dispute with its arch-rival, Procter & Gamble – before withdrawing the catalyst product in early 1995 (see Exhibit 10.1). Rolling out a new product and marketing strategy in a phased manner on a country-by-country or region-by-region basis involves less risk and allows learning to be incorporated in the successive stages rather than if the launch takes place almost simultaneously in all markets and regions.

| Exhibit 10.1 | *Marketing in action case* |

Unilever and P&G Euro-clash in detergents

In February 1994 Unilever launched a new fabric detergent, Persil Power and Omo Power, throughout Europe. Unilever claimed its new product was the biggest advance in fabric detergents in 15 years: it contained an innovative catalyst, crystals of manganese, which would dramatically increase its cleansing power.

Unilever was hoping to close a widening market-share gap in the £6 billion sterling European detergent market between itself, the number 2 in Europe, and its arch-rival and market leader, Procter & Gamble. Persil Power and Omo Power were intended to blaze a trail in the consumer goods business by combining advanced product technology and innovative techniques of global marketing. Exploiting its new pan-European structure, coordinated from Brussels, Unilever planned to launch Power in eleven countries in short order.

Procter & Gamble was more sanguine about Unilever's strategy. It had previously experimented with a manganese additive and found it could speed the bleaching process and also attack fabrics in certain instances. Unilever boasted of having stolen a technological march – P&G believed that Unilever was basing its claim on a formulation which it had reason to believe, from its own experience and recent testing on the new product, was fundamentally flawed. Ed Artzt, P&G's chairman based at its Cincinnati headquarters, took the highly unusual move of calling Unilever's HQ in London to try to persuade it to withdraw the Power product.

Unilever could see no need to take the costly, and humiliating, step of withdrawing a product that had been tested by scientists and consumers for two years without incident. Further, initial sales of the new product were very encouraging. The Euro-clash between the companies soon moved into the public domain and the consumer and consumer associations were informed of what was happening. Claim and counter-claim were reported in the press. There were press conferences held by both sides and lawsuits threatened.

In June, Unilever announced that it was reformulating the detergent, with an 80 per cent reduction in the catalyst to solve any potential dye problem. It also decided to retreat from Power's original broad 'positioning' – a detergent for broad use with all fabrics, water temperatures and colours – and revamped the packaging to focus use on lower temperatures and white fabrics. The move intensified the 'Great Soap War' of 1994. Power was front-page news in several European countries, with Unilever, not surprisingly, blaming P&G's 'well-organized press briefing system' for much of the trouble.

By September, Unilever was admitting that mistakes had been made. Power in its original formulation was withdrawn, and in January 1995 a new flagship laundry detergent was launched without the controversial ingredient. After spending £200 million on developing, manufacturing and marketing Power products, Unilever's share of the European detergent market remained unchanged, and a heavy price had been exacted on brand and company reputations. Unilever's pan-European organizational structures had been found wanting.

To quote a senior Unilever executive: 'I think we were very enthusiastic about a new product and did not look closely enough at the negatives. Somewhere between research and marketing something went wrong – under the pressure to be first to the market.'[15]

The pan-European debate

The hypothesis that European consumers are set on a road of social convergence has already been mentioned. The protagonists of this view argue for a future of 'standardized' demand across Europe which may then be addressed by pan-European companies marketing pan-European brands with scale and depth of resources that cannot be matched by smaller competitors. The argument is a variant on the debate about the globalization of markets sparked by Levitt's controversial 1983 article.[16] Kashani summarizes the globalization hypothesis as arguing that markets increasingly reflect:[17]

1 the disappearance of national market boundaries,
2 declining numbers of competitors and increasing size of survivors,
3 competition between essentially the same set of world-class companies in each national market,
4 interdependence beween local marketing strategies as what is done in one market increasingly affects what happens in another, and
5 growing similarity among segments of customers worldwide as divergence in life-style, tastes and behaviour narrows.

There is evidence to support the existence of the trends that underlie this scenario for the future. Firms' strategies are shaped by the intense pressure to reduce costs and to fund increasingly large investments in R&D and new technology. These forces prompt companies to search for scale by consolidating markets. From the market side there are clear developments in media and communication – for example, *The European* newspaper or Sky television – and in the acceptance of world brands in a manner that suggests convergence in taste and consumption patterns. One might expect all these forces to be even more powerful on a European scale than on a grand global scale. However, the reality of European social, market and industrial structures seems to be such that the hypothesis of convergence receives only partial confirmation.

At a very simple level, European consumer preferences, as represented by food consumption, still differ greatly. Consider, for example, the following contrasts in per capita consumption of some food and beverage products:[18]

- ▶ *Bread* consumption ranges from 131 kg in Italy to 30 kg in Denmark.
- ▶ *Frozen food* consumption ranges from a high of 38 kg in Denmark to a low of 6 kg in Greece.
- ▶ *Yogurt* consumption ranges from a high of 20 kg in the Netherlands to a low of 3 kg in Ireland.
- ▶ Ireland (3.1 kg per capita) consumes five times the EU average for *tea*.
- ▶ Denmark (10.8 kg) consumes twice the *coffee* average.
- ▶ The UK (125 litres) consumes twice the average for *carbonated drinks*.
- ▶ Greek consumers (15 litres) consumes three times the average in *spirits*.

The illustrations of significant continuing divergence in consumer behaviour are, of course, legion – just as it has to be said that all across Europe the familiar names of Benetton, IKEA, Nestlé, BASF, Heineken, Perrier or Swatch are encountered. However, the persistence of significant differences in the marketing environment across Europe appears to be assured for the foreseeable future. In distribution, marketers seeking to implement standardized strategies face the problem of quite dramatically different retailing structures. Retail multiple chain stores account for 51 per cent of retail trade in the United Kingdom but only 10 per cent in Italy and Luxembourg. In 1992 there were 23 retail outlets per thousand of population in Spain compared with 4.5 in the former area of East Germany.[19] At the corporate level, 22 of Europe's top 75 companies have home country sales of greater than 50 per cent which hardly speaks for rampant pan-Europeanism.[20]

Several features of the Single Market are likely to promote the further development of pan-European strategies. The harmonization of product standards, testing and certification procedures, patent regulations, labelling and processing requirements will support greater standardization. Common guidelines on television broadcasting and changes in advertising regulations will make the production of standard advertising material easier. The simplification of transit documents and procedures and the elimination of customs formalities encourage the development of pan-European distribution networks.

Despite the presence of these changes empirical research reveals few successes with pan-European marketing strategies to date. The level of standardization varies among the elements of marketing strategy – product characteristics and brand names may be standardized across borders but pricing, distribution and media decisions vary from market to market.[21] Whitelock shows that tastes and company strategies vary across eight European countries in the market for bed linen.[22] Reichel suggests that while products will be increasingly suited to all European markets in a legal and regulatory sense, deep-seated differences in culture, language and consumer preferences will continue to necessitate country-by-country adaptation.[23] Reisenbeck and Freeling found evidence that while the product, brand, positioning and advertising were likely to be standardized, packaging, pricing, sales promotion and public relations were usually tailored to each market.[24] A study of 'expert opinion' by Daser and Hylton forecasts greater pan-European coordination of brand names, product image, advertising themes, distribution and marketing information systems, but continued diversity by local region in pricing, service and product design and development.[25]

The problem with the debate about pan-European marketing is that it is badly framed, leading participants to argue for a polarized scenario of future markets: either pan-European or local. Bartlett and Ghoshal propose a framework arising from their empirical work with companies that suggests neither viewpoint is right or wrong.[26] They note that in international markets companies seek cost advantage through standardization and centralized control of strategies across national boundaries and that they also seek advantages arising from customer responsiveness through the 'localization' of strategy. Resolving the apparently conflicting demands of these two desires may not be as complex as it at first appears. Drawing on their research with Unilever they map the varying degree to which different businesses, functions and tasks may have to be managed in a centrally coordinated and standardized manner or locally decentralized and responsive (see Figure 10.1).

Figure 10.1 shows, for instance, that the detergent business occupies an intermediate position among the company's activities, requiring less

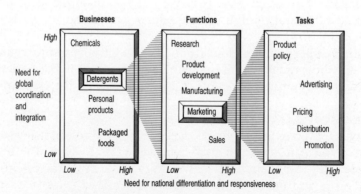

Source: C.A. Bartlett and S. Ghoshal (1989), *Managing Across Borders: The Transnational Solution* (Harvard Business School Press, Cambridge, Mass.) p.97.

Figure 10.1 Integration and differentiation needs at Unilever

coordination and standardization by corporate managers than the chemicals business, but more than personal products. Within the detergents business, research is controlled by headquarters, while marketing decisions are significantly influenced by subsidiary managers. Among marketing tasks, HQ is likely to be involved in product policy, while local promotion decisions are left to the discretion of local managers.

Taking a business system viewpoint, it is apparent that different activities or stages in any value chain – whether for an industry or a company – may respond differently to the possibilities for market advantage based on standardization or local responsiveness. For example, the scale and depth required in R&D in technology-intensive industries almost inevitably argue for centralization and standardization on a European scale. Investing in R&D facilities on a country-by-country basis is almost always an impossibility. In sharp contrast, activities at the other end of the business system, such as sales promotion and selling, must almost always be tailored to local circumstances – reflecting differences in language, culture, legal regulation or distribution structures. Thus, if one isolates marketing in the business system, it is clear that its constituent elements are differentially affected – product policy is most likely to become pan-European; pricing policies are rapidly converging in response to market unification; distribution strategies are still necessarily locally configured because of the radically different national distribution structures across Europe; and sales, service and promotional strategies are most likely of all to be quite localized even where a standardized product is being brought to market.

Pan-European marketing strategies are, therefore, emerging which reflect a combination of both localization and standardization. And that seems entirely appropriate as an adaptation to a Europe that embodies the two themes of broad convergence and resolute and proud adherence to national differences in many areas of behaviour and taste.

REVIEW QUESTIONS

10.1 What are the important competitive characteristics and structures at play in European markets?

10.2 What are the implications of these for the marketing manager?

10.3 How is retailing changing throughout Europe, and what are the consequences?

10.4 What is your view on the so-called pan-European debate?

10.5 Where a product or service has the potential to be a pan-European or even global product, an important issue for the marketers is how quickly and to what degree of simultaneity should they tackle the total potential market. Discuss.

Part III

The marketing strategy process

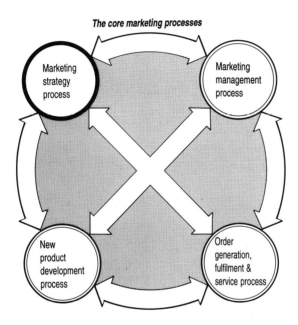

The core marketing processes

CHAPTER 11

Strategic market choice

▶ Business definition
▶ Market choice matrix
▶ Industry and market evolution
▶ Market dynamics and competitive strategy
▶ Segmentation
▶ Market choice and competitive strategy
▶ Technical note

Marketing in action case
William Cook challenges norms in the steel castings industry

ABOUT THIS CHAPTER

Marketing strategy dictates the context for all subsequent marketing activity. This process is embedded in the strategic management of the firm and ensures that overall corporate direction is routed towards customers, markets and competitors. The choice of market in which to compete is a fundamental strategic decision. Through it the manager commits the company to a relationship with chosen customers in a targeted segment.

A market choice matrix (MCM), with its dimensions of market attractiveness and relative competitive capability, can guide the marketing manager in his or her search from broad business definition to specific target market. The dynamics of the MCM evolve over time and this demands an understanding of market evolution, and its characteristic competitive behaviour, from an emergent phase, through growth and maturity, to decline. Innovative and rejuvenescent action is possible, not only in growth but also in mature or unpromising markets.

A significant determinant of relative competitive capability is the stage at which the company enters the market – whether as pioneer, as challenger to an early leader or as late entrant. All these factors influence the evaluation of market segment feasibility, underpin strategic direction and lead to a firm's decision to be a niche or mass market player.

Market choice is crucial

Choosing the market or markets in which to compete results in one of the most fundamental strategic commitments made by an organization. Once the choice is made, the organization's environment, its context for action, is given. It must then strive to compete, survive and prosper within the forces at work in the chosen marketplace and within the general profit potential of that industry. At the same time, it must accept that most of its learning, and therefore the character and value of its resource base, will be shaped by the chosen environment. Both environment and organization will evolve and adapt interdependently.

From a market focus viewpoint, the act of market choice must reflect a well-considered combination of market opportunity with organizational capability. The arena of competition is chosen in a focused manner and the organization's resources are focused on that arena in pursuit of the firm's objectives.

In order to choose markets well and wisely, several steps in analysis are advisable. First, the challenge of business definition must be addressed thoroughly and creatively. This leads to the identification of potential market segments which the company may choose to serve. Once these possible market segments are specified, the necessity to rank them and choose among them must be tackled. This can be done with the help of a market choice matrix which will isolate a short list of prime segments or market sectors. The final choice of market or markets can then be pursued using value analysis, considerations of strategic fit and potential for engendering future capabilities.

Business definition

Business definition is centrally involved with the decision concerning market choice, since it provides the kernel of the firm's orientation about where and how to compete. It provides the starting point for strategy formulation as it indicates *both* the arena of competition and the organizational response or configuration required to compete in that arena. Abell's pioneering work suggests the use of three dimensions: the customer groups that may be served, the customer functions that may be performed, and the technologies that may be used to perform functions for customers.[1] These dimensions define a business in terms of customers on whom to focus, their needs, expressed in functional or performance terms, and the technologies available to satisfy their needs. Day enhances this notion by proposing four dimensions of business definition: customer needs, customer segments, technology or materials to be used in satisfying those needs, and the activities in the value-added chain, including their scale and scope.[2]

Business definition clearly involves identifying the *range of customers* and customer segments on which the company can productively focus its resources and then seek to serve profitably. This aspect of business definition asks the company to answer the question: 'Whom could the company serve?' Asking and answering the question 'What problem(s) could the company solve?' demands that the firm's managers develop a clear insight into *customers' needs and wants* in the identified segments and understand which of those needs can be satisfied by the resources at their command. 'How could those customer problems be solved?' demands a two-part answer. The first part requires thought about the *technology and/or materials* that could solve the customer problem – for example, is it to be mechanical or electronic hardware, fresh, chilled, frozen or dehydrated food, steel or engineered plastic components, chemical or biologically-based medicine? The second part of the answer requires thought about the alternative configurations of the micro, or firm, business system that could deliver the various 'solutions' to the different customer segments. In the latter instance the company must be aware of the macro business system for the industry and must then creatively choose its own particular micro busines system configuration as a focused delivery mechanism, or *organizational technology*, for delivering its competitive promise to serve customers better, cheaper and/or faster. Business definition might therefore be summarized as the act of asking and then answering from the company's point of view the questions:

- Whom could the company serve?
- What problem(s) need to be solved?
- How could those customer problems be solved?

The answers to these questions set the foundations for strategy. They are answers that the marketing team must be involved in providing and answers that top management must consider carefully from a marketing-based perspective. If the many combinations of whom to serve, what problem to solve and how to deliver a solution are reviewed and screened for feasibility, a considerable list of possible market segments that may be of relevance to the company is generated. Because the analysis is multi-dimensional and likely to produce some unexpected combinations, it is also creative in its outcome.

Market choice matrix

The combination of answers to the questions of business definition illustrates the extent to which the market choice decision is based on a matching of market and industry factors with company capabilities. Portfolio frameworks and matrices have been traditionally used to probe and manage business and product portfolios. They may also be used to array and consider market segments. In using a portfolio framework in this manner, the company must think through all the factors that determine *market attractiveness* on the one hand and *company capability* on the other. The relative attractiveness of the segments which the company might choose to serve may be measured in many ways: growth rate, intensity of competition, concentration levels, barriers to entry, accessibility of channels, customer innovativeness, price sensitivity, and so on. It is, in fact, in the determination of the criteria to be used to judge attractiveness that a great deal of the managerial value of using the framework is to be derived.

Assessing company capability requires a shift in perspective if it is to be well used for making market choice decisions. While market attractiveness is judged from a company viewpoint, company capability for these purposes must be judged from a customer viewpoint. What is of importance is not how capable the company thinks itself, but how capable customers think the company is, relative to its competitors, when it comes to serving their needs. These steps from business definition to market choice are summarized in Figure 11.1.

In using a portfolio framework, such as the market choice matrix set out in Figure 11.2, to array and assess market segments, the nature of the market choice decisions faced is greatly clarified:

1 Explicit identification of, and discussion and agreement about, the criteria that make a market segment attractive to the company must be undertaken. Attractiveness will depend on the company's resource base, capabilities and goals, so what is attractive to one company may be unattractive to another. Attractiveness to a large global company may turn out to be very different from attractiveness to a small, entrepreneurial venture. Because of this each is led towards choices that encourage each to stake out different competitive territories and market niches.

2 Identification of the attractiveness criteria may be further elaborated by attributing weightings to each criterion to indicate their relative importance. This is further discussed in a technical note at the end of this chapter.

3 Measurement of the company's competitive capability in each segment must be undertaken from a customer viewpoint. It is only customer perceptions and their view of reality that will drive competitive success. This is an important antidote to the tendency for businesses to make internal, managerially driven, assumptions about 'how good we are'. The discipline created by a market choice matrix is the

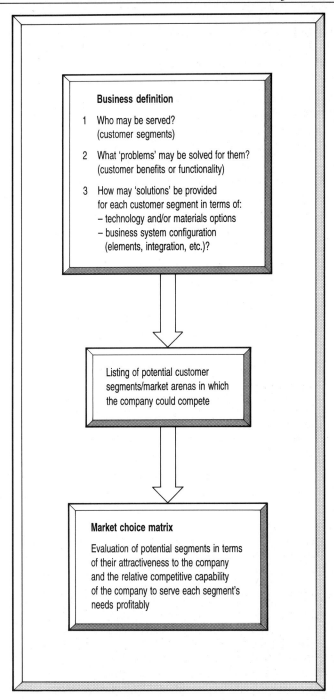

Figure 11.1 Business definition and market choice

essential marketing discipline of seeing the company and its offerings through the customers' eyes.

4 Competitive capability should be measured as *relative* competitive capability – i.e. the ability to serve customer needs compared with competitors' ability to serve those same needs. The mid-point of the relative competitive capability axis, therefore, represents equality with a nominated key competitor or competitors. Measures to the left represent lesser capability and therefore the expectation of competitive loss, while measures to the right represent the expectation of achieving competitive superiority.

5 Relative capabilities, once measured from a customer viewpoint, can also be weighted in terms of their relative importance in customer choice behaviour. This allows the measures of relative capability to be weighted and summed as a single score on the horizontal axis of the matrix.

6 Given an array of segments, each with a weighted assessment of attractiveness to the company, and a weighted assessment of relative capability to compete for customer satisfaction, the essence of the market choice decision is laid bare.

Making the market choice decision

A worthwhile market choice matrix will usually display more segments than the company is capable of serving. A creative business definition analysis should ensure this. A first cut at isolating markets that should be chosen may be made by excluding segments that fall below the diagonal line in Figure 11.2. In such instances the combination of attractiveness

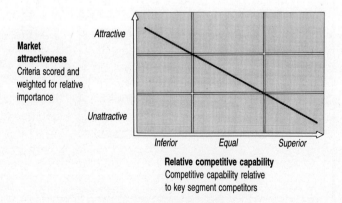

Figure 11.2 Market choice matrix

and relative capability tells a story of inferior markets and company weakness.

The prime exceptions to this are two-fold. Attractive segments where capability is currently weak, but for which there is a strong case to build capability in order to reap future rewards, is one exception. This demands assessing the matrix 3, 5 or even 10 years into the future to visualize whether and how the segment could be moved to the right, by investing in capability while still expecting attractiveness to remain high. A disaster scenario would, of course, be one in which capability is acquired or built through heavy investment only to find that by the time it is available and operational the segment has become unattractive, though this may be qualified by the observation that companies can sometimes thrive in markets that appear unpromising or even hostile (see Exhibit 11.1).

The second exception occurs when attractiveness is currently low, but expected to increase significantly, and where capability is already high. A company might well include such a segment in its portfolio of chosen markets, provided that it is confident of its projections concerning the increase in attractiveness and its ability to maintain relative capability in an evolving marketplace.

If these exceptions from among the segments plotted below the diagonal are included with all those above it, then the set of serious options for market choice is established. In many instances, this set will encompass more segments than the company is capable of addressing. Choices between these options are best addressed by evaluating the economic and strategic feasibility of each segment. A number of broad criteria must be met:

1 The economic value of each segment, based on assumptions about the cost of developing and maintaining capability, effective strategy and market share, is calculated. This involves considerations of segment size, substance, accessibility, defensibility and durability – issues discussed in more detail earlier in Chapter 7. Cashflow forecasts, discounted by the cost of capital, are key. Such a value analysis yields a ranking of segments based on quantified economic considerations and assumptions.

2 The fit between segments and the company's vision, mission and goals can be assessed one by one to provide a more qualitative assessment of the extent to which each supports the broad objectives of the company and its values (for example, Lego has consistently rejected the segment consisting of war toys for its creative construction blocks).

3 The fit between each segment and the learning objectives of the company should be assessed to establish which segments best support

the acquisition of new capabilities that are deemed important for the company's longer-term survival and growth.

This methodology for assessing, ranking and making choices may be quantified and weightings attributed to each of the criteria suggested in order to produce a summary numeric ranking and cut-off point, given stated resource constraints. In many instances, it will prove fruitful to do some elementary quantification of this kind, but it is probably most vital to devote time to the more qualitative discussion and evaluation of the options before exercising a final judgement.

Dynamics of the market choice matrix

Any one market choice matrix will represent a view of attractiveness and relative capability at a particular time. Dynamism may be readily introduced by plotting several matrices for future dates and showing how each segment evolves in terms of its attractiveness and in terms of the expected relative capability of the company as both it and competitors change. Both axes, therefore, demand attention to how assessments will change through time, as market choices made today will normally commit the company to market presence for a considerable period.

One of the fundamental drivers of attractiveness is the stage in the life-cycle of the market segment and its industry. This demands that the nature of market evolution and its inherent competitive behaviour be examined carefully. A significant determinant of relative competitive capability is the stage at which the company enters the market – whether as pioneer, as challenger, as early leader or late entrant – and indeed the stage at which competitors may be expected to enter the chosen market. These underlying factors driving the dynamics of a market are dealt with next.

Industry and market evolution

Emergent phase

It is important to appreciate that markets move, in the broadest sense, through a number of phases analogous to a lifecycle. A new or emergent market is characterized by an innovation. This may be a new product or service which offers clearly superior performance benefits to existing ones, e.g. the microwave oven. It may be a process innovation which cuts costs significantly or improves the availability of a product or service, e.g. the development of fast food business format franchising, like McDonald's. Or it may be a new marketing concept that creates a new set of customers, e.g. the extension across genders of clothing and personal care products formerly of single gender appeal.

For an innovation to succeed it has to offer benefits that buyers perceive as better than current solutions. The customers who see this advantage first and who act on this perception are called innovators. Innovators are normally not very price-sensitive as they value the new benefit highly and are unwilling to wait until competition brings the price down. Marketing's task here is to identify those buyers most likely to benefit from the performance or promise of the new product or service. Typically some potential customers will derive significant gain, while others will perceive little benefit at all.

Initially sales growth is usually slow. Customers have to be informed about the innovation and persuaded of its advantages. Uncertainty, high switching costs (the set of 'costs' the buyer incurs in switching from the old to the new product – for instance, the old one may have no resale value; the new one may involve the purchase of new expensive peripherals and technical advice), and the lack of established distribution and service supports also restrain buyers. The more readily customers can be convinced of the performance advantages of the new service or product, the more easily these barriers to adoption will be broken down. Once the innovators start to adopt the product, the market may grow quite fast as other segments become cumulatively persuaded to purchase.

In the initial stages, the innovating firm has the market to itself. The main competition comes from the older technology or delivery system. New entry is forestalled temporarily by barriers such as patents and other suppliers not having the competence or capital to imitate or follow the pioneer. However, such barriers to entry tend to erode rapidly. Patents are an important economic instrument in wealth creation as they enable and encourage firms that invest in innovation to enjoy a protected stream of benefits for so doing. A pharmaceutical company that spends half a decade developing a new drug is guaranteed a return over the patent's life should the product be a success. But not all industries enjoy this degree of patent protection. Technology is evolving so quickly in many industries that such protection becomes redundant anyway. It is reckoned that the total lifecycle for new products in the electronics industry is as low as three years – which affords little time for the innovator to enjoy an initial monopoly.

Growth phase

The growth phase is characterized by the expansion of the market to new customer segments and new uses. This is facilitated by the spread of knowledge about the service or product beyond the innovator group, the reduction of uncertainty about standards and switching costs, and the inevitable decline in prices. As prices fall the new product becomes increasingly attractive to customers who only perceive a modest benefit in it. At the beginning of the 1980s, video cassette recorders (VCRs) were the preserve of innovators, present in less than 1 per cent of UK homes, while just a few years later, by mid-1988, 51 per cent of households had one.[3]

New competitors come to market as well. They witness the initial success, and profits, of the new product, strive to overcome any entry barriers, replicate the pioneer's offering and possibly develop new segments. By the mid-1980s there were more than a dozen firms supplying VCRs to the market. In addition, the building of a strong infrastructure of sub-suppliers and distributors facilitates entry. Prices generally fall quickly as experience and scale economies lower unit costs and competition forces most of these gains to be passed on to the buyer.

In the later part of the phase, as growth begins to slow down, competition for market share intensifies. The leading players start to develop international ambitions and to broaden their product lines, pushing them into markets and segments occupied by other strong competitors. Companies which have not achieved strong positioning strategies or developed low cost structures begin to see their profits margins falling. A number exit, or are forced to exit, from the market as competitors experience a shake-out.

Mature phase

Market maturity takes place when the number of new users and new uses ceases to grow. Marketing activity then switches from attracting non-users and creating new uses to maintaining or gaining market share. Present users are more experienced and so price and service become more important. Marketing strategy needs to be clearly enunciated as any mistakes cannot be cushioned by the market growth of the previous phase.

The shake-out of less competitive players will continue from the late growth stage. Excess capacity and inroads from international competitors will likely exacerbate events. The marketing manager should expect changing behaviour along the business system. Distributors and retailers may exhibit greater negotiating muscle, playing off alternative suppliers or even introducing own brands. It is more difficult for competitors to reduce costs because most of the scale economies and experience or learning curve effects have already been obtained.

At a later stage of maturity the market may consolidate around a handful of large competitors which effectively creates barriers to entry. These barriers derive from the scale economies they possess, the high capital requirements, the advantage of established brand names and the implicit threat of sharp retaliation which newcomers may face. Markets that have matured into this more oligopolistic pattern include the oil industry, the cigarette industry, retail banking, the supermarket sector, the detergents business and car manufacturing.

The observant reader might point out that these markets account for an ample proportion of all economic and marketing activity. This raises an important point about the nature of mature markets and industries. The decline to which maturity seems the antecedent does not always in reality appear to take place. Why?

The answer lies in the difference between wants and needs. Wants and their ephemeral expression in particular products are distinguishable from long-term durable customer needs for clothing, heating, transportation, as well as for engineering, communication and business solutions – be they a better hole-creating device, phone or software program. Wants and their narrow manifestation in particular products do indeed go into decline and disappear. But at a more generic level, markets and industries will often redefine or reinvent themselves with 'new' products or services, new users or new uses. These may be product extensions or product developments or products with new substitute technologies or delivery systems; but they fulfil a need and provide a performance benefit which the customer needs. Hence, markets and industries, at this broadly defined level, seem to rejuvenate themselves with modest periods of growth which gradually fade, so that era of maturity becomes a gently undulating plateau of troughs and peaks (suggested in Figure 11.3). This has two important implications for the marketer.

First, he or she must continue to match the firm's competences to long-term market need. These competences will often have a life much longer than any individual product. He or she and his or her fellow managers throughout the organization must continually and creatively consider substitute ways of satisfying customer need in a profitable manner. This can be done successfully in slow-growing, mature and even hostile environ-

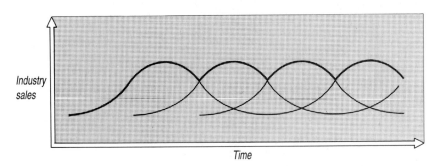

Figure 11.3 Industry lifecycle and generic market need

ments. Indeed, a resource-based view of competitive advantage would argue that there is no such thing as a mature industry, only mature firms; industries inhabited by mature firms often present great opportunities for innovative and rejuvenescent action. The last chapter described how Richardson achieved this in the cutlery industry, inventing the Laser knife along the way. Such resurgence often involves confounding the current industry orthodoxy and changing the 'rules of the game'.

The story of William Cook, outlined in Exhibit 11.1, also highlights the point that organizations can be successful in an industry which seems unpromising. In the early 1980s, UK industry sales of steel castings were declining; there was excess capacity; rationalization schemes had been tried and failed. The firm showed a clear understanding of the roots of generic competitive advantage in refocusing its operations. In less than a decade, Cook moved from being a marginal business to a highly profitable one with some 30 per cent industry share. Cook's performance encouraged new competitors to arrive in the market to copy and rival it. Partly on account of all the actions of the players in the industry, industry sales stopped declining, excess capacity disappeared and the industry looked more attractive.

Second, marketing managers must be aware of business system myopia. Their understandable attention to their own immediate market or industry point of transformation/added value, with its current rivalry, potential entrants and substitutes, may lead them to ignore the wider dimensions of the business system both upstream and downstream. Here they may be neglecting an opportunity where their firm's competences might be profitably rewarded.

Exhibit 11.1	*Marketing in action case*

William Cook challenges norms in the steel castings industry

William Cook is an old-established UK firm which makes steel castings. After a number of boom years which ended in 1978, most of the companies in the steel castings industry were making a loss. Cook's profitability was also poor, and it controlled only 2 per cent of the UK's industry output. It was a small player in a big company industry, where four firms controlled 60 per cent of the industry's output. Industry outlook in the early 1980s was appalling; average industry margin was zero.

In 1983, at a time when capacity was more than double the level of industry sales, Cook embarked on an investment programme to increase efficiency, quality and capacity. Cook's stated objective was to challenge the conventional norms of the industry, especially those held by the industry leaders. Rivals thought that Cook was unwise and predicted disaster.

Conventional thinking would have suggested that Cook either milk the business, or else go for a high-value differentiated niche. There were three segments in the steel castings industry: highly valued steel alloys; more basic alloys; and the casting of unalloyed or basic steel. Many firms competed in the higher valued segments. Cook focused on the lowest valued segment of the market. It aimed to improve its capability and efficiency at this low end of the market. Equally, it emphasized service to its customers and assuring the right quality.

Cook's plans seemed especially foolhardy as it had limited resources, was in a poor position to raise debt and had no particular technology which conferred advantage. Rather, it had a clear-minded resolution and an ambition to succeed on the part of its top management. Its MD commented: 'In the 1970s the industry was grossly overmanned. The slump was good for the foundry industry. Many companies were not fit to survive.'

Its rejuvenation programme yielded results very quickly. In 1984 profits rose to 10 per cent of sales, while the rest of the industry recorded losses averaging 1.6 per cent of sales. Cook continued to invest in efficiency, quality and service. In 1985 it was the first business in the industry to win the quality award BS5750. Over the next three years it acquired two larger competitors which it rationalized, closing parts and investing heavily in others. By the end of 1988 Cook was the largest business in the industry with 30 per cent market share, recording even better profits.

Cook's response of improving quality and service levels saved the customers money and so increased demand. When others realised what Cook had done, they changed too. They sought to catch up with Cook and invoked intense battles. In the 1990s the fortunes of the industry are being transformed and demand has stopped declining. The causes of the transformation were mainly the actions of the firms.[4]

Decline phase

A further stage is reached when the market enters a period where volume looks like declining permanently. This occurs when the pool of potential new users and new uses has dried up, when substitute products have demonstrated clear superiority or when buyers' needs change. Again, circumspection is necessary when predicting, and making strategic decisions about, decline. Many markets have developed new sources of growth after entering what appeared to be the decline phase.

The Western cigarette industry, in decline in First World economies, has found new and profitable markets in Third World countries and in the markets of Central and Eastern Europe. The bicycle market was in decline until the early 1980s until a concern for healthier lifestyles and the environment, and some interesting product development, saw a significant return to pedal power; the motorcycle experienced a similar resurgence two decades earlier as a youthful fun product rather than just a cheap form of transport. Even if the decline phase looks certain, the strategic recommendations are not clear. Porter identified four strategic options for the business in the decline phase.[5]

1 *Leadership*. The firm invests in acquisitions and other share-building policies to rationalize and control the market. However, management must be sure the resulting market structure will enable the firm to recoup its late investment.

2 *Niche*. The company focuses on a segment that is more robust and price-insensitive than the mass of the market. But others competitors may also have the same idea.

3 *Harvest*. Here the firm attempts to optimize cashflow rather than market share. Harvesting strategies involve cost-cutting, raising prices and rationalizing the range of products, customers and channels. This strategy is most attractive if the firm has been a strong player in the market.

4 *Divest*. The business is sold off to maximize net investment recovery. This strategem is only likely to be profitable early in the phase, as later the business is unlikely to be of much interest to a buyer.

Many markets in decline can be highly profitable and substantial cash generators for a very long period if managed properly, e.g. the cigarette market. In recessionary times, with little growth on the horizon, the adroit management of declining businesses is a key area of strategic marketing and management decision-making. In addition, a market does not always decline in a homogeneous pattern. More innovative segments leave the market for new alternatives, leaving behind customers who are reluctant to change and often conservative and price-inelastic. Here, the remaining competitors may be able to push up prices to offset the decline in volume.

Market dynamics and competitive strategy

Studying the dynamics of the market, how they evolve through a number of stages and the characteristics of competitive behaviour provides a basis for assessing market attractiveness and assists the marketing manager in his or her choice of market, market segment and competitive positioning. Underpinning this decision also lies a number of capability considerations. What is the firm's current competitive position – is it a market leader or a challenger? Is it seeking a strong or dominant mass market position or merely seeking to win a small but profitable niche? Does the stage of market maturation strongly suggest or preclude certain competitive initiatives? A number of these issues are now addressed.

Timing of entry: Pioneer

The pioneer is the company that creates the market through a new product or service introduction, through a process innovation which cuts costs significantly or enhances availability, or through a new marketing concept that creates a new set of customers. The pioneer has the opportunity to obtain significant first-mover advantages which can materialize into future market leadership and high returns.[6] Such advantages include:

▶ *Perceived differential advantage.* Usually the innovation has obvious advantages over the product or concept it replaces. But they must be perceived by the customer to be so.
▶ *Higher prices.* The innovator segment is normally not price-sensitive, enabling the pioneer to earn high margins. Later entrants have to offer lower prices as the market becomes more price-sensitive and selective.
▶ *Switching costs.* Once customers have adopted a pioneer's product they are often reluctant to change. The costs and risk of another change make it relatively easy for the first mover to hold on to its early customers.
▶ *Economies of scale and experience.* Being a first mover enables the firm to build scale economies and move down the experience curve ahead of rivals. This cost advantage can be used for subsequent marketing investments and competitive pricing.

There is evidence from a number of research studies that pioneers outperform later entrants, earn higher profits and achieve bigger market shares. The PIMS database confirms that 70 per cent of companies holding the leading share in their markets were one of the pioneering entrants.[7] Other studies show that surviving pioneers in a market hold, on average, a market share of 30 per cent when the industry reaches maturity, compared to 17 per cent for early followers and 12 per cent for late entrants.[8]

But if the pioneer is to capitalize on early success, pre-empt competition and maintain a leading edge, he must display two key characteristics: *ambition for size* and *speed of action*. Pioneers like Bailey's Irish Cream in liqueur drinks, Apple in personal computers, McDonald's in fast food, IKEA in furniture (see Exhibit 12.2), Carrefour in hypermarché retailing, all moved with big intent and speed to achieve and maintain a leadership position as the market evolved. Conversely, Federal Express, which successfully pioneered new air courier systems in the United States, failed in Europe in the early 1990s because DHL and TNT copied the Federal Express system and were already well established in Europe when it entered.

The pioneer acts decisively to expand the market, develop new segments, find new uses for the product and build market share. The target market evolves from the innovators to the more typical segments that constitute the mass market. The product range broadens. Supportive distribution systems are built and strong communications channels established. In the emergent and early growth phase of the market, the successful pioneer is effectively configuring his own micro business system and, to a large extent, the macro business system of his immediate competitive arena. This can present difficulty to smaller innovative firms. Acting fast and big requires resources; to capitalize on their innovation, small companies may have to look at alliances or partnerships to leverage their resources.

Challenging a leader

A market challenger is a firm that attempts to usurp the leadership of the market from the current front runner or runners. The appropriate marketing strategy depends on the competences and resources of the challenger and whether the attack is in the early or late phases of the market. Challenging a market leader is difficult. The leader's share superiority should mean lower unit costs, higher prices and profit margins, and the resources to counter-attack.

Attacking a market leader is easier at the earlier stages of a market's evolution, particularly when the pioneer has not decisively expanded the market beyond a limited innovatory niche. A challenger can have a number of potential advantages over a pioneer. He can allow the pioneer to take the initial risks and then capitalize on his weaknesses and mistakes. He can reap much of the benefit of the early leader's investment in market education and development at little cost. In markets characterized by fast technological change, the challenger can enter with superior second-generation technology to leapfrog the initial mover.

The window of opportunity for the challenger is to identify *new market segments* and/or offer *new attributes* to the product or service. Markets grow mainly through the addition of new discrete customer segments. Focusing on these emerging segments, perhaps with a modified offering and at a somewhat lower price, provides a strong foothold – and may even allow such an early follower to became a pioneer itself in an emerging mass market. A challenger may also succeed if he can augment the basic innovation with a further differentiating attribute, e.g. second-generation and higher performance technology or phased release capability in a newly pioneered drug. Obviously the more resources the challenger can bring to the endeavour the better.

In general, early followers of the pioneer in a still-growing dynamic market are more likely to succeed, in terms of share and profitability, than late entrants into a more established market situation.[9] In particular, the early follower who can enter on a relatively large scale with a high quality differentiated product and a controllable level of direct costs will often succeed. IBM was a successful early follower in both mainframe computers and microcomputers. Conversely, Xerox was an early withdrawal from the mainframe computer market, as was Texas Instruments from the microcomputer market, because their challenges suffered from the dual disadvantages of small scale and poor quality or undifferentiated product. It may be observed that a late entrant may well succeed in carving out a niche and getting a satisfactory return on investment, but is very unlikely to achieve a significant share or leadership status.

Segmentation

The strategies of successful firms are characterized by good segmentation, leading to clear choice of target markets, consistent market focus and continuous adaptation to the shifts and changes in segment characteristics. It is worthwhile to explore the nature of market segmentation in more depth. A market segment is a group of customers whose needs and consumption patterns are very similar to each other while being different in some significant way from other groups in the same general market.

For example, within the market for coffee there are many segments. One segment prefers freshly ground, high quality coffee and responds sensitively to factors such as taste, type of coffee bean, manner in which the coffee is roasted, aroma, appearance and method of preparation. Another general segment prefers instant coffee and responds generally to convenience in preparation as well as taste, aroma and price. Within the instant coffee segment there are various user sub-segments. These include consumers who use instant coffee as a fast convenience drink in the morning or at other times of the day and have little sensitivity to quality or care in preparation; consumers who drink instant coffee at work-breaks and social encounters largely as a basis for socializing with others; consumers who use instant coffee as their principal daily beverage in preference to tea or soft drinks and who therefore search for taste, aroma and visual characteristics that they find attractive; consumers who serve instant coffee after dinner or to guests and who may therefore pay special attention to quality and to using a premium product as a direct taste substitute for freshly ground coffee.

This illustration indicates the richness of insight into a market that may be derived from segmentation analysis. Each segment potentially represents a market opportunity for a different product and marketing strategy and a basis for the company to build a focused competitive advantage.

Market segments are not a characteristic of consumer markets only. They are just as pervasive and important a feature of business-to-business markets. The market for water treatment equipment, for example, normally breaks down into the public sector segment and the industry segment. The public sector is composed of rural district authorities and city or town councils whose needs and buying behaviour are quite special. Water treatment for them is a vital feature of ensuring public health and adequate water supplies and can become a basis for either attracting or hindering new industrial development in their local area. The industry segment typically buys because it has to avoid legal penalties for pollution and therefore approaches purchases with a different motivation. The industry segment also breaks down into sub-groups with different needs depending on whether they are large chemical process plants with high volumes of quite toxic effluent to be treated and perhaps recycled, or whether they are small food processing firms, located in city centres with severe space constraints on treatment installation size and on odours and unpredictable variations in the output of effluent.

Segments are at the heart of understanding all markets. A good rule of thumb for the manager is to remember that there is no such thing as 'the market' for any general service or product form, whether it be coffee or water treatment systems: there are market segments which, if aggregated, form 'the market'. But the information and insight of real value to the marketer lie at the market segment level.

Customer-based segments

The bases on which segments are identified and analyzed are many and varied. In general, however, most companies use either customer-based segments or company coverage-based segments, or a combination of both. Customer-based segments are identified by searching for groupings among customers on the basis of:

1 customers' personal characteristics,
2 purchase and usage behaviour,
3 customer needs and preferences.

Customer and personal characteristics such as age, income, sex, location, occupation, marital status, social class, life-style and personality profile are the traditional measures incorporated in marketing research studies aimed at segmenting consumer markets. Similar characteristics can be collected about organizations to form organizational segments for a business-to-business service or product – the size, location, age, technical expertise and organizational culture of companies in the market. Segmentation variables of this general kind are often categorized into the broad groupings of demographic, geographic, psychographic and gerontographic factors.

It must be noted that these measures are descriptive ones and are useful only when they are clearly related to variations in behaviour: Do older consumers behave differently from younger ones? – Men from women? – Higher social status from lower social status groups? – Urban from rural? – Married from unmarried? – And so on. For many products this is the case. In more recent years life-style bases for segmentation have proved particularly powerful in structuring product markets and in designing matching products. The Swatch watch described below is a case in point.

Purchase and usage behaviour bases for segmentation explore the more specific interaction between customer and individual product – how, when, where and in what quantity they buy; and how, when and where they use the product – variables often referred to as behavioural factors. Segments may be constructed on the basis of the outlet where customers shop, whether they buy frequently or infrequently, and whether they buy large or small pack sizes or large or small quantities on a shopping trip. So, for example, customers who buy cameras in chemists' shops or department stores are different from those who buy in specialist camera shops. Typically, the former is buying a camera in a technically uninformed way, is looking for convenient and simple operation and a reasonable price. The latter is searching for technical performance and sophistication and retailer advice on choosing between brands, models and accessories. Many airlines segment on the frequency-of-use dimension by offering special airport and in-flight services to passengers travelling frequently, such as the 'frequent flier' programmes launched by most European airlines with the onset of deregulation and greater competition.

Heavy users of many consumer products are treated as a special segment by manufacturers which produce special pack sizes and volume purchase promotions and incentives to capture their loyalty. In industrial marketing, many companies find that the 80/20 rule applies to their customer base – 80 per cent of their business comes from 20 per cent of their clients. In response to this they may treat the 20 per cent as a particularly important heavy-usage segment, giving them preferential treatment in terms of delivery, technical service and support and salesforce account management time. Indeed some firms formally structure their marketing organization to reflect the needs of such large customers and key accounts, using category managers and customer business teams to operationalize this approach (see Exhibit 13.1, p.258, about Kraft Foods).

Customer needs and preferences represent yet another set of variables by which markets may be segmented, and ultimately form the 'best' bases for segmentation since they demand a thorough understanding of customer behaviour and objectives. Measurement of needs and preferences can be more difficult than for the other two categories of segmentation variables because they are less easily observed. What motivates customers, what product benefits they are seeking and the nature of their preferences demand more subtlety of marketing research techniques and in managerial judgement.

The coffee example quoted earlier is an interesting illustration of the variety of product benefits that customers may seek from a product category. Each variation in need and in preferences – from the group that uses instant coffee as an emergency convenience beverage (a study conducted by the Carnation company in the UK in the early 1970s showed that many users of instant coffee saw coffee as something they made 'when they didn't want to dirty the teapot') to those that buy it to serve as a taste substitute for freshly ground coffee – can be considered as defining a segment that might be addressed with a unique product and marketing strategy. Indeed, the great variety of existing coffee products and brands illustrates this. Consumers can buy coffee beans of varying origin and varying roasts from specialty outlets such as the *Kaffeehäuser* of Vienna to brew their own coffee; they can buy packaged ground coffee to percolate or filter; and they can buy instant coffees varying from supermarket own-label brands to very expensive premium instant coffees.

The complexity of the segment structure of a market is further underlined by the fact that an individual may belong to more than one segment. Managers are often puzzled by multi-brand loyalty on the part of customers – customers regularly buying two or more competing brands and appearing to have a repertoire of brands to which they are loyal. This feature of many markets is illustrated in the coffee market by the consumer who purchases an average priced instant coffee for use in the mid-morning and afternoons and for occasional single cups of coffee, but who also buys a premium brand sold on quality, taste and aroma, and uses it perhaps to serve after dinner or when guests are being entertained. Here we see two segments of need, with the same customer belonging to each one under different usage scenarios.

Company coverage-based segments

Company coverage of customers forms another basis on which segments may be formed in practice. This approach acknowledges that most companies are limited by their history and resources in terms of their ability to cover the total market for a product. Many small firms start the process of market development with only enough resources to cover a local or regional area of the total market. Others may find that their time and technical resources prevent them from dealing with the sophisticated segment of buyers requiring advanced products and intensive technical support. Many very large companies, by contrast, find smaller and less sophisticated markets a distraction and without enough profit potential to justify application of their elaborate and high-cost marketing approach. All these company coverage constraints may, of course, be changed in the longer term if the company sees economic advantage in entering new segments. In the shorter term, however, they form constraints that make some sectors of the market accessible and others inaccessible. The two sets of segmentation factors – customer-based and company coverage-based – may be further integrated in a matrix format so that the manager can get a broad representation of the segments that exist, those in which the company operates, and those in which it is capable of building a competitive advantage.[10]

Creative segmentation

The innovative marketing manager looks for the unserved segment – the area of need that no one has yet identified or discovered a way to serve cost-effectively. Resegmenting the market is often a key to marketing innovation. Many managers when pushed to think about segmentation of their market will respond that the segments are obvious and require no further analysis. Yet the discipline of starting afresh on a segmentation analysis usually generates some novel ideas about customer groups and unexploited opportunities. For example, segmenting the market for meal-time foods into day of week as well as into breakfast/lunch/dinner segments can radically alter the marketer's perception of customer needs and behaviour and market opportunity. Market research indicates that different days of the week have different food-serving patterns, so that some foods suit some days and not others. Following a detailed segmentation analysis on this basis, the marketer is likely to find new ways of presenting and positioning his or her product to increase its usage perhaps, or to make it a more regular element of weekly diet.

The watch industry provides an interesting example of creative segmentation. The world market has been traditionally segmented into price segments. The 'AA' segment, with prices ranging from over £2,000 virtually to infinity; the 'A' segment ranging from £300 to £2,000 ; the 'B' segment ranging from £150 to £300 ; and the 'C' segment selling for less than £150. Swatch, one of the great successes of the watch industry of the 1980s, was, however, aimed not at one of these traditional segments but at a newly defined lifestyle segment – young-at-heart, fashion-conscious, fun-oriented and a little irreverent. As a result the brand created a new watch category and a segment that drew customers from across all the traditional price segments. Over eight million Swatches were being bought in total each year by 1990 – by teenagers and millionaires alike. Segmentation decisions are therefore never once-and-for-all decisions. They must be reappraised periodically in the search for innovation, new opportunity and greater profitability, and above all in response to change in customer behaviour and values.

Market choice and competitive strategy

Once the nature and number of segments in the market are known and competitive dynamics understood, the decision must be taken as to what kind of strategy to pursue. Serve all segments with a common marketing approach, or serve one or more individual segments with a separate marketing strategy? There are three fundamental options open to the marketer:

1   mass market strategy,
2   niche strategy,
3   multiple niche strategy.

Mass market strategy

A mass market strategy does not imply going for huge markets, but does mean ignoring any segments that may exist and addressing the total market with one marketing strategy (an approach also referred to as undifferentiated marketing). IBM managed in a very short period to dominate the early market for professional personal computers with such a strategy. With its personal computer the firm went from no market presence on introduction in August 1981 to over 26 per cent of the market by the end of 1983 in the United States. In achieving this it sent many smaller companies to bankruptcy with the power of their mass market strategy. With just a reasonable level of technological sophistication in its product, it managed to produce a basic personal computer that most buyers and users of micros could comprehend and use, with confidence in the service back-up and technical reputation of its manufacturer. As this market matured, however, this became a less feasible approach. The evolving customer needs led, by the 1990s, to the necessity for a more differentiated and focused approach. This produced a market structure in which different competitors focused on desktop, laptop, notepad and workstation variations which an increasingly sophisticated and demanding market requested. In addition, the different competitors pursued different sales and distribution policies, ranging from the huge success of Dell as an international mail order microcomputer supplier to that of Sun, with its high technical expertise in selling and supporting advanced workstations.

Many companies pursue the strategy of marketing a package that is almost all things to all people. Successful mass market strategies make very clear and relatively simple competitive claims. Success depends on there being large numbers of customers with more or less common needs, and a product with sufficient features and benefits to provide all with their needed product benefits. Coca-Cola have succeeded outstandingly with such a strategy world-wide for many years. Several motor car companies achieved major cost and quality advantages by pursuing the concept of a world car (Japanese companies in particular but also Ford's world car projects such as the appropriately titled Mondeo, for example). The advantage of this strategy is that it allows maximum use to be made of economies of scale and experience. This should, with good management, result in a low-cost, high-quality product capable of supporting substantial marketing, manufacturing and R&D overhead. The rapid growth of global markets supports the feasibility of such strategies of standardization. The difficulties with the strategy are that it is usually most attractive to large and resourceful companies and especially global and multinational enterprises. It is therefore difficult for small, medium-sized or new ventures to adopt such a strategy in markets that are of any large scale. Where the whole market is of limited size, this consideration need not hold true.

Niche strategy

A niche strategy is the polar opposite of the mass strategy. Here the marketer selects a single segment in the market which represents the best opportunity for the company to serve customers well and build a defensible competitive position against new entrants. The strategy is therefore to focus and seek dominance of a specialist segment. Many high-technology companies producing specialist technical industrial products illustrate this approach. Applied Microelectronics Ltd, for example, a Dublin-based producer of electronic test equipment for companies that manufacture floppy disks, serves world-wide markets across Europe, North America and the Pacific Rim. It has a very specialized product line purchased by a very small number of factories which manufacture disks for the world computer market.

While the company using this strategy chooses a narrow focus, it may still reap significant economies through specialization, and its finely-honed expertise and skills base over time become its key competitive advantages. There are risks involved too. Focusing on a single segment carries all the dangers of having all one's eggs in the same basket! If the fortunes of the segment decline, then the company supplying it goes down too. Typically, the marketer is serving quite a small number of customers, so the necessity to be excellent in serving most of them very well and all the time is intense. Market dominance is an important requirement for significant success with the strategy. There is little room for 'also rans' in niche marketing.

Multiple niche strategy

Multiple niche strategy involves the recognition that several segments exist and the adoption of an objective of serving two or more of them with differentiated products and marketing strategies. Companies such as Kellogg's implement this kind of strategy with remarkable success. Kellogg's cover the many segments of need in the breakfast cereal market from their standard Corn Flakes and similar products to cereals for children, and various health, nutrition amd slimness-oriented cereal brands.

Multiple niche strategies usually appear on the competitive landscape of a market as it goes through the growth stage of the lifecycle. More and more products are launched to cater to, and bring into the market, additional customers by focusing on their special needs. This stage of development most typically results in too many competitors fighting for dominance of too many niches, and the slow-down of market growth inevitably precipitates a shake-out of competing companies. The maturity phase of a market usually marks the stabilization of the number of market niches and a competitive equilibrium among competitors who have carved out their positions in the various niches.

The greatest dangers of a multiple niche strategy lie in the cost of production of multiple products and the overhead and coordination implications of marketing several products with different marketing strategies. Production costs can rise if the many products needed for the different niches all involve small production runs, frequent change-over in the factory and associated set-up costs. However, modern manufacturing methods and technologies are beginning to lessen or even to eliminate such constraints. Manufacturing systems developed originally at Toyota have created the potential to produce small volumes at the kind of cost levels traditionally available only from mass standardized production. In the automobile industry Mazda has become a particularly successful exponent of this combined marketing and manufacturing approach, positioning itself in the world market as a producer for niche segments at very competitive prices. Exhibit 3.1 (p.45) outlines National Panasonic's customized bicycle with its 11 million custom combinations and its unique ordering/delivery system. Yet scale ecomonies in manufacturing and marketing enable this firm to truly achieve mass customization.

Market choice and competitor choice

The marketing manager and the top management team should be mindful that choice of market also determines the choice of competitors. The market choice matrix identifies the key competitors in each market segment, their strengths and weaknesses, and the firm's relative competitive capability. Strategic market choice represents the commercial battleground the firm has decided to embrace and the competitors with whom it has decided to enjoin battle. A significant determinant of relative competitive capability is the stage at which the company enters the market – whether as pioneer, as challenger to an early leader or as late entrant. All these factors influence the evaluation of market segment feasibility, underpin strategic direction and lead to a firm's decision to be a niche, mass market or multiple niche player.

REVIEW QUESTIONS

11.1 Why is the choice of market in which to compete a fundamental strategic decision? Explain why the concept of business definition is centrally involved in this choice.

11.2 What benefits does the market choice matrix offer the marketing manager? Use the matrix to chart the relative competitive capability of a firm with which you are familiar.

11.3 Describe the characteristics and inherent competitive behaviour of different phases of market and industry evolution.

11.4 A significant determinant of relative competitive capability is the stage at which the company enters the market – whether as pioneer, as challenger to an early leader or as late entrant. Discuss.

11.5 Compare and contrast, using examples, a mass marketing and a niche marketing strategy.

11.6 Why is innovative and rejuvenescent strategy sometimes possible in mature or unpromising markets?

Technical note

Constructing a market choice matrix (MCM)

The two dimensions of the matrix are market attractiveness and relative competitive capability. The market attractiveness axis measures the attractiveness of each market segment identified during the business definition analysis. The relative competitive capability axis measures, from a customer viewpoint, the capability of the company to serve each segment relative to competing companies' capability.

The market attractiveness measure is a composite one, based on the management team's identification of the criteria that make a segment attractive to their company and their assessment of each segment on these criteria. There are therefore no universal criteria. One of the principal values of constructing the matrix is that it requires the management team to work together to clarify the criteria of relevance to their organization.

Criteria will reflect features of market segments but also company characteristics. So, for example, size will usually feature as one of the criteria in most exercises. But in the case of a very large company with high fixed costs, large size will be 'attractive' and small size 'unattractive'. On the other hand, a small niche-type company may choose to see the situation in quite the opposite manner. For it, large size may mean inability to serve the market due to resource constraints and competition from global companies, while small size may mean compatibility with firm size and restriction of competition to other niche players.

To get the process of assessing market attractiveness going, it may be helpful to discuss some commonly used criteria such as those suggested below. However, it must be noted that this is just a prompt list to encourage debate. Each company must identify the criteria for attractiveness that are appropriate to its situation and also decide on the measurement of attractiveness on each criterion (e.g. is big attractive or unattractive?).

Possible dimensions of attractiveness include:

- size
- growth rate (volume/value)
- intensity of competition
- concentration level among competitors
- cost of entry
- barriers to entry
- threat from substitutes
- buyer power
- stage in market/product lifecycle
- accessibility of channels
- accessibility of final customers
- customer innovativeness
- stability of demand
- cyclicality of demand
- price sensitivity
- degree of regulation

Once the criteria for attractiveness have been agreed through discussion, it may be helpful to explicitly recognize that not all criteria will carry equal weight in any final assessment. Once again there is great value to be derived from the management team debating the relative importance of each of the criteria they have decided to use. If a five-point scale is used then the team should decide the weighting for each criterion, from 1 = minor aspect of attractiveness to 5 = major aspect of attractiveness. If criteria and their weightings are decided then the only remaining step is to evaluate each market segment on each of the weighted criteria and sum to a total score as shown in Table 11.1.

In Table 11.1 each score = a *rating* for each segment, on, say, a five-point scale where 1 = very unattractive and 5 = very attractive on the criterion in the vertical column, *multiplied* by the weighting attributable to that criterion, again say a five-point scale.

The 'total weighted average for each segment' (**) in the last column is then the addition of each of the criterion weighted scores across the segment row divided by the number of criteria. In this illustration this has a range of 1–25.

This first stage in the assessment process yields a set of weighted average attractiveness scores for each market segment under review. The next step is to assess the company's relative competitive capability in each of those segments.

Ideally, the data for this assessment should be derived from customers since what has to be established is how capable the company of is satisfying customers relative to its competitors *in the eyes of the market*. Some companies will have regular market surveys that provide information on this. The information required is not from customers of the company but from customers representative of the segment at large, whether they deal with

Table 11.1

	Attractiveness Criteria							
	A	*B*	*C*	*D*	*E*	*F*	*n*	*Total weighted*
weighting: (1–5)	*x*	*y*	*z*	*i*	*h*	*g*	*f*	*average for each segment*
Segment 1	score (1–5)(1–5)							**
Segment 2								**
Segment 3								**
Segment 4								**
Segment 5								**
Segment n								**

the company or its competitors. To the extent that this kind of information is not available, or is inadequate, the management team must make the most objective judgements it can on the matter.

Assessment of capability may be collapsed into one general measure of capability for each segment or, more powerfully may be built up through a series of measures on each of the components of 'relative capability to

Table 11.2

	Components of capability: segment 1							
	A	*B*	*C*	*D*	*E*	*F*	*n*	*Total weighted*
weighting: (1–5)	*x*	*y*	*z*	*i*	*h*	*g*	*f*	*average for each segment*
'Our' company	score (1–5)(1–5)							**
Main competitor 1								**
Competitor 2								**
Competitor n								**
						Relative capability index		_____

Relative capability index = ratio of ** for 'our' company to 'main competitor' (or average of all competitors) and will = 0.04–25, where 0.04 = complete inferiority on all components; 1 = equal capability; 25 = complete superiority on all components.

	Components of capability: segment n							
	A	*B*	*C*	*D*	*E*	*F*	*n*	*Total weighted*
weighting: (1–5)	*x*	*y*	*z*	*i*	*h*	*g*	*f*	*average for each segment*
'Our' company	score (1–5)(1–5)							**
Main competitor 1								**
Competiter 2								**
Competitor n								**
						Relative capability index		_____

Relative capability index = ratio of ** for 'our' company to 'main competitor' (or average of all competitors) and will = 0.04–25, where 0.04 = complete inferiority on all components; 1 = equal capability; 25 = complete superiority on all components.

satisfy'. Taking the latter approach a methodology such as that outlined for the assessment of attractiveness is again required.

In the case of measuring relative capability, the assessment for each market segment must be done separately for two reasons. The first, and critical, reason is that the components of capability will vary from segment to segment. Excellent relationship management may be central to satisfying customers in one segment and irrelevant to those in another. Each segment must therefore be addressed in terms of its unique demands on company capability. Second, in order to make the relative position of the company quite clear, measures must be taken for its capability to respond to the market's demands and the same must be done for the main competitors. When this is done the capability measure for the company may be divided by that for the main competitor (or by the average for all competitors) to provide a ratio or index of relative capability. On such an index 1 will always represent equal capability while numbers below will indicate inferior capability and those above superior capability. Table 11.2 illustrates how the measurement may be constructed.

The 'score' in each cell in the table represents the management team's *evaluation* of the relative capability of their company to satisfy the needs of the segment on that component of capability, *weighted* by the importance of the component in the customer's purchasing decision. For example, the scores in the rows for segment 1 might reflect the assessment of the company's and its competitors' capability to satisfy customer demands for speed of delivery, technical assistance, security of supply, competitive price, relationship management and innovativeness. Each of these components might, for example, have been given a relative importance in decision-making by the customer of 5, 2, 4, 3, 4, 2.

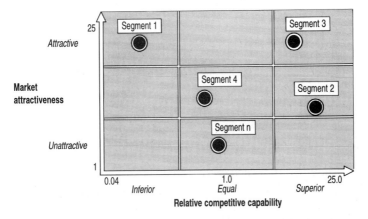

Figure 11.4 Matrix format of measures for attractiveness and relative capability

When the two sets of measures for attractiveness and relative capability have been computed they may be plotted in matrix format. In the illustrations used above the attractiveness axis would range from 1–25 and the relative capability axis from 0.04–25 as shown in Figure 11.4.

CHAPTER 12

Managing strategy

▶ Strategy and learning
▶ Managing the strategy process
▶ Managing the marketing strategy process
▶ Learning loops process

Marketing in action case
IKEA in America

Managing marketing strategy is explored. Consideration is first given to the nature of strategy itself, intended and emergent strategy and the role of learning. How strategy is managed from a corporate or strategic management perspective is described, including the broad phases or stages in the process, the levels of decision-making – corporate, business and functional – and the amount of communication between and involvement of organization members.

The marketing strategy process is described with its various component stages. While similar to many conventional strategic marketing frameworks, a real-time managerial focus shapes its development. The interconnection with strategic management and the marketing management process is highlighted.

Strategy and process

This chapter explores the process of *managing* marketing strategy. This is much more extensive than the process of making marketing strategy or planning marketing strategy. To appreciate this, it is necessary to look briefly beyond marketing strategy *per se* and focus on strategy in a broader corporate context. The practice of strategic management has superseded that of strategic planning over the past fifteen years or more. In doing so it has embodied the learning derived from the successes and failures of the long-range planning, corporate planning and strategic planning move-ments. These schools of thought and practice were especially dependent on assumptions that rationality is a preferred approach to managing; that planning and decision-making are difficult and vital, while implementation is relatively simple and operational; and that formulating strategy and implementing strategy may be separated in time and in execution.

The ascendence of the strategic management paradigm cleaves to the first of the traditional assumptions, but radically alters position on the others. Its commitment is still to rationality. But it builds its practice on the assumption that planning and doing are intertwined, each informing the other in a process of continual learning. It assumes that formulation and implementation are neither practically nor desirably separable. It assumes that planning and strategizing are not the tasks of a leadership or techno-cratic elite but rather the tasks of all those who manage action-taking and learning throughout an organization.

Managing the marketing strategy process is described here in the context of these same assumptions. Its emphasis is therefore on the manager as simultaneously strategist, planner and active learner. Its pre-scription is for managing marketing strategy in *real-time*: reviewing and planning the strategic reality as needed and through continuous learning, modifying, extending or replacing working assumptions and models of cause and effect.

As we saw earlier, an important benefit of the process approach is that it offers a greater simultaneity of intent and operation, of plan and implementation. It does so because as a manager conceives a plan or strategy, he or she must almost simultaneously consider its execution – what are the structures and systems, skills and resources, culture, style and shared values necessary to give action to the strategy? So conception is quickly followed by delivery of product or service. Process overlays strategy; strategy represents the choice of direction, while process is the force which implicitly or explicitly propels the organization in that direction. This real-time interaction was visualized in Figure 4.7 (p. 68).

Strategy and learning

The rhetoric of the professional and academic debate about the practice of strategy in management has been characterized in more recent years by the assertion of a dramatic opposition. On one side stands strategy as a planned, rational, prescriptive activity separated from implementation. On the other stands strategy as an emergent pattern in organizational actions to which managers give meaning and legitimacy by ascribing the label of strategy to what has already happened. This rhetoric probably reached its peak in the early 1990s in a particularly vacuous, very public and highly enjoyable exchange in which Igor Ansoff and Henry Mintzberg were cast as protagonists for the two viewpoints.[1, 2, 3]

With the maturing of strategic management practice and theory, the rhetorical suggestion that rationality and learning approaches to managing strategy are opposites or incompatible has lost most of its sting. While the strategy-making process will always have to be considered as contingent – contingent on the character of the environment and on the nature of the organization – it is none the less clear that current best practice is based on the assumption that rationality, planning, decision-making, action-taking and learning must all be effectively integrated.

The framework presented here for managing strategy at a company-wide level and for managing marketing strategy is similar in process and structural characteristics to many derived from the so-called rational school tradition.[4, 5] This approach to strategy-making supposes deliberateness and intention on the part of the manager and the organization – strategies are set out in advance and are then executed in accordance with plan, and feedback serves to compare actual outcome with intended. However, our framework also views strategy as a pattern in a stream of actions – as a consistency in behaviour – resulting both from intended or deliberate strategies and from emergent strategies where patterns develop in the absence of intentions, or despite them. The framework allows for outcomes that are intended and unintended (planned and emergent) and incorporate continual learning as the heart of the process. Thus emergent strategy and learning-by-doing reinforce the conventional rationalist approach.

Capturing the reality of emerging strategy is important to the effective management of performance. Mintzberg proposes four possible outcomes from action-taking that may confront the manager as strategist (see Figure 12.1).[6] The strategy that has been realized by the company may be either successful or not. The strategy may have been either intended and deliberately acted out, or it may have emerged. Of course, reality is never quite as clear-cut as these categories but the distinctions drawn remain relevant nevertheless.

The outcomes that arise are:

▶ *Quadrant 1*: strategy was developed, acted out as intended and it was successful – the 'classical' strategic planning approach worked.
▶ *Quadrant 2*: strategy was developed and a new strategy emerged through action; the emergent strategy worked; learning was effective and saved the organization from 'the plan'.

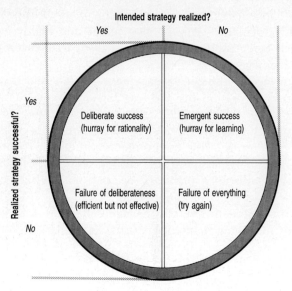

Source: Mintzberg (1994), *The Rise and Fall of Strategic Planning* (Prentice Hall, Hemel Hempstead) p. 360.

Figure 12.1 Outcomes of strategy

▶ *Quadrant 3*: strategy was developed, acted on as planned but failed; here we have classical planning efficiency but consequential ineffectiveness.

▶ *Quadrant 4*: strategy was developed, but was not acted out as intended; the strategy that emerged failed; this leaves nobody with anything to be proud of as both the plan and learning were inadequate.

Taking this perspective suggests that managing strategy – whether corporate, marketing, manufacturing, financial or human resource – and assessing performance have to push beyond comparing intention with outcome (which proves to be more of a test of planning performance than real-time company performance!). It necessitates assessing all the strategies (intended and emergent) that are realized and their effectiveness for the organization in pursuing its vision and mission.

In considering the reshaping of organizations to meet the demands of the late 1990s, Peter Senge, an applauder of the learning organization, suggests that the new role of corporate or central managers 'will be what we might call manager as researcher and designer. What does she or he research? Understanding the organization as a system and understanding the internal and external forces driving change. What does she or he

design? The learning process wherby managers throughout the organization come to understand these trends and forces.'[7]

Managing the strategy process

It is best to study first how and why the strategy process is managed at a
corporate or company-wide level. This enables a comprehension of the
parameters of managing strategy from the chief executive's and the top
management perspective. The ground is accordingly prepared for an understanding of the marketing strategy process, which is then described in terms
of its basic framework, its integration into the firm's broader strategic
management and the steps of analysis, decision-making, action-taking and
learning.

How decisions are made, and even what kind of decisions get made, are
significantly determined by the way in which decision-making procedures
are structured. In a general sense, the structure of the formal strategic
management process, and the marketing strategy process within it, may be
represented as having three underlying principles:

1 Phases or *stages* through which the process must proceed.
2 *Levels* of the organization and decision-making which must be
   incorporated.
3 Involvement and *communication* in the process, both top-down and
   bottom-up.

Stages

The first principle underpinning approaches to strategic decision-making
has a long and often controversial history. The assertion is that strategy
decisions are made by proceeding sequentially through phases in decision-
making, from goal-setting to strategy selection to strategy implementation
through programmes and annual action plans. The principle of sequential
phases is difficult to reject – it represents an orderly and cumulative
approach to problem-solving – what should we do? (goals), how should we
do it? (strategy), what are the details of putting our decisions into practice?
(programmes, action plans) and how can these be quantified or numbered
into an annual company plan? (annual budget or profit plan). Of course,
observation of reality quickly draws attention to the fact that these phases
are much less sequence than interconnected loops. The choice of strategy
will often cause reconsideration of strategy just as the programming of
action is likely to lead to alteration of both goals and strategies. But the
most compelling criticism of the conventional phases principle is that it
assumes that once these three or four phases are complete, action will take

place as explicitly planned. Yet it is obvious that once a strategy rolls into action managers begin to learn about its validity and therefore to adapt and manipulate it to deal with the unexpected and the misunderstood.

More particularly, the clever and observant manager will spot strategies in the making which nobody had anticipated. Pascale's famous account of the real story behind Honda's success in the US motorcycle industry points out that observant managers noticed the wholly unexpected and unplanned – consumers liked small Honda motorcycles and had no time at all for the large motorbikes on which the company's strategy was built.[8] In such ways are many good strategies born. But if decision-making is assumed to end with the phases of programming and budgeting, then this most adaptive and creative activity is excluded. It would seem, therefore, that in addition to the phases in decision-making that are 'deliberate' and deal with what is intended, there is need for a further phase which can capture, give meaning to and incorporate strategy that emerges in real-time. This process, which in turn produces a learning loop, is suggested in Figure 12.2.

So a number of broad phases or stages may be identified as the manager moves from strategic intent and 'grand vision' towards day-to-day performance management. A learning-in-action phase also becomes key. This in effect loops the strategy process. In reality the limited number of stages suggested above may be expanded to a greater number to recognize

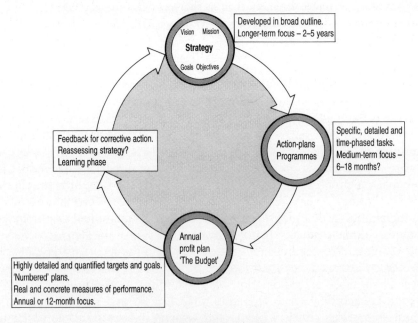

Figure 12.2 'Actioning' strategy

complexity. In particular, the phases of goal-setting and strategy selection are normally 'blown up' into at least four steps of analysis, gap identification, mission setting and strategy choice. Accordingly, the framework suggested in Figure 12.4 (p. 224) for managing strategy has some eight steps.

Levels

The planning and decision-making process in most organizations may be seen as a hierarchical one. An organization may be viewed as having three levels. At the top is the *corporate* or enterprise level. Here, corporate strategy is concerned with issues inherent in business definition and the formulation of company mission – In what product markets will we compete? With what distinctive advantages and competences? With what outcome in terms of market share, return on investment and cashflow? The next level is that of the business unit – the individual divisions or strategic business units (SBUs) within the organization that implement corporate strategy in their related product markets. Business units have the character of independent businesses in so far as they control the resources they need to do their job and are profit responsible through their general manager to the corporate level.

The corporate level may therefore be visualized as managing a portfolio of *business* units, choosing those in which to invest or divest and which to add to the portfolio. Below the business unit comes the product or *functional* level, consisting of related individual products or product lines for which functional strategies and actioning programmes are required. The business unit therefore manages a product portfolio, while the manager at the product level manages the individual product line in its market. Thus, different managers at different levels concentrate on separate although intimately related decision problems (see Figure 12.3). By specializing the activities of strategy-making and managing at each of these interconnected levels, great complexity can be managed in an orderly and relatively simplified manner and without individual managers suffering from both information and decision overload. A second principle of decision process design is therefore advanced: there are different levels in strategy-making and management and different managers and teams should be responsible for each. Of course, in smaller organizations focusing on a single business, there may be only two levels: the corporate and the business unit levels effectively coalesce into one.

Communication

The third principle deals with involvement and communication in the decision-making process. Many traditional organizations were built on the

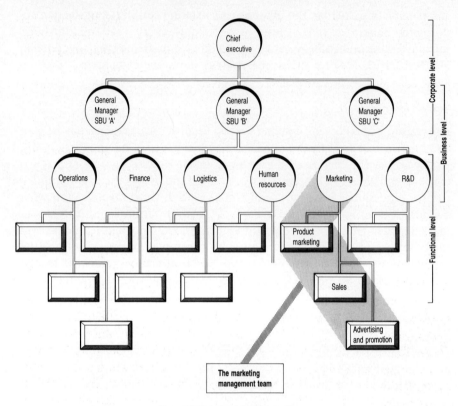

Figure 12.3 Levels of decision-making

assumption that wisdom lay at the top where plans were to be laid and decisions taken and the role of the rest of the company was to enact the strategies and programmes of action mandated from the top. Centralization of decision-making in a powerful and knowledgeable top management group is still sometimes seen as the appropriate design principle despite the evidence that in all but well-understood technologies, in stable environments and under conditions of considerable market power, such an approach is self-defeating. Opposing this approach one finds management history is full of exhortations to decentralize and distribute decision-making power. The most recent fashion package for this view is the selling of empowerment as an organizational panacea. While debating centralization versus decentralization has a happy rhetorical value, it usually turns out to be somewhat vacuous. Few organizations operate at one extreme or the other.

The design principle advanced to deal with this issue is a balance of top-down and bottom-up decision-making. Both centralized and decentralized decision-making are dangerously limited and limiting for the firm. Yet certain decisions must be made at the top, just as others are best made at the bottom – where direct action is undertaken. Even that great advocate of the decentralized, empowered organization, Peter Senge, notes clear agreement with Royal Dutch Shell's former planner Pierre Wack that without a shared common view, decentralized strategic decisions result in management anarchy, that without systems thinking, 'local decision-making can become myopic and short-term' and that the '"tragedy of the commons", where what's right for each part is wrong for the whole' is all too common a condition.[9]

Balancing top-down with bottom-up decision-making seems to be the appropriate design principle. Such an approach minimizes the possibility of vertical communication gaps in the organization. Top management must ultimately set the overall direction – the shared view – for the company. But front-line managers will know far more about the reality of the daily competitive battle for prosperity waged with products, services and brands. Service personnel are the ones who deal most directly with customer concerns and problems and are often in the best position to specify product modifications and new benefits to be developed by the R&D laboratory. Therefore, it is reasonable, indeed necessary, that the essence of strategy and action programmes should rise from those on the front line. It should also be added that such top-down and bottom-up interaction and communication are also crucial in managing performance. Unless it is a reality, major shortcomings arising from lack of integration are likely to occur in the order generation, fulfilment and service process.

Framework for managing strategy

Taking these general design principles into account, strategy may be conceived and managed as shown in Figure 12.4. This process contains some eight phases or stages. Though presented diagrammatically in linear format, these stages may also be visualized as a continuous loop involving learning from action-taking and its consequences; the analysis of the organizational environment and of the organization itself; the identification of a performance gap driven by some combination of environmental demands and organizational aspiration; the agreement of an organizational mission and objectives; the isolation, assessment and choice among strategic options; the programming and budgeting of action; the taking of action and the management of performance; monitoring action outcomes, both intended (planned) and unintended (emergent) – and then back to learning from these outcomes about the validity of the organization's assumptions and 'theories' about itself in its environment.

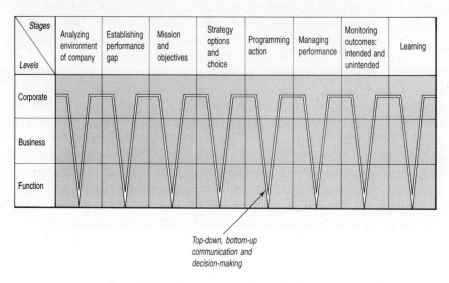

Stages / Levels	Analyzing environment of company	Establishing performance gap	Mission and objectives	Strategy options and choice	Programming action	Managing performance	Monitoring outcomes: intended and unintended	Learning
Corporate								
Business								
Function								

Top-down, bottom-up
communication and
decision-making

Figure 12.4 Managing strategy: a decision-making framework

As this continuous scanning and analysis of the organization in its environment are drawn up through the organization, top management is in a position to act on its fundamental responsibility to establish performance requirements and to set direction. Having done this it must seek the response of the various 'parts' of the organization in terms of their proposals as to what strategic options are available and preferable. The top management team then has the responsibility once again to perform its particular task of integrating and making tradeoffs among the various suggested strategies and to reach a decision on the overall pattern of strategic commitment. When this is done the elements of the organization must respond by programming their parts of the strategy and negotiating the resources and time required. Top management is intimately involved since it must ultimately decide on the allocation of scarce resources across the claims of the many components of the agreed strategy. The management of performance is enacted in a differentiated manner at each level in the organization, as are the monitoring of outcomes and learning from this monitoring. Acccordingly, it is possible to gain the advantages of both top-down and bottom-up consultation while working through the sequence of decision-making from agreement on corporate guidelines to detailed specification of one-year targets and budgets and on to the 'capture' and incorporation of emergent strategy.

The advantage of creating process frameworks of this nature is that they allow great complexity to be handled with relative ease by asking managers at different, but carefully interconnected, levels to concentrate only on what is most vital to the execution of their strategic role and by dividing the decision process – at least for the first pass through – into sequential phases rather than trying to cope with all steps simultaneously.

The extensive delayering and downsizing of business of the 1990s and the associated elimination, or radical streamlining, of planning staff units are sometimes taken as a sign that approaches to managing strategy with a basis in rationalist 'architecture' such as that described in Figure 12.4 are no longer relevant. This is a mistaken impression. Processes such as that shown were developed by companies like General Electric at the height of the strategic planning movement's popularity. But as early as 1981 General Electric had already detected the runaway tendency of staff planning units to over-elaborate the form of strategic planning at the expense of its content. In the 1980s, under the hands-on leadership of Jack Welch, GE dismantled most of the form of its strategic planning system in order to concentrate on its content and to shift from a strategic planning emphasis to a strategic management focus.

However, no matter where one looks at a formalized approach to strategic management practice the phases and levels of strategy-making and management as shown in Figure 12.4 are still fundamental, as is the necessity for both top-down and bottom-up involvement. The fact that fewer people are involved and that they are predominantly line managers – the people who manage strategy are making it as well – generates a more incisive, action-oriented and committed process in which the unfortunate distinction between making and managing strategy, between planning and doing disappears. It therefore remains important to design the process for managing strategy and to design it well. Finally, while the process design principles have been discussed in the context of a larger type of firm, they remain just as relevant for a smaller one. While such firms may be less likely to experience communication layering or vertical and horizontal gaps in operation, they must none the less design process frameworks for managing strategy and performance.

Managing the marketing strategy process

The competent marketing manager has a deep understanding of strategic management and knows all about the process of managing strategy in the firm. There are two reasons for this. First, he or she is ultimately a strategist himself. Marketing activity, no matter how enthusiastically pursued, is unlikely to be much use without being set in a strategic context. The marketing manager's foremost job is to manage the marketing strategy process. This primarily means making the correct choice of markets in

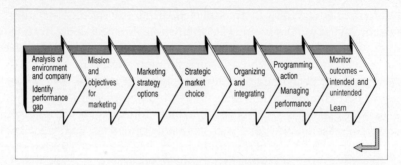

Figure 12.5 The marketing strategy process

which to compete so as to match company competences to customer need. This enables the subsequent marketing management and OGFS processes to be expedited properly.

But strategic market choice also determines the firm's long-term direction and likely competitive advantage. Marketing strategy is inextricably bound up with corporate strategy. This is the second reason why marketing managers comprehend strategic management. They may drive the marketing strategy process but they do not own it exclusively. It is finally shaped in the context of the firm's overall direction and marketing managers work with their fellow senior managers in this pursuit.

Figure 12.5 sets out the various phases or stages in the marketing strategy process. These stages are broadly similar to those in Figure 12.4, the company-wide strategy process, reflecting a movement from analysis and grand vision towards operational detail and monitoring performance. However, corporate strategy is ultimately the responsibility of the chief executive or general manager, and it is approached and understood from his or her perspective. We approach the marketing strategy process from the perspective of the marketing manager and the marketing discipline. The process indicates the concerns, anxieties and interests of marketing and the marketing function – and, more positively, the pivotal role and contribution that marketing brings to wider company fortunes. It is instructive to explore each phase in more depth and to examine the interaction of corporate and marketing thinking, and often the interaction with other functions such as manufacture, logistics, finance, and so on.

Analysis: where we are now

In a formal strategy-making process, learning from the past and attempting to understand the future usually starts with an audit of the status quo, comprising the two steps of internal and external analysis. In general, it is wisest to begin with the external analysis as this allows a fresher and less blinkered assessment of the internal situation afterwards. In order to conduct the analysis, external factors revolving about customers, competitors, industry structure, market definition, trends and channels are scrutinized to isolate the opportunities and threats facing the company and to specify the key success factors (KSFs) dictated by the industry. These KSFs essentially imply and determine the minimum level of expertise or competence that the firm requires if it is to compete with an expectation of success in particular competitive circumstances. The marketing manager is in a position to use the key success factors dictated by the environment as an acid test for any strategy proposal.

Internal factors to do with the company's strengths and weaknesses and its core and distinctive competences (DCs) are isolated by analyzing the company's past and current performance, its resource base and its cost structures. This type of SWOT exercise is discussed in more depth from the marketer's point of view in Chapter 9. Based on this work the manager must be conscious of the need to invest in the company's distinctive competences, since these and these alone confer competitive advantage.[10] For the marketing manager this frequently necessitates working with other managers when important distinctive competences lie elsewhere in the organization – for example in R&D, in design, or in a unique manufacturing mode. It also necessitates working across organizational boundaries when the marketing manager has to persuade others to allocate scarce funds to investment in 'marketing assets' such as brands or distribution channels.

Performance gap: where we want to be

Emerging out of this review of where the company stands it is possible to establish a gap between current performance and that desired by the company in terms of profitability, future growth and risk. Such gap analysis helps to quantify the nature and magnitude of strategic realignment required. It measures what has to be achieved. Too often strategic intent can be seen as some vague aspiration to perform better than is currently the case. Gap analysis puts figures on the aspirations.

Marketing contributes to the definition of this gap. In Figure 12.6 'Business as usual' implies no major change in existing strategies, a steady-as-it-goes regime which is unlikely to lead to significant increases in profitability. 'Doing it better' indicates an intention to improve company performance in its various activities in response to key factors for success in the industry and possible opportunity. 'Doing it different' suggests more – the determination on the part of the firm consciously and continually to realign its distinctive and core competences, and consequently its product

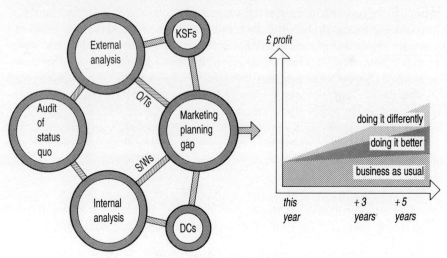

Figure 12.6 Where we want to be . . .

and service offerings, in recognition of lasting and real-time needs in the marketplace – in essence, being a truly market-focused company. This may sometimes involve a very substantial change in how the firm does its business; in other words, a significant reconfiguring or re-engineering of its micro business system. Marketing strategy is a key component of this value chain.

Mission and objectives: saying what it means

'Doing it different' involves an imaginative leap forward – conceiving a vision for the future. This vision describes where the business will be in the longer-term future; the position it will hold in the market and the commitments on which it will have secured its position. This description of a future state of both business and industry is intended to provide a picture of the future state into which managers will guide the company. Its value lies primarily in trying to avoid the traps of extrapolation from past performance and the traps of focusing strategy too narrowly within concepts of adaptation to present market and industry forces. Vision focuses on 'stretching' the company to invent and reinvent its future rather than on achieving 'fit' between existing resources and observable market forces. It is a creative, potentially rule-breaking, approach to managing for the future.

An organization's mission statement seeks to encapsulate this broad vision. It represents a short and pithy summary of the organization's core objective or *raison d'être*, how it intends to fulfil this, and usually identifies its key competences, product/service offerings, markets served and commitment to the customer. A mission statement thus contains a very significant element of marketing intent and strategy. It facilitates the identification of marketing objectives and goals. Such a statement can be used for both external and internal communication – to customers, suppliers, financiers, the community on one hand, and to staff and organization members on the other. Exhibit 12.1 provides examples of two such statements. Note the strong marketing dimension of both.

Exhibit 12.1

Mission statements
Philips Dictation Systems
Office equipment supplier in Austria

MISSION STATEMENT
At Philips Dictation Systems we serve people and organizations around the world in their need to capture ideas, thoughts or information, and prepare these for communication and reference.

To meet these needs we will develop, produce and market products that offer improved ways of capturing and transforming the spoken word so it can be read, stored and distributed as needed.

Our aim is to be the recognized leader in this field utilizing and integrating with new technology to provide exciting innovative solutions for our customers.

Our future success will be founded on our commitment to these guiding principles and commonly shared values:
- **Our focus is our customer**
- **Our foundation is our people**
- **Our core is quality**
- **Our challenge is innovation**
- **We will grow our business**
- **We will be responsible**

In adhering to these guiding principles and values, we will build a company we are proud to be associated with: proud of our ability to meet user needs, of our world leadership position, of our people and of our products.

Our focus is our customer
- **Our users – and their needs – will be the focal point for every decision and action we take.**
- **Where our dealers are our first-line customers, we will do our utmost to satisfy their needs to our mutual benefit.**
- **We will be more effective than our competitors in understanding, anticipating and meeting our customers' needs.**

Our foundation is our people
- ▶ Our people and their determination form the cornerstone of our success. We would rather they try hard and fail than not try at all.
- ▶ We believe in teamwork – our managers will build a team environment, based on caring, honesty and candid communication.
- ▶ Integrity, consistency and decisiveness will be our guide. We will be fair, reliable and trustworthy.

Our core is quality
- ▶ We will only do what we can do properly and thoroughly.
- ▶ We will use our own know-how and experience – and Philips' resources as a whole – to deliver quality, reliability and efficacy in our products and systems.

Our challenge is innovation
- ▶ Innovation – in products, sales and marketing – is an integral component of our formula for growth.
- ▶ We will research and apply current and emerging technologies to ensure that our products integrate with and add benefit to our users' own communication environments.

We will grow our business
- ▶ We will continue as a dedicated organization, with a global presence under the brand name Philips. (In USA, Philips and Norelco.)
- ▶ We will grow our global markets through user-oriented marketing, product development, sales and services initiatives.
- ▶ We will set ambitious goals and be determined in achieving results.

We will be responsible
- ▶ We have a duty to our parent Philips which we will carry out fully.
- ▶ We will always be considerate towards the environment and society in which we work.

Koninklijke (Royal) Ahold NV
Food retailer in The Netherlands

CORPORATE PRINCIPLES

Ahold is primarily a retail organization, distributing and producing consumer goods, and rendering services directly to large numbers of customers directly through its chainstores in The Netherlands, other countries in Europe and the United States.

The objective of the company is to continue to perform this role in society in current as well as in new market areas, and, by doing so, to achieve a proper return on investment, while at the same time providing substantial employment.

To achieve its objective and meet its related responsibilities, the company needs to ensure its continuity. Ahold wishes to be able to determine its own future, and therefore strives to maintain its independence and its own identity.

The consumer is at the very heart of Ahold's policy. Consequently, Ahold monitors the desires of the consumer and the ever-changing market conditions. Here, the basic principle is to give consumers value for money, and at the same time devote a great deal of attention to quality, assortment, safety and information.

For its employees, Ahold wants to be a company that not only offers adequate compensation, but also provides challenges, professional training, education and motivation.

For the stockholders, Ahold aims at a good return on investment. All new and existing activities will be continually tested against this criterion. Ahold makes an effort to inform interested parties, as often as is possible and justifiable, of the course of events in the company.

Ahold strives for a steady relationship with its suppliers that meets the commercial interests of both parties. Social concerns like employment, zoning and planning, environment and public health will be important elements of corporate policy.

Source: T.R.V. Foster (1993), *101 Great Mission Statements*, Kogan Page, London, pp. 81, 100–1.

The consideration of vision and mission and performance gap must be translated into key goals and objectives for the firm. These include not only corporate and business level goals, but also financial, manufacturing, marketing, and so on. Clearly, objectives for each function must be consistent with overall company mission and objectives. This is no less the case for marketing objectives.

Marketing strategy options: how might we get there

If objectives establish the 'goalposts' for strategic endeavour, then a number of potential game-plays and options must be devised to reach the goals. Marketing strategy options are firmly rooted in the company's competences, and in particular in the nature and effective management of its marketing assets. These may include a superior product or brand, an excellent distribution network, a first-rate salesforce, pricing agreements, licensing and trade arrangements and so on. How the firm marshals these competences and other company capabilities to take advantage of market and customer need depends on an array of market-related factors.

As described in the previous chapter, a market choice matrix (MCM), with its dimensions of market attractiveness and relative competitive capability, can guide the marketing manager in his or her search from broad business definition to specific target market. The dynamics of the MCM evolve over time and this demands an understanding of market evolution, and its characteristic competitive behaviour, from an emergent phase, through growth and maturity, to decline. Innovative and rejuvenescent strategy is possible not only in growth but also in mature or unpromising markets.

A significant determinant of relative competitive capability and strategic option lies in the stage at which the company enters the market – whether as pioneer, as challenger to an early leader, or as late entrant. A firm may further consider a mass market, niche or multiple niche strategy. All these factors influence the evaluation of market segment feasibility and finally enable effective strategic market choices.

Strategic market choice: we make up our mind

The decision about what market or markets to serve is the most important decision a firm makes. It commits substantial resources. Changing market or realigning its service takes money and time. Once the marketing manager and his or her team are convinced about the right target market, they must then convince fellow top managers that this is the right decision. The chief executive and all senior managers must believe that the firm has or can develop the resources and competences across all its functions to serve this market successfully.

The marketing manager must consider the full array of interdependencies between marketing strategy and the strategic management of the whole organization. Marketing objectives and strategy are only realistic and attainable if they can be integrated with all dimensions of the overall strategic management task. Hence, marketing proposals must fit with overall strategy and must be consistent with organizational structures, systems, the skills of managers and employees, the style of management, the staff resources and the shared values to which those in the organization subscribe. If there is inconsistency between what is proposed and these factors, then it is inevitable that execution will be ineffective and that marketing objectives, and other of the firm's goals, will remain unachieved.

Organizing and integrating: we start to make it happen

How marketing fits in with other functional domains is also an issue when it comes to how the firm organizes itself to manage marketing and marketing strategy. Strategy and structure are deeply interlinked in the achievement of market focus. How the marketing department structures itself and how those working in it cooperate determines in no small measure strategic outcomes. Decisions to out-source work that might readily be carried out in-house can have strategic as well as operational import. The fact that achieving market focus increasingly requires greater cross-functional activity adds a further dimension of complexity to the issue of organizing marketing. As we see in the next chapter, a number of traditional approaches, e.g. brand management, have been found wanting in the challenging marketing landscape of the 1990s.

Process redesign is at the heart of new approaches to organizing and integrating business activity. Expediting the marketing strategy process, along with the other three core marketing processes, involves overlaying traditional function and hierarchy with process management. Process teams, led by customer or product 'integrators', manage customer value-adding activities and tasks across departments and business units in a manner which simultaneously respects and deepens functional specialism and expertise. Building and providing leadership for such teams is a crucial concern of the marketing manager and top management. In this regard, the concept of internal marketing also takes on a process imperative.

Managing performance: we make sure it works

Making sure the marketing strategy works depends crucially on decisions about competitive positioning, actual product choice, pricing, communication and selling, and distribution. These decisions are part of the marketing management process, and the degree to which they complement one another *and* nest into the strategy process determines in large part the success of marketing strategy outcomes. These positioning and marketing mix decisions are addressed in Part IV.

Decisions about product, price, promotion and distribution in turn get transformed into programmes and action plans, annual budgets and company profit plans. They become yardsticks to assess progress against plan. Performance management systems and controls as well as reward systems both encourage marketing effort and pinpoint shortcoming.

Monitor and learn: we continue to make sure it works

As performance is managed, the uncertainty surrounding the anticipated future resolves itself into present certainty. As this happens those charged with taking action must deal with surprising and unexpected events and manage the strategy process adaptively – in other words, they must learn as their actions lead to both planned and unplanned (intended and emergent) outcomes. The meaning of intended strategy is obvious – the marketing team sets out to achieve certain objectives using agreed strategies and programmes and duly sees these intentions realized as tangible outcomes. Emergent strategy refers to the outcomes of those parts of the intended strategy that are unexpected, due to incorrect assumptions having been made and surprising events having occurred. Part of the art of managing strategically and in real-time is to recognize pattern in such unexpected outcomes and to act in a manner that crystallizes such outcomes as they emerge into new strategies. Thus these two sets of outcomes must be monitored and managed separately, and then reintegrated, through organizational learning, into the new overall and evolving marketing strategy.

Strategic marketing if well managed, is, therefore, a learning process. Learning is one of the most fundamental marks of intelligence whether in the individual or embodied in an organization in the form of embedded knowledge. Much of this learning will be gradual and incremental and thus

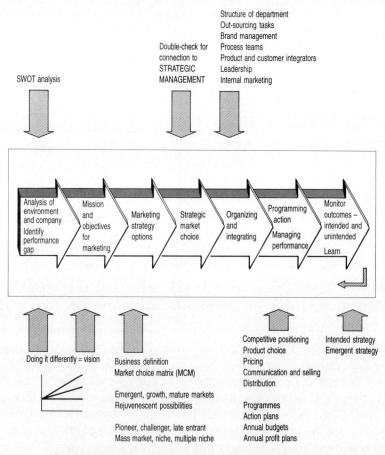

Figure 12.7 Managing marketing strategy: a decision-making framework

strategy will often evolve as a matter of degree rather than experience radical change. Strategy can have as much to do with managing stability as it has to do with managing change. Considerable realignment of strategy is, of course, sometimes necessary and the process described here should inform the manager as to the degree of change that is appropriate.

Figure 12.7 expands the basic process to take on board many of the considerations discussed here. It visualizes a broadened decision-making framework for managing marketing strategy. It reveals complexity, but also a logical and feasible approach for handling such complexity.

Learning loops process

A process approach involves a continuing series of activities and tasks that produce change and development over time; process is visualized in a linear horizontal or lateral form to emphasize both the linear passing of time and its antithesis to hierarchy and function. Of course, process ultimately repeats and reinvents itself and has, as we have seen, a feedback loop or cyclical dimension. It is learning that loops the process and renders it cyclical. (One could, of course, present process in a circular format presenting time in a circular, as distinct from linear format – this would be more in keeping with the Oriental notion of the circular passage of time as compared to the Occidental understanding of linear time.)

Chicken or egg?

Appreciating this dimension of feedback or cyclicity facilitates an answer to a question that often is a source of confusion to those students and managers embarking on planning processes for the first time. Where do we start? What comes first? In a sense, it does not matter. If we accept the learning feedback loop, we can start anywhere. In fact, it may be wisest to start with learning itself. It could be argued that it is difficult to finalize a mission statement before there is a shape on the strategy. This may be so, but if it is possible to loop back to refine the mission statement after strategy is chosen, then the process for managing marketing strategy remains robust. The reality of successful strategy is continual learning. A process approach enables this to be conceptualized and managed.

Exhibit 12.2 recounts the success of the Swedish furniture firm IKEA in the US market. This success took time and perseverance. Much of the strategy which had worked well in Europe had to be relearned and reinvented to cope with the particular challenges of the North American market.

Exhibit 12.2   *Marketing in action case*

IKEA in America

IKEA opened its first non-Scandinavian furniture outlet in 1973 in Switzerland.
From then on it spread with uninterrupted success across most of Europe so that
its huge out-of-town shops, typically decked out in Sweden's national
colours of blue and yellow, became a familiar and welcome sight to young families
furnishing their homes.

IKEA reinvented the traditional furniture business system, through heavy
investment in design for manufacture as well as aesthetics, by building self-
assembly furniture kits (the customer carries the cost of assembly), by sourcing
its products from suppliers in 67 countries, by merchandising its 10,000 products
in its own out-of-town, low-cost stores and by providing a high service shopping
experience for parents and children alike. Its strategy has paid off in competitive
terms, equalling its rivals on quality but undercutting them on price by as much as
30 per cent. It has paid off just as handsomely in growth and profitability terms. In
1994 it had sales of 8.35 billion guilders ($4.5 billion) and estimated profits of
about 6–7 per cent. It operates 108 wholly owned stores in 18 countries with
another 15 stores franchised in the Middle East, Hong Kong and Spain.

In 1985 IKEA opened its first US store outside Philadelphia and six more by 1991.
However, by 1989 the American adventure was in trouble. European experience
had been to produce profits after 2–3 years in any new country, with the third or
fourth store in operation. In America there was no sign of profit. Customers came
to shop but left empty-handed and complained of queues and products being out
of stock. Because products were shipped from Europe and because of the dollar's
strength, its price claim became unfounded.

Having found its established formula for success wanting in the US environment,
IKEA stopped 'trying harder' and decided to learn to 'do it different', but without
abandoning its core commitments and strategy. In 1989 and 1990 Anders Moberg,
the company's chief executive, spent time in the US stores, talking to customers
and discovering that 'we were behaving like Europeans, as exporters, which
meant we were not really in the country. It took us time to learn this.'

European furniture designs did not suit US customers universally in either taste
terms or in physical comfort. Swedish beds were too narrow. Furniture dimensions
were metric. There were no matching bedroom suites. Kitchen cupboards were
too small for pizza dinner plates. Glasses were too small for families that liked to
fill their drinks with ice cubes – in fact some customers bought vases as glasses.
By 1994 IKEA had redesigned 20 per cent of its range for US tastes and usage. In
parallel it began to produce its products in the United States to avoid both the
currency and transportation problems.

So IKEA learned, not just to adapt, but to rethink how it did business without
losing its own unique IKEA tradition and style. Between 1990 and 1994 its US

sales tripled and turned to profitability in 1992. But its learning did not end there. Faced with a slowdown in growth and the puzzle of how to globalize without losing its unique Swedish identity, the company has been involved in 'permanent evolution', according to Anders Moberg.

In 1994, 2 per cent of the world's population visited an IKEA store. At the end of 1994 it announced that it would open in China. This time it had already institutionalized some of its US learning with the result that it had already set up a local supply network. According to Goran Carstedt, then head of North American operations, the company in the United States is 'still blue and yellow, but mixing in the stars and stripes'. *The Economist* magazine noted that one might 'expect a red star to join IKEA's multi-coloured galaxy'.[11]

REVIEW QUESTIONS

12.1 How do the notions of emergent strategy and learning-by-doing alter the conventional rationalist school's view of handling strategy? Give an example in the domain of marketing.
12.2 What general design principles underpin a decision-making framework for strategy?
12.3 Explain the various stages or phases in managing a marketing strategy process.
12.4 Apply such a process to a company or organization with which you are familiar.
12.5 Rather than present these process steps in a linear fashion, try to draw them in a circular anti-clockwise manner. How does this differ?

CHAPTER 13
Organizing and integrating

- ▶ Organization structure
- ▶ Strategy and structure
- ▶ Organizing for marketing
- ▶ Integrators and specialists
- ▶ Teams and team building
- ▶ Internal marketing and the process imperative
- ▶ Internationalizing modes

Marketing in action case
Building teams at Kraft Foods

ABOUT THIS CHAPTER

Organization is the means of managing strategy into action – and of shaping strategy itself for the future. As a firm grows in size and competes across wider horizons, its organization structure evolves in complexity. Strategy and structure are deeply interlinked in the achievement of market focus. How firms organize themselves for marketing is explored. A number of traditional approaches, e.g. brand management, have been found wanting in the challenging marketing landscape of the 1990s.

Process redesign has been at the heart of new approaches to organizing and integrating business activity. Expediting the four marketing processes involves overlaying traditional function and hierarchy with process management. Process teams, led by customer or product 'integrators', manage customer value-adding activity and tasks across departments and business units in a manner which simultaneously respects and deepens functional specialism and expertise. Building and providing leadership for such teams are a crucial concern of top management. In this regard, the concept of internal marketing takes on a process imperative.

In the case of firms which internationalize, a number of typical stages and organizational shapes can be identified. For the large company competing globally, the transnational model balances the needs and advantages of efficiency, responsiveness and global learning.

238

Organizing and shaping strategy

Decisions about strategy and marketing programmes bring the manager to the point of knowing *what* to do. However, knowing what to do goes for nought if the manager is not equally clear about *how* to get it done: about the way to turn decisions into effective action and, in turn, to learn from taking action about what to do next.

Good decisions are never finally made until the issue of seeing them into implementation has been thoroughly anticipated and planned. Thinking through the mode of execution normally leads the manager to alter some aspects of strategy or marketing programming on the grounds that organizational and resource constraints do not support the original proposed decisions, or that even more may be achieved than anticipated. Planning for implementation must, therefore, interact with strategy formulation. Each must influence and shape the other.

However, organizations are not just built and managed to execute decisions taken in advance. Organizations are also designed as a means of learning from doing. They therefore influence the way in which managers discover how their intentions turn into outcomes, and this then shapes the unfolding of strategy and its adjustment and accommodation to the unexpected or poorly understood. Organization is both the means of managing strategy into action and of shaping strategy itself for the future. This point is all the more relevant in an era where speed of response is crucial to positional superiority.

Strategies, plans and programmes are turned into outcomes through organized activity – an organization – and monitored and adjusted with the help of measurement and control mechanisms. Organizational issues are the focus of this chapter; measurement and performance management systems the focus of a later one. Structures, systems and processes are pivotal elements of organizing for marketing action. A number of organizational innovations are explored, such as process-based management and the idea of internal marketing, that have become current during the 1990s and that are likely to hold the seeds of organizational form in marketing for the twenty-first century.

Organization structure

An organization is a group of people and relevant technologies with some degree of permanence or stability that performs specific 'value-adding' tasks in pursuit of explicitly or implicitly shared objectives. Companies are organizations of individuals and relevant technologies that seek a profit objective through serving market needs. Two of the most clear formal traces of an organization are its structure and its transformation processes. An organization's structure defines the way in which its members relate to each other, the specialization of tasks, duties, responsibilities and accountability and the distribution of power among its members. An organization's core processes define the linked activities through which it converts inputs to outputs. For the moment we will focus on the structure of an organization and return later to the relationship between structures and processes.

It is in the nature of a firm's organization structure to evolve (see Figure 13.1). In a small or new firm the owner usually manages everybody else in a *simple* and *informal structure*. As the firm grows, this ceases to be effective and we normally see the emergence of a *formal structure* with managers taking responsibility for specific tasks such as marketing, production, finance or personnel. Administrative procedures and controls become explicit and embedded in systems such as budgets, production schedules or sales forecasts. Further growth in size and complexity may lead to loss of responsiveness in a company where all important decisions must be coordinated by one general manager. For instance, an important sales opportunity may have to pass through the hands of people in several sections and departments preoccupied with other customers, other products, other sales territories or other design and production pressures. By the time their activities are coordinated and a decision is finally made, the opportunity may well have passed. Greater focus, responsiveness and flexibility are then required and the people involved throughout the relevant parts of the organization must be empowered to make and execute the necessary decisions.

Companies will often adapt to increased complexity by reconfiguring their structure into one based on divisions which take care of defined products, territories or customers; take responsibility for performance and profitability; and are managed by a dedicated team with its own general manager. Such divisions, business units or strategic business units (SBUs) are usually coordinated at what is typically called the corporate head-quarters or head office, run by the chief executive and a team of specialist advisers in areas such as finance, planning, legal and public affairs. Divisions enjoy varying degrees of independence depending on their performance, the nature of their businesses and the individual style of the chief executive. For example, Exhibit 23.1 (p. 468) describes ABB, formed by the merger of the Swedish company ASEA and the Swiss firm Brown Boveri, a new kind of global company that makes and markets electrical power generation and transmission equipment, high speed trains, automation and robotics, and environmental control systems. Its president, Percy Barnevic, has established a combination of strategy, structure and leadership style that

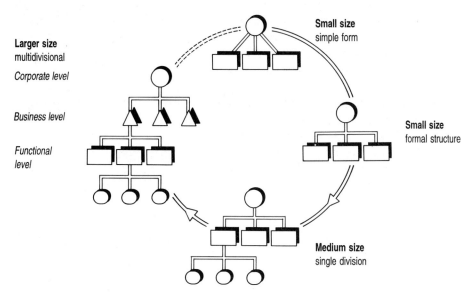

Figure 13.1 Evolving organization structure

has earned him the accolade of one of Europe's most admired chief executives.

Where divisions have considerable independence we usually describe them as part of a *decentralized structure*, with important decisions delegated to divisional managers. By contrast, where the chief executive and the head office allow little discretion and impose strict control we speak of a *centralized structure*. The degree of centralization or decentralization may vary as markets evolve and the company's circumstances change. As markets recede, divisions may, of course, wither and companies may even revert back to to a single 'division'.

In a divisionalized firm one is likely to find that there are three important levels of decision-making and strategic management. At a basic product and programme level (also often called *functional level*), there are decisions and strategies to be made concerning individual products serving specific customer segments. At a divisional level, decisions and strategies which coordinate related product lines and customer groups are made. This is often referred to as business level strategy and the division may be characterized as a strategic business unit (SBU). At *corporate level*, decisions and strategies are concerned with the number and nature of the businesses in which the company should be involved, with providing an overall strategic direction, with the integration of all the businesses of the company and with allocating overall resources as effectively as possible. In Chapter 4 the use of business and product market portfolio approaches was discussed as a help to managerial decision-making at these differing levels, while Chapter 12 examined how strategy was managed through these different echelons.

Historically, one of the most important insights into the nature and form of organizations was provided by Chandler's landmark study of the relationship between organizational strategy and structure. His research indicated that as strategy evolved, structures changed to support the implementation of the new strategies.[1] Thus, growing size and complexity evoked the organizational response of functional specialization. Further expansion and diversification into new products and markets in pursuit of further growth were likely to be followed by divisionalization of organizations to provide a structure that would support the implementation of multi-product and multi-market strategies.

Strategy and structure

The debate about the relationship between strategy and structure has continued over many years. What is clear is that significant strategic change must, almost without exception, be matched by structural change. If this is not done, decisions to change strategy will usually founder as a structure designed to implement a former strategy makes it impossible to implement a new direction.

However, experience shows that structure is not just a consequence of strategy: it may also form and shape strategy. In a curious and, on occasion, in an almost sinister way, the structure of an existing organization delimits the strategies that its managers can envisage. What we are shapes what we can be – and that is just as true for organizations as for people. In this sense organizations are not unlike individuals. An organization with structures characterized by deep vertical lines of specialization; by rigid hierarchy; by commitment to specialized technology and by compartmentalized skills and competences will have great difficulty thinking of strategic innovation and innovative market strategies, never mind implementing those of which it might conceive. By contrast, relatively small organizational units with 'flat', egalitarian structures that resemble an organism rather than a machine are much more likely to change and innovate. In their study of Scottish firms, Burns and Stalker characterized these two contrasting forms of organization as organismic and mechanistic, and noted that the former were more likely to innovate than the latter – the structure of the firm was a predictor of the strategic behaviour of the firm.[2]

The small business context

Before dealing with the specific options for structuring marketing activity, the contrast between structural arrangements in small or new ventures and in large companies demands some further comment. In small, and in most new ventures, structure is very simple. In managerial terms, it may amount to no more than the owner-manager who directly supervises non-managerial staff. More developed small businesses and the typical technology-based new venture will have a small top management team and a supervisory management level. In organizations of this nature specialization of functions into departments usually makes little sense; a small group of key managers is involved in all major decisions, in making and in managing marketing strategy.

Organizations of this nature must be careful to distinguish between the *content* and *form* of marketing strategy and planning. The content is a necessary and essential requirement for success. The form, however, is most usually simple and relatively informal in such businesses. The information base for marketing decisions may often be held in the memories of the managers and updated constantly as they go about doing their business. Equally, the way in which strategies are formulated and modified may be informal in the sense that it takes place during the never-ending series of meetings, debates and confrontations that are the daily life of the smaller business or the growing new venture. Small size and close intimate communication patterns make elaborate formal systems unnecessary. At the same time it is clear that good small businesses and prospering new ventures write down and regularly update marketing plans. This is a regular discipline that focuses and crystallizes the endless strategic debate in such companies – and that is essential to raising finance for growth and development. It is also essential from a corporate governance viewpoint as investors must be reassured through the company's board that the affairs of the company are well planned and directed. It is difficult for a board to take a well-informed view on this matter without the aid of an appropriate degree of formality in strategies and plans.

One of the great mistakes made by observers of small and new ventures is to confuse the form of good marketing with its content – to confuse formal marketing planning with good marketing. Any successful small or new business has by definition got the content of marketing right. Its smallness, the tightness of communication links and the market pressure for flexibility may render many formalized structures and systems not only irrelevant but even counter-productive. As organizations grow to deal with larger markets and greater volumes of business, marketing as a separate function has emerged along with the finance, manufacturing and personnel management functions. This growth in complexity demands more formal mechanisms for sharing information and for arriving at coordinated decisions. Formalized planning and control systems reflect this need.

Structuring marketing activity

There are several options available in choosing a structure for marketing activity. The choice of structure should be made so that:

1 The organization structure fits with the marketing strategy (if it does not, the strategy will not be manageable into intended outcomes).
2 Coordination of marketing processes and their associated activities, and between marketing, manufacturing, R&D, finance, personnel, warehousing and all the other interdependent parts of the organization is maximized.
3 Responsibility for results is matched by authority to determine results.
4 The flexibility of the structure to adapt to new market conditions and strategies is as great as possible (except in conditions of great stability, a structure that fits only one strategy is usually a dangerous structure).

As companies grow in size it is possible for the marketing function to improve its performance by specialization within the function itself. Sales, advertising, distribution, public relations, marketing research, marketing planning are common functional departments in many organizations. Such specialization allows for the accumulation of depth of expertise and should, in a general sense, result in greater effectiveness. Such a centralized functional marketing organization is, however, generally limited in its usefulness to large companies that produce single, or closely related, product lines and market to one or a few target markets. More complex product market situations normally leave this form unable to respond adequately in terms of coordination, flexibility and customer knowledge. What may be required in these cases is a number of smaller, tightly knit marketing departments serving each product market, division or customer group.

Where a company pursues the route of increasing specialization within its marketing function it must regularly confront the age-old 'make or buy' decision. Most of the services that can be incorporated in a marketing department (the 'make' decision) may also be sourced from the market for marketing services (the 'buy' option). Advertising, public relations, database management, mail and telephone selling, merchandising and indeed selling itself are available as services for purchase from specialist suppliers across Europe. The question for the marketer as organization designer is which of the two forms of organization will serve the company best – a hierarchical relationship through which the service is owned and managed 'in-house' or a market relationship through which the service is acquired and managed through contract. This brings us back to our debate in Chapter 2 about the nature of markets and transactions! The manager as organization designer should be guided by the relative costs of the two alternative arrangements compared with their relative effectiveness for the company.

It is salutary to pose matters of marketing organization in these terms regularly to ensure that any given marketing activity could not be more effectively performed by the contrary method of organisation. It is also a critical discipline for any marketing service area in a company to assess itself and its service provision in a market context. If it must answer in the affirmative the question 'could this service be provided just as well and more cheaply by an independent supplier?', then it has no option but to reform itself to become 'competitive' or to disband, move to out-sourcing the service and cease destroying value for the shareholders of the company.

In many companies, a marketing function is created by adding a marketing department or management position in tandem with a traditional sales function. The roles of the two departments may remain unclear and uncoordinated, typically leading to the sales department concentrating on operational matters and the marketing department focusing on planning and market research. This is an unsatisfactory and unproductive state of affairs. The role of marketing must be clearly defined and the selling task integrated within its scope if good marketing practice is to result.

Brand management

Brand or product management structures are common in companies that have many products targeted on many customer segments. A major advantage of this organizational form is that managers can identify with 'their' product and manage it, much as a general manager would run a business. The form can therefore have significant motivational advantages in addition to providing a natural basis for planning and control systems built around products, their customers, competitors, market performance and product profitability.

However, this does not give the brand manager the same role and authority as a divisional general manager since the product or brand manager never controls all the resources vital to the success of the product. A product manager's responsibility may therefore easily exceed his or her ability to influence key determinants of success and profitability. The system depends on negotiation for resources, whether financial, manufacturing or manpower, and skills in negotiation and power brokerage can become vital to the individual manager's success. Without strong strategic marketing at a company level, the system may also behave quite suboptimally: the most forceful and assertive product managers will win resources and support for their products irrespective of strategic merit. Thus large volume brands with good margins very often retain and even acquire resources, while small new products in need of heavy marketing investment may wither for want of resources. A major danger in this structural form is therefore to delegate too much of the strategy-making to the product level. It is vital to retain central strategic marketing control at the corporate level so that resources are more optimally allocated.

Brand management was pioneered in the 1950s by US manufacturers of fast-moving consumer goods. The model worked spectacularly well during the subsequent era of high consumer trust, effective mass advertising, growing prosperity, homogeneous demand and poorly developed distribution channels. Forty years later, a different marketing landscape, characterized by the pressures of prolonged recession, fragmented and deregulated markets, more sophisticated customers requiring more segmented/targeted approaches, multi-media technology, and powerful distributor/retailer networks has led to a questioning of the merits of the brand and product management systems. Brand managers are perceived to be too junior and inexperienced in the managerial hierarchy, too narrowly centred on marketing itself, to provide the cross-functional leadership to cope with this complex marketing environment. Further, they are too overwhelmed with day-to-day tasks and too focused on the short term to consider important sources of value-added in the business system, which are no longer just advertising- or trade promotion-based.

Designing organizations around core processes is a response to this dilemma. In 1994, for example, Lever Brothers, Unilever's British soaps company, abolished the job of marketing manager. Marketing and sales departments were merged and reorganized as a series of business teams focusing on consumer research and product development while a separate customer team became responsible for retailer relationships in general.[3] At Pillsbury, the US food subsidiary of Britain's Grand Metropolitan corporation, the traditional marketing department structure has been replaced by multidisciplinary teams, each garnered around a product group or category – each team involves managers from production and sales as well as marketing.

Procter & Gamble, the original 'inventor' of the brand management system in the United States in the 1930s, has likewise switched to category rather than brand management, i.e. all shampoos or diapers managed as a unit, and evolved customer business development teams. This focus on product category and group rather than on individual product reflects a perceived need to rationalize brand and product ranges and a concern with buyer needs. European firms have also adopted the category manager approach. Another large US food company has replaced the general brand manager with three focused brand managers: business managers, equity managers and development managers (see Exhibit 13.1). This has both strengthened its marketing expertise and avoided the problem of brand managers getting bogged down in daily tasks at the expense of building the business in the long term.

Organizing for marketing

What we observe in these examples are companies grappling with the problems of how to reorganize themselves in response to a complex and fast-evolving marketing and general business environment. Not only is the inherent nature of markets changing, but also types of delivery systems – in particular, technology. As a consequence, speed of response and minimizing the gap between conception and delivery are paramount to competitive advantage. The challenge for firms is how best to organize for this.

Strongly demarcated organizational hierarchies have exhibited significant limitations when faced with market difficulties such as declining margins and increased buyer and channel power. Declining margins have been brought on by recession and by customers who have become less willing to pay sizeable premiums for branded goods or services when compared to increasingly high quality distributor and retailer brands. Under pressure for profit performance, most branded goods companies with no option to increase prices, went in search of cost savings only to find that potential savings were often locked up by inter-functional and inter-department rivalry or plain misunderstanding. Process redesign has been at the heart of much of the change that has ensued. Redesign and re-engineering methodologies cast process ownership and management in a centre-stage role. As a result, the role of marketing personnel as process team members in an interdisciplinary context has become prominent.

Of the core marketing processes, only one is primarily under the control of what would be traditionally regarded as marketing department personnel – the marketing management process (Figure 13.3). The other three core processes – the marketing strategy, the order generation, fulfilment and service (OGFS), and the new product development processes – all involve cross-functional and interdisciplinary teams. The marketing strategy process is part of the overall business strategy process and has to share membership with the business strategy team and with people from other functions that affect marketing strategy performance (Figure 13.2). The OGFS process is co-owned and co-managed by virtually all the main areas in an organization, among whom marketing must play the role of supplying specialist marketing expertise and a constant focus on the objective of profitable customer satisfaction (Figure 13.4).The new product development process has almost equally wide ownership, with marketing once again providing specialist expertise and customer focus (Figure 13.5).

Figures 13.1–13.5 illustrate the interrelationship between organizational

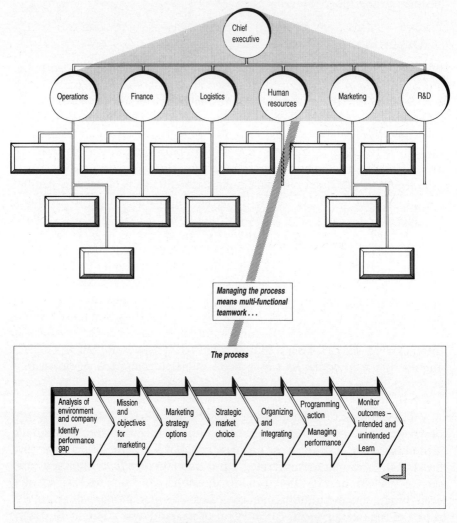

Figure 13.2 Marketing strategy: process and hierarchy

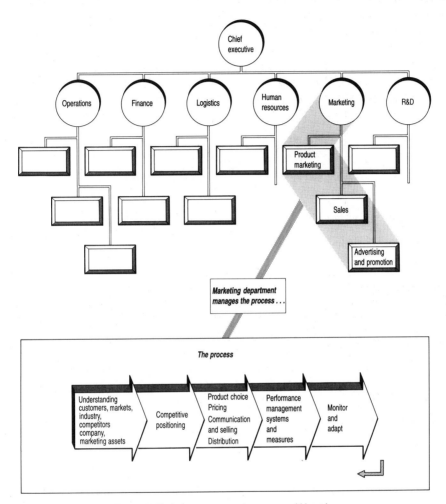

Figure 13.3 Marketing management: process and hierarchy

structure and process and the clear danger of debating the issue of organization design and redesign only in terms of hierarchy. Balanced and interdependent consideration of both aspects of organization design is essential.
The 'fashion' for re-engineering and redesign of organization processes is
too often formulated in language that demonizes hierarchy and announces
process management as the universal answer to organizational and marketing problems. In the occasional rush to organize around processes, the
importance of hierarchy can be underestimated and 'the functions' dis-

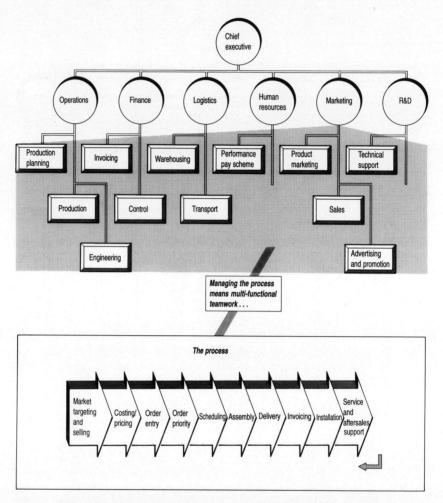

Figure 13.4 Order generation, fulfilment and service (OGFS): process and hierarchy

missed as unproductive overhead costs. But good process design quickly shows that all functions including marketing have two important roles to play:

1 that of co-ownership and co-management of integrated activity chains that convert organizational inputs to value-added outputs for customers; and
2 that of a 'centre' for the consolidation, development and nourishment

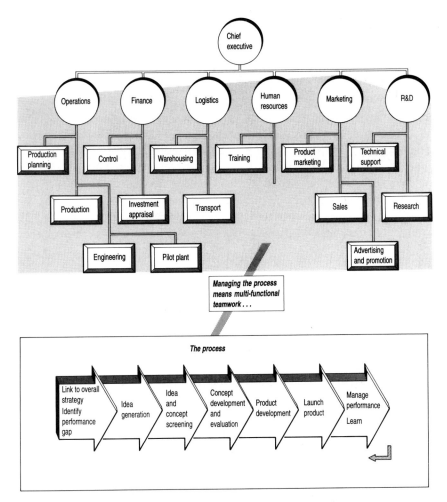

Figure 13.5 New product development: process and hierarchy

of expertise that may be deployed by the company as a distinctive resource or strategic asset to its competitive advantage.

These two roles imply that those working in marketing must organize accordingly – along process management lines and around a functional hierarchy. The organization design must create customer value as effectively as possible and ensure that marketing expertise is managed and deployed to competitive advantage.

Integrators and specialists

While concepts of organizational behaviour and development offer guidance to the firm attempting to reshape itself and cope with market pressures, there is no magic solution that will fit all circumstances or make sense for every company. But two key principles of organization are beginning to emerge. First, the market-focused firm will overlay successfully functional hierarchy with process organization, balance functional specialization with interfunctional integration, and simultaneously deepen and broaden its organizational competences. Second, teams and team leaders will have a key role to play in achieving this.

Recent McKinsey & Company research has explored the characteristics of these team leaders or integrators, and sheds light on the problems inherent in getting a balance between organizational integration and specialization.[4] Integrators play a critical role in guiding activities along a firm's micro business system to ensure long-term profitability is maximized. They are responsible for tearing down the walls that divide function from function, a product manager from product manager, and supplier from retailer. In practice, these integrators:

▶ Understand the real 'drivers' of profitability throughout the business system in order to identify which levers to pull to optimize a firm's share of scarce industry profits.
▶ Work across both the macro and micro business systems to develop genuinely customer-focused strategies.
▶ Lead cross-functional teams resposible for executing these strategies day-to-day.

Such integrators are likely to be senior line managers with experience in a number of the firm's departments and to have the breadth of vision and confidence to take risks – whether that means linking up with sister brands to pursue more effective joint promotion, partnering with a large customer in a new business solution or working with operations to win more efficient supply-chain options.

Companies can consider designing their marketing activities around three different types of integrator. The *consumer integrator* is responsible for meeting the needs of distinct end-user segments. Kraft Foods found that it could not keep up with the fast-growing Hispanic market in the United States under its traditional brand management system. Developing Hispanic programmes was always a low marketing priority of every brand manager. So the company made one of its senior marketing managers responsible for developing integrated programmes to serve Hispanics in each local market. It created special product formulations and set up carefully targeted joint promotions of several brands that enjoy strong Hispanic usage. Results were impressive; more to the point, they would have been impossible to achieve without real integration across brands, R&D, manufacturing and sales.

The *customer integrator* is to be found in business-to-business companies that do not sell directly to end-users. Business customers are often more demanding, more powerful and more fragmented in their needs than are final consumers. The growing strength of top retailers has forced many suppliers to replace salespeople who push products and take orders with knowledgeable key account managers who can help plan their customers' businesses. Procter & Gamble has established cross-functional teams to serve each major account. Replacing the old divisional salesforces, these teams represent all P&G divisions and have significant analytic and operational capabilities. They are led by senior customer team leaders who are former district managers. Further, the organizational layers between these customer integrators and HQ have been stripped away (see Figure 13.6).

Product integrators will also be needed in some companies. The difference here compared to the product management model is that product integrators display much greater cross-functional leadership, are more senior in the organization and have more experience of different departmental tasks than the traditional brand manager. *Bancassurance* has been a feature of European financial services since the late 1980s. The term refers to the

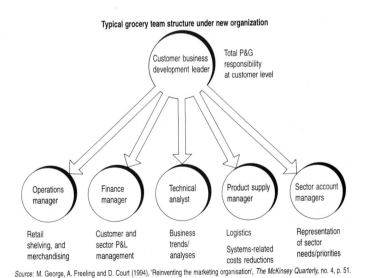

Typical grocery team structure under new organization

Source: M. George, A. Freeling and D. Court (1994), 'Reinventing the marketing organisation', *The McKinsey Quarterly,* no. 4, p. 51.

Figure 13.6 Developing customer integrators at P & G

merging of retail high street banks with life assurance companies to gain economies of scale and cross-selling opportunity. Retail banks come from a conservative, procedural tradition, while the assurance firms from a 'hard-sell', channel-flexible culture. These amalgamated financial services companies have experimented with a number of organizational models to market successfully their products. Teams of advisers or customer counsellors – product integrators of life assurance products – which work closely with retail bank personnel in marketing the life products, have proved to be particularly effective.

In a sense, the 'purest' form of marketing organization should be one structured around consumer segments and customers. Where a company serves several customer groups with quite different needs and buying behaviour, the approach works well. Many companies under competitive pressure in the early 1990s took this course in reorganizing their marketing so that customer groups became the key to structural design, with a company's many products and services coordinated to serve customers' overall needs. Thus, food companies may organize divisions around meals such as the breakfast, snack, lunch, dinner markets. Computer and information technology companies may shape themselves around problems to be solved such as computer integrated manufacturing, financial database management, and so on.

However, the best organization design route to customer focus is to identify the key customer-related processes and to look first to their optimization and second to matters of hierarchy. Figure 13.7 illustrates how this might be visualized in the case of SKF Bearing's approach to the major reorganization it undertook in the late 1980s in order to become more market-oriented. Here the micro business system of SKF is portrayed as it was up to the early 1980s – a single micro business system directed at a segmented market – and then as it was after the CEO, Mauritz Sahlin, reorganized it to direct the business at its different markets (see also Exhibit 4.1, p. 58).

In addition to developing integrator roles, the market-focused firm must also cultivate greater specialist capabilities. In the marketing arena, such expertise enables the firm to respond more quickly – and more accurately – to market need and opportunity. The rapid tailoring of marketing strategies and programmes to consumer segments, and even individual consumers, is key to market focus. In Chapter 7 and Exhibit 7.1 (p. 128) we saw how many companies are upgrading their database marketing skills. Computing innovations capable of scanning huge volumes of data in a flash and neural-network software, able to 'learn' automatically from large sets of data on its own, are facilitating this deepening of marketing expertise. While integrators may lead the process-to-market, specialists provide competences in disciplines like marketing intelligence, pricing strategy, promotion effective-ness, advertising and direct marketing.

Teams and team building

If integrators and specialists are the building blocks of the successful marketing organization, teams and teamwork are the binding mortar. While teamwork is important within each function and specialism, the distinguishing feature of the market-focused organization is cross-functional teamwork, aligned with key business processes, which cuts

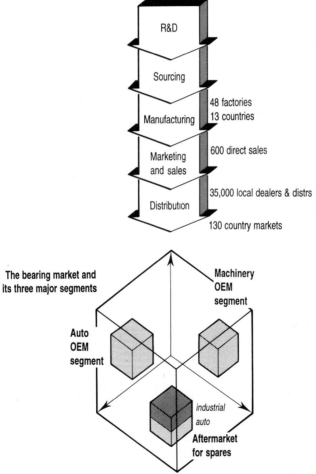

Note: For dimensions of markets, as suggested by the arrows, see 'business definition' on pp. 186–7.

Figure 13.7 (a) SKF: 1985 structure

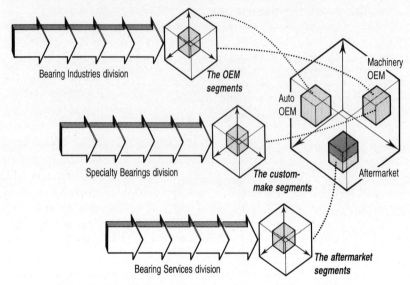

Figure 13.7 (b) After Sahlin's reorganization into three market-focused divisions

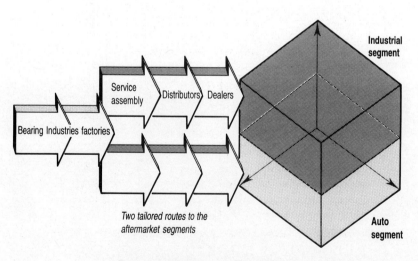

Figure 13.7 (c) The Bearing Services division

across departmental, and on occasion, business unit barriers – the 'silos' which get in the way of serving the customer in a superior manner.

An FMCG firm, for example, might supplement or replace its formal R&D, manufacturing, logistics, sales and marketing departments with teams responsible for key processes such as building brand equity, stimulating consumer demand or ensuring superior customer service. It then organizes a process such as building brand equity around multiple teams responsible for distinct consumer or product segments. Each of these teams is led by a consumer or product integrator and staffed with specialists on pricing, promotions and database marketing (see Figure 13.8). In this case, teams are the linchpin of the marketing organization, because their combination of expertise, experience and judgement inevitably achieves better results than individuals, no matter how talented, working on their own. This team-based structure also enables, if not forces, companies to strip out unnecessary layers, like that of general manager-marketing (marketing VP), which raise cost, create extra work and slow decision-making (see Exhibit 13.1).

Using teams in this way can make managers uneasy. For some, it suggests visions of committees, taskforces and working groups that hold endless meetings, decide only by consensus, and return to their 'real' jobs – and then nothing really happens! Such fears are legitimate, but the problem

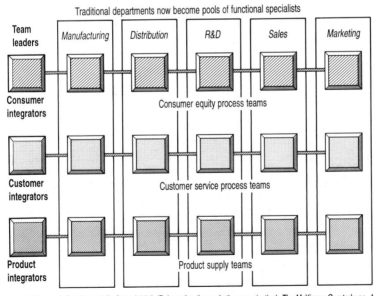

Source: M. George, A. Freeling and D. Court (1994), 'Reinventing the marketing organisation', *The McKinsey Quarterly*, no. 4, p. 57.

Figure 13.8 Teams link process and function

is usually not with the teams themselves, rather with ineffective 'working groups' masquerading as teams.

Genuine teams share a number of characteristics that contribute towards their effectiveness. They have a common purpose, which sets their tone, aspirations and performance goals. These goals, in turn, help monitor progress and hold their members accountable. Real teams also invest time in working out how they will operate together to achieve their shared purpose. They display a healthy mix of technical and departmental knowledge, analytical and decision-making capabilities, and interpersonal skills. Most important, each member holds him or herself accountable for the achievements of the whole team. Such genuine teamwork allows for the 'double solid line' structure of Figure 13.8 – where members 'report' to both the team leader and functional head – and ensures that resultant activity transcends the conventional matrix management mode.[5,6]

To enable such an approach to work, top management must create a supportive culture. Process and task goals must be clearly articulated. Accountability, whether volume, time-based or 'bottom line' product category profitability, must be understood and mutually agreed. Information – technical, customer and competitive – must be readily available to the whole team. As new skills often have to be learned, training and development are crucial. New cross-functional career paths must be offered to integrators, along with long-term specialist careers within departments. Last but not least, such organizational design and its teamwork are likely to be evolutionary in nature. There is no instant blueprint; the avenue to the 'best' approach contains much trial and error. Competences take time and cost to create, but will return such investment over an equally long period – one that is increasingly longer than the lifecycles of many of today's products and services.

Exhibit 13.1   *Marketing in action case*

Building teams at Kraft Foods

In the early 1990s Kraft, like many other food companies, found itself facing declining real growth, limited pricing opportunities, greater retailer power, swelling trade spending and more demanding customers. Its response was to reorganize – reinvent – itself in a way that added up to a profound departure from conventional brand organization. At least four broad sets of changes are to be observed:

1 *From brand managers to category business teams.* Kraft has evolved from a traditional brand management structure, where each brand competed for firm

resources and market share, to a model based on empowered category business directors – 'product integrators' – who lead strong cross-functional teams. Several new structural approaches underpin this evolution:

(a) Related product brands are now grouped into common categories. Thus, rather than compete with one another, they now work together to drive overall category growth at retail level. For example, the sandwich cheese category now oversees three brands of cheese slices: Kraft, Deluxe and Velveeta.

(b) The category managers leading these businesses have been elevated to category business directors, with broadened, bottom-line responsibility. No longer viewed as merely marketers, they are as responsible for identifying ways to improve efficiency of the supply chain as they are for developing the next advertisement. In most cases the marketing VP layer between the category business director and division general manger has been eliminated to streamline decision-making and focus responsibility.

(c) These category business directors are, in turn, supported by a cross-functional team, including personnel from sales, operations, R&D, finance, market information, consumer promotions and brand management.

2 *From functionalized manufacturing to process teams.* Kraft has also set up a series of process teams to complement its category business teams. Team members represent every step in the product supply chain from procurement to conversion and distribution, and work with the category teams to deliver the right products, on time, at the lowest possible cost. The teams incorporate such functions as purchasing, engineering, quality, operations, finance, materials management and plant management.

3 *From geographic selling to customer business teams.* The company has restructured its salesforce, replacing the traditional geographic approach (where account managers covered multiple retailers in their territories) with a customer- and category-based model. Now, each major customer is assigned to a dedicated customer business manager – 'customer integrator' – responsible with his team for maximizing Kraft's total performance with that customer. This approach nurtures long-term category trade planning, the cooperative development of tailored ordering and delivery programmes, dedicated trade promotions, and supply chain savings for both Kraft and the customer.

4 *Greater specialization and focus.* Kraft has replaced the traditional general brand manager with three focused brand managers: *business managers*, responsible for the day-to-day trade tactics and business performance issues; *equity managers*, responsible for advertising and consumer promotion; and *development managers*, responsible for product and packaging innovation. This has both strengthened its marketing expertise and avoided the problem of brand managers getting bogged down in daily tasks at the expense of building the business in the long term.

It should be stressed that this organizational redesign was largely evolutionary. There was no instantly successful 'grand design'. Rather, new role responsibilities, accountability modes and career development paths were explored; new skills learned and training programmes initiated; and information systems transformed radically over a period of a year.

Larger companies with a number of divisions or business units often vacillate between a centralized and decentralized approach to management. A centralized approach usually means a strong functional capability at corporate HQ and close supervision of the business unit and a corresponding inability to respond effectively to local opportunity. A decentralized approach involves greater delegation of responsibility to the business unit and enhanced ability to respond in an integrated fashion to opportunity in its market – though this may involve duplication and scale inefficiencies from a corporate perspective. There is a tradeoff between the two approaches, and the balance chosen by a company at any one time depends on competitive, financial and human resource factors. However, considerable advantage accrues to the company which utilizes process teams of integrators and specialists to deliver customer-added value not only across departmental borders but also across business unit borders. Rather than having to be content with a tradeoff, such firms achieve simultaneous improvements in two directions – increasing functional capability and economics *and* enhancing focus and responsiveness at the business unit level (see Figure 13.9). The traditional tension assumed between central-

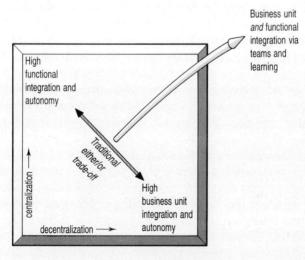

Figure 13.9 Teams mean win-win strategy

ization and decentralization may fade considerably with the use of process-based organization.

Internal marketing and the process imperative

'Making it all happen' – managing strategy into outcome – is a difficult task that requires at least as much effort and creativity as that required in making the strategy itself. Making it happen also demands the creation of an organizational culture and a management and employee team dedicated to achieving agreed goals and to doing so with excellence.

Ensuring that the staff of a firm are committed to the goal of 'actioning' strategy, and in particular of ensuring the best possible treatment of customers, has been labelled internal marketing.[7, 8] This concept involves the application of marketing principles to 'selling the staff' on their role in implementing the firm's marketing policies. It has been suggested that internal marketing has two primary focuses. First, it complements the company's external marketing efforts by ensuring that personal interaction between the company and the people it serves is as conducive to attracting and satisfying customers as possible. Second, internal marketing is directed at producing and maintaining a motivated and satisfied group of managers and employees, who will support the company's external marketing objectives and work towards ensuring quality, productivity and efficiency. This concept is applicable to all organizations, whether in the private, public or not-for-profit sectors, and regardless of whether a product or service is being marketed.

If the task of an internal marketing programme is to 'sell the staff' on the company's plans, programmes and customer service ambitions, then such a programme will require a marketing mix approach. The product in the internal marketing mix is a commitment on the part of staff to the idea of total customer service. The distribution component deals with the concept of marketing consciousness and customer commitment is 'delivered' to the staff. In the context of price it is useful to think not in terms of monetary price but rather to ask what it costs employees, the target market, to participate. The promotional component involves all aspects of communicating messages concerning the programme to staff.

The concept of internal marketing highlights the often substantial gap or barrier between formulating a strategy and putting it into practice successfully. Barriers arise among the people, the systems and procedures, the departments, the business units, and the managers whose commitment and participation are needed to implement marketing, i.e. the internal customers for marketing plans and strategies. Surmounting such barriers involves teamwork which, in practice, amounts to: winning the support of key decision-makers for plans; changing the attitudes and behaviour of employees and managers who work at the crucial interfaces with buyers and distributors; gaining commitment to making the marketing plan work and 'ownership' of the key problem-solving tasks from those units and individuals in the firm, whose working support is needed; and ultimately managing incremental changes in the culture from 'the way we always do things' to 'the way we need to do things to be successful'.

The debate about internal marketing has typically been fashioned around the issue of 'selling the staff' and on the ideas and objectives discussed above. However, it has seldom been associated with a process perspective on business and marketing which highlights other aspects of the internal marketing challenge. The basics of this view remind us of the business system and its micro version at the firm level as a linked set of transformational activities that create customer value. Each of these activities is separated by a transaction – the output of one activity becomes the input of another, either through a market contract or through an internally administered exchange. In so far as marketing is the science of managing transactions, two issues come to mind when the concept of internal marketing is mooted:

1 Within any linked set of transactions that seeks to create customer value and profit for the company, the marketing of the objective of the process activity is an essential task of the team leader and team members. The OGFS or the new product development processes are ineffectual if not imbued with the customer value-creation objective and a commitment to integrated action in pursuit of that end. Much of what has been described above as internal marketing effort must be deployed to this end.

2 For any linked set of activities the designers of the process and associated structure must continuously confront the 'make-or-buy' decision – should each of the activities be performed in-house under company ownership and management, or externally by a supplier? Where the answer lies in neither direction should a quasi-hierarchy be created – a hybrid of market contract and internal management – in the form of a supplier partnership or alliance or joint venture?

The internal marketing issue arises when it is decided that the best way of organizing the individual transaction lies in the form of internal ownership. Internalizing a particular transaction leaves those responsible for the activity of generating an output with the duty to view their internal customer in the same way that an external supplier would have to do – in order to survive as a competitive supplier in an open market. This is, of course, exactly the philosophy of design and operation that a process team urges on those involved at each process stage. Each link activity must be reminded that the fundamental design issue revolves around whether its members can execute their activity – provide their 'product' or 'service' to the next link in the chain – better, cheaper and faster than an external supplier could!

Internationalizing modes

As companies grow and become more involved in international markets their organization inevitably becomes more complex.[9] When a company just exports it remains quite firmly based in its home market. Exporting, even in its literal interpretation, suggests sending products and services overseas. This may well arise as a result of inquiries received from international markets as much as from active selling abroad. An export department or individual responsible for exports may well be established. Many small companies at this stage are characterized by a managing director who travels intensively and takes on the role of export salesperson. The use of agents and distributors in the export markets is a familiar mechanism at this stage of development to enable the company to reach customers beyond its own limited sales and distribution capability. Using channels in other countries brings all the challenges of managing and controlling channels in any marketplace but has the additional complication of uncertainty with regard to foreign business practices, and the difficulty of securing attention for what may be a very small proportion of an agent or distributor's total range of goods (see Figure 13.10).

If the exporter is successful, then a sales office may be established in the main international market. A sales office will ease the problems of support-

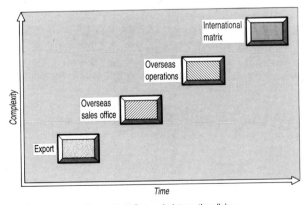

Figure 13.10 Stages in internationalizing

ing distributors and customers and of providing timely service as well as managing routine procedures and selling effectively. Now employees of the company become permanently based in another country and it may begin to think more in the manner of an international company rather than that of an exporter. The sales office will, however, act on the instructions of the domestic head office and receive limited autonomy. It will usually be staffed, and almost certainly managed, by home country nationals.

The next stage in development is likely to be the establishment of some significant production or service operation presence in the company's main international market, or in a location from which many of the key markets may be serviced and supported. For many growing companies this stage is executed by acquiring a foreign company or by entering into a joint venture or partnership agreement. Such entry mechanisms have the advantage of providing not only existing manufacturing and support facilities but also an immediate customer network and local staff with intimate knowledge of market realities. The cost of such acquisitions therefore includes the price of local market knowledge, customer goodwill and managerial competence as well as any physical assets that may be purchased.

Out of such beginnings grow the international, multinational and global companies that are familiar names around the world. As they grow in size and complexity they will most usually adopt some form of matrix organization to cope with the complexities of managing international business. These matrix structures most usually reflect (1) geographic, (2) product or business, and (3) functional dimensions.

The *geographic* basis for organizing international activity often dominates the early stages in companies' growth. This is especially the case in export-led firms, where it may make good sense initially to develop markets one country at a time. Having achieved this, however, the geographic basis for structure may begin to limit flexibility and coordination. This problem is faced by many European international and multinational companies who have had great difficulty in achieving strategic coordination and control across traditionally decentralized country-based divisions or subsidiaries. These problems showed up most actively with the shift to pan-European strategies in the early stages of development of the Single European Market.

The *business* basis for organizing international activity has been much in favour during the 1990s as companies have searched for the benefits of integration and standardization in business and marketing strategy. This is best achieved by having a structure that emphasized unity of strategy across country markets in order to reap the benefits of scale and experience whether in pan-European or in global markets. Structuring around lines of business with their own 'bottom line' responsibilities also helps to deal with the problems of parallel importing and the threat of 'grey markets' that arise if prices vary from one country to another. This is common where marketing strategy is shaped by local country management who respond primarily to the pressures of their own national market. But if price differentials occur between countries, then channel members or smart entrepreneurs will quickly exploit the opportunity by buying in the cheaper market and reselling in the dearer market. The consequence is usually great resentment by distributors, retailers and company salespeople in the country into which the parallel imports are being brought. In some instances this may go so far as to threaten the company's ability to control its channels and to maintain the loyalty of its customers.

The *functional* basis for organizing is a very traditional one, which seeks to ensure that functional practice is adhered to in the company's various international locations. Traditionally, this had two objectives: (1) to control functional activity according to some centrally approved standards, and (2) to provide assistance and support, based on scale and depth of expertise of a specialist nature, to local management. Much of the revolution in head office staff functions, including marketing, of the early 1990s reflected the extent to which such centralized functional areas had ceased to add value to head office, regional or country operations (see Asea Brown Boveri in Exhibit 23.1, p. 468). In general, the functions lost position as strong dimensions of international structures through the late 1980s and early 1990s. During this period of delayering and downsizing, head office functional units and functional staff, including marketing, either disappeared or moved into multi-functional business teams or into country management teams. In doing so however, those who had moved quickly ahead with the downsizing and decentralizing of functional groups also began to reidentify the vital reasons why they had originally needed specialist functional departments:

- to provide depth of expertise in a critical area of competence;
- to provide a source of advice and help for those in businesses and regions who could never have the scale to support adequate development of expertise;
- to provide a place from which standards could be set, maintained and raised;
- to provide a 'home' to which specialists in the field and on the front line of competition could come for regeneration and renewal in their area of technical competence;
- to provide for ownership of the learning activity concerning the functional area within the company and to gather and spread best practice across the company's international operations.

The functions as centralized or head office resources are being recreated in many European multinationals with these objectives in mind. Such companies are betting that reconstituted functions will provide them with significant resource-based, or competency-based, superiority relative to their competitors. The competition to satisfy customer needs profitably is increasingly dependent on knowledge-based advantage.

The transnational model

Bartlett and Ghoshal's five years of research with nine of the world's largest corporations led them to the belief that 'most managers seemed to understand very clearly the nature of the *strategic task* they faced; their main problem was developing and managing the *organizational capability* to implement the new and more complex global strategies' (their italics).[10] They interviewed 236 managers in Procter & Gamble, Unilever, Kao, General Electric, Philips, Matsushita, ITT, Ericsson and NEC, thereby mixing American, European and Japanese corporations evenly as well as the consumer packaged goods, consumer electronics and telecommunications switching industries. Their objective was to understand the organizational characteristics required to manage in the changing, worldwide environment.

Three traditional organizational models were identified in their work: the multinational organization model, the international organization model and the global organization model. They suggest that the multinational model (Figure 13.11a) is the most common. Economic, political and social forces of the pre-war period encouraged decentralization to enable responsiveness to very different national markets and the result is characterized as a decentralized federation. The network of decentralized assets and responsibilities is managed by simple financial controls and a strong informal system of personal coordination, with the whole being viewed as a portfolio of national businesses. In the international organization model (Figure 13.11b), which became widespread in the early post-war period, it is suggested that the underlying pressure was to transfer central expertise to less advanced subsidiary locations. A coordinated federation characterizes such companies and formal systems and controls are used by powerful top management who guide the direction of subsidiaries. The global organization model (Figure 13.11c) is both old and new. It was one of the earliest forms exploited by Ford and Rockefeller who built world-scale facilities to produce standardized products for all. It was then the basis for much of the Japanese approach to organizing for global expansion in the 1970s and 1980s. The global form centralizes assets and responsibilities, and subsidiaries are primarily pipelines to final markets with little independent discretion. The organizational configuration is seen as a centralized hub.

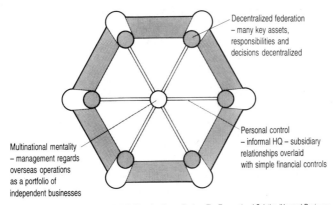

Source: C.A. Bartlett and S. Ghoshal (1989), *Managing Across Borders: The Transnational Solution* (Harvard Business School Press, Cambridge, Mass) p. 50–2, 89.

Figure 13.11 (a) The multinational organization model

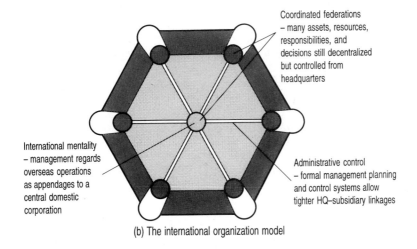

(b) The international organization model

The three traditional emphases in organizing yield different advantages – the global has the potential to generate efficiencies through scale and standardization; the international to generate learning from the array of markets from which lessons may be drawn and then communicated back to other parts; the multinational to be responsive to local needs and to win by being more tailored to the specifics of demand than competitors. Bartlett and Ghoshal propose that current circumstances require that companies should design their organizations to achieve all three strengths simultaneously in order to be fully competitive and call this the transnational model (Figure 13.11d).

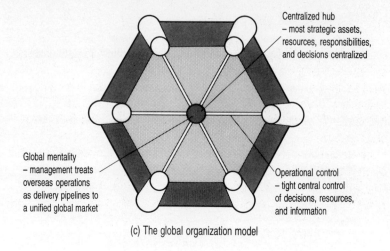

Centralized hub
– most strategic assets,
resources, responsibilities,
and decisions centralized

Global mentality
– management treats
overseas operations
as delivery pipelines to
a unified global market

Operational control
– tight central control
of decisions, resources,
and information

(c) The global organization model

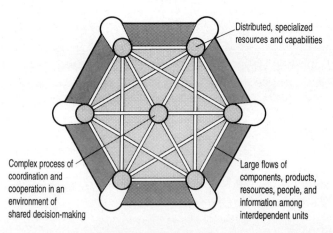

Distributed, specialized
resources and capabilities

Complex process of
coordination and
cooperation in an
environment of
shared decision-making

Large flows of
components, products,
resources, people, and
information among
interdependent units

(d) The transnational organization model

The transnational model is therefore proposed as one which balances integration for efficiency, with localization for market responsiveness and joint development, with sharing of knowledge for learning on a global scale. The individual line of business and its business team and business manager are likely to be the locus of *integration*. The country manager and country management team are the most appropriate locus of *responsiveness* and the function is the most likely centre for shared *learning* and the guidance of central and locally originated *innovation*.

REVIEW QUESTIONS

13.1 Organization is about the means of managing strategy into action and of shaping strategy itself for the future. Discuss.

13.2 What are the implications of a marketing department's decision to out-source some of its activities?

13.3 Are reports of the 'death' of the brand manager, like that of Mark Twain, greatly exaggerated?

13.4 Elaborate on how process teams work in an organization. Provide examples with which you are familiar.

13.5 Why is it necessary to add a process imperative to internal marketing?

13.6 How do the strategy and structure of the internationalizing firm evolve over time?

Part IV

The marketing management process and the order generation, fulfilment and service process

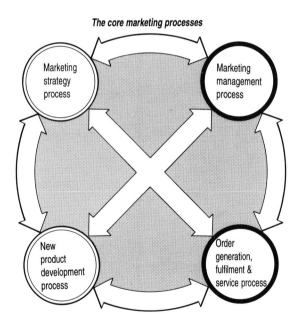

The core marketing processes

CHAPTER 14
Competitive positioning

▶ Analysis for competitive positioning
▶ The competitive positioning decision
▶ Necessary versus superior benefits

Marketing in action cases
Waterford Crystal positions a new international brand
Hugo Boss better suited for good business

ABOUT THIS CHAPTER

The marketing manager and marketing team make decisions about the choice of markets in which to compete, about strategic market planning and about how marketing activity is organized and integrated, in full consultation and cooperation with other functional managers in the firm. The competitive positioning decision is, however, the domain of the marketing department itself. Competitive positioning establishes the context for subsequent concerns about the particulars of product choice, pricing, promotion and distribution. It is rooted in the marketing management process.

Competitive positioning of a firm's product or service involves decisions about who precisely to serve in the chosen market and what particular benefits – or 'bundles' of benefits – to propose to that customer. The manager draws significantly on his or her knowledge of consumer behaviour. Customer purchase criteria and preferences for different competitive offerings must be understood. Three broad alternatives can then be considered: introducing new products or services to fill 'gaps' in the market; altering the position of an existing product; or altering buyers' perceptions of the market. In assessing each avenue the manager is mindful of the distinction between necessary and competitively superior benefits to the customer.

From market choice to positioning

In Chapter 11 the manner in which market choices are made was considered. The choice is a complex endeavour. The manager must select, at a broad generic level, between the strategies of (1) producing a product or service to meet the specialized needs of one segment, (2) producing two or more products to meet the needs of several separate segments, or (3) producing one product to provide general appeal across many segments.

The choice of a target market results in a clear identification of the target group with which the firm wishes to undertake transactions and develop a market relationship. The organization decides *who* to serve. The segmentation analysis leading to this decision yields an essential profile of target customers in terms of their buying behaviour and relevant individual or organizational characteristics – for example, their demographic, socio-economic, psychographic and gerontographic profile.

When the target customer group has been chosen the managerial challenge becomes that of *positioning* the company and its products or services relative to the preferences of the target group and relative to existing and anticipated competitive offerings. The objective is to serve the customer and to outperform competitors by focusing the company's competences in an appropriate manner.

Analysis for competitive positioning

To make a competitive positioning decision the manager must first know:

1 customer purchase criteria;
2 customer preferences concerning service or product performance on each criterion;
3 customer perceptions of competing suppliers and their products on each criterion.

Customer purchase criteria

The discussion of approaches to customer analysis in Chapter 6 stressed the value in application of a simple five-stage decision-making framework of buying behaviour. The third stage involved evaluation by the customer of the alternatives available to satisfy his or her consumption 'problem' or need. The importance of understanding the criteria that are used in evaluating the alternative products or services on offer was stressed, not only because of their central role in explaining customer behaviour, but also because an appreciation of the nature and use of these criteria is fundamental to the positioning decision. Evaluative criteria are usually best conceived of as benefits sought by customers from competing products or services. Customers do not buy replacement car tyres so much as they buy safety, conformity with the law, economy, quick fitting, a reputable brand, and so on. The identification of such criteria which consumers will use in making their evaluations not only allows us to understand their decision-making but also makes it possible to segment the market in terms of customers requiring similar 'bundles' of benefits and to develop products that incorporate the identified bundles. Normally there are several important purchase criteria involved in the buying behaviour of any one target customer segment. In general these may be categorized as:

- price-related criteria (e.g. purchase price, discounts, trade-in allowances, residual value, operating or lifecycle costs);
- performance-related (i.e. functional) criteria (e.g. speed, durability, length of life, precision, cleansing ability, service and support facilities);
- psycho-social criteria (e.g. acceptability to others, fit with self-concept, fit with reference group attitudes, reputability and dependability of supplier).

Specific criteria must, however, be identified on a product-by-product and segment-by-segment basis. For example, a study of the impact of customer service mix on the effectiveness of manufacturers' marketing strategies towards retailers might indicate that the criteria the retailers used in evaluating alternative suppliers included:

- quality of goods when received,
- delivery reliability,
- discounts offered,
- guarantees provided,
- aftersales service,
- credit terms.

The relative importance of these criteria may vary considerably depending on the product studied. Thus, as is demonstrated in Table 14.1, electrical appliance retailers, paint retailers and cigarette retailers might, for instance, attribute different weightings to each criterion and use some different criteria in evaluating their specific suppliers.

The criteria used in industrial purchasing may equally well be identified. For example, mobile refrigeration units used to provide temperature control in trucks carrying perishable foodstuffs are evaluated by purchasers using criteria such as purchase price, running cost, spare parts availability, international service network, expected down-time, and so on. In contrast, the purchase of a mass market consumer item such as a chocolate bar might revolve about the comparison of alternatives on criteria such as advertising imagery, texture, sweetness, wrapper design and perceived nutritional value.

Table 14.1 Rank order of importance of evaluative criteria

	Electrical retailers	Paint retailers	Cigarette retailers
1	Aftersales service received	Quality of goods received	Quality of goods
2	Quality of goods received	Discounts offered	Delivery reliability
3	Guarantees	Inventory reliability	Inventory reliability
4	Ease of contacting supplier	Delivery reliability	Speed of delivery
5	Discounts offered	Guarantees	Guarantees
6	Delivery reliability	Aftersales service	Sales representation

Generalizing from these specific examples, it is clear that for any product or service there exists a set of benefits important to the potential buyer. The extent to which any service or product is perceived to provide the relevant benefits lies at the heart of the customer evaluation process. Possession of an important desired benefit, such as long service intervals for a motor car, is used as a criterion in choosing between competing alternatives.

The first step in formulating a positioning approach is to identify these important purchase criteria. The manager should attempt to complete a basic listing of the criteria important to target customers through formal research or, at the least, through personal questioning of buyers and reflection on experience in marketing to them successfully.

Customer preferences

When criteria have been identified, the next step becomes that of identifying customer preferences concerning product performance on each criterion. So, if 'running cost' is established as an important criterion, the preferred level of running costs must then be measured. When this information is developed for each criterion, the marketer has a profile of the segment's 'ideal', or preferred, product. It is particularly useful to visualize such information in a simple map-like diagram such as the one illustrated in Figure 14.1a, in which the hypothetical preferences for a restaurant service in southern France are shown for a tourism market segment (in this case German holidaymakers). A map of customer preferences such as this is of enormous importance, as it documents explicitly an ideal service from the customer's viewpoint. In doing so it provides one of the essential benchmarks relative to which a service offering may then be positioned.

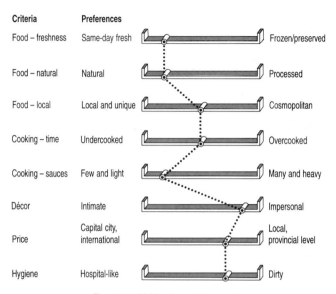

Criteria	Preferences		
Food – freshness	Same-day fresh		Frozen/preserved
Food – natural	Natural		Processed
Food – local	Local and unique		Cosmopolitan
Cooking – time	Undercooked		Overcooked
Cooking – sauces	Few and light		Many and heavy
Décor	Intimate		Impersonal
Price	Capital city, international		Local, provincial level
Hygiene	Hospital-like		Dirty

Figure 14.1 (a) Mapping customer preferences

Analytical and measurement techniques are available to undertake more scientific and detailed research and quantification of perceptions and preferences. These techniques are often referred to in general as perceptual mapping methods.[1] One of particular relevance is conjoint analysis. Conjoint analysis uses customer-derived information to determine the relative importance of one product or service attribute as opposed to another. Customers typically indicate that all attributes are important – in selecting a beer, they want price, alcohol content, taste, quality, aftertaste and image. Conjoint analysis asks them to make trade-offs between these various attributes – is one aspect desired enough to sacrifice another? If one aspect had to be sacrificed, which would it be? Extremely sensitive and useful information may be gathered in this way to assist the manager in choosing the most appropriate *combination* of attributes.

Customer perceptions of competing products

The next step that must be taken before making a positioning decision is to detail the perceived position of each competing product on each criterion. To continue with the restaurant example, the manager of the restaurant should plot on to the map the performance of competing restaurants in the local tourism area (for example, the area accessible to German boating holidaymakers in the Canal du Midi region).The positioning of two hypo-

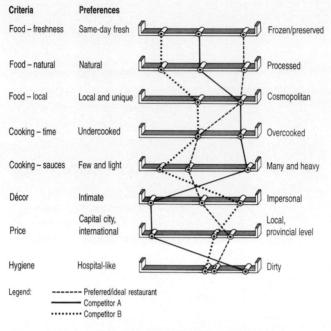

278 *Strategy and process in marketing*

Criteria | **Preferences**

Food – freshness | Same-day fresh → Frozen/preserved
Food – natural | Natural → Processed
Food – local | Local and unique → Cosmopolitan
Cooking – time | Undercooked → Overcooked
Cooking – sauces | Few and light → Many and heavy
Décor | Intimate → Impersonal
Price | Capital city, international → Local, provincial level
Hygiene | Hospital-like → Dirty

Legend: - - - - - Preferred/ideal restaurant
———— Competitor A
·········· Competitor B

(b) Customer perceptions and preferences

thetical competing restaurants is illustrated in Figure 14.1b. Significant marketing implications of the analysis now begin to appear. How the two establishments differ is readily visible, as is their ability (or inability) to match customer preferences. Both have paid little attention to a desire for natural fresh foods, and *A* has particularly misjudged consumer needs by preparing food with many and heavy sauces in an intimate and highly priced environment whereas segment preferences are in fact for few and light sauces in a relatively impersonal environment and at reasonable prices.

The competitive positioning decision

Armed with such information the marketing team next decides how to position its own offering in the market. The position chosen is of a relative nature. It makes marketing sense in so far as it is chosen relative to the identified customer preferences and competitor performance on each important criterion and relative to the company's capabilities. In general, three alternatives are available in considering a positioning decision. The manager may choose to:

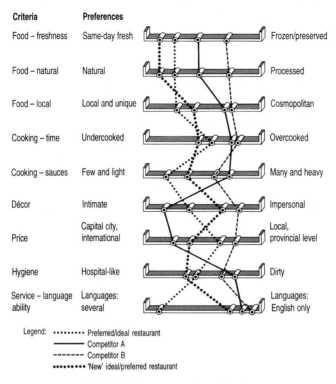

Criteria / Preferences

Food – freshness	Same-day fresh ... Frozen/preserved
Food – natural	Natural ... Processed
Food – local	Local and unique ... Cosmopolitan
Cooking – time	Undercooked ... Overcooked
Cooking – sauces	Few and light ... Many and heavy
Décor	Intimate ... Impersonal
Price	Capital city, international ... Local, provincial level
Hygiene	Hospital-like ... Dirty
Service – language ability	Languages: several ... Languages: English only

Legend: ········ Preferred/ideal restaurant
——— Competitor A
------- Competitor B
•••••••• 'New' ideal/preferred restaurant

(c) Modified customer perceptions and preferences

1 introduce new products or services to fill gaps in the market;
2 alter the position of an existing product or service;
3 alter buyers' perceptions of the market by:
   (a) introducing new criteria,
   (b) changing the importance they attribute to existing criteria.

Introduce new products to fill market gaps

Returning once again to the restaurant example, the positioning analysis suggested a gap in the market: an unsatisfied need for very fresh natural foods with some degree of local uniqueness. An entrepreneur considering opening a new restaurant could develop a product to fill this gap while also providing the other benefits desired by the target customer group. In doing this the new restaurant would address itself to an unsatisfied demand and differentiate itself clearly from competing restaurants. In a more general way, the success of ethnic, health food and vegetarian restaurants illustrates how such market gaps may be exploited.

The truly market-focused firm seeks to exploit new emerging needs as societies change economically, culturally, socially and environmentally. The challenge is to identify the needs, develop a product that delivers value appropriate to these needs and then to carry it via a brand that communicates a unique proposition to consumers. Flora margarine, created by Unilever, provides a classic example. It was originally created in 1964. Its developers foresaw a change in life-styles towards healthier eating. The brand was perhaps slightly ahead of its time. But the company persisted with it, adapting its positioning until the vision became the reality. Within ten years Flora had taken off – and it hasn't looked back. It has consistently been one of the top ten brands in the United Kingdom and the brand concept (although not the name) is worldwide.

Waterford Crystal, part of Waterford Wedgwood plc, provides another instance of an emerging gap in a market skilfully and profitably captured. A major recession in its principal market, the United States, saw its high income target consumers start to trade down, move to lower price purchasing points in the crystal market and modify their tastes. To capitalize on this trend, the company launched a new brand, Marquis, designed in a more contemporary way and positioned in a lower price tier of the premium crystal market (see Exhibit 14.1). It is generally true that innovative and entrepreneurial activity will be more successful to the extent that it is based on a decision to fill a market gap, thereby providing customers with something they desire but cannot obtain from existing suppliers. In doing this the marketer secures an immediate monopoly position until competitors discover how to imitate the innovation.

Exhibit 14.1 *Marketing in action case*

Waterford Crystal positions a new international brand

Waterford Crystal is a renowned name in the international tabletop industry and one of the world's leading brands in the premium crystal market. It was faced in the early 1990s, among other problems, with a major recession in its principal market, the United States, which saw its high income target consumers starting to trade down, move to lower price purchasing points in the crystal market, and modify their tastes. The company responded with the launch of a new brand, Marquis, designed in a more contemporary way and positioned in a lower price tier within the premium crystal market.

Company research indicated that, while the Waterford Crystal brand continued to be highly regarded and in a sense to enjoy superstar status, there was a consumer demand for products at lower price points and with a more transitional design appeal. This encouraged Waterford to forge a new positioning strategy in the US premium crystal business. This market contained three price tiers: 'We saw

Waterford going to market with a top tier that was Waterford Crystal – our traditional range of products but with some price and design repositioning to respond to changes in consumer taste and to re-enter some of the price points we had vacated some years earlier through our overly aggressive pricing strategy,' comments Redmond O'Donoghue, sales and marketing director.

However, this top tier accounted for less than a third of the premium crystal market measured in both price and design terms. Thus despite all of Waterford's success in world markets, it had no product offering in what constituted 70 per cent of the premium crystal market. This second tier was now addressed by an entirely new brand of crystal – a brand that would compete in the price segment immediately below Waterford's segment (which the company dominated); a brand that would be less traditional in design terms; a design that would appeal to younger consumers, particularly young brides (and the vibrant US bridal registration business where brides submit a list of desired gifts to a leading store from which friends and relatives choose); a brand that would conform to Waterford's unparalleled quality requirements; and a brand that would be *endorsed* by Waterford.

This brand became known as 'Marquis by Waterford Crystal'. Less than two years after conceiving the notion of creating the first new brand in Waterford's 200-year history, Marquis garnered the number 6 brand slot in the US crystal sales chart; and the addition of Marquis to the company's brand portfolio translated into a doubling in overall US bridal registrations for Waterford products. Not only was this achieved with great speed, but also without cannibalizing sales of its mother brand, Waterford Crystal.[2]

Alter the position of an existing product

In the case of the restaurant example, if a new restaurant had been opened to fill the market gap identified, it might well transpire that after several years not only would competitors have learned of their own weaknesses, but the customer group might also have changed its preferences. A mapping of the new state of consumer preferences is visualized in Figure 14.1c, showing a changed structure of perceptions and preferences. The positioning challenge now faced by the restaurateur is to alter perceptions of the restaurant's position so as to achieve a better fit with new customer preferences and to obtain some distinct advantage relative to competition. The importance now attached by customers to having restaurant service in their own language presents an opportunity, while it is also clear that gaps have been left in the market by the shift in consumer preferences towards lower price and more intimate surroundings. Our restaurateur's major current strength lies in the provision of unique local food. He might therefore consider repositioning his service by building on this strength and moving to fill the identified gaps.

The repositioning of packaged soup as 'fresh soup' distributed in tetra packs through the chill counter of supermarkets is a further illustration of this approach. When launching its new Marquis range of crystalware, Waterford Wedgwood adroitly repositioned its long-established Waterford Crystal at the same time to increase market share successfully in an essentially static crystal market. This involved adding a more transitional look to the Waterford Crystal range, on the way to contemporary styling but without straying into Marquis's design territory. It added more visual cues to Waterford – gold banding on the rims of glasses, for instance, and coloured products, like its sailboat, shells and hand warmers. These product, price and design initiatives provided product offerings in a much wider span of Waterford's tier of the premium crystal market, enabled an expansion of sales volumes and a gain in market share from competitors (see Exhibit 14.1).

Changing an established competitive position is not always a feasible option because of the difficulty of changing the perceptions and attitudes that customers have learned over time. For this reason many companies will choose to relaunch a modified product, sometimes with a new name and identity, rather than attempt to reposition the old product in the consumer's mind. Despite this caveat, it must be recognized that since all markets are dynamic, owing to changing customer tastes and competitive activity, some degree of continuous repositioning is virtually a necessity. Where this repositioning takes place gradually – for example, in the form of a steady increase in product quality – the company will almost always benefit. Where the repositioning is sudden and major, however, and asks the customer to accept the credibility of a major change in product or service performance, the weight of past experience may render the new position unbelievable, resulting in rejection and sales decline.

Alter buyers' perceptions of the market

Two approaches may be engaged to pursue this avenue. One is to introduce new evaluative criteria into the customer's decision-making. In marketing truck tyres to fleet owners, for example, purchase price, fitting service and number of retreads were traditionally critical criteria. With rapid escalation in the cost of running a truck in the last twenty years, however, the more innovative tyre companies and retailers quickly introduced a new criterion – tyre running cost. The factors determining operating costs associated with the use of a tyre, range from the expected life of the tyre (extended with the introduction of truck radials) to its rolling resistance (which affects fuel consumption) and the number of retreads (while most operators demanded two retreads, many traditional tyres failed before even one retread).

Innovative marketers introduced radial tyres designed to reduce rolling resistance and to ensure at least one retread. By insisting on better quality from their manufacturing divisions and by educating trucking companies to the role that tyres play in their overall operating costs, they introduced a new decision criterion of lifecycle cost and placed their own new tyre ranges in a strong competitive position. Moreover, in some markets they could trade off a higher initial purchase price against the expectation of lower lifetime running costs.

The second approach appropriate to altering the buyer's perceptions involves changing the importance that customers attribute to existing criteria. The discussion so far has generally assumed that each criterion used by a consumer in evaluating competing products carries equal importance or weighting. This is, in fact, seldom true. It is far more common to find that in any customer decision involving multiple criteria, some criteria will be significantly more important than others.

These 'weightings', attributed to the various criteria, are open to influence by the marketing company. A toothpaste manufacturer may choose to influence consumers to attribute extra weight to decay prevention, as opposed to cosmetic effect, thereby shifting market demand towards brands that contain decay prevention ingredients and that are promoted on this basis, and away from brands that stress 'whiteness', cosmetic and social impact benefits. The growth of toothpaste brands formulated to combat plaque illustrates this process. Similarly, the repositioning of Lucozade as a sport and fitness-related drink as well as its traditional appeal to those seeking a health restorative suggests how marketers may seek to broaden perceptions of a product and reposition an older brand to deliver on newer needs.

Lucozade was launched in 1927 as a tonic for convalescents. In the 1980s with sport and life-style becoming ever more popular the opportunity was seized to reposition the brand to satisfy a youth fitness culture. Doing this opened up a whole new and much larger market and with this new look and more dynamic advertising its growth has been dramatic. A new generation has grown into the brand while knowing little of its history. The key to the revitalization of the brand was spotting the trend and finding a popular positioning. Other drinks companies, e.g. cider and cidona firms, have followed suit – brands which have been around for many years are now changing their positioning to reflect the way values have changed and to ensure a continuing market presence. The fashion clothing industry often pursues similar strategies. Exhibit 14.2 narrates how and why the

Boss brand of men's fashion clothing reconstructed itself into three brands, each offering a particular set of values to different customers.

Exhibit 14.2	*Marketing in action case*

Hugo Boss better suited for good business

Just three months after taking over as chief executive officer in March 1993, Peter Littmann split the Boss product into three new brands to find a new market role for the company whose branded clothes had become synonymous in the 1980s with the yuppy market. Littmann, an outsider to the clothing market and a teacher of management, marketing and marketing research at the University of Cologne as well as *professeur honoraire* at the University of Witten/Herdecke, took a fresh view of the consumer for men's clothing in the 1990s.

It was believed that yuppie bosses wanted a Boss suit to show their power and wealth. The beginnings of the 1990s, however, saw the fall of the yuppie and a Boss searching for a role in the new, more caring 1990s. To find it, the new owner, Marzotto of Italy, which took control in 1991, went outside the fashion industry and headhunted Peter Littmann for the post of president and CEO. The move was a shock to the fashion establishment. Littmann, who was born in Prague, moved from Vorwerk & Co., where he was president and CEO of the carpet division. At Littmann's first board meeting, the decision was taken to create three brands from the previous sole Boss name. It marked a fundamental change in the company. Boss had suited the macho outlook of the 1980s. Even the name could have been tailor-made for its position in the market. Boss meant being the boss.

The 1990s are different. 'I believe that women emancipated themselves in the 1960s and 1970s,' says Littmann. 'Men are becoming more individual and self-confident – I would like to be different from my colleagues. This means we have to approach different target groups in different ways. If you just have one brand, it is very difficult to do this, so we needed to split the brand.' In the 1990s, he says, customers do not want to make a statement about being the boss. Teamwork, friendship and family values are more important than money and conspicuous consumption.

The first move was to change the name of the company from the stern statement of Boss to the more friendly Hugo Boss. The next move was to split the range into three brands. The three brands devised by Boss are equal but aimed at different types of people. The new Hugo Boss brand is for the traditional, conservative businessman: 'The Hugo brand is more focused. The target is a man who is probably younger, and is very interested in fashion. He is not the type of man a mother would like as a son-in-law. While the Hugo Boss customer would take his wife or girlfriend along to help him choose, the Hugo customer does not need anyone to reassure him.' The third brand, named Baldessarini after Boss's

Austrian-born chief designer, is a more expensive line of handmade clothes from the best fabrics. The choice of the Italian-sounding name was deliberate and this line competes with Italian designer clothes.[3]

Necessary versus superior benefits

Finally, the fact that several competitors have all converged on some of the ideal points of consumers will usually be visible on any competitive positioning map – i.e. they all provide an equally satisfactory response to one or more of the customer's criteria. Where this is the case the market-focused organization must understand that while performance on this criterion is necessary to compete effectively, it yields no competitive advantage. For example, consumers now assume that any watch they buy will keep time with considerable accuracy and electronic watch technology makes this benefit universally available. To compete in the watch market one must therefore market a watch that keeps time, but there is no competitive advantage in this feature – it is a necessity for entry to the market but no aid to success. Companies do not always make this distinction and can fool themselves into thinking that having a required feature is the same as having a basis for superior competitive advantage.

The same point must also be made about the nature of the company's capability or competence which generates a perceived benefit for a customer. A firm may have a core competence in a particular area of business activity. But so also may another competitor or competitors. It is a distinctive competence, one that competitors cannot easily replicate, which confers true positional superiority. It is the task of marketing to seek ways to build the competence of the function into a source of competitive advantage by deepening and extending its knowledge resources and skills. If it can encourage other functions in the firm to do likewise, distinctive competences – and their concomitant benefits to customers – will follow.

REVIEW QUESTIONS

14.1 The competitive positioning decision is part of the marketing management process. Why?

14.2 What are the three analytical requirements for effective positioning? Explain each one.

14.3 What positioning approaches are available to the manager? Find an example of the application of each and discuss its effectiveness.

14.4 Under what circumstances might you consider attempting to alter buyers' perceptions of the market? How could such a strategy be implemented?

CHAPTER 15

Product choice

- ▶ What is a product or service?
- ▶ Branding
- ▶ Brand equity
- ▶ Product lifecycle
- ▶ Product portfolio analysis

Marketing in action case
España: an international tourist brand

ABOUT THIS CHAPTER

When the marketing team has made the strategic choice of target market and decided on the competitive positioning of the product or service in this segment, the time has arrived to develop a marketing mix programme – the so-called 4 Ps. The product element of the marketing mix consists of the physical, service and psychological benefits that buyers demand. Each of these sets of attributes must be carefully designed and balanced with each other, and the complete bundle of attributes may then be branded so as to communicate to customers assurances about availability, consistency and value.

Branding essentially attempts to decommoditize a product – adding value to it in some way that will be perceived by the customer who will in turn confer his or her purchasing loyalty. Multi-branding, brand stretching and the development of distributors' own brands (DOBs) are important. A process approach encourages firms to deepen brand equity and view branding as a multidisciplinary task.

Managing the evolution of products over time is aided by the product lifecycle concept, which stresses the changing performance and strategic characteristics of products as they are launched, grow, mature and decline. It also underlines the temporary nature of most competitive advantages and leads growth-oriented firms to consider the creation and management of a product mix. In a multi-product company, product portfolio techniques become important managerial instruments.

From who and *how* to *what*

Two foundation stones of successful marketing practice have now been addressed. The market has been segmented and the target market(s) chosen. Within the chosen target market a competitive position has been selected for the company's product or service. This position locates it in relation to customers' needs and competitors' offerings. The company has therefore decided *who* to serve and *how* to outperform the competition.

The next step in the marketing management process involves what are generally called marketing mix decisions. The marketing mix refers to the four essential elements of a marketing programme that are necessary to execute the strategic market choice and the competitive positioning decisions. Most commonly referred to as the 4 Ps – product, price, promotion and place – the components of the marketing mix represent vital and interdependent decisions.[1]

The origin of the term marketing mix is attributable to an analogy with cooking. To bake a cake the cook must have all the necessary ingredients and then mix them in correct proportion. So too with marketing. All four elements of the mix are essential, but must be used in an appropriate balance with each other. Just as you cannot make a marketing decision without considering price, so too you cannot decide the price without careful consideration of the product's quality and the way in which it will be distributed and promoted. In this and the next three chapters each element of the mix will be reviewed under the headings product, price, communication and selling (including promotion) and distribution (including both channels and physical systems of distribution).

What is a product or service?

The words service or product will be used interchangeably, as all the issues raised in this chapter apply equally to both. From the marketer's point of view, a product is *a bundle of physical, service and psychological benefits designed to satisfy a customer's needs and related wants*. The physical aspect is the tangible, performance-related element of the product – the bodywork, transmission, engine, wheels, etc. of a motor car, or the payroll programme written by a computer software house. The service aspect consists of all the product benefits that make the physical product saleable – sales assistance, warranties, and so on. The psychological benefits consist of the symbolic aspects of the product and its brand or manufacturer's name – its reputation and associations with important or symbolic people, values or uses.

The physical product

Good decisions concerning the physical aspect of any product are usually a reflection of good design – an area too narrowly understood by many marketers. Design decisions incorporate choices about functional characteristics, structural characteristics and aesthetic characteristics.[2]

Functional characteristics are those that provide the expected performance benefits to the customer – the length of life of a car tyre and its grip under various driving conditions, or the warmth and washability of an item of clothing. Guaranteeing that a product has the correct functional characteristics demands that the marketing, design, manufacturing and R&D areas work very closely together. A child's anorak that is poorly cut or inadequately stitched will not perform when in use. The result is angry customers and a declining reputation for the manufacturing company. The development of new and better functional characteristics is often a key to competitive success, and many companies pursue it as the basis of their product strategy. During the 1980s many European dairy companies decommoditized milk by offering a range of improved product variants, such as better-tasting, creamier, low fat and vitamin-enriched milk. These products involved designing new farm-to-customer chilled delivery systems. The innovating firms enjoyed considerable first mover advantage. The search for better functional performance is continuous and demands effective cross-disciplinary relationships within a company.

Structural characteristics can deliver the functional features of the product in a variety of different ways – in different shapes, sizes, colours, materials, and so on. The innovating dairy companies pioneered the inherent space and stacking benefits of Tetra Pak packaging, a development which increasingly took milk off the doorstep and onto the supermarket shelf. The children's ice-pop is regularly reinvented in a structural sense by companies seeking positional advantage in this lucrative market, producing bizarre combinations of shape, colour and texture. The structural form of electronic products such as computer terminals is increasingly a basis for competition as manufacturers search for more cost-effective materials, easier-to-use keyboards or finger-input mechanisms.

Aesthetic characteristics are most obviously important for fashion dependent products where visual quality is extremely important. Aesthetics are, however, an important part of any product or service design, as evidenced by the impact of design on products such as Cross pens, the uniquely rounded Japanese car shapes that emerged in the early 1990s, the styling of Gucci leather items, and the visually pleasing and distinctive yellow, egg-shaped form of Atlas-Copco's mobile air compressors.

Service attributes

The service attributes that accompany and back up a product and that are central to a service are, from the marketing perspective, integral to product choice. These services may include guarantees, warranties, installation, training, maintenance, spare parts assurance, replacement, technical advice and upgrading or updating facilities. In markets where it is difficult to differentiate the functional aspects of the product from competitors' offerings, and especially in industrial markets, service features are often the key to market success. Investment in providing appropriate service features is likely to pay off in customer loyalty and market share gains. The battle for market share in earth-moving equipment or in long-distance haulage trucks revolves significantly about rapid and unfailing spare parts availability. Caterpillar, for example, has been a world leader in earth-moving with a spare parts policy of 48 hours' delivery in any market it serves in the world and an ability to fill 97 per cent of emergency parts orders within 24 hours. Warranty and guarantee arrangements are critically important in competition among car manufacturers as consumers' expectations of product quality, reliability and rust-proofing rise continually.

For services such as banking, air travel or retailing, service attributes are, of course, the very heart of what is offered to the market, but all these also require physical attributes too – bank branches, automatic teller machines, aircraft, food, shops, merchandising displays, and so on. The difference between products and services is much more a question of the balance between physical and service attributes than anything else: all services are partly product and all products are partly service.

The psychological product

Customers buy psychological benefits as well as the more tangible physical and service benefits of any product. This is especially true of mass market consumer items. In the jockeying for position in the lager market, gains by the various brewers result from advertising campaigns featuring desirable lifestyles, novel situations or storylines rather than changes in physical or service aspects of the product. The Marlboro cigarette brand is the largest selling brand in the world, primarily owing to imagery of the 'great outdoors' and of masculinity encapsulated in the cowboy symbol. The strategy of the marketers of Bailey's Irish Cream Liqueur, aimed at creating and defending a global brand position, has stressed the creation of psychological associations for the product with a relaxed, sophisticated consumer life-style through aggressive investment in coordinated advertising, packaging and merchandising images.

For some products, image is all. Beer, cigarettes, soft drinks and confectionery are typical examples of products that customers differentiate primarily on psychological grounds. Thus blind-taste tests of competing beer brands will show that large numbers of consumers cannot distinguish one brand from another when their names are concealed. Yet when brand names are provided, many of these same consumers will insist that there are radical differences in taste. The name and all the associations it has created with various symbols and images overwhelm perception of physical characteristics.

Psychological product characteristics are most obvious in the kinds of products discussed above. They are, however, a vital part of almost all products and services. The psychological attributes of industrial products such as machine tools, turbines, gears or electronic components are vital to market success. Here the attributes are usually built around market perceptions of the supplying company – its reputation for technical excellence, delivery reliability, customer advice and problem-solving, and so on. The competitive position of products from new companies is sometimes weakened by worries in buyers' minds concerning the frequent problems encountered with entrepreneurial ventures – patchy quality assurance, part-delivery of orders or unreliable supply. A marketer may find these psychological associations already established, irrespective of his or her planned performance, and has to work doubly hard to establish a good image.

Customers pay for relevant psychological product attributes. It is therefore quite possible to add value to a product through design and delivery of its psychological features. It is important to note this. Value inheres not just in tangible, functional characteristics. Most of the money consumers pay for a perfume product is for its psychological content and as a result most of the investment in cosmetics is in advertising, packaging and merchandising and not in the physical product or its manufacture. Some commentators will dismiss marketing activity of this nature as wasteful and frivolous while others will argue that it is necessary to enable consumer choice and market efficiency. Ultimately, the question revolves about whether customers perceive value in benefits created in this manner and whether they have freedom to make other choices. Where consumer choice is ultimately sovereign, trivial, false or unethical psychological claims will prove ineffective in all but the short term.

The psychological attributes of services are most often created by the service experience – by the human contact that is so central to most services. Jan Carlzon, as President of Scandinavian Air System (SAS), popularized the term 'moments of truth' to characterize the moment of contact between a customer and the provider of a service – a ticket desk clerk, a steward or stewardess, a telephonist handling an inquiry. Because services are very often 'produced' on the spot by service company employees, these personnel must be trained and have the relevant ability to convey the psychological as well as the more tangible benefits of the service they provide. Thus, airline cabin staff must not only provide passengers with whatever food and drink is included in the flight but also with the sense of being valued and cared for as customers.

All marketers, and especially those in durable consumer goods and industrial goods, must remember to design and deliver the non-tangible product benefits that customers inevitably demand. Excellent physical and service characteristics alone are seldom enough to guarantee customer satisfaction and competitive effectiveness. Achieving the seamless balance of these product components, in the manner of a Club Med holiday offering, a Gillette shaving product, or a piece of Sony electronic equipment, is a complex but ultimately rewarding endeavour.

Branding

Branding a product through use of a name, symbol, design or a combination of these is a fundamental step in differentiating a product from those of competitors and in communicating to customers in a shorthand manner the kind of benefits they may expect to derive from using the product. A brand name encapsulates the physical, service and psychological attributes of a marketer's product. Think of the wealth of product information and expectations conveyed by motor car brand names such as Saab, Rolls Royce, Rover, Volvo, Renault or Volkswagen, or among microcomputer suppliers such as Toshiba, Compaq, Olivetti, Philips or Apple. That a carefully and well-developed brand name is a major asset for any company is best illustrated by the money value placed on it in the event of an acquisition or takeover deal. In 1988 Nestlé, the world's largest food manufacturer, paid £2.5 billion for Rowntree Mackintosh, a leading UK confectionery manufacturer. Nestlé effectively paid five times the stock market value of Rowntree – an extraordinary premium by normal financial standards. The reasoning behind its decision was the power and reputation of the brands created and nurtured by Rowntree Mackintosh over the years, e.g. Kit-Kat, Polo, After Eight.

Although the word 'brand' originated in Europe in the Middle Ages as a distinguish mark or 'burn' on craft products to distinguish one craftsman from another, modern usage dates from the turn of this century and the beginning of mass manufacturing. At that time the dominant force in the distribution sector was the wholesaler, whose power base was due to his ability to extract solid margins from weak manufacturers who had no direct access to consumers and widely scattered small retailers with no bargaining power. A fortuitous coincidence of a number of key manufacturers who intrinsically understood the nature of brands, and the emergence of the mass media tilted the balance of power. In 1881 Harley Procter, one of the founders of Procter & Gamble ran the first advertisement for Ivory soap. Full of imagery and brand claims – '99.44% pure' – the brand was an immediate success. Meanwhile in Britain, Sunlight soap was launched four years later by a company which ultimately evolved as Unilever. By establishing strong evocative brand names backed up by unique selling propositions manufacturers eroded the power of wholesalers and became the dominant force in consumer markets for the next three-quarters of a century.

Gardner and Levy, writing in *Harvard Business Review* in 1955, argued presciently that

> a brand name is more than a label employed to differentiate among the manufacturers of a product. It is a complex symbol that represents a variety of ideas and attributes. It tells the consumer many things, not only by the way it sounds (and its literal meaning, if it has one), but more important via the body of associations it has built up and acquired as a public object over a period of time. The net result is a public image, a character, or personality that may be more important for the overall status (and sales) of the brand than many technical facts about the product.[3]

Thus brands represent not only the physical product and its service attributes, but also a set of emotional associations which are built up over time in the minds of consumers through the brand name, packaging, advertising, PR, promotion and other methods of communication used to inform the public of its value.

The addition of emotional values creates a complete personality so that brands can often almost be envisaged by consumers as real people. Although this aspect of branding is now much more clearly understood, there is still some confusion surrounding the roles that brands play in people's lives. This is due partly to the fact that different brands play different roles, but also the same brands can play different roles for consumers in different purchase or usage occasions. In general, brands are used by consumers to fulfil the following three functions:

1 *Convenience* – ease of decision-making; in many markets branding plays a low level but often crucial role. Faced with a range of alternative products where some have had a degree of branding or added value from marketing communication and others have no provenance at all, consumers are not only likely to choose the brand which they have heard of, but are likely to pay a little bit extra. Here

the brand offers a solution to a familiar purchasing dilemma – how to decide between a variety of choice.

2 *Guarantee* – here branding operates at a slightly higher level of consciousness and offers a genuine bargain to consumers by a kind of unspoken guarantee – 'as proof of the care and attention we took in making this product we also took equal care and attention with the packaging, advertising and promotion'. Consumers in many markets are forced into judging the book by the cover.

3 *Personal statement* – branding operates at its highest level when the choice of a particular brand in any market is also making a personal statement about the consumer. 'Brands not only frame the environment in which I live, but also enrobe me and by doing so help depict who I am.'

While marketing managers have no choice about whether to design and manage the physical, service and psychological attributes of a product, they may choose to brand or not brand a product. Sometimes this is at the request of the distribution channel. Jewellers, for example, often prefer to carry silverware that is unbranded (except for the hallmark if solid silver) to give the impression to customers that they are still in the business of producing silverware. Silverware producers, in contrast, are probably better off if they can create a brand name and have customers coming to a jeweller's shop asking for their products by name, such as Christofle of Denmark.

This example illustrates how branding is related to the creation of market power. For a marketer who must distribute products through middlemen or retailers, the successful creation of a brand name creates power over intermediaries. If customers come to shops or wholesalers demanding a named product, the middleman will typically feel compelled to carry the product in stock. If no brand has been created, the customer will ask for the product type and the wholesaler or retailer is in a powerful position to stock and promote the product that best serves his own needs.

As we saw in Chapter 2, in the context of the business system, the emergence of branding in a market usually coincides with its transition from a commodity to a non-commodity status. In a true commodity market, all products perform similarly and price is generally the only factor determining sales; the customer buys the cheapest. Branding may be seen essentially as an attempt to decommoditize a product – trying to add value to it in some way that will be perceived by the customer who will in turn confer his or her loyalty on it rather than a competing product, *and* pay a premium to reflect this added value. Earlier, it was described how during the 1980s many European dairy companies decommoditized milk by offering a range of improved product variants, such as better-tasting, creamier milk, low fat milk and vitamin-enriched milk. The same is true of many other food products where firms add value to the basic raw material by further processing. Petrol companies continually seek to win the loyalty of car drivers by claiming that their latest formulation offers genuine performance advantage, so breaking the shackles of a mere commodity.

In industrial and in many service markets, the producer company's name frequently acts as a brand identification and is carefully nurtured to perform many of the functions of a brand. The name Siemens, for example, is perceived among engineers and purchasers of electrical engineering equipment as standing for quality, reliability, technical excellence, advice and aftersales service. Many small businesses in industrial markets throw away the opportunity to build customer loyalty and customer endorsement of their products by paying no attention to building their 'brand' or company image through product labelling, promotional material and the creation of brand names for individual products. And this is often not a particularly difficult job, amounting to no more than establishing a consistent firm logo, livery and advertising support. Branding concepts are being increasingly applied to other sectors, for example, not-for-profit organizations, voluntary agencies and even countries themselves. Exhibit 15.1 provides an interesting outline of how Spain has marketed itself successfully as a national tourism brand.

Exhibit 15.1   *Marketing in action case*

España: an international tourist brand

For over a decade, Spain has been developing and positioning its national brand, recognizing the importance of managing the market perception of Spain as a tourist destination. In doing so, it has addressed the issues involved in capturing the essence of a country in a sustained marketing programme, in involving the travel trade, and in managing its marketing communications. The Spanish government has invested heavily in the brand of the country over this period, and foreign visitors have increased by over a third. Other countries, such as Greece, Australia and Malaysia followed suit in developing such national tourist brands.

In 1983, the Spanish tourist board commissioned a strategic plan for Spanish tourism. It set a European precedent by becoming the first country to brand itself consistently and invest in a comprehensive promotional campaign. Two important elements in the branding concept were identified from an investigation of the country's tourism product and the market's needs: diversity and sun.

Basic branding concepts included the name, logo and the development of a unique value proposition. As it was branding the country as a tourist destination, the nation's name – España – was used. The logo was based on a work, *Sun*, by the famous Catalan abstract painter, Miró. It suggested themes relating to holidays and to Spain, mainly the sun, but also the beach, nature, fiestas and abstract art. Thus, it stressed the brand values of sun and diversity contained in the proposition: 'Spain . . . Everything under the sun.' Advertisements highlighted this diversity, including golf, cuisine, scenery, tradition and culture.

In 1992 Spain reviewed its positioning in line with changing tourist market trends and to build on major events in Spain. The objective was further to boost, not only the sun and beach mass tourism, but also other regions and products. 'España . . . Passion for life' was the new positioning statement, developing a new aspect of brand personality for Spain. Dynamism and creativity were added as additional brand values. This enabled the brand to be repositioned in consumer perceptions in light of emerging competition from other destinations, such as Greece, Turkey and long-haul destinations.

Using the 'Passion for life' concept, all the activities, such as sports, entertainment, leisure, culture, craftsmanship, cuisine and creativity, contribute to tourism. Again, award-winning advertisements in print and televisual media represented different tourist products, including art, sport, fun, the climate, nature, resorts, cuisine, imagination, e.g. paradors, the Santiago pilgrim trail, fishing in the Valencia region, and so on.

In executing such a branding strategy, collaboration and coordination between public and private sectors were crucial factors. Further synergy was created by international events. A key feature of Spain's success has been the ability to integrate specific tourist products and events, – such as the Olympic Games, EXPO '92 and the European Cultural Capital, into the existing national brand. This has a dual benefit. The national brand offers an 'umbrella' branding for these events, and the events also build into the values of the brand itself. It also integrates with developments in the country's tourist infrastructure and benefits local communities.[4]

Multi-branding

If a company succeeds in establishing a brand name in the marketplace, it has a valuable asset. It often seeks to widen this brand franchise into other related markets and/or products. Multi-branding occurs when a company targets several brands into the same broad market. In some cases it will carry the same name over the brand family; in others, it will choose to use independent brand names.

The growth of multi-branding derives from a number of reasons. The most important is the increasing segmentation of markets. In the earliest stage of the development of a market a single brand will often be sufficient. Demand is normally homogeneous and too small to warrant a company employing a multi-branding strategy. Then, as the market develops, new segments emerge, consumer requirements fragment and multi-branding opportunities occur. As customer needs diverge, differentiated distribution channels evolve, providing a further stimulus to separate branding. Further momentum has been given to multi-branding by the development of new flexible manufacturing and delivery techniques and more imaginative out-sourcing arrangements. These have lowered the cost of product variety and specialized customer segments can be accessed by new targeted marketing and advertising media.

Multi-branding can be categorized into two types: horizontal and vertical. Horizontal multi-branding is aimed at differentiating distribution channels rather than consumers. By giving different retailers or distributors specific brands, the manufacturer aims to increase distribution and market share. Horizontal multi-branding is often low-cost because the brands may have only cosmetic differences, for example, the retailer or distributor's name along with different packaging being put on the manufacturer's existing product.

Vertical multi-branding targets different customer groups and uses differentiated branding strategies. In this case the distribution channels may or may not be the same. Vertical multi-branding is more powerful than horizontal. Its major problem is often the cost of building distinct brand identities. Developing a brand image for a new marque of car is significantly more expensive than simply stamping a retailer's name on a white good. However, if successful, it is likely to be much more profitable for the company. Thus, while vertical multi-branding can generate sizeably greater revenues in the longer term, it offers fewer opportunities than horizontal multi-branding for economies of scale and shared purchasing, marketing, distribution and service costs.

In servicing these different markets, customer segments and channels, a company can use an existing name or promote a different brand name. *Brand extension* means using a brand name, successfully established for one segment, to enter another within the same broad market. Kellogg's provides a prime illustration of this in the cereals market, as does Pierre Cardin in fashion lifestyle products. *Brand stretching* involves transferring the winning brand name to quite different markets. Marks & Spencer moved from clothes into foods and again into financial services. Mars moved from sweets to ice cream. The Virgin name covers air travel, music, computers, software and drinks.

As markets segment and a multi-brand approach suggests itself as more effective than a single-brand strategy, a cautionary caveat must be entered. Companies must ask themselves an important question: Is the new brand offering likely to impact negatively on sales of the existing one? If so, by how much? Such *cannibalization* may be disastrous for the company. The positioning and market strength of the flagship brand may be damaged significantly by the attempt to multi-brand. There may even be a case of double jeopardy if the new introduction itself fails to take off and justify the investment in new product development, channels of distribution and promotion.

Exhibit 14.1 (p.280) described how Waterford Crystal, one of the world's leading brands in the premium crystal market, successfully launched a new brand called Marquis by Waterford, designed in a more contemporary way and positioned in a lower price tier of the premium crystal market. This new product did not cannabilize the existing Waterford product range; rather, it afforded an opportunity strategically to reposition this range. Companies considering a multi-brand approach must do so with considerable circumspection. Rigorous market research must establish that there is not only a new market segment, but that this segment has a viable dimension worthy of a specially targeted approach. Any danger of cannibalization must be minimal. Therein lies the nub of a successful multi-brand strategy.

Distributors' own brands

If manufacturers eroded the power of wholesalers and retailers towards the end of the last century and became the dominant force in consumer markets for the next three-quarters of this century, retailers have won a new strength and bargaining power over the last two decades. Throughout most of Europe retailing structures have become concentrated and the grocery and clothing business systems have become smaller with fewer intermediate players. One result, if not also a cause, of this concentrated retailer power has been the growth in private label or distributors' own brands (DOBs).

These first appeared when the larger supermarkets and clothing retailers began to market products under their own private brand names and thereby transferred customer loyalty and trust to the retailer away from the manufacturer. A further development was the cheap 'no brand' (generic) product – typically contained in white or yellow packs from which the cost of superior packaging was removed to reduce costs and prices further. Retailer brands have steadily increased in quality and sophistication so that now many match, if not surpass, those of manufacturers. Market analysts indicate at least four categories of DOB:[5]

1   *Generic* – simple packaging, no branding except retailer name.
2   *Price-led retailer brands* – carrying the retailer name but package design giving an overt signal of lower prices. Product quality often below par.

3 *Quality-led retailer brand* – packaging designed to reflect product quality, which in turn is on a par (or even above) manufacturer brands.

4 *Exclusive retailer brand* – manufacturer-based, but sold only through one retailer.

In building its own brand and managing the supply and distribution of a portfolio of DOBs, the retailer has two clear advantages over the manufacturer. One is the lower costs derived from lower expenditures on product development and marketing as he or she tends to adapt rather than start from scratch; hence many DOBs often have a 'lookalike' appearance to manufacturers' brands and mimic their trade dress. A second, arguably more important advantage, is the capacity for direct contact with the consumer. Modern EPOS technology provides a capability for nearly instantaneous feedback of consumer preferences. The possibilities here are extensive and make some traditional market research methods look primitive.

The pattern of DOBs varies considerably across countries. US penetration of DOBs is far lower than that typically seen in Europe. And within Europe there are significant differences, for example, between the relatively low levels in Italy and the relatively high levels in Switzerland and the United Kingdom. This is due in large part to the varying concentrations of retailing. In the United Kingdom Sainsbury and Tesco account for more than one-third of all grocery sales, whereas in Italy retail distribution systems are relatively fragmented, thus allowing a supremacy of manufacturers' brands.

Manufacturers' secondary, (as distinct from premium) brands are particularly vulnerable to usurpation by retailer brands. Symptomatic characteristics of such vulnerable brands include loss of distribution through key retailers, no clear market position, little innovation and an increasing proportion of expenditure on trade promotion at the expense of above-the-line advertising spend. Their manufacturers face the dilemma of continuing to invest in such trapped brands or considering becoming sub-suppliers of product for branding by retailers. Another consequence of increased retailer power has been a growth in trade marketing expertise. Manufacturers are developing new competences in managing relationships with distributors and retailers in terms of pricing, long-term agreements, merchandising, advertising, inventory and supply arrangements.

For a small business there is a particular challenge in becoming a supplier of private brand products, especially in areas such as cheaper ranges of clothing or food items for large multiple stores and department stores. The danger is that the manufacturer becomes totally powerless and survives from contract to contract at the whim of the large buyer. It may also lose contact with the market and with customers, since both of these are analyzed and serviced by the retailer alone, who then supplies product specifications to the subcontractor manufacturer. The manufacturer can easily become a single function business – all manufacturing and little marketing. On the positive side of such relationships, a first-rate subcontractor can create power for itself through first-rate operation, so that the retailer comes to value and depend on his quality, reliability and cost-effectiveness. Under such circumstances, the retailer typically begins to invest in the subcontractor through transfer of technology and through advice and financial assistance. The intelligent small business will use this power to learn about manufacturing excellence and (through the retailer) about market conditions. By building a solid resource base in this way, the choice to go direct to market with a manufacturer-branded item to a more premium segment of the market becomes a realistic option.

Brand equity

One of the ways in which marketing activity creates organizational assets is through investment in branding. Branding must be seen as an investment decision and, if properly managed, yields an asset of value which will ultimately appear as a balance sheet entry.[6] How precisely a brand is valued in accounting terms is a complex issue, but at a minimum a successful brand is worth sizeably more than the traditional notion of a firm's goodwill. It was described earlier how Nestlé, in acquiring Rowntree Mackintosh, effectively paid five times the stock market value of that firm because of its brand franchises. Philip Morris's $13 billion takeover of Kraft General Foods in the United States in the same year also cost considerably more than the stock market valuation of that company.

However the rise of DOBs, along with increasing consumer sophistication, have thrown into focus the difficulties of measuring brand equity precisely. Philip Morris's Marlboro brand, estimated by accountants as the world's most valuable brand ($30 billion), faced aggressive competition from cheaper private label cigarettes in the early 1990s. On 2 April 1993 Marlboro was forced into the humiliating position of having to reduce prices by 20 per cent to counter this growing threat. Over $13 billion was wiped off Philip Morris's stock market value. The subsequent months saw many pundits speak apocalyptically of the death of brands.

The reality was different. The brand was far from dead. Rather, Marlboro Friday, as it came to be known, symbolized the end of the exclusive hegemony of the manufacturer's brand and the challenge to it by the distributor's own brand. The competitive arena of branding changed profoundly. The two sets of brands are fundamentally different in their origins, strategic management functions and contribution to consumer well-being. Yet they share the essential characteristics of a brand from a marketing perspective.

Manufacturers claim that retailers rapidly imitating their brands effectively amounts to the theft of intellectual capital. As innovators, they are not being allowed the time to appropriate the full economic benefits of their innovations. In some cases they have challenged lookalike brands in law courts. In other cases, such developments motivate manufacturers to strive harder to innovate and create products and brands which are more difficult to imitate. They are aware that their company's manufacturing history is a potentially powerful defence which no retailer can match – and consumers have always responded to messages about genuine pedigree and provenance. Manufacturers are increasingly recognizing the strategic importance of corporate branding and the need to celebrate the company behind the brand as well as the brand itself.

Retailers and distributors argue, for their part, that they offer the consumer better value; their brands are as good as manufacturers yet more keenly priced. But the competence to develop and manage brands effectively is not equally distributed among all retailers. Few retailer brands are as good as, let alone surpass, those of manufacturers. Retailer brands are not homogeneous; at least four categories can be identified. Not all retailers embrace brand management, conscious that it is an expertise developed by manufacturers over generations. Developments in retailing, whether the growth in discounting and discount stores, like Aldi, or the development of new modes of shopping, such as home shopping using multi-media technology, are benefiting manufacturers' brands as much as retailers'. Many discounters prefer to offer manufacturers' brands and the remoteness of virtual reality shopping often favours the manufacturer.

Brand as marketing's DNA

The battle between manufacturers' and DOBs' brands deepens brand equity in effect. Firms acquire new expertise in nurturing brands in a manner that is advantageous to them – *and* to the customer. A process approach to business encourages firms to look across departmental boundaries in organizing their business. In this sense brand management becomes a multidisciplinary task, and not that just of the marketing department. Chapter 12 elaborated on how some firms are replacing traditional brand managers with product integrators. The concern is to augment the brand franchise by better matching, supplying and delivering product to customer need. To consider branding as marketing's DNA is a useful metaphor, reflecting a process or re-engineering approach to business activity. As DNA contains the unique and inherited codes which determine the shape, form and function of an organism, so branding may be viewed analogously as a business process which integrates optimally the physical, service and psychological benefits of the brand and determines the particular combination of product quality, innovation, technology, trade partnerships, logistics, and so on crucial to a firm's sustainable competitive advantage.[7]

Finally but importantly, it is critical to remember that building substantial brand equity is usually a very expensive undertaking. It must, therefore, be embarked on with the same care and analysis as any major investment decision. In some markets, especially fast-moving consumer markets, the cost of brand building will equate in scale to a major capital expenditure project. This represents a particular dilemma for many small and medium-sized companies, particularly as they internationalize. They must make choices between the expensive process of developing their own international brand identity or developing deep supply partnerships and relationships with those who already have access to final markets via their own brand assets. Ray Ban sunglasses exemplifies a brand-building choice, but one must remember that the resources of its parent company, Bausch and Lomb, were available in doing this. By contrast, a small food company with very limited resources might more appropriately choose to invest in supply relationships with large brand-owning manufacturers, distributors or retailers.

Product lifecycle

So far, the product has been discussed in a static manner. But most products are in fact dynamic, almost living, things. Recognition of this reality is the basis for the product lifecycle concept. Just as most things in nature are conceived, gestate, are born, grow, mature and eventually die, so too with products. New products are conceived in marketing managers' minds, in R&D labs and on the shopfloor. They are developed as concepts, prototypes built, and are finally launched onto the market. If they prove successful, they grow as more and more consumers learn about them and repurchase them. At some stage all those customers needing the product are already buying it and growth ceases: the product has reached maturity. And inevitably the mature product is challenged by a better one based on newer technology, better design, a more efficient manufacturing process or a better fit with changing customer requirements. Decline sets in and leads to the ultimate withdrawal of the product from the market. The S-shaped curve shown in Figure 15.1 reflects the most common sales pattern, but products can be found that grow in a straight line through time, or that experience immediate and rapid growth followed by sudden maturity.

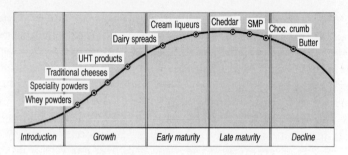

Figure 15.1 The lifecycle of processed dairy products

Figure 15.2 shows the typical relationship between sales revenues and profitability over time. The typical pattern of profit is important to note. It illustrates the fact that, for most products, their development (pre-launch) and introduction phases require marketing investment, while revenues are not yet sufficient to cover costs and generate a positive return. Ignorance or disregard of this typical pattern leads to marketing decisions based on grossly over-optimistic initial sales projections, to misjudged cash-flow deficits, to underestimated working capital provisions, and sometimes, in small or new ventures with very limited resources, to financial collapse and liquidation. This is especially tragic where the new product or service is inherently good and acceptable to the market, but where the company is short-changed by bad planning and management.

Before the implications of managing the product lifecycle are explored it is necessary to enter some qualifications about the concept. Lifecycle theory fits well with experience at individual product or brand level. But it is a very weak and imprecise tool when analyzing the dynamics of a product

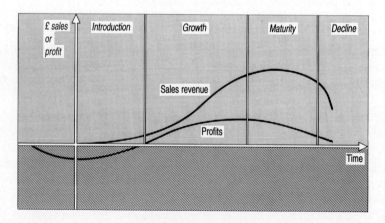

Figure 15.2 A product lifecycle

category. Thus it is much more powerful in analyzing the life of a motor car model than in analyzing motor cars as a generic product group. As one probes more deeply into generic demand – the need to be clothed, to eat, to be transported, to write, to furnish houses, and so on – one finds generic products that are always in demand. The specific form of that demand evolves over time and through generations of consumers, but a lifecycle pattern is not to be found. In this sense, there is no such thing as a dying industry, only industries that have slipped out of line with the evolution of generic demand, as much of the European auto industry did during the 1970s, or as European (but not Korean) shipbuilders have done. The distinction is the same as that made between needs and wants in Chapter 1. Wants will usually follow lifecycle patterns, but needs are reflected in stable underlying demand patterns that do not conform to a normal lifecycle profile (see Figure 11.3 p.195).

Timing is also a problem in the application of lifecycle concepts. There are no standard rules for forecasting the time-scale of a product's lifecycle. Some survive profitably for many, many years, while others come and go on the wave of a fashion fad, lasting months or only weeks. This holds true even within product categories. Brands such as Heineken or Guinness have seen, during their continuing life, the birth and demise of many brands of beer on the market.

Forecasting is the biggest problem with managerial use of the lifecycle concept. At the individual brand or product level it is at its most amenable, but even here most of the factors that determine the shape and time-scale of the lifecycle are beyond the marketer's control: competitive reactions and innovation; technological change; consumer tastes and disposable income, and so on. For the introductory and growth periods the manager depends primarily on judgement to forecast the shape of the sales curve. Which of the three patterns shown in Figure 15.3 will reflect market reality? Pattern (a) is the one favoured by most marketing scholars and derives theoretical justification from what is known about the social diffusion of new products. Yet many new product sales budgets show figures more in line with (b) and (c). Indeed, budgets predicting a pattern such as that in (a) are very often greeted derisively with comments that timid managers always predict success in the more distant future and tough times in the next planning or budgetary period. Effective forecasting of the shape of the lifecycle curve can only be based on a very deep knowledge of the market and well-researched assumptions about how many customers there are, their willingness to try a new product and switch from an old one, the conversion of trial into repeat purchases, and the frequency of repeat purchase. This can and should be done by any professional marketing manager, and an increasing number of computer-based models exist that help the manager

(a)   (b)   (c)

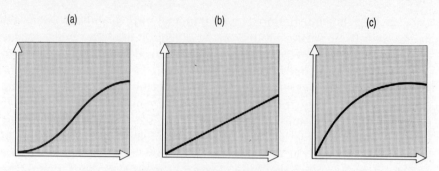

Figure 15.3 Alternative sales growth patterns

to integrate estimates of these factors with marketing mix proposals and likely competitive reactions in order to produce forecasts of future sales.

Forecasting the time-scale of the maturity phase is also difficult, as good innovative marketing decisions and manufacturing and design improvements can continuously extend the phase. When to categorize a product as approaching decline is sometimes easy, based on clear technological and customer demand trends. More often it is not so clear, so that the decision to manage a product quietly into retirement or to drop it from the company's product line is a most difficult one in terms of timing.

Lifecycle phases and marketing practice

Introduction stage

In general, it is clear that products at different lifecycle stages should be marketed with different strategies. The following guidelines are generalizations, and there will always be exceptions. Any such guidelines should therefore be used with caution and more as a stimulus to further thought and analysis than as mechanical rules.

At the introductory stage, market risk and uncertainty are normally at their highest. The new product is offered to customers, and the marketer must invest in market development. Customers and members of the trade must be informed of the product's existence and of its unique advantages. Net cash outflows are characteristic of this stage, and adequate funds to cover working capital requirements must be carefully arranged. The vital initial sales to key customers must be made and their reaction to the product monitored. If they dislike or reject it, the process of product recommendation among customers will begin to work against it and repeat purchases will not develop. Gaining product trial is a vital objective at this stage if customers are to accept the product for long-term repeat purchase, and innovative methods to facilitate trial at low financial and psychological risk to the customer are often central to early success. Weekly monitoring of orders and sales to final customers is vital to staying in control of the introductory process because it allows the manager to check trial purchases against budget and to identify the emergence and volume of repeat purchases in a fast-moving consumer good.

Growth stage

Entry into the growth stage is normally signalled by a rapid increase in the rate of sales volume growth. Typically, repeat orders are flowing in, and the less innovative but large majority of customers begin to enter the market. Strong attractive growth usually brings imitators or 'me too' products from marketers who have seen the success and try to obtain some of the market growth with cheaper or differentiated versions of the product. Because growth is strong, the severity of the competitive pressure that may be building up is easily ignored. If the new product is expanding the market, there may well be temporary room for many competitors in the marketplace. However, in the late growth phase, at the approach of maturity, the battle for market share and survival typically precipitates a shake-out among competitors, leaving only the strongest to survive. During growth it is important to continue to improve the product and to innovate if possible in order to stay one step ahead of imitators. Growth normally requires continued investment in the product's future, and it is inappropriate to manage it for maximum profit or cash throw-off during this stage. Doing so will usually shorten its lifecycle and weaken any leadership position created.

Maturity stage

When the rate of growth in sales volume slows down to one roughly equivalent to the general rate of economic growth in the market, the product has well and truly matured. Ideally the marketer wishes to have a product in a leadership or strong competitive position in the chosen target market by this stage, as strategy during maturity largely revolves about defending position and prolonging the period of maturity. To enter maturity with a weak market position is generally a recipe for futher losses of market share and weak financial performance. The objective of prolonging the maturity phase is usually tackled through product improvement and adaptation (as often seen in the 'new improved' versions of popular consumer goods); through further segmentation of the market; through the development of line extensions (variations of the product to cover additional segments and shifting consumer needs); and sometimes through price decreases to bring in more price-sensitive segments of demand provided that the price/volume/manufacturing cost relationship allows the company to maintain profitability. While the introductory and growth phases demand marketing investment, the maturity stage should see strong positive cashflows to provide a return on the earlier investment and the creation of reserves from which to fund new product innovation.

Decline stage

The management and inevitable burial of declining products are a task from which many marketing managers shy away. Yet if the product lifecycle concept is accepted, then products must inevitably begin to decay. Careful management of the process of decline, involving curtailment of product models, variations and options, and maintenance of reasonable margins, can produce significant positive cashflows for the company to invest in new and growing products. On the other hand, mismanagement of decline, especially when it involves investment in the product and its retention beyond its profitable life, can become a serious financial trap for the business and damage its reputation among customers. It is as important – and quite often as difficult – to bury an old product as it is to launch a successful new one.

Multi-product firm

Few firms manufacture and market a single product. Multi-product activity is more typical of business life in general and of individual companies as they evolve from new small ventures into established mature companies. The pressures to become a multi-product company have several origins. The lifecycle process and the ever-shortening length of individual product or brand lifecycles create an obvious pressure. If the manager waits until the demise of a first product to launch a replacement, the interim period of minimal revenue and substantial cash outflows shown in Figure 15.4(a) can easily trigger financial collapse. The remedy is to begin the development and introduction of a new product well before the original product begins to decline. Figure 15.4 (b) shows how this will help to smooth revenue and profits and to maintain a healthier cashflow status.

A second major pressure towards multi-product companies comes from the increased uncertainty and risk inherent in many of today's markets. One way to reduce this risk is to avoid putting all one's eggs in the same basket. Several products spread over several markets or market segments reduce risk, since the likelihood of their all failing together is usually low. The company's commitments and investment are spread much in the way that private investors will spread stocks, shares and other asset holdings in order to balance risk and return, current income and future profits in their financial portfolio.

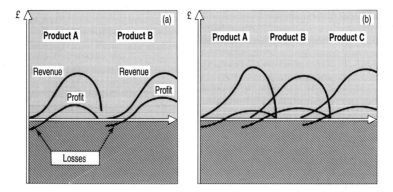

Figure 15.4 Overlapping lifecycles

Finally, multi-product companies develop in response to much more positive or aggressive forces revolving around objectives of company growth. Any one product has inherent limits to its size and growth potential. For the company to expand beyond these limits, it is necessary to add further products to the product mix.

For the multi-product company, careful management of each product in relation to the other is vital to achieving objectives of risk reduction, of balanced cashflows and of company growth. Essential to any product management system is accurate and up-to-date information on the market position, cost, revenue and profit profile of each product. Without this information at the manager's fingertips, he or she can never tell which products are at what stage of the lifecycle or which are absorbing or generating cash. He or she cannot therefore plan the product mix and is effectively out of control of his or her business.

Product portfolio analysis

The complexity of managing multi-product companies and of making decisions about an optimal mix of products is reduced through product portfolio analysis. In Chapter 4 the development and certain applications of the Boston Consulting Group (BCG) growth-share matrix was described. It was first used by the chief executives and corporate strategists of large diversified companies faced with making decisions about investment allocation and corporate support across a large portfolio of businessess, divisions or SBUs. The BCG matrix helped to lessen the complication involved. Gradually the matrix was adapted for use at product portfolio level where senior managers, including, of course, the marketing manager, employ it to assist in evaluating products and product lines and making decisions about their development, maintenance or deletion.

Each product in a company's product mix is classified on two dimensions: the rate of growth in the product market (to indicate lifecycle stage), and the market share dominance of the product. The reasons these two dimensions were chosen illustrate the basic conceptual foundations of product portfolio techniques of analysis. Market growth rate as a proxy for product lifecycle stage is used because of the implications for cash management and strategy formulation discussed earlier in this chapter. In a period of rapid growth, market share can be captured relatively easily, but at the expense of considerable investments of cash to fund growth and to win share. In maturity, however, the structure of the market hardens and market share is expanded with great difficulty, but maintenance of a strong position should, by the same token, be quite achievable and should generate a cash surplus on trading.

Market share dominance is used as the second dimension because of the evidence that market share is strongly and positively correlated with profitability and with net cashflow. Share dominance is used to indicate not absolute market share but a product's market share relative to that of the largest competitor. This acknowledges that there is a vast difference between having a 30 per cent share when the next largest competitor is 20 per cent, compared with when the largest competitor has 50 per cent of the market. The evidence for a strong relationship between share and profitability derives principally from the PIMS research programme. The BCG matrix allows the manager to categorize products into four quadrants, as shown in Figure 15.5.

1   *High-growth/low-share (question mark)* products generate an enormous demand for cash to keep up with market growth and to improve

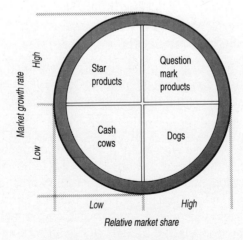

Figure 15.5 BCG product portfolio matrix

share. If cash is not invested, the product will become a 'dog' as market growth slows down. The strategy recommendation for getting out of this cash-absorbing position is either to invest aggressively in order to gain share or to acquire competitors and turn the product into a 'star', or to get out of the market.

2   *High-growth/high-share (star)* products are market leaders which typically return significant profits but absorb all or most of them in the process of maintaining leadership and keeping up with market growth. Recommended strategy is to hold share by reinvesting the product's profits in product improvement, market coverage, manufacturing efficiency, and perhaps price reductions to expand the market and pre-empt low-cost competitors.

3   *Low-growth/high-share (cash cow)* products are, or certainly should be, profitable products with strongly positive cashflows. Low market growth places no demands on the funding of growth, and the high market share should normally yield above-average profitability for the industry. Strategy should revolve about protecting share, while avoiding undue investment in product innovation and market expansion. Any investment whether in manufacturing or marketing should be limited by the share maintenance objective. Excess cash should therefore be generated to support research, new product development and the funding of worthwhile 'question mark' products into 'star' positions.

4   *Low-growth/low-share (dog)* products normally have below-average profitability. Low share brings about below-average profitability and cost disadvantages in manufacturing. Lack of market growth means there is little new business to capture and market share gains will be vigorously fought by other competitors. Strategy options are more diverse here and include:

  ▶ segmentation of the market to find a niche that can in fact be dominated;
  ▶ harvesting the product, i.e maximizing net cashflow by minimizing product support;
  ▶ divesting the product to a buyer who sees possibilities for it;
  ▶ deleting the product from the product mix to curtail cash losses.

The simple share/growth portfolio matrix therefore allows the marketer to analyze the market and competitive position of each product and to derive guidelines for action. For such an apparently simple tool with all its visual attraction, it promises major insights into the product mix and into future policy alternatives. Managers commonly find that the effectiveness of the matrix is considerable in communicating complex information in condensed and graphic form. Before accepting it at face value, however, the manager is well advised to understand its basic assumptions and to check their validity for the conditions in which he or she operates.

Market share is used as an indicator of relative profit performance in the market and net cashflow position: high-share products have higher relative profitability than low-share products. The experience effect – the decline in unit cost with increased cumulative output of a product – is invoked to explain how high-share (and therefore higher cumulative volume) producers should have lower costs and better margins. The PIMS programme findings are also used as evidence of the impact of market share, although these findings show a less significant impact for share in consumer than industrial products. For any one industry and a product market within it, the marketer must therefore evaluate the relevance of these general findings about the impact of share on profitability. In markets where entry and exit for competitors are easy, where there is little proprietory technology and where customers perceive little risk in purchasing the product, the relationship is likely to be weak. The assumptions concerning market growth rate must also be checked before the technique is applied. The key assumptions are that shares stabilize in mature markets and that share gains are a more reasonable objective in growth markets. While these are reasonable general assumptions, specific markets may provide conditions in which they do not hold.

Composite portfolio approaches

The original BCG portfolio uses the two dimensions of relative share and market growth. Most of the elaborations of the portfolio analysis approach that followed BCG's innovation revolved around generalizing from market share to *competitive position/capability* and from market growth to *market attractiveness*. As discussed earlier in Chapter 4, the most widely used of these portfolio techniques include the business portfolio popularized by General Electric with McKinsey & Co., A. D. Little Inc.'s product market evolution portfolio and Royal Dutch Shell's directional policy matrix.

Chapter 11, which explored the firm's strategic market choice, introduced a market choice matrix (MCM) as a guide to the marketing manager in his or her search from broad business definition to specific target market. Its dimensions are market attractiveness and *relative* company capability. This dimension of relative competitive capability – i.e. the firm's ability to serve customer needs compared with competitors' ability to serve those same needs – is an important innovation as it enables the firm to focus in a knowledgeable way on market segments where it might win substantial competitive advantage.

As well as understanding the assumptions underlying these matrices and assessing the validity of implicit conditions, the prescient marketer is also aware of the company-wide context in which they are being used. The market choice matrix is rooted in the strategic marketing process where the marketer works closely with other senior managers. Using the product portfolio matrix is part of the marketing management process, essentially the bailiwick of the marketing department. Portfolio analysis is used at corporate management level, at SBU level and at a marketing or product management level. The portfolio tool, in all its various forms postdating BCG's initial innovation, must be viewed in this hierarchical manner. The levels of analysis are nested within each other and are deeply interconnected. When a marketing team uses the tool it must be conscious of the nature of, and set of policies attaching to, the corporate portfolio; of its own role in configuring the product portfolio; and of its direct responsibility for the balancing and rebalancing of the product line portfolio.

REVIEW QUESTIONS

15.1 Identify two car rental companies, one an international company and the other a local company. Analyze the products of both companies in terms of their 'physical', 'service' and 'psychological' components, identifying the differences between them and the related marketing consequences.

15.2 In the context of a business system, the emergence of branding in a market usually coincides with its transition from a commodity to a non-commodity status. Elaborate.

15.3 What are the implications for manufacturers' brands, and branding in general, of the rise of distributors' own brands (DOBs)?

15.4 Branding as marketing's DNA reflects a process or re-engineering approach to business activity. Is this a useful metaphor and what are its implications?

15.5 Why and how might a country be branded?

15.6 Identify four products, one at each stage of the product lifecycle. Explain your choice and evaluate the way in which each product is being marketed in relation to the general recommendations about lifecycle management strategies.

15.7 How might a marketing team use portfolio analysis?

CHAPTER 16

Pricing

- ▶ Basics of pricing
- ▶ Price decision-making
- ▶ Price as a profit lever
- ▶ Transaction pricing
- ▶ Price wars

Marketing in action case
Apple Computer: what price glory?

ABOUT THIS CHAPTER

Setting price necessitates understanding the firm's cost structure, the nature of customer demand and the characteristics of competitive activity – and good judgement on the part of the marketing manager. As price is just one element of the marketing mix, it is finally determined in the context of the firm's overall marketing objectives and strategies. Cost-leadership approaches, premium niche pricing, skimming and penetration policies may be relevant options.

Pricing is an important profit lever for the firm. The payoff of improved pricing decisions is high, whereas incompetent pricing or price erosion can have disastrous profit consequences. Engineering the 'pocket price waterfall' – the drift or erosion from a firm's list price to the actual achieved, left-in-pocket price – involves the astute management of the order generation, fulfilment and service process. Aggressive price discounting and entry into a price war are strategies on which a firm embarks only after much scrupulous consideration.

Pricing is complex

Pricing decisions ought to be simple. Calculate the cost of supplying a product or service at various levels of output; find out how customers respond to variations in price level; decide that the firm wants to maximize profits; and calculate, with a little mathematical help, the price that gives the highest profit level.

Market realities and professional practice, unfortunately, are not quite so simple. Costs are sometimes difficult to allocate to individual products. Few marketing managers can, in fact, estimate with accuracy the way demand responds to small price changes. Very often the objective for an individual product is not to maximize profit but to complete a product line and maximize profit across the whole line of products. The theory of pricing that is generally at the marketer's disposal has to make simplifying assumptions about market conditions and company objectives that render it difficult to apply with practical effect. The theory is nevertheless important in identifying the key relationships and objectives involved in all pricing decisions.

In practice, most pricing decisions are made on the basis of determining costs and adding on a profit contribution. Other approaches based on what the market will bear and competitive parity pricing are also common. No one of these taken alone is a justifiable approach. Taken in combination they do begin to provide the parameters for a reasonable approach to setting price in the complex and uncertain conditions of most product markets. Pricing decisions reflect strategic imperatives as well. The company pursuing a market share building objective will have a different policy towards pricing than one trying to recover its investment in a new product in the shortest possible time. These are the factors which ultimately complicate the pricing decision.

Basics of pricing

It is important to identify the essential objectives and relationships involved in a pricing decision in a simplified manner before the complexity of real markets and of professional practice is explored. The price for a product should reflect:

1 the company's cost function – how much it costs to make products or services at various levels of output;
2 the product's demand function – how customers respond to different price levels in terms of their volume of purchases;
3 the profit objective of the company.

A *cost function* consists of both fixed and variable cost elements. The fixed costs do not change as the company varies its output in a given production facility. So these are the standing overhead costs that must be paid whether the firm produces one or 100,000 products or services in a year. The variable costs are those that vary directly with the number of units produced. As more wooden chairs are produced in a furniture factory more timber is used – and it is used in direct proportion to the number of chairs involved. The total cost is therefore the combination of the fixed element plus the variable element. This is illustrated in Figure 16.1 (a).

Turning to the market, it is obvious that for most products price significantly determines the level of sales. As price increases it is generally valid to expect the volume of purchases to go down. There are, of course, exceptions to this, and there are ranges of small incremental price increases, where customers may not notice or may not be sufficiently sensitive to change their purchasing behaviour. The opposite is also generally valid: as prices go down more of the product is likely to be sold.

The nature of this relationship determines the product's *demand function*. What is especially interesting to the marketer is the price elasticity of demand – that is, the sensitivity with which customers respond to price changes. If price is increased by 1 per cent, does demand drop by 10 per cent, or does it perhaps not change at all? The difference between these two outcomes has a major impact on the formulation of pricing decisions. Figure 16.1 (b) shows two simple demand curves. One is highly sensitive to price changes, the other quite insensitive.

When the manager knows both the cost and demand functions, total revenue can be calculated, since it is a function of the price charged and the quantity the market will buy at that price level. Total *profits* may then be calculated as the difference between total revenue and total cost. Figure 16.1 (c) shows all the basic relationships necessary to calculate the profit-maximizing price with the help of a little calculus.

The real world of pricing, unfortunately, does not look like this. If it did, good costing, some statistical estimation of the demand function and a little algebra would turn every marketing manager into an infallible pricing expert. Nothing would go wrong. But in reality the objectives pursued are usually not as simple as profit-maximization for each product. Costs may not be known with complete accuracy. Above all, the demand function is difficult to estimate and moreover alters with changing customer and competitor behaviour. To cope with this, most pricing decisions usually reflect one, or a combination, of the following managerial approaches:

▶ cost- or profit-oriented;
▶ demand-oriented;
▶ competition-oriented.

Costs and pricing

By far the most widely used methodology is the cost-oriented one. Its wide use, however, is in no way a justification for its application to any

(a)

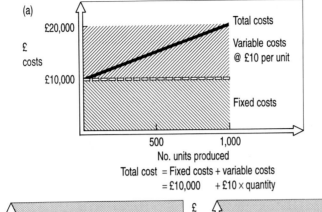

Total cost = Fixed costs + variable costs
= £10,000   + £10 × quantity

(b)

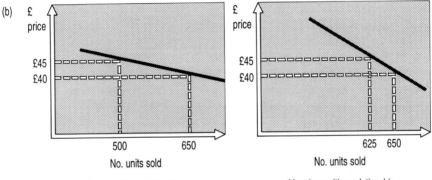

Very sensitive relationship   Very insensitive relationship

(To estimate such demand functions it is necessary to analyze historical data
on prices and volumes sold, using statistical methods)

Such a demand equation might be: Quantity purchased = 850 – 5 × price

(c)

Cost equation: TC = FC + VC
                          TC = £10,000 + £10 × quantity

Demand equation: D = 850 – 5 × price

Total revenue: TR = Quantity bought × price

Total profit: Profit = TR – TC
                          = Price [850 – 5 × price] – [10,000 + 10(850 – 5 × price)]
                          = 850P – 5P^2 – 10,000 – 8,500 + 50P
                          = – 18,500 + 900P – 5p^2

Profits therefore reach their maximum at a price of £90, as may be ascertained with the use of calculus.

Figure 16.1 Pricing: important relationships

individual pricing decision. The most typical approach is to calculate the total cost of the product and to add on a margin to cover profit for the producer or seller. This 'cost-plus' approach is, for example, typical of much of retail pricing where standard mark-ups or margins are applied to many retailed products. In large projects such as major construction works the practice is also common of developing total project costs and then negotiating between contractor and client the profit margin to be added on to costs.

The value of the method lies in its focus on accurate cost estimation. At worst, the manager will not set a price below total costs and bankrupt the business. This possibility is not as far-fetched as it may seem, since many small and medium-sized businesses do not yet have adequate cost accounting systems. They often trap themselves as a result of ignorance into pricing products based on the direct variable cost of production without allocating fixed costs. If this becomes habitual, total costs are never recovered and the business will collapse unless subsidized even more irrationally by the introduction of further capital.

Where cost-plus pricing is done well, it still involves serious flaws. It takes no account at all of the demand function! The cost-plus price may well result in only a few or even no purchases. Equally it may result in less profit than is possible because customers are sometimes willing to pay more for the value of the product to them than the cost-plus price.

A variation on the cost-plus approach is target profit pricing. Here the manager estimates how much will sell, the unit cost at this volume of production, and the return on total costs that the company wants to earn. The focus becomes a target profit level. Have you spotted the flaw? The logic of this decision approach demands that the manager must determine the quantity that will be purchased before setting price. Yet price is a fundamental determinant of purchases in almost all markets! So this approach introduces a concern for profitability as well as costs, but totally ignores the demand function once again.

Customers and pricing

In order to incorporate the demand function in the decision, customers and their behaviour have to be taken into account. Taking a customer- or demand-oriented approach on its own shifts the focus to what the market will bear. Intense demand is likely to be met by high prices, and weak demand by low prices – even though the cost structure is constant under both conditions of demand.

Approaching pricing decisions from this perspective requires knowledge of customers' price perceptions and their perceptions of value for money. As discussed in Chapter 15, customers pay not just for the 'physical' product features but also for service and psychological attributes of the product. The value they derive from consumption therefore represents the total of values – or utility – they derive from each of the product's attributes. These perceptions of value may be explored by various marketing research methods. One of the most sophisticated methods which enjoys widespread acceptance, as we saw in Chapter 14, is conjoint analysis, which allows the researcher to identify the individual product attributes or benefits, to assess their individual utility or value to the customer, and then to construct alternative products by varying the combination of attributes or the amount of each attribute.

Buyers' perceptions of the prices they pay for various products differ considerably in accuracy. Regular purchasers will have very accurate knowledge of prices for some products – for example, staple grocery items they purchase weekly. For other products, the typical customer will only be able to estimate a price range within which he or she expects to find the product. This latter phenomenon has important pricing implications, since it implies that within the price range demand will be quite insensitive to price variation – a product priced at the upper bound of the range will be at no disadvantage to one priced at the lower end. Many marketing research studies question buyers about their price expectations to establish this price range and give one indicator of the pricing discretion available to the marketer.

For some products, the generally assumed inverse relationship between price and purchases becomes quite distorted. Some customers use price as an indication of quality and purchase a higher priced product to reduce the risk they take in making the purchase and to assure themselves of good quality. This might be viewed as consumers paying an 'insurance premium' in the form of a high price to protect themselves against the risk of making a bad choice. This is perhaps also part of the explanation for the market power that high market share, high quality producers acquire in many markets. Because they are dominant competitors, and because they compete on quality, they command premium prices and typically earn above-average profits for their industry. This phenomenon is especially strong in consumer durables and infrequently purchased products where the customer is more likely to rely on supplier reputation in making a purchase than on long experience of making many repeat purchases from several competitors.

Customer- or demand-oriented pricing also raises the issue of price discrimination – charging different prices for the same product but in different locations or at different times. Most hotel pricing is very complex because of its basis in price discrimination policies. It is far more expensive to stay in most hotels in August than it is in February – unless the hotel is in a ski resort! Suppliers of tourism services respond to the seasonality of their industry by pricing high when demand is high and low when demand is low. This policy is implemented through different rates for different seasons of the year. It may also be applied within a weekly time-scale. Hotels that depend on business traffic do well during the working week, but may price their rooms and services at bargain rates for weekends to attract a different segment of the market and contribute towards the fixed costs they must incur on Saturday and Sunday as well as from Monday to Friday. Watch how some of your nearby city hotels will offer special weekend deals to the non-business guest.

The positive features of the customer-oriented pricing decision are its concern with the fundamentals of marketing – consumer or buyer behaviour. It probes the nature and determinants of the demand function which none of the cost-oriented approaches consider. It can, of course, also be used unethically or exploitatively to reap excessive temporary monopoly profits. Companies in business for the long run do not exploit this potential, as it inevitably generates customer resentment, public regulatory reaction and the entry of competitors to gain access to some of the profits.

Pursued singlemindedly, customer-based pricing may also lead to a disregard for profitability. It is possible to sell almost anything if the price is low enough! Such a policy, however, is unlikely to result in profitable operations.

Competitors and pricing

Many small businesses, especially those with products they have not succeeded in differentiating, base their pricing decisions on what the 'going rate' is in their sector of industry. Tendering and bidding situations are also characterized by emphasis on judgements about what competitors' tender prices or bids will be. There are, therefore, circumstances where there may be little choice but to orient the pricing decision towards competitors' price levels. Under such circumstances, the marketing priorities are two-fold:

1 to do everything possible to become cost-effective, since if price is a given, cost is the only managerial variable in determining margins and profits;
2 to attempt, if possible, to differentiate the product in some way so that some managerial discretion may be created in the pricing decision.

Competitor-oriented pricing raises the issue of price leadership. Price leaders pursuing an experience curve approach may gain substantial advantage (as may be seen in Exhibit 16.1). Most markets have one strong, respected competitor who 'leads' prices. Typically, such a company is the first to increase prices in response to cost pressure, and the rest of the industry then follows suit. In recessionary periods this is a difficult strategy to execute, as competitors with unused capacity are always tempted not to follow but to build their volume and market share at the expense of the leader and any followers. Price leaders may also lead prices down in an attempt to expand the market and precipitate a shake-out of small inefficient suppliers.

Exhibit 16.1

The experience curve
How the price/cost relationship evolves over time

From studies in many industries, the Boston Consulting Group found that the cost and price histories of a product are frequently directly related to the cumulative production (or 'experience') of that product. This can be quantified by plotting, over a period of time, the logarithms of unit cost or price against the logarithm of cumulative production. Cost and price are expressed in constant money values.

When this is done, it is usually found that cost decreases smoothly with experience – commonly by about 30 per cent for each doubling of cumulative production. However, price moves through four phases as experience develops.

This type of plot is useful in interpreting the price history of a product, understanding the phase reached in its development, and developing appropriate strategies for the period ahead.

In Phase 1 price lies below cost of production due to low scale of manufacture and the need to compete with established markets.

Phase 2 is that in which the original market entrants make increasingly attractive profits.

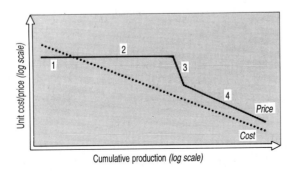

In Phase 3 increasing competition causes price to fall rapidly – often by 50 per cent for each doubling of cumulative production. It is associated with rapid growth, big improvements in technology and scale: negative cashflows and frequently a blood-bath leading to the exit of some of the contenders.

Phase 4 is more stable with prices and costs falling so that there is just sufficient margin to keep the marginal producers in business. This is the period in which some of those surviving make handsome profits and positive cashflows. It is, however, important to realize that in this final phase, costs and prices in real terms should still be expected to fall due to increasing scale of operations and improvements in production processes.

The ramifications of these general findings are considerable and have been successfully employed by the Boston Consulting Group. The most important of these are as follows:

▶ Market leadership is extremely important. The market leader typically has lower costs due to his greater cumulative production or experience. These give him the iniative in deciding how the market will develop, particularly in Phase 4, and can put him in an unassailable position.

▶ The leader can set prices such that the marginal producer is just kept in business. This makes it unattractive for the latter to invest heavily and deters new entrants. Prices lower than this may dislodge the marginal competitor but cost the leader heavily in absolute profits since his volume is larger.

▶ Alternatively, the leader may choose to set prices such that his profitability is high. This may make the market attractive also for others who will invest heavily, catch him up and in so doing reduce their costs to the same level as his. In this case he has taken a shorter-term profit at the expense of longer-term dominance.

▶ Being a number 2 or 3 in the market can be moderately attractive. However, catching up a leader with intelligent pricing policies can be an extremely expensive business. Being a marginal producer, with relatively high costs, is an unsatisfactory position and usually a case for disinvestment.

▶ All competitors, but particularly the leader, must ensure that their costs (in real terms) are constantly reducing or their profitability will be eroded and competitors will be able to gain market share.

Source: Shell Chemicals UK, *Techniques of Business Analysis* (1979), p. 5.

In the personal computer market during the mid-1980s IBM cut its prices, expanded the market and built its market share very rapidly at the expense of smaller microcomputer manufacturers in North America and Europe. As it built market share, manufacturing economies of scale and experience drove its costs well below most of the smaller competitors, who could not as a result compete successfully on price let alone on product design and marketing. By the early 1990s, Apple Computer adopted a similar price-cutting strategy and had to face the dilemmas illustrated in Exhibit 16.2.

Exhibit 16.2   *Marketing in action case*

Apple Computer: what price glory?

In the autumn of 1990, Apple Computer reversed a 6-year-old policy of charging high prices for its Macintosh line of computers and slashed prices by about 40 per cent. Six months later, though quarterly sales of Macintoshes had nearly doubled, the firm was forced to sack 10 per cent of its workforce. And, after years of fierce independence, Apple was negotiating a technology-sharing arrangement with the company its salesforce once loved to malign – IBM.

Apple's abrupt and painful about-face dramatically illustrated just how tricky pricing decisions can be. For better or worse, its new pricing policy transformed the company. Optimists argued that lower prices would at last make the Macintosh popular enough to enjoy the sort of virtuous circle of innovation that IBM-compatible computers had enjoyed. Because about 90 per cent of personal computers run the same software as IBM'S machines, software companies were increasingly focusing their efforts on these computers – which sells more computers, which attracts more software, and so on. But sceptics saw only gloom ahead. Despite its self-proclaimed innovative prowess, Apple's share of the market had possibly already shrunk too far for the company to influence the development of the next generation of technology. And rivals were far ahead of the firm on the price and cost-cutting curve, making it difficult for Apple to gain the volumes and profits needed to stay ahead technologically.

Apple got itself into this mess with a key decision made back in 1983. It was then that it decided to set the price of its new Macintosh personal computer well above that of competing models made by its rivals. This was at a time when learning-curve pricing was the order of the day in the computer industry – setting prices as low as possible in order to capture market share. But then the Macintosh was a unique product with its user-friendly windows, icons and 'mouse' – a 'bicycle of the mind', in the words of Steve Jobs, Apple's founder and its then president. The design goal for Mac's creators was to build a machine that could be sold for $1,000. By the time production plans were drawn up, the minimum selling price had crept up to $2,000. It was decided to add a further $500 to the price of the machine in order to pay for a high-profile marketing campaign to tout the Mac's advantages.

This advertising and selling strategy flopped, largely because the first version of the Mac was not all the marketing had cracked it up to be. Despite an encouraging start, Mac sales nosedived, just as Apple ramped up production to meet what it thought would be booming demand. In the ensuing mêlée Jobs was forced from the company he founded.

However, Apple continued to persevere with its premium pricing policy, pushing prices up in order to pay the high cost of going it alone on innovation. Over the next few years, holding gross margins above 50 per cent – well above those of most competitors – became a key concern of Apple managers, who needed the profits to pay for their ambitious research programme. The main thrust of this research policy was to develop increasingly powerful computers. In 1987 Apple launched the Macintosh II range of computers with colour screens and super-fast processors.

Powerful, costly Macs were popular with several constituencies. The high margins available on big machines appealed to the network of dealers who were entrusted with the job of selling Macs to businesses. Fast machines were also popular with the smallish, but fanatically loyal, group of companies developing software for the Macintosh. Graphic designers liked the Mac. But many others ignored it. The machine's overall market share remained tiny throughout the late 1980s. IBM computers were far more popular with big companies. They may not have been as easy to use, but they worked well enough. Apple justified a premium for the Macintosh because studies showed that new users could be brought up to speed more quickly, with less training, than on IBM machines. But many corporate customers would only consider switching to the Mac if the machine were cheaper than an IBM personal computer. That was because either the Mac would have raised the cost of administering their computers, or it would have forced them to write off their existing machines.

Also, so-called open systems, which enabled the products of many different vendors to work together, spread the costs and opportunities of innovation. The success of IBM's personal computer was not entirely IBM's doing. Because they could build machines like IBM's, companies like Compaq picked up the pace of innovation when IBM faltered. And extra competition pushed prices down – so boosting market growth – just as Apple was pushing up prices to pay for its R&D.

Cheap, not cheerful

Proposals for low-cost Macintoshes were made several times in the late 1980s, and shot down each time. Though various reasons were given, executives say that the real reason for rejecting a low-cost strategy was that smaller margins would simply not support Apple in the style to which it was accustomed. In the pursuit of high margins, Apple refused to invest in its low end-product range, the Apple II, with the predictable result that the firm was overtaken by IBM in the educational market in 1989.

By 1990, Apple's market share was near the point of no return. Software houses simply did not see a big enough market in Macintosh software to develop new products for it. Equally important, a new program from Microsoft, called Windows 3.0, provided cheaper IBM-compatible PCs with many of the Mac's once exclusive capabilities, undercutting the justification for the Mac's higher price. After an executive reshuffle, Apple decided to launch low-cost Macintoshes and cut prices on existing products. This proved even more painful than the apostles of high gross margins had predicted. Lower prices did generate extra demand: unit sales in the second quarter of 1991 were running 85 per cent above the same period of 1990. But all the extra demand had come at the low end of the product range. Apple's attempts to predict the price elasticity of demand for its products had suggested that price cuts would spur sales across the entire Macintosh range, and it was hoped that this would have given the company two or three years to adjust to its new lower gross margins. Instead, Apple was forced to adjust much more quickly and the pain hit Apple squarely in its profit and loss account.

In the spring of 1991 Apple started sacking workers and began reshuffling its dealer network to accommodate high volume, low margin box-shifters alongside the traditional Apple dealer, who had been encouraged to avoid price-cutting and to provide lots of expensive service for the machines he sold. And it reshuffled its R&D priorities. Instead of developing everything in-house to keep the edge on its proprietary technology, Apple began negotiating joint development deals to share R&D costs. Chief among these was the deal with IBM. But it also negotiated a deal which would mean that Japan's Sony would make low-cost home computers for the US firm. It was also considering letting other firms manufacture Macintosh imitations or 'clones' in order to increase market share.

Judged against the assumptions of its previous high price strategy, Apple was now in considerable difficulties as it moved into the 1990s. It could neither afford to spend heavily on proprietary R&D nor to spend heavily on evangelizing the efforts of its research laboratories. Most of the proprietary technology it was developing would be shared with IBM and with Sony, companies which had more marketing clout and enjoyed greater economies of scale in manufacturing, and whose long-term interests lay, arguably, in competition with Apple – not cooperation.[1]

Pricing decisions must therefore take competitors' prices into account to a greater or lesser extent. If the product is a commodity-type product, then all prices will move towards a single value. As products become differentiated the key consideration ceases to be competitors' prices and becomes the value-for-money trade-off that they offer. And that brings the decision-maker back to developing an understanding of the demand function.

Price decision-making

Good decision-making under normal circumstances of uncertainty about cost and demand functions usually reflects all the approaches to setting a price – cost, customer and competition-based – and an integration of these considerations into a judgementally optimal price, as shown in Figure 16.2. Central to the process of integrating these considerations are the kinds of marketing objective and strategy the company is pursuing.

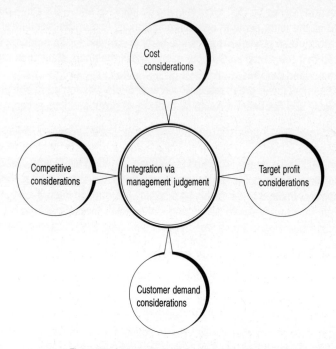

Figure 16.2 An integrated approach to price-setting

Company objectives and strategies

Price is just one element of the marketing mix and is therefore partly determined by the other components and by overall marketing strategy. For example, a highly differentiated product based on advanced technology, quality manufacturing and distributed through an exclusive channel backed up by extensive service must lead to premium pricing to recover costs and to create consistency in the customer's eyes between the elements of the mix. Waterford Crystal's hand-cut glass is an expensive product, yet its very expensiveness is an important part of the bundle of psychological attributes of the product that consumers throughout the world demand when purchasing a premier product.

Pricing decisions reflect portfolio management priorities too. Lower prices may be used to build market share as a company tries to turn a 'question mark' product into a 'star'. Interestingly, the research evidence from the PIMS (Profit Impact of Marketing Strategy) programme suggests that, in general, price is not as effective in building share as other variables such as product quality and innovation. As leading products mature and begin to become 'cash cows', margins normally come under pressure in a market that is no longer expanding. The cash cow has to be managed so as to defend margins and generate cash for R&D and new products. This defence is usually conducted by improvements on the cost side and by reducing the extent of the product line. With products that are in low-share positions in low-growth markets, price-cutting strategies are normally suicidal. Such products are, in most markets, at a cost disadvantage against the share leaders, who therefore have the flexibility to outbid any price reductions if smaller competitors choose to start a price war. The normal consequence of such action is that the marginal products and companies in the market become even more marginal, eat up their own capital and are left bankrupt or in a weaker position to survive in the long run. The way out of 'dog' positions in the portfolio is through segmentation and innovation to dominate a new segment. Price is not a good offensive weapon in this context.

Cost-leadership

Price is on certain occasions used to great effect as an offensive weapon. Its use has been highlighted since the 1970s by the strategies of many Japanese firms, especially those in electronics markets. US companies such as Texas Instruments (semi-conductors) and European ones such as BIC (ballpoints, lighters, razors) also became leading exponents of using price as the key weapon in the battle for market share during the early stages of product and industry lifecycles. It is important to note that such strategies were not based on low margins or poor quality. Quite the opposite is, in fact, the case. These strategies are therefore more accurately called *cost-leadership* strategies rather than low-price strategies. A typical approach in an industry where there are significant scale economies and experience effects is to set price at a level that will yield an attractive profit if substantial volume can be sold. Because of scale and experience effects, the high volume will yield low costs of production. The vital initial assumption that must be made is that setting the low price will in fact stimulate the market to buy in sufficient volume to drive the costs down to profitable levels! Under such circumstances, the marketer is very often hoping to stimulate primary demand – to bring new customers into the market. This happened with Texas Instruments in the case of the demand for semi-conductors and microelectronic components. BIC did the same with the writing instrument market with the introduction of the throwaway crystal ballpoint and repeated the strategy with cigarette lighters, razors, and more recently with wind surfboards. The dominance of modern consumer electronics by Japanese producers is also largely attributable to the same process.

What must never be overlooked about cost-leadership strategies is that they are also high-quality strategies. The BIC crystal pen, trivial as it may

seem, is a very high-quality product based on great excellence in manufacturing. The engineering tolerances and quality control involved in producing and assembling the ballpoint to assure smooth continuity of ink flow
are of a very high standard. Marketers should therefore appreciate the
necessity to match low-price strategies with low-cost manufacturing and
high quality. The combination of low price for low quality is never
acceptable to the market as a value-for-money trade-off over the medium
to long run.

Penetration and skimming policies

Entry strategies for new products are frequently formulated in the context
of a debate among managers on the implementation of penetration or
skimming price strategy. Penetration pricing opts for a low price to capture
a large market share, to encourage as many customers as possible into the
market and to generate volume to drive down costs. A skimming strategy
sets price high and targets on segments of the market that pay premium
prices. The objective is usually to obtain rapid recovery of new product
development and marketing costs. This latter strategy is most often invoked
by companies with very high R&D costs and a period of temporary
monopoly granted by patents. Many pharmaceutical products are launched
in this way. Problems do arise when the monopoly position disappears and
the company is forced to make a major change in pricing policy to match
new entrants, such as producers of generic drugs in the pharmaceutical
industry. In such cases failure to abandon the old premium price will result
in a rapid loss of market share.

A skimming policy is probably at its most effective in the highly
innovative company with excellent technological and marketing resources
that keeps producing innovative products, reaping premium prices and
then innovating again as competitors begin to imitate the first product and
drive down its price.

Price as a profit lever

Getting the price right – managing price performance expertly – is a crucial
function for the marketing manager. He or she is also aware of its company-
wide implications – the payoff of improved pricing is high, whereas
incompetent pricing or price erosion can have disastrous bottom-line profit
consequences for the firm. The marketing manager has ultimate responsibility for setting price, but in doing so and in maintaining consistent price

levels over time, he or she consults and operates with others in the firm whose decisions will affect the 'real' price achieved and revenues earned.

Credit control is normally a financial function in a firm, and the credit controllor reports to the chief financial officer. A valued customer who always pays within an agreed time often enjoys a price discount. Is this a marketing or financial decision? It is both in effect. Indeed, in certain firms credit is viewed as part of the pricing mix and credit control decisions are taken primarily in the marketing department. In some organizations, a quality control and customer care function, perhaps not in the marketing department, makes decisions about refunding customers' money as a consequence of possible dissatisfaction about a product purchased. This effectively reduces overall revenue.

The marketing management process determines the price that will be sought in the marketplace for a product or service as part of an overall marketing strategy. However, operationalizing this policy and achieving the price are part of an order generation, fulfilment and service (OGFS) process, which involves many others, both within and beyond the ambit of the marketing department. This is an important factor when one considers the major role of pricing as a profit lever.

Research by McKinsey & Co. suggests that improvements in price typically have 3–4 times the effect on profitability as proportionate increases in volume. Consider, for example, the profit implications of a 1 per cent increase in volume and a 1 per cent increase in price. For a company with an average cost structure and economics, improving unit volume by 1 per cent yields a 3.3 per cent increase in operating profit, assuming no decrease in price. But, as Figure 16.3 shows, a 1 per cent improvement in price, assuming no loss of volume, increases operating profit by 11.1 per cent.

But, of course, the price lever is a double-edged sword. The messages of Figure 16.3 also apply in reverse: a mere 1 per cent price decrease for an average company, for instance, assuming no increase in volume, could destroy 11.1 per cent of profits. Managers must always remember that a price reduction is immediately reflected in a corresponding drop in profits unless there is a sufficient increase in volume sales to make up the margin loss. If anticipated extra sales do not materialize it will cost the company dearly. Moreover, it is very unlikely that a company will be able to raise its prices back to their original levels. A ratchet-like mechanism characterizes price reductions in most markets.

The basis of pricing policy can often be forgotten or become unclear with the passage of time. For this reason it is important regularly to revisit the logic of pricing decisions. The aggregated nature of accounting and information reporting systems often fails to alert the manager to the precise profitability of individual items. Careful scrutiny may be required to identify

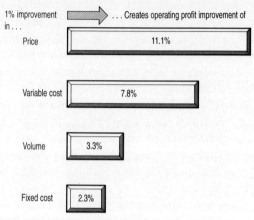

1% improvement in . . .   . . . Creates operating profit improvement of

Price   11.1%

Variable cost   7.8%

Volume   3.3%

Fixed cost   2.3%

* Based on average economics of 2,463 companies in Compustat aggregate
Source: M.V. Marn and R.L. Rosiello (1992), 'Managing price, gaining profit', *Harvard Business Review*, Sept/Oct, p.85.

Figure 16.3 Comparison of profit levers

products as unprofitable. These may have to be dropped, repriced, cost structures reappraised or a clear decision made to sell them at a loss as part of a profitable line.

Transaction pricing

Pricing issues are seldom simple and isolated; usually they are diverse, intricate and linked to many aspects of a business. While managers are competent in handling many of these issues, there is one key aspect often overlooked – transaction price management. Most companies use invoiced price as the reporting measure of firm price levels. Yet significant differences can arise between invoice price and net realized or transaction price. This erosion between invoice and actual transaction can vary sizeably between different customers and different sales orders. Minimizing this revenue leakage can be a valuable profit lever. A number of factors explain this erosion between the set invoice price and the final transaction cost, including:

▷ Prompt payment discounts – for example, a supplier may give a customer a 1 per cent payment terms discount if the invoice is paid within 30 days.
▷ Volume buying incentives – for example, a firm may offer buyers an annual volume bonus of up to 5 per cent based on their total purchases.
▷ Cooperative advertising allowances – for example, a retailer may receive joint advertising allowances of up to, say, 3 per cent if he

features the manufacturer's products in his advertising. Other types of off-invoice promotions may similarly lower net price to the manufacturer.

▶ Special shipping arrangements – a firm may pay the freight for transporting goods to a distributor or retailer on all orders exceeding a certain value.

While each of these factors may appear small, once they start to come together the overall effects are substantial. (It should be pointed out that we are dealing here with erosion from the agreed invoice price. This invoice price may already have been reduced from the list price by sales or marketing personnel to allow for order size discount or competitive discount. So transaction price shrinkage from the list price is likely to be even greater than that from the invoice price!) When these transaction-specific elements are subtracted from the invoice price, what is left is called the *pocket price* – the revenues that are truly left in a company's pocket as a result of the transaction.

Pocket price waterfall

Pocket price, not invoice price, is the right measure of pricing attractiveness of a transaction. This cascading down of revenues from list price to invoice price to pocket price is called the pocket price waterfall.[2] McKinsey & Co.'s research found close to a 20 per cent average decline from invoice to pocket price alone in a sample of firms across a range of sectors. Companies that do not actively manage the entire pocket price waterfall, with its multiple and highly variable leaks, miss many opportunities to enhance price performance. Firms' shortcomings in this regard are understandable. Formal management information systems, which tend to report in the aggregate, often do not allow such elements in transaction pricing to be readily identified. Some senior managers perceive such pricing decisions as unimportant and relegate them to low-ranking managers or even clerical administrators, with some flexibility at the salesforce level. Poor communications may further exacerbate matters. The net effect is lost profit opportunity.

Firms find that not only is the erosion from invoice to pocket price substantial, but that its size can vary enormously from customer to customer and transaction to transaction. On closer scrutiny customers they thought were highly profitable may not be so, and vice versa. Indeed, many experienced customers may be able subtly to work the pocket price waterfall to their advantage. To remedy the situation, firms must actively engineer the pocket price waterfall to their advantage. This requires greater scrutiny of constituent pricing elements and potential revenue leaks during the order generation, fulfilment and service process.

More information and tracking are needed to uncover or unbundle key, price-related decisions in the process. This extends both vertically and horizontally in the organization. Quite junior personnel, possibly not even within marketing's conventional remit, may be making decisions about promotional, transport or credit discount to the customer – decisions which in the aggregrate eat into bottom-line profit. Marketing and sales should target customers producing high, and thus attractive, pocket prices for increased volume. Buyers with low pocket prices are identified for actions that will result in improved price levels or their possible termination as customers. Incentive schemes are designed and managed to support these objectives.

The firm's pricing mindset should focus more on pocket price realization than on invoice price or list price. Managing the pocket price waterfall to advantage involves little investment or risk. The keys to success are mostly executional – doing a number of small things right. A harmony between the marketing management process and the order generation, fulfilment and service process is crucial. For instance, the importance of pricing in the marketing mix might be reflected in having a pricing analyst as part of the OGFS process team.

Price wars

Price wars have been a feature of many markets, especially since the mid-1980s. A protracted recession kept consumer and organizational buyers' emphasis on price as they sought to minimize their costs. The many industries characterized by high fixed costs and overcapacity such as pulp, paper, chemicals or airlines were caught in the vice of unavoidable standing costs on the one hand, and a buyer's market on the other. Such circumstances led to recurrent bouts of price warfare. While the pulp and paper industry was enjoying rapidly rising prices and an absence of price warring in 1995, companies were already prepared to anticipate the next outbreak, once additional production capacity comes on-stream in about 1998 from investment decisions made in 1995.

At another level, price wars are precipitated by the entry of new specialist discount competitors such as happened in food retailing across Europe, led by companies like Germany's Aldi or Lidl & Schwartz and Denmark's Netto. A new form of competitor, based on new, low-cost structures, attacks the traditional competitors on price and they are forced to respond in kind or watch their market share erode rapidly. This process will often produce a 'step-change' in the pricing structure of a market – all prices in all segments adjust downward as a result of the new expectations created by the discounter.

In terms of consumer behaviour some would argue that European consumers are now less convinced by the claims of premium and branded products after two decades of watching private label and generic products being transformed from second-rate goods into top quality offerings. Sophisticated, knowledgeable, well-informed customers may, in many instances, rely less than their counterparts in earlier generations on the brand to signify quality and trust more in their own independent evaluation. Any such underlying shift in consumer behaviour necessarily produces a market that is more price-sensitive and more tempting to some competitors to deploy price as an offensive weapon in the battle for market share.

However, the most vicious price wars break out between industry peers rather than as a result of underlying shifts in market structure or the entry of newcomers. One commentator recently commented: 'The casualty list can be appalling. Customer loyalty? Dead. Profits? Imploding. Planning? Up in smoke. Given the massed armies of capital and capacity that most competitors command today, there's less hope than ever of winning a price war.'[3] In their study of price wars, Garda and Marn note that there are seldom winners, and indeed few healthy survivors, of an outbreak.[4] They argue that price wars are to be avoided at almost any length because:

1 The impact on profit is huge: for products with a 29 per cent marginal contribution, a 5 per cent price decline as a result of price warring will require a 20 per cent increase in volume– just to break even on operating profit. Price elasticities seldom support any such response.
2 The advantage is fleeting as competitors can and will usually respond immediately. There is almost no barrier to rapid response on price, unlike most other marketing variables.
3 The customer re-establishes expectations concerning the range of 'normal' or expected prices and the overall price level in the market shifts downward. As a result, the average profitability of competitors shifts downward, triggering cost restructuring, which will seldom restore profitability to its former levels. The long-run profitability of the industry therefore changes, and with it investors' expectations and willingness to lend or invest in companies.
4 Because price wars often become obsessive stand-offs between rival companies, product or service benefits are frequently forgotten and price becomes the dominant marketing tool. This leads to commoditization of the product in the customers' eyes.

5 The shake-out of weak competitors that the initiator of a price war often predicts seldom happens because of the intervention of regulatory agencies or government, because of various barriers to exit, or because of the sheer emotional content of the battle which can override the economic logic of exit. Even where some competitors are shaken out, their capacity may not be retired but rather redeployed by an acquirer in even more aggressive fashion.

Garda and Marn suggest that the best routes to avoiding price wars involve:

1 avoiding strategies that force competitors to respond with price;
2 reading competitors' pricing moves with great care to avoid over-reaction;
3 avoiding over-reaction and especially the use of price as a counter-offensive if at all possible;
4 price for the value provided to the customer, not for competitive parity;
5 communicate pricing decisions very carefully so that they cannot be misread by customer or competitor;
6 communicate publicly about the inefficiencies and competitive damage of price wars;
7 segment aggressively to avoid the open field of price combat which is so often in the unsegmented and poorly differentiated areas of a market.

The world tyre industry in the early 1990s provides an interesting example of a price war where the major players found themselves in a lose–lose situation. It is estimated that the leading tyre makers lost more than $2 billion between 1990 and 1993.[5] Changes in the world automobile industry had led tyre companies to merge and acquire in a race for market share to fund the increasing cost of R&D. By 1990, 75 per cent of the world market was controlled by six top companies. A price war broke out between Michelin and Goodyear over the supply of tyres to General Motors after it discontinued its contract with Firestone. The war spread rapidly to replacement tyres – traditionally the high margin sector of the industry. As the situation worsened, competitors claim that Michelin cut European prices by as much as 25 per cent in a push for market share. However, everyone in the industry moved in lock-step on prices, so there was little change in market share. A spokesperson for the Hannover-based Continental tyre company noted that 'the whole industry went crazy. There was absolutely no economic rationale behind our pricing.' Finally, in mid-1992, Michelin raised its prices and competitors quickly followed suit.

REVIEW QUESTIONS

16.1 In theory, how can a profit-maximizing price be set? Illustrate your answer using hypothetical figures. Identify the items of information that are most difficult to estimate accurately in reality, and explain why.

16.2 What alternative approaches to pricing are most often found in practice? Evaluate the strengths and weaknesses of each approach.

16.3 What are the pricing implications of a cost-leadership strategy? What lessons can be learned from Apple Computer's pricing strategy of the early 1990s?

16.4 In what regards is price an important profit lever?

16.5 How might the order generation, fulfilment and service process impact on price?

16.6 A price war is a strategy on which a firm embarks only after much scrupulous consideration. Why?

CHAPTER 17

Communication and selling

▶ Developing a communication programme
▶ The elements of the communication mix
▶ Integrated marketing communication
▶ Advertising
▶ Personal selling and sales management
▶ Relationship marketing

Marketing in action case
EMI Records – marketing means money

ABOUT THIS CHAPTER

Informing the market accurately, clearly and persuasively about the company and its products or services is the role of marketing communication. It is necessary to integrate in a synergistic way the various elements of the marketing mix – a challenging task in the context of marketing's changing landscape. While advertising remains the most important communication medium for many companies, greater consumer sophistication and expectation, new and fragmenting media, the availability of highly targeted communication modes and rising advertising costs have conspired to see a rise in sales promotion and below-the-line expenditure and a greater use of instruments like direct mail and sponsorship.

The firm must consider carefully the role of personal selling in this mix. It is a very expensive medium yet one that can be highly effective in achieving buyer loyalty and in generally nurturing the relationships and networks key to sustained market focus. Genuine relationship marketing involves both the marketing management process and the order generation, fulfilment and service process in winning and retaining customers.

Coordinating the communication mix

Before customers can respond to the services or products that a company has for sale they must be aware of their existence and their performance characteristics. They must be informed about the products and persuaded of their relevance to their consumption needs. The task of informing the market accurately, clearly and persuasively about the company and its products or services is the job of the communication mix.

The communication mix consists of all the methods available to the company to achieve this objective. Just as with the marketing mix itself, there exists the necessity to choose the components of this mix and to ensure their compatibility with each other. The communication mix consists of the elements of advertising, publicity, public relations, sponsorship, sales promotion, merchandising, direct mail and personal selling, as well as participation in exhibitions and trade fairs, as summarized in Figure 17.1.

The complexity of developing a specific mix for a company and managing its adaptation over time can only be tackled effectively if the marketing manager approaches the task analytically and logically. This demands that an identification of a target market or audience should be the first step in decision-making, followed by decisions on communication objectives, message, media, budget and execution of the communication programme. Following this stage, measurement of the effects and their evaluation against the objectives set are necessary.

Elements of the mix are often seen as separate and independent areas of decision-making in marketing. Such a viewpoint can lead to uncoordinated activity in several communication media – advertising and the salesforce, for example – and to a sacrifice of the mutual support each element of the

Figure 17.1 The communication mix

mix can give to the other. Coordinated planning and integrated decision-making should produce synergy – the total impact on the market should be greater than the sum of the effects of the individual components taken alone. Within the communication mix personal selling is of special importance. Personal selling is an extremely effective element of marketing strategy, but it is also one of the most expensive communication media that a firm can use and, if badly managed, it can have disastrous and expensive consequences.

Developing a communication programme

Figure 17.2 summarizes the elementary logic of arriving at a justifiable communication programme. Each step in the framework is important and necessary, and while the decision-maker will modify some earlier decisions in the framework as later ones are made, there is a necessary sequence in the decision-making involved.

Choice of target audience brings the marketing manager back to the customer analysis stage discussed in Chapter 6 and the crucial decisions made about the segment that is to be the company's target market and the competitive position chosen for the company's product in this segment. These decisions are discussed in detail in Chapters 11 and 14. In formulating the communication programme, the manager begins with these considerations. Their implications for communication decisions are immediate and far-reaching. If a marketer's objective is to position a new breakfast cereal product in the mass market for morning cereals, the target market will be family households nationwide. Within the households it will be important to understand that purchaser (typically a housewife) and consumers (children plus parents) may have different preferences (parents may prefer healthy nutritional products, while children may prefer sugared novelty products) and that each perhaps has to be persuaded to consume the product. Distribution through supermarkets will be essential to success, so for this and for cost reasons personal selling to final consumers is not a relevant consideration. Advertising, however, is probably the main mechanism by which so many final consumers can be informed of the product, and this will have to be backed up by good merchandising and store promotions within the supermarkets. The supermarkets themselves will have to be persuaded to add yet another cereal product to their shelves through intensive personal selling by the company.

Knowledge of the target market and the competitive positioning decision, therefore, begin to dictate the heart of the communication programme. The essential outcome of this step in the procedure must be a clear statement or specification of the customer's profile and buying behaviour.

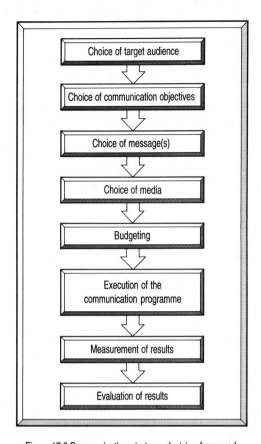

Figure 17.2 Communication strategy: decision framework

Choice of communication objectives is possible once the audience has been specified. Objectives must reflect what is the desired outcome of the strategy – to inform people, to create an awareness of the product, to get consumers to try it out, to achieve a specific sales revenue impact. There are, therefore, typically multiple objectives, and these objectives will change over the product's lifecycle, with competitive reactions and with shifts in buying behaviour.

Taking the new breakfast cereal example, the key objective at launch of the product may be to make consumers aware of its existence and of its unique features compared with existing brands. A second objective might be to induce maximum possible consumer trial in the weeks immediately after launch. If the product becomes successful, these objectives would change to emphasize building brand loyalty, increasing product usage rates among loyal customers and winning new users from competing products.

This path of analysis and decision-making applies as effectively to business-to-business products as it does to consumer products. Thus, in launching a new venture to manufacture lenses for use in cameras and other optical equipment, the entrepreneur and his marketing manager or adviser would have to specify clearly who purchases such lenses in Europe or around the world for incorporation into optical products. They would next have to develop their communication objectives just as the cereal manufacturer must. In this case key objectives would concern establishing relationships with the buying or procurement managers of major international optical goods firms in order to have the venture's ability to produce lenses assessed and its name added to the list of approved or acceptable suppliers who are asked to compete for business. The framework of decision-making is the same across products, services and industries; only the specific details vary.

Choice of message grows from the objectives to be achieved and the nature of the consumer. The optical lens producer has to design a message that will convince purchasing managers in sophisticated international companies that a relatively small new venture can meet their standards of quality and reliability. The message will therefore have to communicate the technical competence of the firm, its manufacturing scale and resources, and its ability to deliver a product of consistent quality, on time, every time. If the buyer is initially convinced of these factors, then samples of the lenses will be provided for testing and technical features discussed and explained as this testing takes place. The required message through all these avenues of communication is therefore one that features the new venture's technical excellence and managerial ability to organize production and delivery.

Choice of medium/media requires a decision on what channel or channels should be used to get the message to the target audience so as to achieve the established objectives. The word media is used here in the general sense of alternative channels through which the message can be delivered. It therefore includes all the elements of the communication mix.

The marketer of optical lenses will probably rely heavily on personal selling as a medium because the message is complex and technical and must be adapted in response to the customer's questions. Other media are important to support the personal selling one. Brochures and technical data sheets would be essential to effective communication, and direct mailing of these to buyers along with advertising in specialist trade journals could also be vital in establishing an entry to potential customers for personal selling activity.

In the breakfast cereal example, by contrast, heavy reliance on television and radio mass advertising might be more appropriate and cost-effective in communicating relatively simple messages to a mass audience. The important outcome of decision-making at this stage is a clear decision on what mix of media to use and on how they should be combined to achieve the company's objective.

Budgeting is the next step. What is to be done, how it should be done and the intended results of the programme are known, so the manager is in a position to assess costs and benefits. If objectives have been set in terms of sales effect, then very clear assessments may be made of the profitability of any one communication programme. Poor budgeting is a problem that bedevils many aspects of the communication mix decision and especially components like advertising. To the extent that the marketing manager does not build up and evaluate a programme budget in the manner described here, it becomes impossible to defend the budget as a justifiable economic expenditure. Inadequate discipline of this nature is characteristic of companies where the advertising budget is the first item to be cut in times of financial difficulty. If nobody can justify logically and quantitatively the need for a given budget level, then no rational manager can approve the budget.

The budgeting decision therefore becomes the financial summary and yardstick of the decisions taken in the four preceding steps. Because most companies have very limited financial resources, it is normal to introduce limits on what is an affordable budget, given the company's finances. To the extent that an initial communication programme proposal exceeds this limit, the manager has to evaluate two factors:

1 Are benefits expected from the budget such that the company should consider reallocating resources internally to fund the programme? Or,
2 Are the benefits such that the company should consider raising additional funds to implement the programme?

If the answers to both these questions are no, then the manager must return to the cycle of decisions about audience/objectives/message/media and find a valid programme that fits within the budget constraint. The lens manufacturer might choose, for example, to limit initial marketing to companies located in his or her national market. If success is achieved during the first budget period, then additional financial resources will have been created to address buyers on a European or global scale.

The budget decision must therefore reflect the strict disciplined logic of what has to be done and how, and the payoff to the company from undertaking the communication programme, as well as any financial constraints on budget size.

Execution of the programme must be actively pursued, whether through interaction with an advertising agency, through supervision of a salesforce, or design and printing of brochures. The programme, its details and its budget commitments have to be relentlessly managed to make it all happen. Not only is the marketing management process involved here, but also the order generation, fulfilment and service process. Marketing communication may be initiated and organized by the marketing department, however, its successful administration involves personnel throughout the firm – from the general manager officiating at a public relations event to a front-of-house assistant orchestrating a successful 'moment of truth' for a potential new customer. No amount of good analysis and planning will compensate for a lack of thorough professional implementation.

Measurement of the results of the communication programme is essential to knowing whether objectives have been achieved and the budget profitably spent. At the heart of measurement activity is the establishment of standards against which to measure performance. By going through the decision framework described, many if not most of these standards will have been set. Thus the communication objectives, the media, the message and the budgeted expenditure have all been decided upon. These factors, in the case of the hypothetical cereal example already discussed, might look like the following in terms of a managerial action plan:

Objectives for new breakfast cereal launch, April 1997
1 Achieve 70 per cent awareness of the product among all target housewives in the region by end of first four weeks.
2 Achieve sell-in of product by start of April to all supermarket chains, symbol groups and cash-and-carry wholesalers.
3 Execute merchandising and sales promotion programmes in 25 supermarkets in main cities and major provincial towns.
4 Ship cases of cereal to the trade by 1 April and second orders by end of April.
5 Achieve consumer sales of 2,450 cases by 30 April, based on a two-week repurchase cycle, initial purchases by 5 per cent of households in the target market, and repurchases by 50 per cent of these within four weeks.

Message
1 'Bran Nu' is a healthy, nutritious breakfast meal made from pure natural ingredients.
2 ' "Bran Nu" is the NATURAL way to start the day.'

Media
1 Regional TV and radio advertising commencing 31 March 1997 targeted at the housewife with an intensive schedule for first two weeks of April and a 'reminder schedule' for last two weeks.
2 Salesforce sell-in of product to trade commencing 1 March.

3 Advertising to trade during March in key trade journals and press.
4 Promotional and merchandising materials for supermarkets to highlight the new product and support consumer trial in 25 supermarkets.

Budget

1	Advertising: media plus production costs	160,000 ECU
2	Trade incentives	40,000 ECU
3	Allocation of salesforce time	70,000 ECU
4	Contract promotional personnel to conduct 25 in-store promotions	50,000 ECU
		320 000 ECU

With these stated objectives, costs and planned sales consequences, the programme for the launch of the product may be monitored closely. If actual results diverge from budget, the cause of the variance can be traced to (1) poor implementation of the programme, (2) bad assumptions about the response of the market to the programme, or (3) unpredicted changes in the market such as a competitive launch of another new breakfast food. Under these circumstances, the next step in the framework can be tackled.

Evaluation of results is possible because standards were set and performance against them measured. If variances have arisen between budgeted and actual performance, their origin can be diagnosed with some accuracy. The marketing manager is therefore in a position to learn from experience and to take rational corrective action if it is needed. Going through these steps is essential to eradicating the tendency in many companies to view budgets for communication strategy as very judgemental and impossible to justify with conviction. As long as a company conducts the communication element of its marketing mix under these circumstances, its implementation of this vital decision is likely to be subject to sudden changes and reversals, uninformed decision-making and confusion about the cost-effectiveness of the activity.

The elements of the communication mix

These elements, illustrated in Figure 17.1, are the media alternatives referred to in the decision-making procedure described. Each element has its unique strengths and weaknesses, and in practice one seldom encounters a single element mix. This reflects the complexity of most communication decisions, which demand several media or channels to achieve the several objectives or to reinforce each other in pursuit of a single objective.

Advertising in itself is a complex of alternative mechanisms for communicating with and persuading potential customers. While television, radio, press and popular magazine advertising are part of everyday life, and indeed part of a country's popular culture and lifestyle, there are many non-mass media advertising vehicles. Trade and professional journals and magazines reach specialist target audiences with a narrow focus such as doctors, grocery store owners, purchasing managers, and so on. Specialist magazines reach select segments of the consumer population such as camera enthusiasts, yachtsmen, motor sport addicts, home improvement amateurs, and many other groups to whom the marketer of a specialty product can communicate directly via the appropriate magazine. Outdoor advertising in the form of billboards and posters has been a staple of advertising in many European countries for generations but is increasingly subject to strict regulation in order to preserve the visual environment.

The implementation of an advertising programme can be undertaken independently by the firm. When a significant amount is being done and creative help is needed with the message and choice of media most companies will employ the services of an advertising agency to produce the content of the advertising, to advise on the message and on the optimal choice, and scheduling, of media within a given budget.

A considerable body of information exists on the media habits of various consumer and specialist audience groups which can be accessed by the marketer via advertising agencies or directly from the media themselves. The Joint National Media Research study conducted annually in most European countries details the viewership and readership profiles of the main mass media alternatives. These profiles typically illustrate who watches/listens to/reads what media in terms of their demographic and socioeconomic characteristics and their ownership/use of a range of consumer durable and non-durable products.

Sales promotion and *merchandising* cover activities such as demonstrations, special offers, price-offs, samples, coupons, customer and trade competitions, bonus packs, stamp plans, continuity premiums and affiliation clubs, in-store displays, special shelving and presentation mechanisms that stimulate short-term sales and customer interest. Sales promotion mechanisms are particularly important at the early stage of a product's lifecycle to encourage consumer trial and withdrawal of loyalty from old products. They are also widely used in the maturity stage to maintain product interest and to combat competing new product launches. With the greater importance of trade marketing, sales promotion is developing in a range of innovative ways.

In addition, sales promotion instruments may be employed as tactical weapons in the battle for market share throughout the lifecycle. They are also used on occasion to achieve a company's end-of-year sales budgets where actual sales are running behind forecast sales. This is a particularly short-sighted use of the tool, as it typically transfers demand from a later period to an earlier one, leaving trade or consumers stocked up with the product and the marketer with a very bleak sales period at the beginning of the new budget while customers run their stocks back down to normal levels. Merchandising is increasingly important in retailing because of the pressure for shelf space from more and more competitive products. Many companies therefore employ full-time or temporary merchandising personnel to look after the effective presentation of their products in supermarkets and to arrange periodic special displays.

Public relations and *publicity* are chosen as part of the communications mix to inform selected groups in the environment about the company and its products and to build a backdrop of trust and understanding for the more specifically product-related and annual plan-based communication activities. Public relations involves activities planned to create, maintain or enhance the company's reputation in its environment among groups whose goodwill and understanding are important to its future prosperity. Such groups may range from the government to the banking community, from schoolchildren to employees. Large, well-established companies whose prosperity is intimately tied to that of a whole economy pay particular attention to public relations, as can be observed in the extensive range of PR and sponsorship activity undertaken by companies like Philips, Volvo, Alfa Laval, Royal Dutch Shell, Nestlé, and many others.

Publicity is closely linked with PR in seeking unpaid coverage of the company's activities and products in public media. Media coverage of annual general meetings, of new product innovations or of export successes by firms can be obtained with a little care and planning and has the value of giving the market a positive evaluation of the company from an objective and detached third party. Public relations and publicity activity may be organized by the company itself or through the specialist services of a public relations consultant or agency.

Sponsorship is a rapidly growing area of marketing communication. It involves a firm paying funds to be associated with an event, activity, organization or person in the public domain where the firm derives goodwill and prominent exposure from the association – typically a sporting, artistic, entertainment or societally oriented event. Commercial sponsorship has witnessed a dramatic increase for a number of reasons: regulatory policies on tobacco and alcohol; more leisure-related activities in society; and greater media coverage of sponsored events.

Direct mail and *direct response marketing* are other rapidly developing modes of marketing communication. They seek to appeal to the final user or consumer directly by shortening the downstream end of the business system – cutting out middlemen. Direct mail shots, telemarketing, direct response TV and radio using 1–800 numbers and direct response print appeals are highly useful in markets where traditional mass market appeals are ineffective and too costly, and where sophisticated databases permit access to highly targeted, and fragmented, customer groups. They also have the benefit of the marketer being able to assess their effectiveness in a very measured and accurate manner.

Exhibitions and *trade fairs* involve the marketer in presenting his or her company and its products or services at a venue where many potential customers can conveniently gather. This is usually done at industry exhibitions or fairs such as the London Boat Show or the Frankfurt Book Fair. The list of such events is extensive and constitutes something of a reversal of personal selling activity. Here the customer comes to the exhibition or fair, whereas under normal circumstances the salesforce has to go out to call on customers one at a time. Exhibitions or 'roadshows' can also be organized by the company on its own. This is often done by hiring space in a hotel in the centre of a market area and inviting present and prospective customers to inspect and perhaps try out a product range or a new product or service.

Trade fair participation is often the first step into international markets taken by a small firm. If well planned and undertaken with realistic objectives, it can be a very productive means of learning about buyer needs in export markets and testing product acceptability. At a later stage in international marketing growth it should be undertaken with more sales-related objectives as well as the market research and learning objectives.

Personal selling is perhaps the most powerful, certainly the most sophisticated, and often the most expensive element of the communication mix. Its power and sophistication derive from the use of intelligent, flexible human beings to act as the communication mechanism. The salesperson who understands the sales and communication objectives of the company can adapt the communication message as the need arises, applying it to the unique behaviour pattern and product needs of each customer. Personal selling is therefore extremely effective where good and close relationships and communication flows must be maintained between customers and company. It is particularly effective where the product or service is complex or technical and where it is used in a customer problem-solving context. Under such circumstances, the salesperson acts as consultant, diagnostician of customer problems and needs, adviser on specifying problem solutions, and support person during use of the product. Such characteristics are expensive. If they are good, they readily justify their overhead cost, but if they underperform, they become a serious burden.

Integrated marketing communication

It is evident that some elements of the communication mix have moved to the fore at the expense of others, in terms of perceived effectiveness and company expenditure. For example, in 1978 advertising in the United States accounted for 42 per cent of consumer packaged good companies' marketing budgets, and sales promotion for 58 per cent. By 1988, advertising spend had slipped to 31 per cent, against 69 per cent for promotion.[1] A similar picture exists in Europe, where there has been a greater movement towards the use of sales promotional techniques in recent years, largely because of the focus of business on short-term profits and value and the perceived need for promotional strategies that produce short-term sales boosts – often in the face of growing retailer power and own-brand development. This is not to deny that sales promotion can play a valuable role in sustaining a brand franchise, especially when allied to advertising.

This trend away from above the line to below the line, as well as the rapid growth in beyond the line spend in areas like sponsorship and direct response marketing, are characteristic of a changing landscape in marketing. This has impacted significantly on communication modes and their support agencies. A number of contributory factors are to be considered.

Media fragmentation
Technology, greater leisure time availability and changing socioeconomic and demographic factors have resulted in a fragmentation in traditional advertising media in particular. New magazines and newspaper titles, extra national, regional and even global television channels, along with regional and local radio have all conspired to make the marketer's job of communicating with the target audience more difficult. This complexity is further compounded by the increasing heterogeneity and segmentation in customer profiles.

Innovatory media
The explosion of cable and satellite broadcasting has been replicated in the development of the 'super highway' where opportunities for marketing communication are manifold. The Internet, multi-media instruments, even video games, have become stable modes for commercial exchange. Other media, such as commercial sponsorship of major sporting events, have been facilitated by this growth.

Other novel access channels to target markets include product placement, the presentation/inclusion within programmes, normally film and TV, of goods and services as part of realistic scene creation. Ray Ban sunglasses dramatically increased sales in the early 1990s by complementing traditional advertising through the placement of its products in over 160 movies per year.[2]

Escalating costs of traditional advertising media

Rates in the traditional advertising media have risen sharply over the last decades. This in part reflects the desire of such media owners to maintain profits in the face of declining revenues, and so becomes a vicious circle. As well as this, actual production costs of advertisements, especially for TV, have also risen. The net result has been to encourage the search for other, more cost-effective modes of communication.

A sophisticated, more autonomous consumer

The customer to whom the market is appealing is becoming increasingly sophisticated, sceptical and literate – in short, harder to persuade. This is particularly true of younger consumers for whom consumption is often an act of self-expression and empowerment. Further, the consumer confronted with a barrage of advertising or 'clutter' simply switches channel or zaps. The propensity of marketers to segment, allied to the increasing array of communication modes, has both produced and responded to audience fragmentation and decreased effectiveness in traditional mass marketing appeals.

Managing marketing communications in transition

Such changing circumstances challenge the marketing manager and his or her team to manage marketing communication in an effective way. While the boundaries of this change remain unclear, one factor is certain: communication management requires an integrated approach. Communication strategy must be handled resourcefully within the context of the framework set out in Figure 17.2, and the selection of media used must be synergistically and mutually supportive.

Integrated marketing communication is also identified by imagination and speed of response. It may be a small food manufacturer which launches a new product with a judicious mix of sales promotion and public relations – as indeed the UK makers of the Covent Garden brand of tetra packed fresh natural soup did. Or it may be a large manufacturer, like Heinz, which has chosen to supplement its above-the-line advertising with direct, and highly targeted, marketing to win customers' affiliation and to establish mutually satisfying relationships. This ability creatively and optimally to select communication modes, and to do so in a timely fashion, is also a feature of the leading companies in the popular music business (see Exhibit 17.1).

Marketing services providers are also affected considerably by these developments in communication media. There has been a growth in specialist agencies in the fields of direct marketing, promotions and sponsorship. Traditional advertising agencies, attempting to provide their clients with coordinated communication mix programmes, have had to develop these skills in-house or acquire specialist agencies. Escalating media rates have seen the establishment of media specialists which undertake the placement of advertising at low commission levels and thus undermine a traditional key role of the advertising agency. Indeed, the successful advertising agency provides a classic example of an organization being forced to reappraise its core processes and activities and re-engineer itself.

| Exhibit 17.1 | *Marketing in action case* |

EMI Records – marketing means money

The marketing machines of major record labels are well-oiled operations, and there is usually little left to chance when a new album is released. The market is thoroughly analyzed to tell the company how popular the record will be, and large amounts of money are then spent on promotion to encourage purchase. The marketing and distribution campaign begins well before a record is actually brought out, and continues long after the initial hype has died down. A tour is usually planned six months in advance, to coincide with the album's release; the main aim of the tour is to promote the new album, not to make money.

At EMI Records in the United Kingdom, a monthly sales meeting is held to plan for the releases of the following month. Promotional campaigns for the label's artists are devised for the various media. The next stage sees company reps visiting the record shops or contacting them by phone – telesales – to encourage retailers to order copies of new EMI releases. The reps also provide tour information, sell merchandising such as T-shirts and arrange for in-store displays featuring the artist.

Normally, a first single is released a month or two before the album comes out. The number of copies of the album that are manufactured depends on the sales of the artist's last album and the performance of the single. Most albums need the release of two or three singles in order to build up sales. For the lucky few a first best-selling single can lead to a flying start.

The machinery of pop promotion really moves into action once an album has been brought out. In-store displays are put up, the artist is interviewed in the media, and newspaper, radio and perhaps TV advertising is paid for. Even for a small release, it is vital to try to get on regional or national radio, to have the song's video shown on national TV, and to promote by playing gigs around the country and appearing on local radio.

In the pop business MTV is now the dominant channel to international success. Record companies display considerable resourcefulness in advertising, promoting their 'stars' and arranging sponsorship liaisons with MTV. The logistics of actual record, tape and CD distribution are swift. Retailers can phone in additional orders at any time, and these orders are processed on a weekly basis by the record distributors. Further single releases keep the momentum going behind a promotional campaign. Advertising is particularly heavy at Christmas, when huge numbers of records are sold. And, of course, record companies frequently re-release records when it suits them.

Record companies are frequently accused of ripping off their customers (and even their bands) and of hyping their product. With some justification, the companies defend themselves by saying that records and CDs are no different from any other products, and are promoted in the same way, using advertising, public relations, sponsorship, merchandising and other marketing techniques.[3]

Advertising

Some special issues arise in the development of policy for the advertising element of the marketing mix. These are the use of advertising in industrial product markets, the development of advertising objectives and the advertising budget.

The use of media advertising is generally associated with consumer products. Industrial marketers often underestimate its usefulness and cost-effectiveness in promoting their products. Many business-to-business marketers use advertising in specialist and even on occasion in general media to achieve objectives such as:

▶ creating awareness of a new industrial product;
▶ creating awareness and credibility for a company so that personal selling activity starts from a base of customer knowledge of the company and product;
▶ generating inquiries and leads for the salesforce to follow up;
▶ reminding customers and prospective customers of the company and its products so that when a purchase need arises the company will top the list of potential suppliers to be contacted;
▶ building customers' confidence and loyalty by positively reinforcing their decision to purchase and use the company's products.

Even traditional mass media, and some of the newer direct response channels, can cost-effectively achieve some of these objectives. Over the last decade, many products previously promoted only through personal selling in a business-to-business context found new ways to market through the mass media and direct marketing. This was particularly instanced in the case of personal computers where Apple and Toshiba made major investments in television advertising and Dell built its business on mail order promoted through newspapers and general interest magazines. Exhibit 6.2 (p. 99) described an imaginative use of TV advertising to promote roof tiles by a Spanish firm. Creativity in the use of the communication mix is therefore important, and managers should never be deterred from considering media traditionally avoided by their own company and its competitors.

The development of advertising objectives requires the manager to develop at least a basic analysis of the various kinds of communication results he or she may wish to achieve. In Chapter 6 a framework for customer decision-making was used as a basis for exploring consumer and buyer behaviour. An issue which emerges clearly from such an analysis is that different customers and indeed whole segments of the market may be at different stages of the decision cycle and therefore need different information. Communication aimed at triggering need recognition is likely to differ from communications intended to help customers evaluate competing products or to reassure them if they have had second thoughts about the wisdom of their purchase at the product usage stage.

A company trying to develop a new commuter air traffic service faces an interesting variety of communication needs. Past users of commuter air services would need reassurance that trying another service reflects good decision-making. The company would also have to fight for its share of the market, so potential customers need information on how to evaluate the competing modes of travelling and the advantages of air travel. Many people travel by car or train between main cities who could be encouraged to fly if their decision-making behaviour were altered from choosing between ground transport alternatives to choosing between ground and air travel.

The development of an advertising strategy in such a context, therefore, demands that thought be given to which target audience, at what stage of its decision-making, should form the object of the exercise. Separate objectives are required for the different groups, although separate advertising programmes may not necessarily be required. Objectives may also be specified at various stages on a continuum stretching from creating awareness to precipitating a sale, as shown in Figure 17.3. The five steps shown in the diagram represent just one of many models of communication effect. These models are usually called *hierarchy of effect models* because the audience is likely to go through the steps sequentially, although impulse purchases could well jump from initial awareness of the existence of a product in a shop to immediate purchase. The value of these models is in their clarification of the many levels at which an advertising objective may be set. Advertising to create awareness of a new product may have to be different from advertising aimed at helping consumers to evaluate the product they now know about. Equally, such a framework may highlight inappropriate objectives. For example, to return to the example of the new enterprise set up to produce optical lenses, it is not appropriate to set a sales objective for any advertising that may be undertaken. Closing sales in this company is a personal selling task. However, it may be a very valid advertising objective to achieve the awareness step and part of the comprehension step. The job of helping the customer to comprehend the product fully, to evaluate it accurately and to form an intention to purchase it is much more a task for personal selling in this kind of technical product market.

Each of the stages in the model shown in Figure 17.3 is measurable by relatively simple marketing research methods, so achievement of such objectives can be monitored with accuracy. Consumer goods firms have the opportunity to measure advertising effect in terms of changes in intentions to purchase, since final purchase is heavily dependent not just on advertising but on distribution and in-store location, merchandising and retail selling.

Advertising budgets are determined in practice by several methods. The percentage-of-sales method is an arbitrary approach that has alarming popularity. Using this method, the manager applies a fixed percentage to sales to set the advertising budget, usually justifying it on the grounds that there is an accepted advertising/sales ratio in the industry. The method

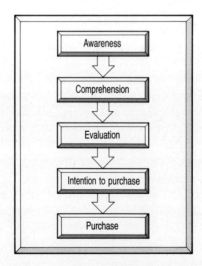

Figure 17.3 A hierarchy of communications effects

assumes a constant relationship between advertising expenditure and sales results and can lead to a pattern of decision-making that allows sales revenue to determine advertising where one might more reasonably expect advertising to be a determinant of sales. Budgets are also frequently set with reference to competitors' budgets, allowing little for the different strategies being pursued and the different market positions of competitors.

The objective-and-task method is the most valid approach in common use. This demands that the budget emerge from a logical determination of objectives and a specification of the advertising tasks that must be undertaken to meet these objectives. The tasks are costed and the budget estimated. If the budget level is higher than the company can afford, the manager must adjust objectives to a more realistic level. Some computer-based models have been developed, usually based on the statistical estimation of relationships in a product market between advertising and sales response. While these budgeting models have limited currency as yet, their contribution to analytical decision-making is growing continuously, especially with the development of EPOS (electronic point of sale) and EDI (electronic data interchange) technologies.

Personal selling and sales management

The implementation of an effective personal selling strategy depends on good sales management. For sales management to be effective, it must be based on a sales management strategy with the eleven basic components set out below:

1 identification of selling tasks,
2 selling objectives,
3 selecting strategy for selling,
4 salesforce size,
5 territory design,
6 salesforce structure,
7 recruitment and selection,
8 training,
9 remuneration,
10 supervision,
11 evaluation.

Identification of the personal selling task involves the specification of what exactly has to be done by a salesperson to achieve a successful sale. This demands knowledge of the customer's buying behaviour and circumstances and what actions are required of the salesperson to help solve the customer's problem and present the company's product or service as a solution to appropriate problems. These tasks should be specified in simple behavioural terms. In the case of selling water treatment equipment to local authorities and to industry, for example, the salesperson's tasks will include:

▶ analyzing the water treatment requirements of the customer;
▶ developing with the local authority engineer or production manager specifications for the water treatment system;
▶ developing with the consultant engineer (if any) extensions of these specifications for inclusion in any tender invitation;
▶ identifying all the key decision-makers involved at different stages in purchase activity;
▶ selecting and providing technical and financial and general performance documentation for transmission to different members of the buying group;
▶ helping to solve technical design problems as the design project evolves;
▶ liaising with the engineer in charge of installation and commissioning of the system after the purchase to ensure that full technical and other forms of assistance and support are made available;
▶ maintaining ongoing contact with the customer after successful conclusion of the sale to identify further sales opportunities.

It can be seen how specification of these tasks can be readily translated into personal selling objectives.

Objectives for the salesforce emerge from an analysis of the tasks necessary to make a sale and generate further business, as well as from the overall marketing programme concerning how many sales must be closed for what particular products. Objectives, therefore, contain selling activity standards and revenue and volume sales targets.

Personal selling strategy is developed to achieve the stated objectives through performance of the required selling tasks. To achieve volume and revenue targets, the number of customers to be called on, the regularity of calls and the procedures for closing sales and managing customer accounts must be specified as a personal selling strategy – the means by which the objectives will be achieved.

Decisions on *salesforce size* can be addressed by considering the information available on the workload involved in implementing the strategy to achieve stated objectives, and by evaluating the productivity of a salesperson and the consequent costs and contribution to profit arising from the hiring of each additional salesperson.

The determination of salesforce size is normally approached in one of two ways. The first is the salesforce productivity method. In most established markets the productivity of a salesperson in terms of sales achieved over a sales period can be estimated with considerable accuracy. However, when more salespeople are added to a market, their productivity eventually must begin to decline as they saturate the market with selling activity. The revenue produced by each additional salesperson can be used to calculate the profit contribution from his or her sales efforts, and this can in turn be compared with the additional cost of having the salesperson on the sales-force. As salespeople are added the contribution on the sales they make will initially cover the cost of hiring and maintaining them on the payroll. However, as saturation begins to set in, the additional return to each new salesperson will begin to decline until one more addition just covers its own cost with profit contribution. At this point it ceases to be profitable to employ any more salespeople.

An alternative and more widely used method is the workload approach, which starts with a management decision about the number of sales calls required per customer per year. The total number of customers to be called on is multiplied by the call frequency to give a total required number of calls per year. The average number of calls a salesperson can make per day can be determined from the nature of the selling task and travel distances. This calls-per-day rate is then translated into a call capacity per annum which, when divided into the total required number of calls per year, yields a necessary salesforce size:

$$\frac{\text{Total calls required per annum}}{\text{Annual call capacity of salesperson}} = \text{Salesforce size}$$

While the first method mentioned may be difficult to implement in many circumstances, management should always check on the contribution generated per individual and per average salesperson and compare this with the total direct cost per salesperson. If the two figures begin to converge, action to limit salesforce size or to increase its productivity will become necessary. This need to evaluate salesforce contribution becomes all the more apparent when the cost to a company of running its sales personnel is considered. Table 17.1, based on research in one European country, item-izes the typical cost of a sales representative. Converging prices and costs in the EU suggest that this cost of almost 40,000 ECUs per year is not untypical in many European salesforces. If this figure is multiplied by 10 to allow for a very modest level of sales representation, and increased approximately by a third to allow for the cost of sales management and sales administration, a total cost of over half a million ECUs is reached – a very substantial investment for any company. Thus issues of salesforce size and productivity are key.

Table 17.1 Costs of a sales representative

The average cost of having a sales representative on the road may be estimated as follows:	ECU
Basic salary	14,635
Pay related social insurance	1,478
Pension	1,463
Commission/bonus	4,376
Travel expenses	5,098
Car purchase and tax	5,063
Car insurance	1,040
Services and repairs	885
Postage and telephone	840
Training (1 × 1-week course)	516
Sundries (entertainment, etc.)	400
Total	35,794 ECU

Source: *Profile of a Salesforce* (1995), Sales Placement Ltd., Dublin.
Note: Figures are converted into ECUs at the exchange rate of IR£1 = 1.25 ECU.

Territory design and *allocation* are often done in a non-analytical manner and can result in conflict and bad feelings within a salesforce, with immediate repercussions on sales effectiveness. For example, if territories are allocated on simple geographic boundaries such as counties or regions the sales potential of different areas will vary radically. This typically leads to disputes over who gets the 'good' and the 'bad' territories. If a significant part of the salesperson's income is in commissions and bonuses tied to sales volume, conflict can become particularly strong and emotional. In general, therefore, the aim should be to design territories with equal sales potential, thereby avoiding such a basis for conflict and providing a simple framework within which to evaluate performance. This approach can break down, of course, when the workload involved in covering two equal-potential territories begins to diverge for reasons such as variation in geographic size. For some products, a city market might well equal the sales potential of a large rural region. Yet to allocate one salesperson to the city and one to the rest of the region would produce very different workloads in terms of travel time and time spent away from home. For this reason some companies design territories on the basis of equal workloads and try to manage any conflict arising from the unequal sales potentials that inevitably follow.

Salesforce structure addresses the issue of whether personal selling should be focused on products, on customers, on territories, or on a mixture of these three. Many salesforces are organized around products: salespeople sell one product or a related line of products, but not the company's other products. They therefore become product specialists. This may be necessary where products are very complex and there is little overlap or complementarity between the various products of the company. It can, however, lead to problems of salespeople identifying more with the product than with the customer's needs, and to the situation of several salespeople from the same company calling on one customer in a quite uncoordinated way.

Territory-oriented structuring results in a salesperson carrying all the company's products within a given geographical area to all customers. Salespeople can respond to this very positively by accepting 'ownership' of the territory and its long-term development and by becoming the company's representative in all senses of the word in the area. This works well where the product range is limited and similar and customer characteristics do not vary greatly. Where the opposite applies, it becomes difficult for one salesperson to be all-knowing about all products and all-competent to deal with every type of customer.

Customer-based sales organization is an approach being increasingly adopted by firms keen to overlay a process approach to their marketing. Customers are identified individually or clustered into similar groups in terms of their needs, and the salesforce is then structured around these individuals or groups. Many grocery salesforces reflect the need for (1) high-level sales and negotiation work with buyers of supermarket multiple and symbol group chains; (2) a different kind of selling into individual chain and multiple outlets and cash-and-carrys; and (3) yet another sales task in servicing the independent grocer.

Selling and the process imperative

The growing strength of top retailers has forced many suppliers to replace salespeople who push products and take orders with knowlegeable key account managers who can help plan their customers' businesses. It was described in Chapter 13 how Procter & Gamble established cross-functional teams to serve each major account. Replacing the old divisional salesforces, these teams represent all P&G divisions and have significant analytic and operational capabilities. They are led by senior customer team leaders who are former district managers. Sales personnel play a crucial role in these process teams dedicated to achieving market focus in a fluid and complex business environment.

Where customers are large buyers when taken one at a time and where they divide into distinct groups with identifiable needs, a customer-based approach suggests itself. For a company with a wide range of complementary products that can be sold as a system as well as individually, it may also be a very necessary structure. IBM, for example, changed its worldwide sales structure from a product-organized one to a customer-organized one, believing that it had to coordinate all the company's products to address the overall system problems of individual clients and avoid uncoordinated and on occasion conflicting sales activity by product salespeople selling to the same company.

Recruitment, selection and *training* of the salesforce should be undertaken when the decisions on the areas already mentioned have been taken. It is possible at this stage to specify a job description and personal profile for the person who could perform the required tasks, meet objectives and fit into the chosen territorial and organizational structures. The company can choose to buy in experience by hiring trained and expert salespeople or to invest in the training and development of younger, less experienced persons. This decision must reflect the urgency of immediate sales generation requirements and the necessity to socialize people into the company and to make them expert in the details of its products and services.

A process imperative stresses the notions of networks, longer-term buyer–seller relationships and basic sound business practice. This in many ways devolves more responsibility to sales personnel, and also to the process of selling itself, than is often the case in more conventional approaches to marketing. The successful sales representative complements his or her skills in persuasion with these in negotiation, bargaining and organizational empathy. The prudent company invests in training and development to nurture these competences in its saleforce.

Remuneration should be based on the nature of the selling task, the motivational role of money payments, and the control and supervision requirements of the business. Selling jobs that involve long lead-times before sales are concluded, as well as extensive customer liaison, servicing and advisory work, are generally best dealt with by remuneration schemes emphasizing a guaranteed salary. Where sales are made daily and there is little need for deep involvement with customers, commission and bonus elements should generally play a much stronger role. Most situations require a mixture of both.

Money, especially in the form of commissions and bonuses, is not always the great motivator to higher achievement that it is sometimes naively claimed to be. Sales personnel respond very positively in terms of job commitment and productivity to much less tangible motivators such as intelligent and attentive *supervision*, senior management recognition of achievements, fair and transparent *evaluation* and a supportive company environment which makes them feel part of the enterprise and the vital final link between it and the market that ultimately is its only source of revenue and prosperity.

Remuneration systems heavily geared towards variable elements such as commission and bonuses generally require less managerial supervision – they are self-regulating in a rather mechanical way. If the salesperson does well, rewards automatically flow to reinforce the behaviour. If performance is poor, remuneration shrinks and the behaviour is punished. The difficulty with such relatively 'automated' supervisory and control systems is that nothing is done to help the salesperson understand what is causing success or failure so that he or she can learn by the experience, and as a result high staff turnover rates are typical of such salesforce systems. This can also reflect the extent to which salespeople in highly pressurized environments experience 'burn-out'. The alternative approach is depth in managerial supervision and motivation and is a high-cost approach, but will often be justified in high productivity performance, lower staff turnover rates and deeper customer relationships.

International selling and group marketing

The nature of personal selling and the type of salespersons required for international marketing very much depend on where the firm is in the sequence of internationalizing. The experience of many small ventures entering international markets for the first time is that top management must shoulder the burden of much of the early personal selling to develop its knowledge of these markets and to demonstrate its serious commitment to serving international customers. As this business begins to grow and a loyal base to develop, specialist international sales talent becomes more affordable and can be hired in on the basis of a clear knowledge of the selling tasks that must be performed and realistic performance objectives.

At an early stage smaller companies may find it possible to finance international selling by cooperating with producers of complementary products to support an export salesperson, perhaps also by gaining assistance from a state trade board for initial personal selling investment. Such firms may also consider dealing through a company that specializes in developing export markets and product ideas and coordinating the efforts of several small businesses. Such group marketing has to overcome the barriers to cooperation between independent-minded firms but the payoff can be well worthwhile.

Relationship marketing

The market-focused firm views marketing in a context which emphasizes mutual profitability for the two parties involved in a market relationship. A basic objective of the marketing management process is to achieve a sale and effect a transaction. But good marketing practice is also about retaining a customer in a manner satisfying to both the firm and its client. Relational marketing focuses on customer retention. Christopher *et al.* suggest that the objective of relationship marketing is to 'turn new customers into regularly purchasing clients, and then to progressively move them through being strong supporters of the company and its product, and finally to being active and vocal advocates for the company, thus playing an important role as a referral source'.[4] Figure 17.4 depicts such a loyalty 'ladder'.

There are good economic reasons for winning customer loyalty. It was noted in Chapter 1 that in mature markets it may cost five times as much to attract a new customer as to maintain the goodwill of an existing customer.[5] Under such circumstances, sound established relationships are of great value. Much recent research argues that the longer customers stay with a business, the greater their contribution to profitability. This arises from both cost savings and additional revenues.[6] Reichheld and Sasser show, using a range of examples, how a 5 per cent decrease in defections can contribute from 12 per cent to 85 per cent more profits.[7]

There are clear benefits to a firm from a relational approach. But a relationship is by definition a two-sided affair with mutual advantage to both parties. What are the benefits to customers? Ideally, they gain from the

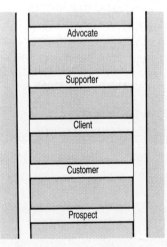

Source: M. Christopher, A. Payne and D. Ballantyre (1991), *Relationship Marketing* (Butterworth-Heinemann, Oxford).

Figure 17.4 The relationship ladder of customer loyalty

firm having a deeper and ongoing understanding of their wants and needs which allows it to offer a value-for-money bundle of benefits over time such that they remain happy to bestow loyalty on the firm. An example might be a financial institution which courts customers over a post-adolescent lifetime by providing a tailored range of services and products to meet their changing needs. However, customers do not always perceive such mutuality of benefit nor indeed do they always want to enter into a 'relationship'.

Some kinds of transaction make the initiation of a relationship problematic, for example, a good purchased on impulse, on a one-off decision, or the case of low-involvement products. Indeed, relational marketing is most likely to be successful where both firm and customer perceive the purchasing stakes to be rising – where purchase decisions require more buyer involvement, and order generation, fulfilment and service require greater investment on the part of the firm. Many firms attempt to lock in customers in a variety of ways, e.g. through the creation of switching costs, exit barriers, training schemes, even affiliation clubs. While such approaches do indeed achieve repeat purchase, yield profit to the firms, at least in the short to medium term, and represent a type of structural bonding, they cannot be categorized as exercises in relationship marketing. Buyer loyalty and repurchase must be won on a voluntary not coercive basis in a true relational exchange. Further, some customers simply do not want a relationship with a company for whatever reason. In the case of financial services, some clients prefer to deal with a bank at arm's length and purchase services from a number of institutions. Other customers may be well disposed to the idea of a relationship with a firm. But the firm fails to deliver from its side, and the customer defects to a competitor. Such an occurrence is often indicative of a firm's incompetence at listening to its customers' grievances and failure to understand the nature of consumer complaint behaviour.

From transactions to relationships

Firm–buyer relationships are complex in their nature, varying considerably in their viability, intensity and length. The firm considering a more relational approach with its customers assesses at least three important factors:

1 *The nature of the exchange* – is the transaction one where a mutually satisfying relationship can indeed be nurtured, or one where it will always remain difficult to establish? A personal service like a retail bank has many possibilities to foster a relational approach. A seller of holiday souvenirs to tourists has few.

2 *Building blocks of the relationship* – if a relationship looks feasible, how is it best pursued? What actions will enhance it, given the particular array of product, market and competitive behaviour? A car dealer, for example, may place a customer who has purchased a particular model, and who has indicated certain lifestyle interests, on a mailing list for regular information updates about new model innovations in order to enthuse him or her about a possible new purchase. A specialist component manufacturer may work very closely with a number of client companies, providing first-rate service back-up, liaising on R&D and offering the clients new and better solutions in their operations. A local grocer may use friendliness, personal service, delivery and credit availability as the basis of relationship building with his customers in winning their loyalty away from competing supermarket chains. In fact, it is to be observed that many smaller local firms seem intuitively better at relationship management than bigger companies. The large firm can usefully imitate aspects of small firm practice in relationship marketing.

3 *Researching customer needs* – a thorough and unrelenting ambition on the part of the firm to understand the precise, and changing, needs and wants of its customers characterizes successful relationship marketing. Firms display great innovation in pursuing this, from running focus groups, commissioning lifestyle research, using point-of-sale terminals and 1–800 telemarketing, to simply going into the marketplace and listening and observing buyers and consumers. Current research methods facilitate an increasing ability to segment markets and customers on a variety of bases.

The growth in database marketing has already been described. Exhibit 7.1 (p. 128) illustrated how General Motors Corp. joined with Mastercard to offer the GM Card. As a result, GM now has a database of over 12 million GM cardholders, and it surveys them to learn what they are driving, when they next plan to buy a car and what kind of vehicle they would like. If a cardholder expresses an interest in, say, sport utility vehicles, the card unit mails out information on its jeep line and passes the cardholder's name along to the appropriate division. Such targeted offerings garner a considerably higher response rate than the typical 2–4 per cent for normal, unsolicited junk mail, and may be seen as way of nurturing closer firm–customer relations. However, not all database marketing should be equated with relationship marketing. Much of it involves direct mail techniques and telemarketing where the notion of a mutually satisfactory relationship is very tenuous.

Figure 17.5 may assist a firm to understand more fully the nature of relationships it may expect to cultivate.[8] It maps a continuum from pure transaction to very close relationship between firm and purchaser. For example, it may be assumed that a customer's relationship with his or her hairdresser or dentist would be closer to the genuine relationship end of the continuum, while that with an electrical utility or a fast-food restaurant may be closer to the transaction end. The depiction of each of the customer–firm relationships as a distribution rather than as a single point on the continuum suggests that not all customers want the same type or intensity of relationship with a particular firm or industry. For example, some customers will want a very close, friendly relationship with a hairdresser, while another may view the purchase of a haircut as more of a transaction. However, the nature of the interaction between hairdresser and customer will almost certainly mean that the relationship will be more personal than that between a telephone company and a customer.

The firm first asks if, indeed, a relationship is possible considering the nature of the exchange. It is fair to say that at some point along the relationship continuum, a transaction approach to marketing ceases to be appropriate and the possibility for the establishment of a genuine relationship begins. The firm then identifies the building blocks of the relationship and ascertains the information and research necessary to comprehend fully the client's needs and level of interest in a relationship.

The examples on Figure 17.5 refer chiefly to final users or consumers. But relationship marketing is as much, if not more, about establishing win-win relations on a business-to-business basis – in fact, all along the business system. Consider again Figure 2.1 (p. 23) which places alternative ways of managing transactions also on a continuum from classical 'open' market to a fully 'managed' market. Here it is to be observed that relationship

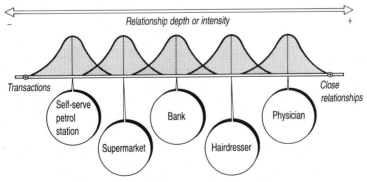

Source: J. Barnes (1995) 'Establishing relationships – Getting closer to the customer may be more difficult than you think', *Irish Marketing Review*, vol. 8 p. 112.

Figure 17.5 The relationship marketing continuum

marketing itself may evolve over time into another form of market arrangement, e.g. alliance, joint venture, franchising, or even to single ownership where former seller and buyer merge together into one trading and organizational entity. Managing relationships is crucial to achieving and sustaining market focus. Such management is crucial across the business system and in expediting the four core marketing processes.

REVIEW QUESTIONS

17.1 What are the principal steps of decision-making involved in developing a communication strategy? Show how each step must necessarily be taken before the succeeding one is decided on.

17.2 Elaborate on the various elements in the communication mix. Are you aware of any trends in the choice of communication media by companies?

17.3 How is integrated marketing communication best achieved?

17.4 How should advertising objectives be developed?

17.5 Personal selling is an extremely effective element of marketing strategy, but it is also one of the most expensive communication media that a firm can use. Discuss.

17.6 What factors must be considered by a firm seeking to embrace relationship marketing?

CHAPTER 18

Distribution

- Selecting a distribution channel
- Evaluating alternative channels
- Managing the channel
- Channel strategy
- Physical distribution

Marketing in action cases
Firstdirect – the branchless bank
ISPG reconfigures the aquabusiness value chain

ABOUT THIS CHAPTER

Distribution in a marketing context addresses two broad issues. The first concerns whether the marketer will deal directly with the final customer or use intermediaries or middlemen to bring the product or service of the company to market. The second is concerned with the physical management of the product or service flow from company to customer – what stocks should be held and where and what transportation arrangements are appropriate.

The first concern, deciding on a channel, is a crucial step. How channels should be chosen, managed and controlled is considered. Channel choice has considerable strategic import amd often involves the marketing manager in broader corporate decision-making. Channel of distribution decisions necessitate a deep understanding of the macro business system, and strategic advantage is to be gained by imaginative reconfiguration of this system and the firm's micro business system.

Physical distribution considers the selection of service level standards, the minimization of the total cost of physical distribution and the effective integration of the order generation, fulfilment and service process.

Channels and customers

The purpose of a channel is quite simply to get the product or service of the company to the customer in a manner which best suits the customer while also fitting in with company objectives and resources. Who customers are and where they are is therefore the best starting point in making a decision. Think of the customer for a simple headache remedy. The ultimate consuming unit for this product is really the family group. Purchases are typically made in two ways. A consumer will frequently buy a supply of analgesics (aspirin, paracetamol) during her main weekly shopping trip to the supermarket. This purchase then becomes a stock item in the home, to be used as needed and replaced on another supermarket trip. Other purchase situations arise, however, especially when someone suffering from the pain of a headache or cold or flu wants an immediate remedy. Under such circumstances, if they are away from home, they are likely to want to purchase the analgesic in a convenient tobacconist, sweet and newspaper (TSN) shop, or perhaps in a chemist shop where they can ask for the pharmacist's recommendation.

Choice of distribution channel for analgesics must be fundamentally governed by these underlying patterns of consumer behaviour. Here the manager immediately has to consider three retail points at all or some of which he or she might make the product available. Furthermore, the choice will have an impact on the product packaging decisions that must also be made – perhaps large packs for the supermarket to last the family some time as a stock item and small convenient pocket or handbag-size packs for the TSN, which are easily carried during the day and at work. Some marketers confine their analgesic brands to chemist outlets alone, giving the product strong associations with the professional and paramedical nature of the pharmacy outlet.

Selecting a distribution channel

So the first issue in selecting a channel is to return to the fundamentals of marketing analysis to understand the customers – who they are, where they are and where they would prefer to purchase the product. This normally provides immediate guidance for the choice of retail channel. There are, however, many instances in which the channel chosen is direct from company to customer. This is particularly common in the case of industrial products and services where the company is selling to another organization which is the final customer, as is the case of most engineering sub-assemblies, circuit-boards sold to an electronics company, machine tools sold to an engineering works, plastic moulds sold to a moulding firm, and so on. Here the marketing manager is typically faced with a relatively small number of final customers and a customer need for a high level of interaction with the supplier about product design, performance, installation and service. This does not mean that all industrial goods are distributed through a direct channel. A great deal of all industrial equipment and consumables, such as cutting tools, is brought to market through channels consisting of at least a distributor and not uncommonly of an import agent, distributors and sometimes retailers. Electrical cable may go through this latter channel to reach the small electrical contractor.

Direct distribution is not ruled out for consumer products either. Some companies, such as Avon Cosmetics and Tupperware, have made direct selling of their products to customers their vital competitive advantage in very intensely competitive markets. Mail order and 'factory shop'-type operations also take this direct route with consumer products. The last decade has witnessed the extensive growth of direct marketing and direct response techniques of communication and distribution. Such approaches, facilitated by the development of large databases and the wider availability of computing resources, have proved highly successful in a number of markets.

Distribution innovation can therefore be a powerful weapon in the fight for competitive advantage. It was described in Chapter 8 how the long-standing hegemony, and profits, enjoyed by UK chemists or pharmacists in developing and printing amateur photo film were suddenly challenged in the mid-1970s. Larger film processing companies used innovative mail order techniques to bypass the chemists, whose position was further eroded by high street mini-processors or one-hour photo shops, as well as by local newsagents becoming collection agents for film processors. The market for amateur film developing and printing changed profoundly with a number of traditional players, mainly chemists and inefficient film processors, losing out to new distribution practices, new technology and a revamped macro business system.

The essential channel choices are illustrated in Figure 18.1. The key to choosing the right channel lies in three considerations:

1 customer behaviour,
2 desired customer service level,
3 tasks to be performed by the channel for the marketer.

The meaning of the first is already clear. Choice of the *desired customer service level* reflects the marketing team's knowledge about customer needs plus consideration about how well it can satisfy these needs and how competitively it can do so. Choice of service level usually demands a careful decision on (1) where and how widely and how conveniently the product will be made available; (2) how long, if at all, the customer will have to wait for delivery of a purchase; (3) how often, if at all, a situation can be tolerated where the product is temporarily out of stock; and (4) how much service has to be made available with the product in terms of advice on

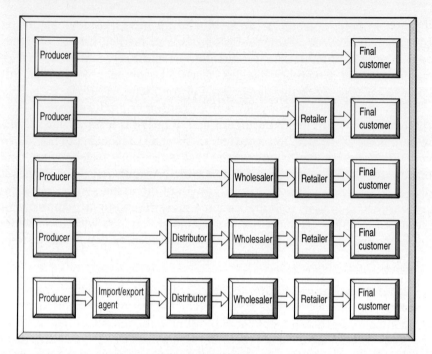

Figure 18.1 Channel choices

choice of product, installation, maintenance, repair, spare parts and support.

The relationship between the channel and the final customer is not the only important one, however. That between the marketer and the channel is also vital and must be carefully designed or chosen in structuring a distribution channel. This leads to the third consideration – the *tasks to be performed* by the channel. What is it that the channel should do for the marketer? And especially, what can it do better than the marketer's own company? The range of tasks that may be performed includes:

▶ transportation,
▶ storage/stock-holding,
▶ selling,
▶ collection of payments for goods,
▶ credit and financing service to customers,
▶ marketing and collection of market and customer information,
▶ promotion, merchandising, publicity,
▶ transfer of legal title.

Which of these tasks must be performed by the channel to attract and hold loyal customers, and what quality of service is required under each head-ing, are issues to be examined in detail. The marketer must then utilize the results of this examination in selecting channel members who can effectively execute the mix of tasks.

Evaluating alternative channels

Consideration of the many factors discussed above is likely to lead to the identification of channel alternatives rather than to a single option. How can alternatives be evaluated and the best decision be made? Five criteria for evaluation will help to clarify most choices of this nature:

1 fit with customer behaviour and preferences,
2 fit with rest of marketing strategy,
3 economic performance,
4 control,
5 adaptive capability.

Customer behaviour and preferences dictate the essential features of where and how the channel should make products available, and especially the required customer service level.

Overall marketing stratagem and the components of the marketing mix demand that the channel used is consistent with the nature of the product, its price and the way it is sold, advertised and promoted. Sophisticated hi-fi equipment is sold through specialist hi-fi retailers, but stereo rack systems are most appropriately distributed as a package purchase through department stores, electrical retailers and general electronic retail shops.

The *economic performance* of different channel alternatives may vary considerably. By going direct to the customer, the producer retains all the margin between cost of production and the final price to the customer. But under such a direct channel arrangement the producer must also incur all the costs of holding stocks of finished goods, transportation, customer credit and customer servicing and selling. By working through an intermediary or intermediaries, the marketer yields part of the total margin to the intermediary in payment for its specialist services. The justification for this and the reason why it may be cost-effective are that the intermediary, through specialization, should be able to undertake the distribution tasks at lower cost than the manufacturer can hope to do. The decision on whether to go direct or through a more complex channel must, therefore, reflect an evaluation of the relative cost-effectiveness of the alternatives.

Channel control is also an important consideration in arriving at the channel decision. With own or direct distribution, the marketer is in total control of the channel. As more intermediaries are built into the channel between marketer and customer, control becomes diluted and increasingly regulated by contractual relationships. The danger inherent in a dilution of control is that the marketer can no longer fully determine customer service levels; he or she must trust to the intermediaries and retailers the effective delivery, presentation, selling and promotion of the product. As more control is transferred to the channel, it is vital that the marketer chooses the best possible channel members, and exercises great care in negotiating the terms of the relationship and the responsibilities of the channel members.

This problem is seen in its most urgent form by many small and medium-sized exporters which have to face the decision and management challenges involved in finding a channel into international markets. Because of a need for market expertise based in the overseas market, the choice of an agent or distributor is frequently an essential step in market entry. Ensuring an appropriate level of control over how their product is brought to market is a vital consideration for such firms if their product is not to become just one more incidental item on a poorly motivated agent's or distributor's product list.

The *adaptability and flexibility* of the channel alternatives open to the marketing manager must be examined to assess their ability and willingness to change as markets, competition and customers change. For example, the traditional bicycle retailer proved, with very few exceptions, quite incapable of effectively retailing the new generation of leisure-oriented bicycles that emerged after the oil crises and the growth of health and environmental consciousness. Supermarkets, department stores and new bicycle outlets stepped in and radically changed the distribution system. Those bicycle suppliers that stayed too long with the traditional outlets lost sales and market position.

In order to enable the marketer to cater for the unforeseeable changes in markets and customer preferences, it is also generally appropriate to retain flexibility in the terms of any contracts with channel members. This can be achieved by keeping the term of such contracts limited and subject to regular renewal and renegotiation and by retaining flexibility within the terms of any agreement. This is not to advocate a short-term attitude towards distribution arrangements. Channel decisions have strategic import: they have long-term implications and cannot be changed easily without far-reaching repercussions for all elements of marketing. Once this orientation is accepted, however, specific channel choices and agreements should be made with a view to maximizing flexibility to cater for the unforeseeable, but inevitable, changes that will occur in the marketing environment, within the company itself, and within the organizations of channel members. Firstdirect, the world's first branchless nationwide bank, interestingly illustrates these channel evaluative criteria in action, not least adaptive capability (see Exhibit 18.1).

Exhibit 18.1   *Marketing in action case*

Firstdirect – the branchless bank

Firstdirect is the world's first branchless, nationwide bank and the first bank to offer a telephone-based, person-to-person service 24 hours a day, 365 days a year. Operating since 1990 from an unprepossessing building near Leeds – its only 'branch' – 170 miles north of London, it has over half a million retail accounts throughout the United Kingdom.

In the late 1980s a group of younger executives at Midland Bank, its parent, was assigned the task of finding new ways for the bank to improve business. The industry was oversupplied, profits were hard to come by, cost-cutting was widespread and hostile customers were demanding higher levels of service.

The taskforce concluded that there was a need for an altogether new approach to consumer banking: traditional processes needed to be totally re-engineered. As team members researched consumer opinions and studied changing life-styles, they found that customers were making progressively less use of the retail branch network. A national survey showed that 51 per cent of all respondents preferred to visit their branch as little as possible and that 27 per cent wished there were more things they could get their bank to do for them by telephone. But over three-quarters of those interested in a telephone banking service wanted a real person on the other end of the line, not a computer.

The team found that in other countries large numbers of transactions were being conducted by telephone. But most such transactions were simply extensions of the branch network and often limited to normal working hours, or in many cases required the customer to interact with a voice-activated computer. It concluded that none of the existing telebanking models could be adapted to supply the desired range of services. Instead, an entirely new type of bank was created – a 24-hour bank accessed entirely by telephone (or mail) and offering a full array of retail services, with very competitive charges and interest rates.

Creating the necessary human and technical systems presented a particular challenge. One telephone link had to replace the functions normally delivered by five or six employees in different departments. Moreover, as one officer puts it, 'we have to be able to respond in seconds, not minutes – normal banking procedures simply do not apply. We have had to create a workable system that is the servant, not the master, of those using it. It is a high-performance system that is both flexible and easy to use for both our front line employees – banking representatives, we call them – and our customers.'[1]

Managing the channel

When a company has chosen a channel consisting of one or more inter-mediaries it must actively address the need to manage the channel so that marketing objectives are achieved. Management of the channel demands that the marketer selects, motivates and evaluates channel members. Selection of members has already been discussed, but it is necessary to explore the other two aspects of channel management in greater detail.

Channel motivation

Channel motivation might be compared with the job and necessity of motivating a salesforce. Without motivation, the channel will not actively sell the marketer's product and will deliver an inadequate service level to the final customer. Careful selection of channel members is the first step in ensuring their later motivation to handle a company's product and so provide an excellent service to its customers. Selection involves finding a three-way match between customer needs, the company and chosen channel member.

Customer and channel member must fit in terms of matching customer needs and the channel member's ability to respond to these needs. Can delivery requirements be met? Can the product be made available in the right place? Can sufficient stocks be held? Can the channel member's sales team communicate effectively with the chosen customers? If there are negative answers to questions like these, the successful operation of other elements in the marketing mix is unlikely to compensate.

The relationship between company and channel member must also be carefully planned at the selection stage. A channel member capable of dealing successfully with the company's chosen target customers may not necessarily work well with the company itself. This is an issue which frequently confronts exporters. For example, having chosen a large distributor for one of the regions of Germany for fashion clothing, a small Belgian clothing firm may find as time passes that the distributor is accustomed to dealing with much larger suppliers. As a result, the distributor prospects and sells large orders to department stores and clothing chain stores. Then it becomes apparent that the Belgian company cannot respond to such large orders, and the relationship of exporter and German agent begins to deteriorate. The fault in what has happened under such a circumstance lies in the decision to form the relationship between two companies with different objectives in mind. The marketer must therefore ask of the prospective channel members: How will we fit together? Are our respective scales of operation compatible? Is my product complementary to, rather than competing with, other products in the distributor's product range? Do we share common objectives in terms of how to conduct business and serve customers?

Once a satisfactory channel has been selected, it becomes the marketer's task to motivate it so that both parties' objectives in establishing the relationship are achieved. The straightforward contractual terms of the relationship are the starting-point. The wholesaler, agent or retailer, just like the company itself, is in business to earn profits. The terms of the relationship must therefore assure a profit provided that the required tasks are carried out. This demands a careful negotiation of how the intermediary is to be paid. Is he to be paid an agreed margin or commission on sales? Is he to take title to the product (i.e. buy it from the marketer) and then resell it at an agreed price, or at whatever price he wishes? What margin should he expect on resale, and what therefore can he reasonably expect to pay the marketer when he buys in the product? What credit is to be given, and taken, if any? Should there be bonuses or special discounts for sales above agreed levels? The list of relevant questions continues and is quite extensive, but it is critical for the marketer to remember that a well-motivated channel member is one who can make a reasonable business out of distributing his product. It is therefore important in negotiating a relationship that the marketer puts himself or herself in the shoes of the middleman or retailer and identifies what would constitute a profitable and worthwhile financial arrangement.

Motivation draws on much more than the profitability of the relationship between company and channel. Channel members also respond positively to motivational efforts concerning the long-term quality of the relationship. Many distributors of imported products who have taken on good Japanese product lines remark on how satisfied they have been with these relationships. This satisfaction derives from dealing with suppliers that make a long-term commitment to developing good partnership and investing in educating the distributor, training the salesforce and supporting it fully with technical back-up. A relationship of trust based on factors such as these will result in above-average attention to the supplier's products and customers. There is, of course, value too in short-term promotional initiatives to create excitement and increase short-run sales. Competitions between distributors or wholesalers, or between sales personnel at distributor, wholesaler or retail level, are common tactics in generating enthusiasm and achieving short-term sales goals and, if well managed, can lead to longer-run additional commitment to the marketer's products.

Channel evaluation

Channel evaluation, like all control-oriented procedures in management, can only work if standards of performance are set and behaviour measured against these standards. The relationship with a channel member is therefore fundamentally out of control if there has been no agreement for a planning period concerning such basics as:

- sales volume,
- revenue after discounts and allowances,
- personal selling activity,
- market coverage,
- stock levels,
- delivery standards to customers,
- technical service and advice,
- handling of returns, defective products, warranties.

The relationship with each channel member should be planned yearly in advance in conjunction with the company's marketing planning activities, and should result in agreed budgets, terms and activities. These factors should then be reviewed regularly and departures from the planned programme investigated to determine whether the variance is due to changes in the market, to the performance of the channel member, or to the performance of the company itself. By following this procedure, the effectiveness of the channel can be evaluated and ineffectiveness traced to identifiable sources. Accurate diagnosis therefore becomes possible and solutions can be developed that reflect the real problems.

Channel strategy

Choosing the channel through which to bring a product or service to market is inherently strategic. It is so in the sense that the channel decision is best made for the long term, involves substantial commitment of resources to develop and maintain, and in general cannot be easily or quickly changed. It is also strategic in that an imaginative channel choice can confer significant competitive advantage on a firm. The fact that distribution and channel decisions are conventionally presented as part of the marketing mix – and at the last stage or fourth P for that matter – belies the importance of this set of decisions to the fortunes of the firm.

Distribution innovation can thus be a powerful weapon in the fight for competitive superiority. It was described earlier how larger UK film processing companies profitably used innovative mail order techniques to bypass chemists, the traditional distibutors of amateur film products. Exhibit 3.1 (p. 45) outlines National Panasonic's customized bicycle with its 11 million custom combinations and its unique ordering/delivery system; its success dramatically reversed the company's fortunes. Exhibit 1.1 (p. 14) narrates how in one European market, in the face of declining match sales, Swedish Match successfully exploited long-established distribution channels to market a compensating range of FMCG products. Leading US retailers, Toys-R-Us and Wal Mart, display deep understanding of the value chain and distribution activity in their business systems and an ability to reconfigure them to their positional benefit (see Exhibit 19.1 p. 405).

Marketing strategy and distribution

Issues of distribution mode and channel choice impact not only on channel efficiency *per se*, physical distribution costs and marketing pre-eminence, but also on overall company strategy. Such issues are traditionally presented as part of the marketing management process where the marketing manager and his or her team are generally the final arbiters. But these concerns have corporate implications and involve all senior management; the wise company considers them also as part of the marketing strategy process, enabling company-wide consultation and input into this crucial domain of decision-making. To do so in no way diminishes marketing's contribution. Rather, it recognizes the importance of distribution in the firm's prosperity. It broadens our understanding of marketing and, ironically, returns it to its seminal roots in distribution economics.

Such thinking is evident in Firstdirect's decision-making in setting up the world's first branchless bank. It underpins the trend in many European countries whereby high street retail banks have merged with life assurance firms in order to benefit from the synergy of one grouping providing a full range of financial products. These organizations, known as Bancassurance in France and Allfinanz in Germany, have met with surprising success despite the traditional differences in culture, sales expertise and distribution practice. Such reshaping of the business system is not limited to large firms. ISPG is a small Irish aquaculture firm which has successfully re-engineered its industry's value chain – primarily downstream distribution practice – to its advantage. It has done so from a peripheral location while serving markets in continental Europe (see Exhibit 18.2).

| Exhibit 18.2 | *Marketing in action case* |

ISPG reconfigures the aquabusiness value chain

Irish Seafood Producers Group (ISPG) is the largest aquaculture marketing firm in its country and the first EU-recognized producer organization (PO) in fish farming in Europe. From its peripheral location in the west of Ireland, it supplies profitably a quality range of salmon, trout and shellfish to markets on continental Europe.

A visitor to ISPG's headquarters in Connemara witnesses business being transacted in at least three different languages, English, French and Gaelic (the

374 Strategy and process in marketing

language of the staff and the supplying producers), and a salesforce using the latest telecommunications and computer equipment to sell and do deals in the international auction argot of commodity floors, weekly and spot prices. The company's marketing personnel are charged with nurturing relationships with primary and secondary customers. This involves much 'shoe leather' marketing – extensive travel both nationally and internationally. Thus ISPG's organization reverses the traditional relationship between selling and marketing, where selling typically takes place in the field and marketing is directed from head office.

ISPG was established in the 1980s by producers as a cooperative sales agency to channel their products to market in a more efficient manner. Aquaculture in Ireland was then essentially a 'cottage' industry – fragmented, undercapitalized, with uneven product quality, and at the mercy of larger, often foreign-owned, distributors. Today, a rapidly growing aquaculture industry is achieving profitable prices for a quality product in competitive international markets. Key to this success has been a fuller understanding and reshaping of the aquabusiness 'value chain' – the chain of value-adding activities from raw material to final consumer which characterizes the industry. Producers, using cooperative and relationship-based marketing approaches, have essentially changed the rules of the game and won more control over and profit from downstream distribution activities.

ISPG's commercial strategy involves managing key components along the value chain in order to ensure the best supply of product *and* achieve more control over and profit from the value-adding activities of selling and distributing. Essentially, the firm has reconfigured the value chain by supplying a quality range of seafood products, with considerable logistical expertise, to its trade partners across Europe, 52 weeks of the year. First, fish supply is crucial – the consistent provision of high quality fish product. Second, information is also critical – information regarding clients (i.e. distributors/agents), the retailer/caterer and the end-consumer. A company maxim is 'Get to know your customer's customer's customer'.

Relationship marketing on the selling/distribution end of the chain involves more than a bilateral approach. The company seeks to build trilateral trade relationships with distributors and the retail/catering chains. For instance, ISPG occasionally negotiates directly with a large supermarket to offer a special salmon promotion, particularly during peak periods of production. This has the benefits of generically promoting salmon, thus extending the overall market. However, the distributor is not excluded from this negotiation process and is happy to accept lower margins for guaranteed high volumes.

ISPG is a tightly run, lean, flexible operation. The company relies on a process-driven approach, which identifies four key activities in the firm's aquabusiness chain. This approach organizes and empowers the staff into four teams which manage the firm's activities of product supply, sales, market development and administrative support.[2]

Exclusive, selective and intensive distribution

Channel strategy should also reflect the marketing manager's objectives with regard to market coverage, the character of the product itself and the quality of selling and aftersales service that is appropriate to it. Such considerations demand that a choice be made between exclusive, selective and intensive distribution.

A strategy of *exclusive distribution* involves giving one middleman or retailer exclusive rights to distribute and sell the product in a well-defined and usually quite large territory. This may be combined with an agreement that no competing products are to be handled by the intermediary. The logic for such a strategy usually lies in the assumption that it will give greater motivation to the channel member to develop business and look after customers. What is invested in the product will result in a payoff to the channel member, since there are no other intermediaries to gain from the effort. Arrangements such as this are most typical in two sets of circumstances. In the first case a very prestigious marketer can enhance product quality image and depth of customer service by such an arrangement. The second case is a less happy one and may arise where the firm is small, not well known and possesses little bargaining power compared with the intermediaries or retailers. Under such circumstances, the channel may force an exclusive arrangement on the firm, which is left with no choice but to agree. Such occurrences are frequent in the experience of firms entering new international markets with a product that shows potential. Care must be exercized at such a time not to give too much away to the channel and not to commit the company to such a distribution straitjacket.

A strategy of *selective distribution* involves a limited form of exclusiveness. This is illustrated by the traditional distribution arrangements of many clothing manufacturers. Such manufacturers often supply only one clothing shop in each city district or provincial town, thus giving the chosen retailer some competitive differentiation compared with the other shops in the area. Such arrangements help to build a cooperative relationship between marketer and channel member and also limit the resource commitment the marketer has to make – only a fraction of the total potential intermediaries has to be serviced and managed.

An *intensive distribution* strategy is quite the opposite of the exclusive strategy. The objective is that of covering the market as extensively as possible and having the company's product available to customers wherever they may be. Typical of mass-marketed FMCG products, this strategy is most often seen implemented for products such as cigarettes, which will be found on sale in tobacconist, sweet and newspaper shops, street kiosks. supermarkets, grocery stores, cinemas, pubs, and so on. Whenever customers expect to buy a product conveniently without having to spend time searching, and when the purchase is a frequent one, intensive strategies are generally appropriate.

Competition law and distribution arrangements

EU Competition Law has significant effects on many aspects of distribution practice. A number of traditional distribution (and implicit pricing) arrangements are viewed under this legislation as distorting competition, amounting to undesirable concerted practices and generally inimicable to the consumers' interest. Exclusive distribution agreements come under particular scrutiny and have to take on new forms and arrangements. However, while this causes some firms difficulties, it also presents the imaginative firm with the opportunity to adapt quickly and successfully to the legislation and win an advantage in the marketplace. A number of small European airlines have taken advantage of this legislation to compete on previously cartelized routes.

A 'push' or 'pull' strategy?

Channel strategy, design and relationships can be built around two generic orientations. A 'push' strategy assumes that the best way to get a product to market is to push it towards the customer by carefully selecting the channel and motivating it actively to recommend the product to final customers. A 'pull' strategy, by contrast, builds on the assumption that the best approach for the marketer is to communicate directly to the customer about the merits of using his or her product and then to allow the power of market demand to pull the product through the channel – even when channel members may not be wholly enthusiastic about either the company or its products.

Not many marketing approaches reflect just one approach or the other. The push approach relies on building what is sometimes called a trade franchise, while the pull strategy relies on having a consumer franchise. Few good marketing strategies are ever built on just one of these alone. What does vary considerably is the relative emphasis on the two strategies. Marketers of mass market items that channel members basically stock and present for sale must have a strong pull strategy, as they cannot expect a newspaper and sweetshop or a supermarket to sell their products actively in the retail outlet. In the shifting market for products branded by retailers (DOBs) and those branded by manufacturers, a pull strategy is essential to maintaining the viability of the manufacturers' brand. Without extensive advertising for Andrex toilet paper products, there would be little consumer pull to prevent such a manufacturer's branded product from being usurped by retailers' own-label offerings.

Emphasis on a push strategy is particularly appropriate when the product or service being marketed requires skill and commitment in the selling process. Most industrial products and components exemplify the need for a push orientation. Caterpillar Tractor, the world market leader in earth-moving equipment, implements this strategy with particular success by selecting its distributors with great care, training them, monitoring and evaluating their performance and providing in-depth technical support on a worldwide basis. Through this avenue of channel support the company built from the end of the Second World War a uniquely effective dealership and a dominant world market position that went unchallenged until the Japanese Komatsu brand began to expand overseas in the early 1980s.

A channel strategy that is exclusively push- or pull-oriented is unlikely to be successful, but the relative emphasis between the two strategies will change between product markets and will reflect marketing objectives and the marketer's resource base. For example, discount electrical superstores regularly advertise aggressively to pull customers into their shops and then use their strong personal selling skills to push products that they and the manufacturers wish to promote.

Physical distribution

Physical distribution management is an area of traditional weakness in the practice of marketing management. Revolving about the central issues of inventories and transportation, it is an area that many marketing managers regard as somebody else's problem within the company. Unfortunately, this is often the attitude of other functional managers too, with the result that responsibility for stocks and their movement can become subdivided and never adequately integrated. Yet the physical distribution performance, a key part of the order generation, fulfilment and service process, fundamentally affects how well the customer's needs are served and the company's cost structure.

Physical distribution objectives are set in terms of customer service levels on key factors such as delivery time (from customer order to receipt of goods) and policy with regard to whether and how often being out of stock is acceptable. Such objectives are constrained by the cost of offering various service levels: the higher the service level, the greater the cost of providing it becomes. Running counter to this cost relationship is the normal experience that as direct costs are reduced and service levels compromised more and more, sales are lost. So one must carefully account for the cost of lost sales.

Overall, therefore, the objective in managing the physical distribution system is to minimize total cost, taking into account the direct cost of providing various service levels plus the cost of lost sales at each service level. This relationship can be grasped quickly by inspecting Figure 18.2. In (a) it can be seen that as the service level to the customer (measured in terms of days' delivery time) increases, the direct cost of providing the service increases too. In other words, the shorter the delivery that is promised, the greater the cost of transportation becomes. However, (b) indicates that when the promised delivery is very short very few orders are lost, whereas when delivery is extended over a longer period more and more orders are lost to competitors that offer a better service level or to substitute products that perform the same function and are quickly available. Figure 18.2 (c) shows how these two contrasting cost curves when added yield a total cost curve that is typically U-shaped. The manager's objective is to manage the system so as to operate at the minimum point on this total cost curve.

Cost of physical distribution

Physical distribution costs are sometimes difficult to trace, especially in accounting systems that have not been designed with management accounting uses in mind. The typical costs that should be collected and reported for physical distribution include:

- ▶ order processing,
- ▶ packing,
- ▶ shipping,
- ▶ warehousing/stockholding, in the company and in the field,
- ▶ transportation.

These costs include the cost of financing the stocks held in company and in the field. A careful analysis and evaluation of these costs are essential to any sensible decisions about customer service level standards and to decisions about whether to do the physical distribution job within the company or to subcontract it. A channel member may be able to deliver the required customer service level at lower total cost because of specialist skills, investment and experience in physical distribution. Companies must consider the tradeoff between the cost efficiencies of subcontracting or using hired haulage as against the service quality benefits but likely overhead costs of company-owned transportation.

Estimating the shape of the cost of lost sales function is a much more difficult task because it demands information and managerial judgements about how customers respond to various levels of service. The shape of the curve shown in Figure 18.2 (b) assumes that customers are indifferent to improvements in delivery service of better than four days. The company providing a one-day service is therefore incurring extra cost to give the customers what they do not particularly want. However, considerable sensitivity sets in as delivery time goes beyond five days: sales are lost rapidly, and when delivery is quoted at nine or ten days most sales are lost and few won. Beyond ten days the company is out of business!

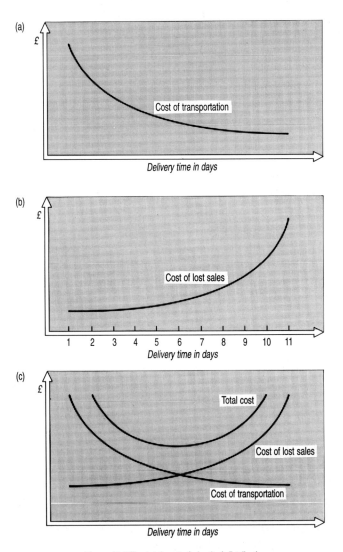

Figure 18.2 The total cost of physical distribution

Estimating the shape of such a curve can be done by market research methods. It can be done by asking customers for the probability of their buying at various service levels. It can be done by examining historical data if different service levels have been offered at different times and if sales records are available as well as the service levels of competitors. Managerial judgement, based on years of experience with customers, can also be quantified to estimate the curve's shape.

The physical distribution decisions of warehouse location, stock levels and transport routeing are well suited to mathematical modelling and optimization methods. Once the manager has specified the service levels he or she wishes to achieve to meet marketing objectives and the resources he or she has to spend on their attainment, a variety of models may be applied to find optimal or least-cost solutions.

Order generation, fulfilment and service (OGFS) and physical ditribution

One of the most common problems that arises in attempting to manage physical distribution more effectively in a company is the typical confusion over responsibility for the area, for elements of customer service, and for elements of the cost of providing the service level. The execution of the physical distribution task is usually a matter for several areas or departments ranging from office administration, accounting, marketing and sales to the transport office, warehouse, and perhaps a dispatching office if the company has its own fleet of vans or trucks. The imperative is for management to coordinate across all such areas to achieve the objective set for the system. In organizations with rigid or excessively hierarchical structures and where responsibility for distribution-related tasks is divided across many people and departments, such coordination can be difficult to achieve. Situations then arise where the warehouse manager may begin to reduce stock levels to reduce his working capital costs while marketing personnel are attempting to expand sales by increasing service levels! If they do not coordinate closely and design an integrated process, the customer and the company will both suffer. The potential for conflict between different areas of the company pursuing contradictory objectives is very considerable.

Such potential problems have been exacerbated by changes in technology and organizational design. Much scholarly research and writing has been recently addressed to how distribution and logistics might be understood in a more holistic manner, and at least two influential European books have explored how such operations might be integrated more seamlessly into overall company activities.[3,4] This thinking argues that a process approach must overlay traditional views about functional responsibility and hierarchy. Studying the firm's value chain or micro business system emphasizes the need to concentrate on key customer-focused tasks and to empower the relevant employees involved in fulfilling these tasks. Such tasks of their nature are often cross-functional. For instance, it is clear from Figure 3.8 (p. 50) which shows the micro business system of a printing company, that the work involved in physical distribution will impact across a least six cells in the diagram. Thus coordination and a process frame of managerial mind are crucial. In larger companies it may be advisable to create a physical distribution management position to coordinate the process and possibly lead a cross-functional team, provided that the cost of the manager is recovered by the greater efficiency arising from his or her work.

Best marketing practice is ultimately achieved through order generation, fulfilment and service. This OGFS process operationalizes the objectives, programmes and aspirations of marketing management. It involves, as we shall see in Chapter 19, a generic range of tasks and activities, many of which are outside the domain of the marketing department. These tasks, including shipping and physical delivery, must be co-managed across functions, with the customer being the continuing, if not obsessive, end-point of activity.

REVIEW QUESTIONS

18.1 Explain the difference between channel decisions and physical distribution decisions.
18.2 Identify five criteria for use in evaluating alternative channels of distribution and show how they help the marketer to choose the most appropriate alternative.
18.3 Issues of distribution mode and channel choice impact not only on channel efficiency and physical distribution costs, but also on overall company strategy. Discuss.
18.4 Distinguish between exclusive, selective and intensive distribution policies.
18.5 Explain the concept of customer service level as used in the context of physical distribution decisions and show how an optimal service level may be chosen.

CHAPTER 19

Managing performance

▶ Performance management systems
▶ Rewards
▶ Managing the order generation, fulfilment and service (OGFS) process
▶ Contingency and performance management

Marketing in action case
How Wal Mart optimizes its performance

ABOUT THIS CHAPTER

How performance is best managed in firms is explored. Performance management sytems – and not just control systems in the negative sense – are fundamental to good marketing management and central to managerial and organizational learning. Rather than focusing on one 'best' measure of corporate and marketing performance, a 'balanced scorecard' approach is proffered. This enables a range of yardsticks to be considered, including financial, customer, internal process, and innovation and learning measures. The design of rewards systems is also crucial.

Order generation, fulfilment and service (OGFS) process operationalizes marketing management. It involves a series of steps – a process – from an order being won from a customer to a point, subsequent to any aftersales service or query, where the customer may be deemed to be satisfied with the exchange. It thus brings marketing activity full circle and closes the loop between strategic intent and final customer satisfaction.

The activities and steps in this process must be clearly understood and mapped. They involve much cross-functional activity. Where and how gaps or cracks are likely to occur in the system must be identified and the whole process designed and managed to maximize performance both vertically and horizontally. Performance management is, of course, contingent not only on the nature of the industry, but also on the complexity of the market and the resources available to the firm.

Performance outcome is key

Performance management and control systems are fundamental to good marketing management and central to managerial and organizational learning. To learn, the company is self-conscious about what it wants to do, about its assumptions, about linkages between its own behaviour and the reactions of the market, and about its expectations concerning the outcomes of each strategic move. It must learn in 'planning mode' – that is, by doing the things it sets out to do and studying the consequences – and in real-time 'learning mode' – that is, by studying the things it does that it did not set out to do, but which proved necessary in the event. It is in the combination of learning in both these modes that results in the best marketing practice.

Control modes are vital at both the strategic and operating levels. Operating-level control is based on the development and monitoring of programmes and the annual profit plan. Variances require an explanation. What went wrong? Does the cause lie in the company's implementation of planned action? In unforeseen changes in the environment? Or in bad assumptions about customer or competitor behaviour? Short-term changes in tactics and direction are the stuff of operational performance management. But it is by searching for causes of performance variances that the true strategic value of the control system can be realized.

Control systems are at the heart of the successful management of strategy and its performance outcomes. Performance management depends on clearly articulated company mission, goals and measures of desired performance in each functional area. Achieving such articulation is not easy and finding metrics for the multi-dimensional features of first-rate performance is a major challenge currently faced by management throughout Europe. Shaping performance outcomes requires the design of human reward systems that encourage people in a company to be both hard-working and creative, to strive and to learn, emphasizing the necessity to design for human interest and motivation.

Performance management systems

Control systems, by virtue of their very name, carry a weight of meaning which is not always amicable to their underlying objectives. A good control system embodies a clear sense of intended direction and the outcomes that will signal movement in that direction – it embodies targets and associated measures. A good control system also embodies methods through which realized outcomes are compared with those intended, and discrepancies are used to learn about how effective the organization is in its direction setting and in its management of the processes needed to pursue that direction.

Targets, measurements, assessment and learning are the essence of good control and good performance management systems. However, control systems are too often seen and designed and managed in a negative manner, as if their essential point were to 'police' and 'audit' the implementation of strategy. To the extent that this is done they usually have great difficulty in contributing to a strategic learning process – they become centred on historical data rather than real-time data; on quantifiable, or hard data; they tend towards problem-seeking rather than opportunity-seeking in their emphasis; and they persistently turn into modes that excel in 'fixing the blame' rather than 'fixing the problem'. Control systems, in so far as their fundamental role is to support learning, are positive processes. Looking at them as performance management mechanisms captures this approach and draws particular attention to the necessity that they be managed actively and that the way in which they are managed is at least as important as their 'architecture'.

Establishing targets and measures

The most critical job for those concerned with performance management is to establish targets that:

▶ Provide a consistent and coherent hierarchy reaching from the organization's vision and mission to the operating targets for the individual or team taking action in support of that mission.
▶ Are measurable in a manner that is timely and that maximizes clarity of meaning for the individuals and teams taking action, while minimizing complexity and the probability of error.
▶ Are balanced in terms of customer, competitive and internal orientation, short- and long-term horizon, individual and group responsibility, financial and non-financial perspective, current and future resource adequacy.

Managers generally recognize the impact that measurement has on performance – everyone is familiar with the notion that 'what you measure is what you get'. But measurement can all too frequently be disassociated from strategy and from the objectives, goals, mission and vision that underpin strategy. Achieving coherence between mission and goals on the one hand and operational measures of performance, on the other, is a vital task for all managers and no less so for the marketing manager. The marketing manager is part of the senior management team that shapes the company's vision and translates this into a mission and set of organizational goals that are market-driven and market-focused. Within his or her own area of direct responsibility, along with a team of marketing professionals, he or she interprets the vision, mission and goals of the company in terms of their implications for the marketing function. With customers and relevant 'suppliers' (internal and external) he or she communicates, shapes and where appropriate agrees the customer-related mission, goals and standards of performance – the customer promise must be fulfilled in a manner that provides consistency and coherence between the conduct of each successful market transaction and the organization's mission. With related areas in the company he or she also interprets the company's vision and goals for the core processes over which there is shared responsibility for performance outcomes.

In moving from vision and mission statement to goals and detailed objectives the predominant tendency is to turn to financially stated commitments. But financial objectives and their associated measures deal only with a subset of the activities that constitute strategy and the fundamentals of business success. Furthermore, financial measurement methods have an historical rather than a future-oriented emphasis. However, the main danger lies in the tendency to use one-dimensional financial goals and measures – for example, return on investment measures such as RONA (return on net assets). A major problem with RONA-type goals and yardsticks is the difficulty in dealing with the short term versus the long term. A clever manager is almost always able to improve RONA in the short term. This may be done, for instance, by minimizing inventories at the cost of customer service or maximizing sales in a given period by discounting to fill distributors' and customers' warehouses with demand that would normally have been expressed in a later period. One action reduces net assets employed at the expense of future market share. The other increases turnover and total margin (if the discount to volume relationship is carefully calculated) at the expense of these two factors in the next period. Taking both actions simultaneously could increase RONA considerably to boost end-of-period performance yet spell disaster in succeeding periods. Conversely, the manager who sets out to secure the long-term profitability of a business by investing in new technology, building inventories to grow the business and cutting margins to meet competitive attack may well be 'punished' under a set of business goals that emphasize year-on-year RONA or a given hurdle rate.

The balanced scorecard

The answer is not to propose one better or best goal or measure, but rather a balanced set of measures. Kaplan and Norton suggest such an approach with their 'balanced scorecard' framework which, they claim, 'provides executives with a comprehensive framework that translates a company's strategic objectives into a coherent set of performance measures'.[1] They argue that their balanced scorecard approach differs from traditional measurement approaches in four important ways:

1 It is based on the company's strategic objectives and competitive demands; by demanding that managers select a small number of critical indicators, it promotes greater focus on strategic vision.
2 By including financial and non-financial measures it provides a basis for managing both current and future success.
3 It balances external and internal goals and measures and reveals tradeoffs that managers should or should not make.
4 It facilitates coherence among various strategic initiatives and special projects (such as re-engineering, total quality and empowerment initiatives) by providing a goal-related context and an approach to integrated measurement.

Kaplan and Norton suggest four sets of goals and associated measures, which provide answers to the following basic questions:

1 How do customers see us? (customer perspective)
2 At what must we excel? (internal business perspective)
3 Can we continue to improve and create value? (innovation and learning perspective)
4 How do we look to our shareholders? (financial perspective)

The four elements of the scorecard are visualized in Figure 19.1. The great potential advantage of this approach is that it can overcome the two most pervasive problems with establishing measures and goals: the lack of coherent articulation between objectives and performance measurement, and the use of unidimensional measures. How this framework seeks to deal with these problems is clearly illustrated in Figure 19.2. Four questions are posed, which are fundamental to the shaping and management of strategy:

1 What is my *vision* of the future?
2 If my vision succeeds, how will I *differ* in terms of shareholder perceptions, customer perceptions, internal management activities and my ability to innovate and grow?
3 What are the *critical success factors* from a financial, customer, internal and innovating perspective?
4 What are the critical *measurements* that I should use for each of the four goal and result areas?[2]

Each of these questions is of central importance to the marketing manager as custodian of the marketing management process and as a member of the strategic management team. The marketer must be assured of the inclusion of appropriate financial goals and measures and must understand their implications for marketing management. The customer perspective is, of course, the special responsibility of the marketing manager; to bring customer focus to the vision and mission; to articulate the way in which value will be created for the customer; to nominate and defend the factors that are key in creating customer value; and to establish measures which will tell whether customer-related goals are being achieved. The marketing manager is totally reliant on internal management processes to deliver the customer promise that the business makes and to create the value the customer expects. Therefore the design, redesign and co-management of these internal processes that ultimately create customer value are work that is central to marketing's remit. Setting goals for innovating and learning, establishing the keys to success and operationalizing measures of performance in this area underpin marketing's contribution to the creation of a worthwhile future for the business – in terms of customer satisfaction, shareholder value, employee satisfaction and general stakeholder satisfac-

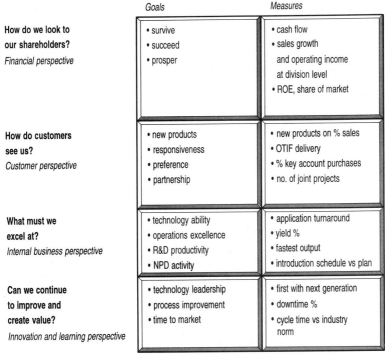

Source: adapted from R.S. Kaplan and D.P. Norton (1992) 'The balanced scorecard – measures that drive performance', *Harvard Business Review*, Jan–Feb, p. 76.

Figure 19.1 The balanced scorecard

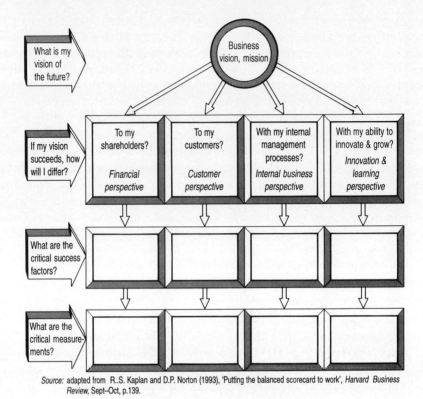

Source: adapted from R..S. Kaplan and D.P. Norton (1993), 'Putting the balanced scorecard to work', *Harvard Business Review*, Sept–Oct, p.139.

Figure 19.2 From vision to scorecard

tion. Thus, it is important to explore these questions and their consequent operationalized measures in more detail.

Financial measures

The marketer must influence the choice of appropriate financial goals and measures for the company as a whole and establish the financial sub-measures that are appropriate to managing marketing's performance in areas of sole control and shared control. Typical measures that the marketing manager uses are sales volume and value, market share, sales and market share trends, advertising and promotion spend, sales representation cost allocation, margins and trends in margins, inventories and receivables. These latter financial efficiency measures are sometimes collected into margin management measures and asset management measures. Margin management measures track the factors that contribute to the net profit margin – sales and cost of goods sold which form the basis of the gross margin and variable and fixed expenses which represent the costs that must be more than covered by the gross margin. Asset management measures track the relationship between sales and the capital employed to support those sales. Capital employed reflects both fixed and current assets, and the latter is especially dependent on inventory levels and accounts receivable.

Customer measures

The customer perspective is, of course, the special responsibility of the marketing manager. Establishing measures that will tell whether customer-related goals are being achieved is a critical task. Rockwater is a US company used as an exemplar by Kaplan and Norton. It is in the international engineering and construction business and has a special leadership position in underwater work. Its customer measures recognize a difference between two types of customers – one group that seeks value-added services and a second that purchases primarily on price. Rockwater uses a price index measure to ensure that it maintains its goal of being able to deal with price-based customers when it is opportune. For its critical value-based customers it uses an annual, independently undertaken, rating of customers' perceptions of its services relative to competitors' as well as monthly satisfaction and performance ratings taken directly by the company. Market share by key account is taken as a measure of whether improvements in service are being translated into direct financial performance.

Defection rate, or, more positively, customer retention rate measures are widely used to index customer loyalty. Since retention rate is generally highly correlated with profitability this is a powerful measure that is linked strongly to profitability measures, but more importantly provides an often direct link between direct managerial intervention – to increase retention rate – and the outcome measure of profit. Reichheld and Sasser document how decreases of 5 per cent in defection rate can boost lifecycle profit by 85 per cent in the case of branch banking deposits or 75 per cent in the case of credit card business.[3]

Internal process measures

It has been observed many times that the marketing manager is totally reliant on internal management processes – and especially in the order generation, fulfilment and service (OGFS) and new product development processes – to deliver the customer promise that the business makes and to create the value the customer expects. The OGFS process alone includes at least ten activities for most companies: order planning, order generation, cost estimation and pricing, order receipt and entry, order selection and prioritization, scheduling, fulfilment, invoicing, returns and claims, and aftersales service. This represents a challenging set of tasks to coordinate, measure and monitor.

Measurement of these processes is still not very common, although specific attention to cycle time, quality and completeness of process metrics is growing rapidly. Time critical markets demand the use of cycle time targets, measurement and continuous improvement. At Rockwell, cycle time is measured for the launch-to-completion time on any construction project. This process is broken into its five constituent stages so that targets can be set for each and management held responsible for continuous improvement:

Development cycle:
1 Project identification (prospecting and selling time).
2 Win (tender success ratio).

Supply cycle:
3 Project preparation (effectiveness, time).
4 Project delivery (effectiveness, safety/loss control, rework, time).
5 Close-out (time to close out project).

While time-based measures are increasingly important across most markets as companies seek to add customer value and build advantage on the basis of speed of response, quality-related performance is already unambiguously established as a key to competitiveness. It is a key to marketing performance as quality determines much if not most of the customer's satisfaction with the product or service received. Completeness measures have to do with the provision of promised transactions on time and in full. One of the platforms of ICI's competitiveness as a global leader in the area of decorative paints and of its reputation with retailers is its OTIF measurement and performance management system. This system measures response to customer orders in terms of their being delivered to retailers 'on time and in full' (OTIF) with expectations that performance be pushed continuously closer to 100 per cent.

Innovation and learning measures

Setting goals and measures for innovating and learning in and through the core marketing processes underpins marketing's contribution to the creation of a worthwhile future for the business. These measures typically deal with new product and service activity and with performance in continuous improvement of established products and services and the processes that produce them. A common measure is the proportion of sales attributable to products that are less than some specified age – a figure which will have to reflect the industry and its technology. Another measure is the proportionate spend on R&D and/or new product market research. Continuous improvement as an indicator of learning how to do existing marketing work ever better can be measured by improvements in customer critical product performance factors or improvement in service provision such as waiting or queuing times, or OTIF as used by ICI Paints.

Since learning and innovation are entirely dependent on human commitment and enthusiasm, measures of staff attitudes and morale, investment in training and development, staff involvement in teams, participation in and output from suggestion scheme activity, are often considered important to monitoring and managing the root system for organizational learning.

Assessment and intervention

If targets are set and measurement undertaken, then a performance management system must deal with the comparison of actual relative to intended performance. For example, a company wishing to achieve market leadership must translate this strategic intent into component programmes which might include a new product launch. To implement this programme or action plan, the marketing function must, among many other activities, set specific volume, price and revenue targets on a weekly, monthly and annual basis for the year of introduction. If this is done properly, the activity of the individual sales representative, for example, will be planned on a weekly basis and his or her performance monitored against budget/target. Variance from budget is then managed for improvement by the sales manager. In this way, even the most specific daily actions are driven by the company's marketing strategy and its overall corporate intent.

Equally important the performance of the company may be addressed directly by managers at appropriate levels of intervention. In the example above, the sales manager will intervene directly to counsel, motivate and assist the individual salesperson. If, however, the sales manager realizes that underperformance is not the 'fault' of the salesperson, other factors under the manager's control must be considered for action – perhaps the structure of the salesforce's incentive scheme or the product distribution back-up that is being provided. If the cause of the performance variance goes beyond his authority, then the manager must begin to seek a remedy with fellow team members concerning a core process area or through the marketing manager with other parts of the company with which the sales manager has no direct link.

Learning

Learning is both a short- and long-term process, about improving existing systems and creating new ones. Short-term, tactical learning takes place as the anticipated future resolves itself into present reality. Performance measurement systems must act in the manner of real-time control systems in order to support appropriate short-term response. In this sense performance management must proceed in the way in which an airliner's flight deck with its extensive battery of controls and visual displays allows the crew to take immediate action to deal with keeping the aircraft on course, comfortable for the passengers, economical in its operation and safe for all. At the same time, experience of flying an aircraft over hundreds and thousands of hours contributes to longer-term learning, which allows modifications and better crew routines to be designed to improve performance. Ultimately, the accumulated experience with one generation of aircraft contributes to the design of a new generation. Even though the new generation may be a major departure from the past, it will still rest on the shoulders of what has been learned from the old generation and all its successes and failures.

The performance management system for marketing must have the same features of learning to support short-term corrective action and learning to provide the basis for long-term adjustment or redesign. In this latter sense the process must allow marketing managers to learn about the 'theory of the business', as Drucker puts it – it must help them to gain self-consciousness about, and ever deeper insights into the 'theory' of their firm and its markets which govern their assumptions and strategy.[4] For this reason in particular the performance management system and the measures on which it is based must trace the chain of assumed causality which links vision to mission to goals and objectives to critical success factors, to measures, to targets, to action taken and outcome observed. It must lay bare the assumptions of the marketing team. It must allow them, even force them, continuously to challenge and refine or change these assumptions. It is only in this way that effective learning to support long-term survival can take place.

Rewards

Performance management and control systems also involve the rewards and incentives that a company uses to motivate and channel the energies of managers and staff and of other third parties on whom it relies – suppliers and channels of distribution, for example. It is important to develop reward systems that support the desired goals and behaviour of the company. Many companies fail to integrate coherently and consistently their remuneration mechanisms with strategic and operational intent. This can have unfortunate results. For example, an objective of building up a new product into a 'star' position will inevitably fail if the relevant product or brand manager is rewarded on the basis of annual contribution to profits. The manager will, under such circumstances, almost certainly produce a first-year contribution from the product and, almost equally certainly, ruin its long-term potential for gaining share, which may require perhaps 12 or 18 months of negative cashflows. Rewards and punishments are, therefore, designed for consistency with strategic objectives, and in a multi-product, multi-market firm this demands quite complex arrangements, as objectives will vary considerably from one product and market to another.

Individual reward systems

Individual systems have always been the most common approach to linking the behaviour of sales and marketing personnel to performance. Commission systems tie incentive payment to how much is sold, although more sophisticated schemes may relate payment to product gross margin or profit contribution. While commissions are usually calculated on a percentage basis, bonuses may also be paid on a fixed-sum basis, tied to achievement of specific targets or threshold levels of sales or contribution. Commission systems stress the short over the long term and can be dangerous where long-term market development is a key to success, where customer relationships are more important than individual transactions and where the relationship between employee and company is better not based on a predominantly market transaction foundation. Performance-related pay schemes must be considered with special care for this latter reason. Undue emphasis on performance-related pay schemes and especially on individually-based ones turn the employment relationship into a market relationship – the employee performs and the company pays. This can run the risk of dismissing all other factors from the employment contract – such as loyalty, commitment to learning, group solidarity – as effort comes to be seen purely as a commodity to be bought and sold in a labour market.

Group reward systems

Group rewards have become more common amd more important as companies have placed more stress on process management, on teamwork and group endeavour, on shared commitment to learning and continuous improvement and have tried to avoid the dangers of sub-optimization involved in purely individual effort being rewarded. Group-based bonus schemes, profit-sharing and employee stock options are common forms of group reward. Group reward schemes are most likely to be relevant to marketing in situations where customers are served by marketing and sales teams – for example, a relationship manager, product specialists and technical service representatives in capital goods marketing, or where management is trying to improve the new product development or OGFS process. In such cases, it is the group that determines the performance of an integrated and interdependent process and if monetary incentives are to be used, one must either reward the whole team or avoid money-based incentives completely.

Reward systems are usually discussed on the implicit assumption that employees, suppliers and distribution channel members are best motivated by money incentives. However, the reality of organizational life indicates that there are a variety of ways in which people are encouraged to be involved and to contribute productively to a company's goals. Market mechanisms provide one way of managing human performance. They are based on the assumption that effort, commitment and enthusiasm are behavioural outcomes that can be bought and sold. They depend on setting up a monetary equivalence for individual performance: sell 100 and you get paid 10DM; exceed your sales quota by 120 per cent and you get a bonus of 300 guilders; work overtime and you get 90 Swedish kronor per hour; save 80,000 French francs in annual inventory holding costs and you get 5 per cent of the cost saving in the first year, and so on. While these systems can provide a very sharp and fast-acting operational control on behaviour, they have a tendency to deflect attention from the core task to the job of maximizing gain from the system – 'game playing' takes over – but more critically they implicitly or explicitly put it to the employee that his or her relationship with the company is a purely market-based one. This has a habit of rebounding to the disadvantage of companies who can find themselves facing employees who approach all requests for action with the question 'How much is it worth to you?' Under such circumstances the employment relationship degenerates into continuous bargaining about the value of each individual behaviour and its relativity to every other behaviour. It was in such a morass of employment and then industrial relations agreements that Europe almost drove itself bankrupt in the world marketplace of the 1970s.

Organizations also use bureaucratic mechanisms to control and manage employee performance. Bureaucratic systems depend on rules, standard operating procedures and precedent to guide and channel behaviour. In stable market, technological and organizational environments, good bureaucracy supports high performance. Where tasks are well defined and may be broken into their constituent parts, a bureaucratic process may be very appropriate to dealing with performance management. Better performance will typically be a result of better design of the task and its constituent elements, as when a salesperson is 'programmed' on the steps and stages in selling or a technical sales support representative is schooled in a technical diagnostic process to trouble-shoot for malfunction in a computer network or a printing press. In such circumstances it is assumed that the individual will take satisfaction from knowing what exactly to do, how and when, and is not required to relearn behaviour except when the system is redesigned. Some particular marketing tasks will always respond well to bureaucratization. Order entry processing, credit checking, invoicing and accounts receivable management, safety, health and environment compliance, customer support scheduling and many more activities where the precision of bureaucratic design and management are both appropriate and important. However, bureaucratic approaches to managing human performance break down under conditions of change and under circumstances where the tasks involved are difficult to analyze and programme. Bureaucratic systems also assume that performing the established task well is the basis of motivation. They are likely to have 'negative rewards' – punishments in plain language – for non-performance of the specified task but no positive rewards for performance.

Clan mechanisms, by contrast with those discussed above, deal with the management of performance through social mechanisms – performance is something valued by the group and rewarded through a stronger sense of affiliation, status or belonging. Non-performance is discouraged by the converse – disaffiliation from the group, lowering of status and a diminished sense of belonging. Marketing departments, sales teams, brand management groups, customer or key account teams, and technical sales units often respond most powerfully in terms of performance to the degree of clan membership that they feel. Strong identification with a company, its vision for the future, its mission and its marketing strategy and programmes can produce a degree of motivation, enthusiasm, commitment to learning and sheer performance that cannot be encouraged by any other means. Achieving this requires the kind of clarity in goals and measures discussed earlier, combined with a style of management that communicates a sense of 'family' and belonging to all employees. Clan mechanisms are very important to process management tasks and especially to the management of teams with interfunctional and interdisciplinary roles. In these circumstances, the performance of the team is dependent on the combined and integrated effort of the team and, in general, the best way to encourage this is through a strong sense of process ownership and considerable devolved responsibility and authority. Empowerment is the catchword for such an approach and it works best where the group that is empowered acquires a clannish, almost tribal, sense of identity, solidarity and pride in its own achievements.

Managing the order generation, fulfilment and service (OGFS) process

A business process approach by definition seeks to organize and link key tasks in a customer-oriented way – the participants are aware that a satisfied loyal customer is the end-point of the activity. Most of the performance management, control and reward systems discussed so far are cognisant in some way or another of the customer. However, the focus of order generation, fulfilment and service (OGFS) – one of the four core marketing processes – is relentlessly on the customer. The marketing strategy process enables customers to be identified in a 'ballpark' context – where they are in the market and what their characteristics and requirements are. The marketing management process sets the agenda for delivering to those customers – the type of product, its broad price level, promotion and feasible distribution outlets. But the OGFS process actually reaches the customers. It reifies them. It thus brings marketing activity full circle and closes the loop between strategic intent and final customer satisfaction.

In a generic sense, OGFS involves a series of steps, a number of procedures – a process – from an order being won from a customer to a point, subsequent to any aftersales service or query, where the customer may be deemed to be satisfied with the exchange. The exact steps involved and the precise nature of the process vary from industry to industry and from product to service. But managing this order process shares broadly the same activities and characteristics in each firm. Figure 19.3 suggests some ten stages which typify many European firms.

If this process reflects generically the same broad tasks across different types of firms, so also does it reflect a similar possibility for error and inefficiency. Every time an order is handled, the customer is handled. Every time an order remains unattended, the customer waits unattended. Thus

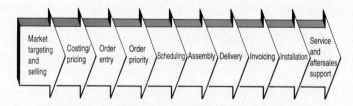

Figure 19.3 Order generation, fulfilment and service (OGFS) process

ironically, the best way to be customer-focused is to go beyond the customer and the product to the order. In a sense, a 'moment of truth' occurs at each stage of the OGFS process, and every employee in the firm who affects OGFS is the equivalent of a frontline employee. In the final analysis, it is the order that connects the customer to the company in a systematic and company-wide manner.

Managing the OGFS process is crucial. Failure to do so properly leads to disgruntled buyers and/or ailing profits. Even if customers are satisfied, it may be at a cost to the firm in terms of inefficiency that renders the exchange pointless. Primarily, it involves movement across the organization and considerable interdepartmental liaison and cooperation. Many other than marketing personnel are charged with its execution. But buck-passing, unclear responsibilities and a 'not my job' syndrome can make execution problematic.

It is the dedicated customer focus of the OGFS process that leads us to categorize it as a marketing process rather than as a general business or administrative process. It ultimately smooths or facilitates the way to market so that the firm can creatively match arenas of market need with unique competences through durable and profitable relationships – the basic task of marketing and market focus. Of course, marketing does not own the process; it must work with other departments and functions in managing it, but unless marketing can specify the outcome in terms of a satisfied customer, much overall marketing activity is simply ineffective and a waste of time and resources.

Key activities in the OGFS process

Research at Harvard Business School has sought to unbundle this process and explore areas of conflict and inefficiency, in particular as order management moves across the firm.[5] Ten typical activities were observed which sometimes overlap and interact and which are often the subject of interfunctional wrangling.

Order planning
The reality, if not the paradox, in most firms is that order planning commences long before an actual order is received. The requirements of planning systems dictate that at the beginning of each year, sales and marketing personnel prepare a forecast which becomes the basis for the company's annual profit plan. But the preparation of this plan is usually subject to self-interested lobbying by departments, negotiation, and plain error such that, ultimately, production planners, the people furthest from

the customer, may decide the final 'forecast' for manufacture and inventory purposes.

Order generation

It is the job of the sales and marketing functions to generate orders whether by advertising, sales promotion, personal selling or direct marketing. In doing so such personnel can often ignore other functions which 'get in the way'. This produces a gap between order generation, order planning, and later steps in the process.

Cost estimation and pricing

At this third step, disputes and misunderstanding can arise between the marketing department which oversees pricing, a field salesforce that actually wins a price, engineers who estimate and accountants who calculate costs. In Chapter 16 it was described how this failure to liaise properly can lead to significant price erosion through the pocket price waterfall.

Order receipt and entry

This typically takes place in a low-profile department called 'customer service', 'order processing' or 'internal sales'. Such personnel are in daily contact with customers, yet often have little clout in the organization, and do not know what is going on at the top of the company, including its basic strategy. And top management for its part does not know much about what its customer service department, the function closest to the customer, is doing.

Order selection and prioritization

Firms derive substantial financial benefit from considered order and customer selection and from linking it to their general business policy – 'good' customers can be nurtured while 'bad' customers can be renegotiated with or shed. Further, firms can also gain by the way they handle order prioritization – how they decide which orders receive faster, more complete attention. However, these decisions are usually not made by senior executives who are conversant with corporate strategy but by customer service representatives who know little of strategy. These latter decide which order gets filled when and often which gets lost in limbo.

Scheduling

Here the order gets slotted into an actual production or operational sequence. Again, interdepartmental dispute and lack of communication can manifest itself. Production people seek to minimize equipment change-overs, while marketing and customer service reps plea for special service for special customers.

Fulfilment

This next step involves the actual provision of the product or service. It can be a very complex part of the process. Order fulfilment may involve multiple functions and locations; different parts of an order may be created in different manufacturing facilities and merged on yet another site. In some cases, fulfilment includes third party vendors. In service operations, it can mean sending people with different competences to the customer's site. The more complicated the assembly activity, the more coordination that must take place across the organization – and the greater the chance for error and cracks appearing in the system.

Invoicing

After the order has been delivered, billing is typically handled by finance, which sees its role as getting the invoice out quickly and getting the money in. The billing function is designed primarily to serve the interests and needs of the company, not those of the customer. It may also be inefficient in that there may be erosion, as described earlier, between invoice and actual net achieved or pocket price.

Returns and claims

These are important in some businesses because of their impact on administrative costs, scrap and transportation expenses. They are also important in customer relations. OGFS processes in most firms are designed for one-way merchandise flow: outbound to the customer. Returns can face difficult and unfriendly hurdles.

Aftersales service

This includes elements such as physical installation of a product, repair and maintenance, customer training, equipment upgrading and disposal. In this final step in the OGFS process, service representatives can truly get inside the customer's organization. Because of the information exchanged and intimacy involved, aftersales service can affect customer satisfaction and firm profitability for years. But in most companies, the service personnel are not linked to any marketing strategy, internal product development effort or quality assurance team.

Finding and filling cracks

In company after company, the Harvard researchers traced the progress of individual orders as they travelled through the OGFS process from beginning to end. What they observed was inefficiency, frustration, missed opportunities, dissatisfied customers and underperforming companies. Four key problems emerged:

1 Most firms never view OGFS as a whole process or system. People in sales think that someone in production scheduling understands the entire system; people in production scheduling thinks customer reps do. No one really does, and everyone can only provide a partial description.

2 Each stage in the OGFS process necessitates an at times confusing array of overlapping functional responsibilities. Figure 19.4 illustrates why orders 'fall through the cracks'; each step is considered the primary responsibility of a specific department, and no step is the exclusive responsibility of any department. Given the reality of overlapping roles, cracks do occur and customers are disappointed.

3 To top management, the specifics of the OGFS process are vague if not invisible. Senior managers in all but the smallest operating units simply do not understand its finer operating points. Further, the personnel with the most crucial information, such as customer service specialists, are at the bottom of the organization and cannot communicate with the top. Thus there are vertical gaps in the system as well as horizontal ones.

4 The customer remains as remote from order generation, fulfilment and service as senior management. During the process, the customer's main tasks are to negotiate price, place the order, wait, receive delivery, possibly complain, and pay. In the middle stages of the process, the customer does not figure at all.

How can these shortcomings and gaps in the process be remedied? In the first instance, the order management process must be clearly mapped, designed or in some sense visualized. This can involve a number of methods from a simple Gantt Chart to a computerized operations model. This visual tool makes it possible for different people from different functions and levels in the organization to accept the OGFS process as a tangible entity. Obsolete or unnecessary tasks that hinder coordination are identified and parts of the system are slotted together to meet customer needs in a seamless fashion. In some firms such process instruments do indeed exist. But they are often flawed and in serious need of some re-engineering.

In shaping the process, the perspective of the customer, and not just the firm, is adopted. Those involved, in a metaphorical sense, 'staple themselves to an order' and move through the various stages concerned about how each step impacts on the customer. Company personnel and a customer can have quite different views about what constitutes first-rate performance. A 99 per cent shipment rate may seem highly satisfactory to the company, but

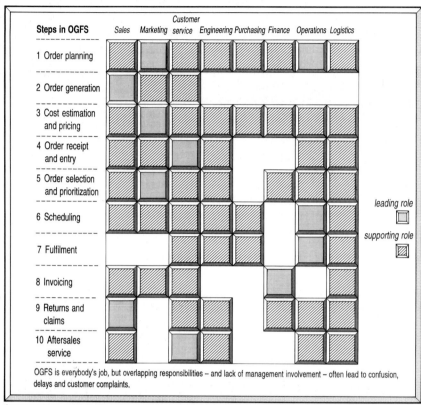

OGFS is everybody's job, but overlapping responsibilities – and lack of management involvement – often lead to confusion, delays and customer complaints.

Source: adapted from B.P. Shapiro, V.K. Rangan and J.J. Sviokla (1992), 'Staple yourself to an order', *Harvard Business Review*, Jul–Aug, p. 118.

Figure 19.4 Why orders fall through the cracks

the customer who fails to receive a crucial part in his delivery is much less complacent. An invoicing error appears a small issue to a finance department; it involves the customer in highly troublesome corrective measures.

Not only is OGFS conceived and envisaged as a process, it must also be managed as a process or system. This means allocating responsibilities, establishing performance systems, setting goals and measures, and rewarding outstanding conduct. Joint reward schemes encourage employees to take a system-wide view of company performance. In designing performance measurements, managers can include yardsticks that reflect coordination across departmental boundaries. Working horizontally in a vertical organization is always difficult. Intention often fails to get translated into actual cooperation. Such an approach involves the firm deepening its understanding of organizational behaviour, of how teams and project groups best operate, and of how the work of integrators complements that of specialists. In short, it learns new modes of organizing.

Senior management, especially the chief executive, must fully endorse the OGFS process. If it does, and managers descend from the executive heights into the organization's depths, they come into contact with critical people like customer service representatives, production schedulers, shipping clerks and others who are custodians of much fine-grained information about customer needs. In this way, vertical gaps as well as horizontal gaps are bridged.

The micro business system and the OGFS process

A micro business system is the chain of value-adding activities that a firm seeks to configure in a manner which yields competitive superiority. As is described elsewhere, such a micro business system disaggregates a firm into a series of strategically relevant tasks and activities in order to understand

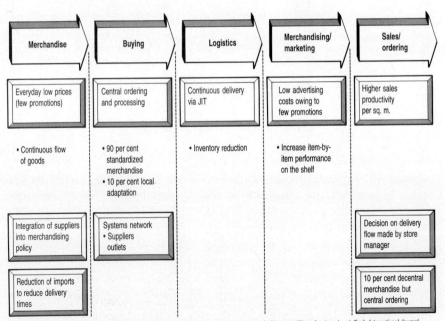

Source: J. Maximov and H. Gottschlich (1993), 'Time–cost–quality leadership: new ways to gain a sustainable competitive advantage in retailing', *International Journal of Retail and Distribution Management*, vol. 21, no. 4, p.9.

Figure 19.5 Micro business system of US retailer Wal Mart

better their structure and interrelationships, the behaviour of costs, and existing and potential sources of positional advantage. It identifies the key tasks and core processes where the firm wants to build exceptional competence. In a generic sense, the micro business system maps the roots of the firm's potential strategic advantage. Whether we examine such a system in an early Porterian format (e.g., Figure 3.8, p. 50) or in the more process-oriented form of US retailer, Wal Mart's, business system in Figure 19.5, we can identify strategic activities and their key underpinning operational dimensions.

Order generation, fulfilment and service process closes the loop between strategic intent and final customer satisfaction. The OGFS process is the vibrant heart and blood circulation of the micro business system. It drives it, breathes life into it and translates the broader strategic dimensions and aspirations of this value chain into the everyday operational reality of satisfied customers.

Contingency and performance management

The manner in which performance is monitored and managed has to take account of the circumstances in which the company finds itself. Depending on the nature of the industry and market circumstances and the company's own resources and competitive position, different approaches to management may be necessary. Chakravarthy and Lorange propose a scheme for considering such contingencies and their implcations for performance management.[6] If the context of a business is taken as defined by first, the complexity of its industry and environment, and second, the distinctive competences it has in that industry or segment, then a simple contingency framework may be suggested, as in Figure 19.6. Four broad categories of direction are suggested for the four contexts – a pioneer strategy, an expansion strategy, a domination strategy and a reorientation strategy. For each of these strategies in their related contexts, different necessities for approaching the tasks of monitoring, control and learning are proposed. The main differences proposed are:

1 the frequency with which monitoring should be repeated;
2 the manner of strategy validation – whether through consensus, experimentation, negative feedback or performance outcomes; and
3 the form which control interventions should take – whether go/no go, contingent control or gradual modification.

In the case of a firm pioneering a new product – where the trading environment is quite complex and the firm may not as yet have developed

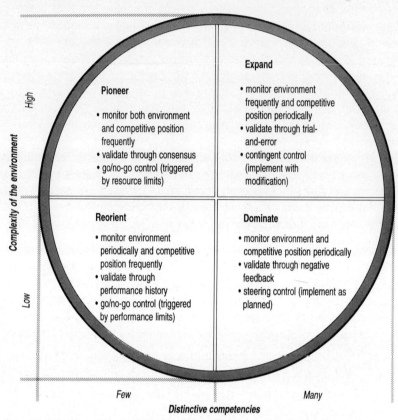

Source: B.S. Chakravarthy and P. Lorange (1991), *Managing the Strategy Process* (Prentice Hall, Englewood Cliffs, NJ) p. 116.

Figure 19.6 Contingency and performance management

a full range of business competences – performance management involves monitoring both the environment and competitive position frequently, making policy through consensus, and having a 'traffic light' approach to control triggered by resource limits. Such a framework serves to remind us that markets are different and evolve, and that strategic and marketing success means adapting to particular circumstances. What is right for a small knife manufacturer, like Richardson, in a mature business (see Exhibit 9.1, p. 153) is inappropriate for a large retailer in a fast-growing industry. Wal Mart is one of the most successful retailers in the United States. This success is built on a low delivered cost (LDC) strategy emphasizing quick turnover, high sales space productivity, superb JIT inventory management and close supplier relationships (see Exhibit 19.1). The firm attests to clear strategic vision and first-rate performance management.

Exhibit 19.1   *Marketing in action case*

How Wal Mart optimizes its performance

Wal Mart is one of the most successful retailers in the United States. Since the early 1980s its turnover and market share have grown dramatically, with sales reaching $44 billion in 1991. Whereas its main competitor, K-Mart, realized a return on sales (ROS) of 3.7 per cent, Wal Mart achieved a 5.8 per cent ROS, which even for US standards is considered to be outstanding.

Wal Mart's success lies in the integrated optimization of its business system. It ensures the uncompromising orientation of the entire system towards client value. It enjoys a clear market identity as a discounter with 'every day low prices', and has achieved an outstanding price competence, an image which also distinguishes Aldi in Germany.

The company boasts very high sales space productivity ($ sales per square metre), resulting in a superior cost position. These relative cost advantages are accumulated, however, not as profits within the firm, but are reinvested in the market, in the form of further price reductions, consequently creating attractive purchase offers. Lower prices/margins here again bring about further growth in the sales space productivity, as a result of the continual increase in customers. This productivity 'loop' enables it continuously to improve performance.

Such performance is realized by optimal process management through the entire value-added chain. Every effort, for example, is made to integrate suppliers as fully as possible into the system. Product managers of Procter & Gamble are always present in the purchasing department of Wal Mart and sit at the same table as their prospective buyers. At the same time, double clearance sales data are made available, so that the suppliers can coordinate their production lines to best advantage. This continuous flow of merchandise, with a just-in-time delivery rhythm, facilitates its pricing policy – and also enables Wal Mart to work with fewer suppliers and achieve an approximately 50 per cent higher inventory and merchandise turnover than its main competitor, K-Mart.

At every stage at which creation of value occurs – whether buying, logistics, merchandising, selling, ordering, etc. – analysis is undertaken to ascertain where competitive advantages can be won (see Figure 19.5). For instance, in merchandising, shelf optimization is developed by scanning systems and advertising expenses are minimal since few bargains or special promotions are offered. Within store management, decisions are made about the form of delivery by the branch manager who is responsible for the 10 per cent of total mechandise ordering to guarantee the necessary local touch – while the other 90 per cent of merchandise is determined by central planning.[7]

REVIEW QUESTIONS

19.1 What is meant by a 'balanced scorecard' approach to the challenge of goal setting and performance management?

19.2 Is it possible to 'measure' innovation and learning in an organization?

19.3 The OGFS process brings marketing activity full circle and closes the loop between strategic intent and final customer satisfaction. Discuss.

19.4 What are the key activities in order generation, fulfilment and service? What gaps are likely to arise in organizing these activities, and how might such shortcomings be overcome?

19.5 How might group rewards be used to improve functional and cross-functional performance?

Part V

The new product development process

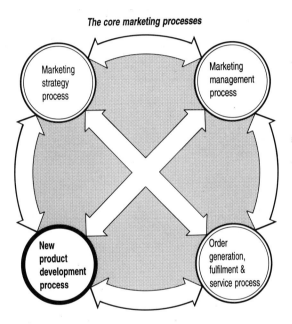

The core marketing processes

CHAPTER 20
New product development

ABOUT THIS CHAPTER

Discussion now focuses, not on the existing products and services in the firm's portfolio, but on the introduction of new ones. A new product development (NPD) process is set out. Developing a strategic orientation for the new product process is a vital and necessary starting point. The various phases or stages in the process are then explored, as is the nature of product diffusion.

How the NPD process is managed depends in large part on whether the phases and activities involved take place in sequence, overlap and/or occur in parallel. There is evidence of increasing simultaneity in new product development. This has implications for organizing new product introduction – the product champion of the 1970s has metamorphosed into the process champion of the 1990s.

Ways of speeding up new product introduction are discussed, e.g. expeditionary marketing, as well as the benefits and risks attaching to such approaches. The growth in strategic alliances to bring new products and services to market reflects the need to partner both deeply and widely in the NPD process.

New product marketing

The development and successful launch of new products present some special challenges. Risk and uncertainty are normally much higher for new product marketing than in managing established or mature products. The rate of new product failure is high; two out of three new products still fail in the US market.[1] It has been estimated that it takes 58 new product ideas on average to yield one successful new product.[2] Yet the ever-shortening lifecycles of individual products or brands in most industries, the rate of technological change and the rapid evolution of consumer tastes and preferences all demand an active new product development or product adaptation response from the individual firm. This is especially true for national companies that go international. Products designed and developed for local or regional customers will not automatically meet the needs of overseas markets. This means that as a company begins to internationalize, it must of necessity become involved in some degree of new product development activity. Having internationalized many firms will then find that the markets of Europe, North America and Asia demand a continuously innovative approach.

The new product development process

How should firms go about developing new products and services? The approach may be structured in many different ways to fit with the unique features of any company and its market. A typical new product development (NPD) process starts with developing a strategic orientation for new product activities, and then moves through steps of new product idea generation, idea screening and evaluation, concept development, product development and product launch (see Figure 20.1).

A strategic orientation

First, it is necessary to examine the logic of launching a new product or service. New product development becomes a confusing and uncontrollable mess for the company if the first step – the development of a strategic orientation – is not undertaken. Without this step, almost any new product idea is a candidate for analysis and potential commercialization; the product

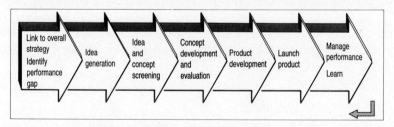

Figure 20.1 The new product development (NPD) process

market search becomes endless. The reality of corporate life, however, is such that only very specific products for quite specific markets are appropriate for development at any period in the company's life. New products must build the company's competences in the marketplace. They must reduce its long-run risk by balancing the product market portfolio and increase the survival and growth potential of the organization. New product development can absorb an enormous quantity of corporate energy and resources. Both resources and managerial energy are in limited supply and must therefore be allocated in the most productive manner.

Developing a strategic orientation for the new product process is, therefore, the vital and necessary starting point. The company must compare its general and marketing-specific objectives with the performance it is likely to produce given its present product or portfolio of products and services, and given the business strengths and weaknesses it possesses to respond to market threats and opportunities. This process of analysis and comparison reveals likely gaps in future performance compared to objectives.

The product portfolio may now be examined to identify the product and market opportunities that may close the performance gap, as shown in Figure 20.2. The lifecycles of products A, B and C are such that A, a star performer, is shifting into a more mature cash-generating position, while B as a cash cow product has a reducing life expectancy and may soon have to be withdrawn. Product C is a net absorber of company cash and management energy and is to be managed out of the portfolio within the planning period. The need for a new product or products to guarantee the future viability of the company is therefore quite clear. An entry in the portfolio, such as E, might allow the company to become involved in a high-growth market with which it is not completely familiar but in which it believes it

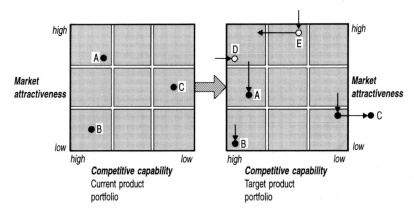

Figure 20.2 Identifying a performance gap

can and must build competitive capability. New product concept D builds directly on existing company strengths to enter perhaps the high-growth segment of the market in which A now competes.

With a target portfolio in mind and corporate and marketing objectives clear, objectives specific to the new product development process can be stated and criteria listed which will determine the strategic fit or non-fit of any new product idea. Once the manager reaches this stage in thinking about new product development more than three-quarters of the new product ideas that may arise may be dismissed as unsuitable even if they have profit potential when considered independently. Remember that the objective in new product development is not simply to introduce a product successfully on a one-off basis. The aim is to introduce a product success-fully that fits with the firm's array of competences and enhances its long-term growth and profit potential. Such a portfolio approach also highlights the need to manage product deletion in an orderly manner, a different though related activity to new product introduction.[3]

When strategic direction has been set, the more operational aspects of product development begin – searching for and evaluating ideas on through to product launch. At each of these stages the company has, and should examine, the option to undertake the process internally or via external acquisition of resources. Top management in expanding companies reg-ularly face the question of whether to develop by a 'greenfield' route or by purchasing an existing company or resources. The use of strategic alliances and joint ventures to support new product development is finding greater popularity throughout the 1990s. This issue is discussed in more detail towards the end of the chapter.

Idea generation and concept screening

The two stages during which ideas are generated and screened and the survivors converted into product concepts that may be evaluated with more rigour form the creative heartland of the new product process. Creativity and mould-breaking thinking are crucial – trying 'to do it different'. Given the agreed direction and criteria for product development, managers should think and search as widely as possible to ensure that all relevant product and market ideas enter the process. Ideas come from customers, various departments in the firm, and even from competitors, and the process may be assisted by the use of various creativity techniques such as brainstorming and morphological analysis. Primary idea screening is performed using the strategic criteria already set (these may specify product technology, market and market segment targets, resource constraints, sales volume and profit potential, etc.).

Concept development and evaluation

When an idea survives screening, it is worthwhile and necessary to develop the idea into a product concept that provides a reasonably detailed picture of its performance and other characteristics and its target market and customer benefit profile. This may take the form of a written product concept, a crude prototype, or it may be visualized in drawings and mock-up versions of the product may be assembled. Developing the concept in this way allows for detailed and quite practical evaluation of the new product proposal in marketing, technical, financial and manufacturing terms. The concept may be tested with potential customers for market acceptance. Manufacturing management can assess in a practical manner likely costs of product development and production, and thus the firm has the fundamental revenue and cost estimates necessary for the financial appraisal of the proposed product.

Product development and launch

Developing the final product, marketing and manufacturing strategies may be undertaken once the product concept passes the basic marketing, manufacturing and financial evaluation of the previous stage. Manufacturing must now gear up to move from prototypes to final product design and production method design. Marketing must begin to formulate intensively its detailed programmes for product launch and management including the completion of a new product marketing plan stating target market, product benefits, market positioning and marketing mix, with associated budgets for revenues and costs set out carefully over, say, the initial three years to identify working capital needs, cashflow requirements and profit performance.

Product launch should be a much less anxious event from the marketing manager's perspective than it normally is if all the above steps have been completed. While it may be less anxious if the process is well managed, it is difficult to reduce the amounts of energy and time and careful attention to detailed arrangements that must be devoted to a successful launch.

For a consumer product all the practical details of packaging, of advertising and promotion planning and scheduling, of selling in the product to wholesalers, distributors and retailers, of producing samples and customer trial-inducing offers must be organized and scheduled with great exactness if the launch is to take place smoothly and on time. For an industrial product the company usually benefits from working with selected customers on final product design and testing prior to launch. Field trials are vital for most industrial and durable products if the marketer is not to be faced with the likelihood of having to recall and replace products that do not perform to specification in customers' hands. Very few new products survive such an event – the market gives very few second chances. A small company that launches a product without adequate pre-launch field trials will usually threaten its own total survival in the process. Big companies, if lucky, can afford a few new product mistakes. Small companies cannot afford any.

Performance management

The rate of adoption of the new product or service must be closely studied. Performance against budget is monitored at the very minimum on a monthly basis for the first year and variances examined as a matter of urgency. Customer experience with the product should be evaluated via formal marketing research or through managerial and salesforce contact with wholesalers, distributors, retailers and final customers. In the case of products that are purchased regularly, the emergence of repeat purchases must be followed with great care. For such products, it is the repeat purchases that determine success or failure, not first purchases – although these must, of course, be achieved before there can be any repeat purchases!

New product diffusion

Product launch marketing should take special account of what is known about the way that new products are accepted and spread in a market. For example, it is found that the sales profile of most new products over time is like that shown in Figure 20.3 – the familiar S-shaped curve of the product

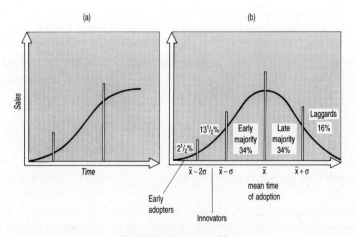

Figure 20.3 New product diffusion

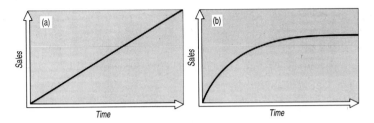

Figure 20.4 Alternative sales curve

lifecycle. This has important implications for forecasting sales, cashflows and working capital requirements. It is vital that the likely shape of the sales curve through time be assessed. If the budget shows a pattern such as one of those in Figure 20.4, then very specific evidence must be produced to justify the assumption that sales will not adhere to the more general S-shaped pattern. The implications of forecasting any one of these three sales patterns for cash management are very critical.

Figure 20.3 also shows in (b) the distribution usually found of customers adopting a new product over time. If all the customers who ever adopt a product for repeated usage are considered, then it is possible to find the average time to adoption (x) of the product by customers in the market – it may be, say, two months or two years. Most studies of this cycle of adoption find that the distribution conforms to what statisticians call a normal distribution, and that typically the customers who initially adopt the successful new product are different from those who adopt it later. Thus it is generally realistic to think about segmenting the market for a new product into time-and-customer 'slices':

1   *Early adopters and innovators* typically constitute about 15–20 per cent of all those who eventually adopt the product for long-term use. Because they are first into the market, and because they usually contain many opinion leaders, they are the vital target for initial marketing attention. If these people do not accept the product, the rest of the market is unlikely to do so. Innovators, as a group, can usually be identified, especially for products that involve significant commitment or risk for the customer. Farmers, for instance, who are early adopters of new agricultural products or practices are typically younger, educated, commercially oriented in their farming, and well networked to other innovative farmers and relevant state support agencies.

2   *The middle majority*, both early and late, constitute the bulk of any market and enter the market at progressively later dates as they see first the innovators and then others buying and successfully using or

consuming the product. Marketing strategy for these groups should shift in emphasis from that aimed at innovators to provide more reassurance, and, in the case of industrial marketing, to use reference sales as a means of demonstrating the product's effectiveness.

3 *Laggards* are the last to enter the market, providing an opportunity to expand the market further, but also on occasion necessitating a higher cost of marketing to convince them, and perhaps even the acceptance of reduced margins in order to 'buy' them into the market.

Exhibit 20.1 provides an interesting case history of new product adoption as well as relative success and failure in the video tape recorder market.

Exhibit 20.1   *VCR versus Laservision*

Winning and losing in product innovation

In *Diffusion of Innovations*, E.M. Rogers suggests that the likelihood that a novel product or idea will be adopted by a population (or indeed, a new product by a market) is dependent on five factors: *relative advantage, compatibility, complexity, divisibility* and *communicability.* The case history of the video tape recorder (VCR) and the Philips Laservision system provides an excellent object lesson of how this model might be applied to the key decision of whether an innovative idea or prototype is likely to succeed, and indeed, what could be done to increase the chances of speedy and widespread adoption. The case also attests to the veracity of Rogers' model for new product decisions.

The conclusion is that VCR succeeded because its launch into a latent market gave it a high relative advantage, because it was compatible with pre-existing TV watching behaviour, because its similarity in principle to audio tape recorders, as well as support from rental companies, assured a perception of low complexity, because an extremely favourable chain of circumstances quickly gave rise to a large rental market that increased divisibility, and because the advantages of VCR ownership were easily communicated.

By contrast, Laservision failed because it had a negative relative advantage compared to VCR, because it was not compatible with the TV recording habit engendered by VCR, because its leading edge technology was seen as relatively complex, because, in the absence of a rental market and due to the need for a supply of laser disks, it suffered low divisibility, and because its shortcomings were easily communicated.[4]

Managing the NPD process

Managing the new product development process poses two important and interrelated questions. First, are the stages or phases in the process carried out in sequence? Or to what extent do they overlap or are they carried out simultaneously? Second, NPD activity obviously crosses many departments and functions, so what is marketing's role? Marketing has obviously a crucial role to play. But it does not own the process exclusively and must co-manage it with many other departments. So who is responsible for managing this process and ensuring smooth and cooperative interdisciplinary working?

From sequential to simultaneous NPD

The process in Figure 20.1 may suggest that the various stages in new product development are sequential. Movement from new product idea generation, to screening and evaluation, to product development, testing and product launch flows smoothly. As one department or function concludes its task, the work is handed on to another department. Each has its own expertise and mode of operation, and so NPD moves through a series of fairly discrete sequences. Such an approach may work in some traditional mature industries where new product development is largely of an incremental nature. It may suffice where the firm is undertaking only limited product development, perhaps a product extension.

However, for the knowledge-intensive industries of the twenty-first century driven by an exponentially growing information technology, such an approach has serious shortcomings. It is slow and fraught with communications problems; it represents a 'chimney stack' vista of NPD. In order for a firm to respond strategically to market opportunity and to match its competence to a market need in a competitively short period of time, the process of new product development invariably involves a sizeable numbers of tasks or phases which must overlap in time in their execution, or which must occur simultaneously and in parallel.

This is all the more evident when it is considered that the representation of the new product development process in Figure 20.1 is very much simplified. In larger firms, each of the main stages or phases would be further subdivided into more tasks and activities involving many functions and departments. Overlapping and simultaneous activities are likely to become a reality, especially in the later stages of product development and launch. At this juncture the new product or service project is moving into a higher gear with engineering, process design, manufacturing, logistics and marketing all simultaneously involved.

A sporting analogy may be used to visualize the management of product development. At one end of a spectrum there is the 'relay race'. This describes the traditional sequential pattern; the various functions are compartmentalized from each other with different specialists carrying the baton at different stages in the race before they hand it on. It is time-consuming and will also be deficient if barriers between departments are high.

This functional relay approach of managing product development may be contrasted at the other end of the spectrum with the 'rugby team' approach. Here new product development is undertaken by a multi-disciplinary team working simultaneously and in regular communication with each other. An attempt is made to break down functional barriers so that all participants in the process, from product designers to marketers, are on the same side, working towards the same goal with a high level of collaboration and integration. This approach involves a hand-picked multi-disciplinary team, with its members working together from start to finish of the development process; the team goes the distance as a unit passing the ball back and forth.[5] The team usually has a high degree of autonomy, and often includes representatives from key suppliers and perhaps customers.

In reality such smooth-running simultaneity is extremely difficult to achieve for most firms. Certainly, a considerable amount of overlapping in the various tasks of NPD is required and firms are managing such process activity with increasing skill. It can also be observed that more and more firms are moving along the spectrum towards greater levels of parallelism in new product development. The European car industry illustrates this. By the end of the 1980s Europe had become the biggest market for automobiles, ahead of North America. The Japanese had garnered some 12 per cent of this market despite quota restrictions. They had also shortened the lifecycle and the development phase of new vehicles: in 1990 the average development phase lasted for about 5 years in European companies compared with 3.5 years in Japanese companies; the average lifecycle of European cars was about 6 years as against 4.5 years for Japanese cars. Top managers in many of the European firms agreed with industry experts that a quick renewal of models was a condition to gain market share. Here, for instance, design capacity was obviously critical; but in 1990 there were 280 designers at Toyota compared to 70 at Peugeot SA and 108 at Volkswagen.[6]

Ford of Europe confronted this challenge in the early 1990s and restructured its entire new product development process in an effort to regain a competitive edge. Exhibit 20.2 describes this and highlights the importance of simultaneity and integration in the process. The Peugeot SA Group with its two marques, Peugeot and Citroën, also saw a revival of its fortunes at this time with some imaginative process re-engineering and marketing. The development of the Citroën ZX showed the case in point.[7] The Citroën ZX would compete in the lower-medium segment along with the Peugeot 309. This segment represented almost a third of the European market, and the success of the ZX was seen as a major challenge for the whole group at the beginning of the 1990s.

Exhibit 20.2   *Marketing in action case*

Ford of Europe designs and manufactures in the same gear

The restructuring of Ford of Europe's R&D operations goes to the heart of its efforts to regain a competitive edge in the fierce battle for European car market leadership. The US car maker's record loss in Europe in 1991 – the worst financial performance among the big six European car makers – has been a bitter pill for a company which led the West European car market in the mid-1980s and which prided itself as the European industry's most efficient volume car maker.

To revive its fortunes, Ford has launched an optimistically titled 'drive for leadership' campaign. High on the agenda is the implementation of so-called simultaneous engineering in the reform of product development. Simultaneous engineering seeks to bring together design and manufacturing engineers to work in a project team (instead of their working in sequence and passing responsibility down the development line) so as to improve the speed, efficiency and quality of the complex process of developing a new vehicle.

To this end, Ford embarked on a controversial programme to concentrate by the mid-1990s all its R&D activities at two sites, one in the United Kingdom, the other in Germany, in place of the present six locations, four in the United Kingdom and two in Germany. At these sites are gathered not only the design engineers and the manufacturing engineers, but also the support staffs, purchasing engineers, finance and quality control specialists.

'Product engineers and manufacturing engineers must be in the same country, and ideally in the same office,' says John Oldfield, Ford of Europe's vice-president for product programmes, vehicle engineering and design. 'You cannot achieve simultaneous engineering by telephone or video-conferencing.'

Mr Oldfield's concerns are underlined by a recent study by two professors at the Harvard Business School and Tokyo University, which identifies gaps in lead-time and engineering productivity between Japanese and Western car makers.[8] The study found that the average Japanese firm had almost double the development productivity and could develop a comparable product a year faster than the average US firm. On average, Japanese car makers needed 1.7 million engineering hours to develop a standard car compared with 3.2 million hours in the United States and 3 million hours for a European volume car maker.

According to Oldfield, US and European car makers still take up to five years to develop a new car. 'The Japanese have about a three-year development cycle and the best Japanese are even a little better than that. We have started on that route.

Product development lead time

US average (months before start of sales)

| 70 | 60 | 50 | 40 | 30 | 20 | 10 | 0 |

62   44   Concept generation
57   39   Product planning
56   30   Advanced engineering
40   12   Product engineering
Process engineering   31   6
Pilot run   9   3

European average (months before start of sales)

| 70 | 60 | 50 | 40 | 30 | 20 | 10 | 0 |

63   50   Concept generation
58   41   Product planning
55   41   Advanced engineering
42   12   Product engineering
Process engineering   37   10
Pilot run   10   3

Japanese average (months before start of sales)

| 70 | 60 | 50 | 40 | 30 | 20 | 10 | 0 |

43   34   Concept generation
38   29   Product planning
42   27   Advanced engineering
Product engineering   30   6
Process engineering   28   6
Pilot run   7   3

Source: Kim B. Clarke and Takahiro Fujimoto (1991), *Product Development Performance* (Harvard Business School Press, Cambridge, Mass).

We have not yet delivered a major programme in three years, but we now have some on the books.'[9]

New model developments methods of Peugeot and Citroën had already been revised with an earlier collaboration between manufacturing, designers and the main subcontractors in order to match style, engineering and production feasibility. For instance, in the case of the ZX the project started in 1985; at the end of 1985 the pilot production phase of the first model was named; several versions were presented in March 1988; then a project leader was named, and the designers also participated in the final phase of the master model. It was planned that the new organization of product development would be applied to the next model (which would replace the existing AX range) to shorten again the lead-time for the development and industrialization from five years to three years. A project manager was named from the beginning to be in charge of quality, cost, scheduling and specific performance targets. The aim was to extend the cooperation between designers, process engineers and the manufacturing and marketing function from the beginning to the end of the project. A new marketing policy was also introduced for the ZX. Until 1990 Citroën used to market many 'special' versions of a given basic model; with the ZX, the product line was to have four brand identities: Reflex (young, modern), Avantage (family), Aura (men, older people) and Volcane (higher social classes).

Organizing for new product development

Organizing an NPD process presents challenge for all involved. Each step can be problematic. When steps begin to overlap and to be expedited in parallel, further complexity is added. Commitment to the end-point of the process is the driving force. Once a NPD project commences and members are 'appointed' to the team, their activities must overstep mere functional loyalty. They are part of and remain committed to a process with clearly defined objectives and must work together in a highly collaborative mode. These players understand the nature of matrix management, but in reality what they do transcends the traditional matrix management approach. Function and task coalesce. The process with its desired outcome is paramount.

Companies attempt formally to structure their approaches to creativity, new idea generation and new product or service development in a number of ways. An R&D department may be charged with developing or scouting for new product ideas. Innovation may be institutionalized in 'skunk works' where a unit or group enjoys a high degree of operational independence in the search for new market opportunities. A service supplier to a retailer may set up its own 'shop' in order to understand better the needs of his customers. But these activities are all at the early stages of new product development. The whole process from conceptualization to full commercialization, from mind to market, is a more complex journey. It is a process that has to be shaped, managed and integrated in a formal way. Multidisciplinary project teams are likely to play a key role, and marketing and the marketing manager must play a key role in the process; if this does not happen, the process is likely to fail.

How formally structured should the team be? How long does it remain as a team? The answer is largely situational. In certain oriental cultures it may be possible to engender a 'rugby' spirit in a company without adopting a formal project team structure. In many large and successful Japanese electronics companies, project teams are not the norm. Yet they display the cooperative modes and outcomes typical of smaller entrepreneurial-spirited companies in the West. The reality is that most European firms do not intuitively exercise this collaborative or organic interaction. It must in some way be structured.

The key appointment is the team leader or project manager who ideally will have responsibility for the process from A to Z. The qualities of leadership, the enthusiasm and personality which he or she brings to the project will in many regards determine its success. He or she will hopefully have the mindset of the product champion, but he or she must have more. The process champion of the 1990s understands that the markets and organizations of the future are significantly different from those of two or three decades ago. Also, while it may seem somewhat obvious to say it, the team leader must have the full support of the top management. He or she probably reports directly to the chief executive. If he or she does not, then he or she must have an executive champion with equal enthusiasm at the top of the organization who can guarantee the necessary corporate support to ensure the process is expedited in a smooth and timely fashion.

Speed to market and new product development

Speed of response, whether in designing a logistics system, counteracting a competitive manoeuvre or in bringing a new product to market, is a powerful basis of competitive advantage. Quick response time involves mastering the art of time-compression or time speed-up, and has even been referred to as 'turbomarketing'.[10] Distribution is an area which has seen considerable time-compression achieved in recent years. Smart manufacturers are working hard to develop faster supply systems. Just-in-time (JIT) operations, quick reporting of orders, EPOS computer systems, flexible factories with low reset-up time, and faster shipment modes all help to speed up distribution.

Retailing is another frontier of time speed-up. Years ago, customers waited a week to have a roll of film developed or to receive a pair of glasses. Today, both a film and a new pair of glasses can be delivered in an hour. The key concept has been to turn the retail store into a mini-factory. Home service delivery times have also been compressed. Domino's Pizza's success is due in large part to its promise to deliver pizza to any customer in its trade area within a half hour.

Cycles for new product development are also speeding up. The primary purpose of simultaneity in NPD is get to the marketplace before competitors and enjoy first-mover advantages. Chapter 11 described how such initial superiority can materialize, through perceived differential advantage, higher prices, switching costs and economies of scale and experience into future market leadership and high returns. It was observed earlier how Japanese car manufacturers, in being able to bring a new model of car to the market 18 months faster than their competitors, achieved a powerful position in the European car market.

Speed to market means that not only has each stage in the NPD process to be executed well and linked in a sequential, overlapping and/or simultaneous way, but that all of this be done at great speed. Success in doing this brings obvious benefit. Exhibit 20.3 recounts how Thermo King Europe stole a march on its competitors in response to changing EU transport legislation and designed, developed and dramatically launched its SMX transport temperature control unit in a short period of time.

But haste can also lead to error. Speed to market is a high-risk undertaking that can backfire. GM's Cadillac division experienced a painful lesson with its Allanté, launched with great expectations in 1987.[11] Cadillac managers hoped the $54,700 coupé would bestow Euro-styling on the division's whole line and expand its customer base to the younger buyers being lured away by BMW and Mercedes-Benz. But the Allanté went to market the apparent victim of a too hasty launch and a failure to offer the right mix of price, quality and features to discerning customers. It was underpowered compared with foreign rivals. The body, handcrafted at the Pininfarina workshop in Turin, was attractive, but not especially distinctive or well made. The roof leaked, and squeaks and wind noise marred the luxury car hush. These were all clear signs that the car's manufacturer should have waited and ironed out the bugs. It did not, and the result was a car which was too small and expensive for core Cadillac buyers,but not really good enough to lure import buyers. It was withdrawn five years later.

Exhibit 10.1 (p. 177) recalls how Unilever launched a new detergent, Persil Power, on the European market in 1994. It contained a special manganese catalyst which, the company claimed, dramatically improved the cleansing power of the detergent. Despite growing evidence that the special agent could bleach and damage some fabrics, Unilever persisted with the pan-European launch of its new brand and got embroiled in an acrimonious dispute with its arch-rival, Procter & Gamble, before withdrawing the catalyst product in early 1995.

These case studies show that speeding to market with a new product has its inherent dangers. To minimize these, two considerations are relevant. First, the NPD process should have a number of 'gateways' where there is clear agreement, including top management's, that the project is meeting specific criteria of manufacturing viability, customer acceptance, sales support and budget planning. Freewheeling momentum is to be avoided. Second, the company must link the process at times back to its strategic roots. What might be the implications for corporate aspiration and fortunes if the new product fails? If these appear significantly negative, it may be wise to abort the project.

Exhibit 20.3   *Marketing in action case*

Thermo King Europe's quick response with its SMX

Thermo King enjoys world leader status in the transport refrigeration industry. The actual industry was 'invented' by Thermo King in 1938 with the development of the first mechanically powered refrigeration system fitted to an articulated truck body. Today, Thermo King equipment is used around the world in the daily transportation and protection of perishable produce. The product itself sits on the front wall of a large semi-trailer and provides accurate temperature control from +15 °C to –30 °C.

In 1989 the EU Transport Commission introduced new legislation governing the total length of the trailer plus tractor. Immediately, it became obvious that the trailer could realistically extend in length from the standard 12.6 metre to 13.6 metres, enabling 33 Europallets to be carried in this new trailer where the maximum was previously 32 or even 30. However, the EC also limited the swing radius of the tractor/trailer combination and this directly affected the space normally occupied by the front-mounted refrigeration unit. Indeed, at the time the legislation was introduced, no such unit existed that would fit inside the dimensions prescribed by the new legislation and deliver the capacity and airflow required to protect the cargo.

Thermo King Europe took up the challenge to introduce such a new unit to the market. It also determined to get the whole project designed, engineered, tested, launched and selling within 18 months – quite an undertaking considering that a typical Thermo King product development cycle up to then was 3–5 years, and involved 6 months of rigorous field tests and thousands of hours of real-life application.

To achieve this, a whole new approach to product development had to be adopted. Thermo King Europe's manufacturing operation was based in Galway, Ireland, but typically, all design and development had been done at the corporation's headquarters in Minneapolis. As this unit was destined for Europe, it was decided from the outset to have European marketing, engineering and manufacturing personnel totally involved in the process.

The concept of a design 'cluster' was born. The first such cluster was formed in early 1990 with a senior trailer unit engineer, supported by specialist engineers in the various disciplines that make up a unit – diesel engine technology, compressor, refrigeration and electrical. These were for the most part based in Minneapolis. In addition, a senior manufacturing engineer from the Galway factory represented the needs for design for manufacturability, and he in turn was supported by a small group of specialist manufacturing engineers. The marketing input to the cluster was largely European, and this group was to be the voice of the marketplace. All in all, there were twenty key individuals in the cluster. A dedicated office and workshop area were created in Minneapolis for the cluster, and satellite communications were established between Galway and Minneapolis for the transfer of CAD drawings from the design group directly to the CAD-driven manufacturing systems in Galway. This meant that as a part or component was designed in Minneapolis, it was being built *in Galway the same day.*

In early 1991, Thermo King Europe's marketing personnel started to prepare what was to be a high visibility product launch in September 1991, the date the development team was confident that the new units would be in production. This involved getting a number of key trailer manufacturers to provide new length trailers with the final customers' livery. (These own equipment manufacturers – OEMs – are the primary distribution channel as they often supply the whole vehicle, trailer plus unit, to the final customer, and are therefore frequently consulted by the end-user as to choice of refrigeration unit.)

In secret, Thermo King mounted the newly branded SMX units to these trailers for a spectacular unveiling at the industry association's annual conference near Barcelona in September. The firm had stolen a noteworthy march on its competitors and continued to modify the SMX to enable it to use environmentally friendly refrigerants and on-board microprocessors with satellite interfaces and trip recorders.[12]

Expeditionary marketing

The term 'expeditionary marketing' has been coined to describe an interactive approach involving the speedy repeat of the *whole* new product development process after receipt of customer information about its use following product launch in the marketplace.[13] This process of real-time reinvention and re-adaptation has been used to great effect by a number of Japanese companies.

JVC's success and Sony's near-success in opening the consumer market for VCRs in the late 1970s came on the back of a long string of product launches, many of them less than outstanding successes, over a decade.

More spectacularly, Toshiba's staggering pace of product introduction in its laptop computer business during the late 1980s allowed it to explore almost every possible market niche and to outpace rivals like Grid, Zenith and Compaq. Between 1986 and 1990 Toshiba introduced no fewer than 31 new models to the market. Further, when one particular model failed, its withdrawal hardly caused a ripple in customer confidence. In fact, by 1991 Toshiba had discontinued more laptop models than some of its tardier competitors had launched (see Exhibit 8.1 p. 136). The key to such expeditionary marketing depends on minimizing the time and cost of product iteration. Speed of iteration depends on the time it takes a company to develop and launch a product, accumulate insights from the marketplace, and then redesign and relaunch. Flexible manufacturing processes and low plant-tooling costs are critical in this context.

Strategic alliances and new product development

The need for efficiency and effectiveness dictates that the market-focused firm should continuously evaluate decisions about whether to carry out a particular value-adding activity within the firm, to outsource it or to perform it in partnership with an outside player. New product development involves making such decisions extensively. A firm may find that it has shortcomings and underdeveloped expertise in certain key parts of the process, for example, channel management, technology, process engineering or customer service. It can choose to buy in such expertise and use outside support. It can also choose to work closely with an outside partner to develop and manage certain aspects and activities in the process or, indeed, in some cases the whole NPD process. This enables superior competences of the partner in certain important domains to be fused to great advantage with those of the firm. It also helps to spread the risks of new product development, particularly in large projects.

Such joint ventures and strategic alliances are of growing importance in many industries, particularly in high technology sectors. There are many examples of alliances between hardware and software firms, or between large and small software firms, in the global computer industry; one partner brings a competence or asset underdeveloped or absent in the other. As a new product development venture grows in scale and takes on wide international dimensions, the attractions of partnering increase. The management of the Chunnel project wisely involved an Anglo-French partnership. Another interesting example of Euro-scale alliance is the Association of European Research Establishments in Aeronautics (AEREA) formed in 1994 by seven European nations to combine their aeronautics research programmes to build a strong new technology base that coordinates the skills of nearly 20,000 staff menbers. The objective is to deepen the European aeronautics industry's research competence to compete against what managers perceive as the US technology threat.[14]

Operating such joint ventures and co-managing these alliances present difficulties for both partners. New skills and expertise have to be learned. Not only are managers managing their functional responsibilities along with many activities across functional boundaries, they must also embrace the different styles and values of the partner firm. But more than most activities and processes in a firm, NPD demands creative adaptation and innovative working modes. It involves partnering deeply and widely – deeply within the firm to draw out every available resource, and widely outside the firm to take advantage of superior expertise.

REVIEW QUESTIONS

20.1 Elaborate on the various stages or phases in the NPD process. Why is it necessary to start with strategic considerations?

20.2 What is meant by simultaneity in new product development? What evidence do you see of it in a chosen market?

20.3 What are the benefits and risks of speed to market tactics in new product or service introduction?

20.4 Discuss how the NPD process might be best organized in a firm.

20.5 New product development involves partnering both deeply and widely. Consider this comment.

CHAPTER 21

Design as strategy

▶ Design and strategy
▶ Design and marketing
▶ Understanding design activity
▶ Organizing for design

Marketing in action cases
BMW designs for disassembly
Apple's Newton MessagePad strives for the 'Ferrari' effect

ABOUT THIS CHAPTER

Good design has an input at many stages and in many forms in the progress from conceptualization of a product or service to its full and ongoing commercialization. Design and marketing, in particular, have a symbiotic relationship in this process from 'mind to market'. To understand this is to appreciate the strategic role of design in creating competitive advantage.

Such a broadened appreciation requires the marketer to see design in its totality – at its core product or service level, at its augmented product level and at the corporate level. The marketing manager benefits from understanding more fully the nature of design activity. The organization of successful design involves the coordination of multidisciplinary tasks and relationships not only within but also outside the organization.

A neglected domain

The role of design in new product development, in the sense of creating form as well as function, in its aesthetic appeal as well as its engineering vision, may at first regard seem self-evident and requiring of little further elaboration. The product or service must be designed to offer the consumer or buyer certain performance characteristics. It will likely be designed in a way that is aesthetically pleasing to the consumer. In sum, it must work or deliver well, and it must look good. However, to state the role of design in this summary way is to misunderstand greatly its contribution to successful NPD and indeed to successful marketing practice.[1]

Marketing, as an eclectic discipline, can lay claim to a number of foundation stones. Few would deny an understanding of consumer behaviour and research methodology as two such keystones. Yet it is undeniable that at the heart of any good product or service lies good design. But design is rarely perceived as a foundation stone of best marketing practice. It is seen as a distant cousin rather than an intimate partner – something somebody else does.

Design and strategy

What exactly do we mean by design in the context of marketing and marketing strategy? The diversity of answers one is likely to receive from marketing practitioners in large part explains the confusion over the role of design. The marketer does perceive design in physical product design; it's about engineering or industrial design. He or she possibly sees it in dimensions of the delivery system; it's about well-orchestrated logistics to minimize waiting times. He or she observes design at the point of sale; an architect has created a pleasant shopping mall or environment. He or she also sees it in aspects of the communications mix; the advertising people have developed some clever advertising or packaging. But this understanding is often cursory and fragmented. Design appears to be of an 'other world'.

In a number of regards this is understandable. Design has a different provenance. It speaks a different language. Yet successful commercial design and best marketing practice share similarities in the need for creative origination, disciplined processes of management and an ultimately satisfied consumer. Consider this quote from the eminent design professional, Wally Olins, chairman of Wolff Olins, the large UK design company responsible for the corporate logos and identities of many European firms:

> Design can add value to products and services by distinguishing them from otherwise identical products and services of other companies . . . in many cases, customers favour one company over another because of the design used to differentiate that company's products or services.[2]

Successful design thus has a strategic dimension that can confer positional advantage like a manufacturing process or a distribution system.

Good design has an input at many stages and in many forms in the progress from conceptualization of a product or service to its full and ongoing commercialization. Design and marketing in particular have a symbiotic relationship in this process from 'mind to market'. To understand this is to appreciate the strategic role of design in creating competitive advantage.

Design and marketing

One way of understanding design from a marketing manager's perspective is to see it operating at three interrelated levels: *the product level, the augmented product level* and *the corporate level*. The first level represents actual product design itself – physical components, shape, size, performance characteristics and certain structural characteristics as well as the aesthetics of the product or service. Here the design input is by industrial designers, product engineers, technical specialists and even inventors. When the phrase 'product design' is mentioned by marketers, it usually refers to this step in new product development or existing product re-engineering.

As we move along the NPD process towards the marketplace and exchange activity, design continues to play a crucial part at the augmented product level. This includes the development of packaging, advertising in different media, technical support literature and sales promotion. Here design input is by graphic designers, art visualizers, creative directors of advertising agencies, film directors and multi-media experts. Good design has a role in creating retail outlets and other service delivery points or channels where intangible elements – the personal dimension – must often complement the product offering.

Design at a corporate level underpins corporate communications in areas involving the company logo, diaries, calendars, exhibitions, sponsorship arrangements and corporate advertising, all of which speak for the company at an overall level rather than just about one specific product or service. This is a domain of increasing strategic importance as firms seek to internationalize. There is a need to maintain a consistent identity across countries which may also have to be balanced with a sensitivity to local or regional needs.

The 1990s have seen a dramatic growth in international design consultants and strategic public affairs agencies. Large firms, in particular, are developing very considerable expertise in the management of their corporate identity. Many have visual communications departments or corporate identity units to ensure consistency of corporate design in the 'trade dress' of all products and services, the livery of fleet vehicles and the use of the company logo by internal divisions and external agencies. Exhibit 21.1 shows Nestlé's general guidelines for the use of its logotypes. An increasingly sophisticated consumer passes judgement on and tempers his or her loyalty towards an organization in the light of every encounter with it. This involves not only using the product or service, but also reacting to its marketing communications from TV ads to letters and calls exchanged.

Exhibit 21.1

Guidelines for the use of Nestlé logotypes

The corporate identity

1 *The Nestlé Horizontal Corporate Logotype.*
Where the first priority is the legibility and the recognition of the Nestlé name, this version, which puts emphasis on *the Company name*, should be used for stationery, fleet vehicles, annual reports, etc.

2 *The Nestlé Vertical Corporate Logotype.*
Where the Company philosophy or its corporate role needs to be expressed, this version, which puts emphasis *on the nest as a Company symbol*, should be used on sign-posting, buildings, etc. Preference should be given to this version wherever possible.

NB These versions are not to be used on packages (see below)

The colour for the NESTLÉ corporate identity is always grey as defined in the NESTLÉ Corporate Identity Guidelines.

The brand logotype

When NESTLÉ appears as a corporate, range or product brand, the solid version should be used. Positive or negative, any colour can be used.

Where NESTLÉ appears as a corporate brand, it shall, in all applications, be given *increased* prominence in size, position and colour.

The Nestlé seal of guarantee

This version is *exclusively for use on packaging*, on the side or back panels only of the unit pack, display or shipping carton.

It should *never* appear on any other material.

For exact application, refer to Nestlé Corporate Identity Guidelines.

Any use of the Nestlé logotype and/or the 'nest' device not in line with the above has to be approved by the Trademark Owners.

If design is to be used as a strategic instrument, it is important that the marketer perceives design activity in its totality, and realizes that this

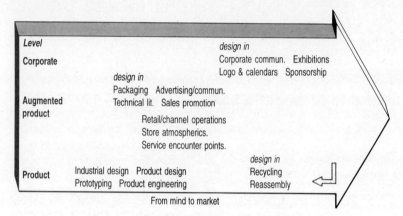

Figure 21.1 Design in NPD

totality is greater than the mere sum of its parts. The perceptive marketer understands the full nature and potential contribution of design, and interacts where relevant with design activity. Figure 21.1 highlights the activities and inputs of design along the value-adding chain from mind to market. It emphasizes the design dimensions in new, and existing, product development at the different levels and stages in the process. It also suggests that design plays an important role in 'green' marketing in recycling and in design for disassembly. (Exhibit 21.2 describes such design at the car manufacturer BMW and at General Electric's plastics division.) For a firm to position its product or service pre-eminently, all three levels of design must be successfully interrelated and managed. All combine to build a brand franchise. In short, a successful brand involves a symbiosis of good design and best marketing practice.

The Danish firm Lego provides an illustration of this interaction of marketing and design. Lego is a toy system in which all the pieces are compatible with each other. The firm has stuck to its basic product idea without chasing fads, but has creatively developed a vast array of variations on that basic idea. Technical improvements in materials, basic brick design ('for better 'grip') and processing have also been important. This, allied to innovative marketing strategy, lies behind its continuing success.

Exhibit 21.2   *Marketing in action case*

BMW designs for disassembly

Problem: You manufacture cars, computers, washing machines, refrigerators, even teapots – complex, durable products. You use plastic, lots of it. But plastic waste is piling up all over the country. Social and political pressure to recycle the material is growing fast. What should you do?

Solution: Design for disassembly. Simplify parts and materials and make them easy and inexpensive to snap apart, sort and recycle.

Assemble for disassembly? Construct to destruct? Counterintuitive as it may sound, design for disassembly has arrived. If the l990s is the decade of the environment and recycling, then taking things apart efficiently may soon become as important as putting them together right. Whirlpool, Electrolux, Digital Equipment, 3M and General Electric are just a few of the corporate giants beginning to incorporate design for disassembly (DFD) in their thinking and their products.

But the leader of the DFD pack is BMW. Its sporty two-seater, the Z1, has an all-plastic skin that is designed to be disassembled from its metal chassis in 20 minutes. This limited production car, currently being sold in Europe, has doors, bumpers and front, rear and side panels made of recyclable thermoplastic supplied by GE Plastics, a division of General Electric. Glue and screws, for example, are enemies of DFD. 'Pop-in, pop-out' two-way fasteners are the way to go. At BMW, it is now becoming *verboten* to use dozens of different kinds of plastics in manufacturing because it makes sorting expensive and the reuse of materials almost impossible.

One great surprise coming out of the BMW experience is the rediscovery of repairability. In a throwback to the Tin Lizzies of the 1930s, when cars and everything else were built to be repaired, design for disassembly allows cars to be worked on faster and easier. Put in a wider context, the throwaway society is having a rethink about itself.

In the United States, trailing behind Europe in 'eco-*angst*', and behind in DFD by about a year, recent legislation has prompted many firms to take recycling seriously. Whirlpool Corp., for one, has a DFD project under way in which the parts of a new appliance will be designed to be quickly taken apart with ease, and coded for easy sorting. Indeed, many companies are beginning to see the 'greening' of products as a marketing tool. To give people easy access to recycling information, 3M has put an 800 number on all its products.

GE Plastics serves the durable goods market, working only with engineering thermoplastics, the kind used in the BMW Z1. Thermoplastics can be reheated and remoulded; like cats, they can have many lives. GE Plastics, in fact, already has buy-back deals for thermoplastic with a number of car and computer companies. It reprocesses the material and sells it back to the manufacturer, competing with Dow Chemical, Du Pont, Hoechst Celanese and other suppliers of virgin plastics. Now, GE Plastics plans to set up a nationwide plastics recycling network buying back recycled thermoplastics from all over the country, regrinding and recomposing the materials and reselling them to manufacturers at large.

None of this would make much sense, however, if GE had to tear apart products to get at the plastic material and recycle it. The key is design for disassembly which makes it cost-effective to segregate the materials in durable goods. To that end, GE Plastics has set up a joint venture with one of the United States' largest industrial design companies and a winner of some of the product design profession's top accolades.[3]

The Italian firm Olivetti has enjoyed the reputation as a thoroughly 'designerly' firm.[4] From its first functional yet elegant typewriter introduced in 1911 by its founder, Camillo Olivetti, the company has always been a trendsetter, which much larger companies were then forced to follow. Having burst into IBM's supposedly impregnable territory in the late 1970s with the world's first fully electronic typewriter, it immediately took the lead with the slimmest and most user-friendly computer keyboard. Olivetti's industrial designers employed highly advanced electronic circuitry to develop the easy-to-use, imposingly wedge-shaped black ET range of typewriters in 1978 – a design which the Japanese and other competitors sought to imitate. The L1 keyboard was born two years later. These two machines symbolize the firm's long-standing ability to enhance the value of its products in the marketplace through the use of good industrial design. Its entire range of computers, terminals, typewriters, screens, printers and other peripherals are not only sleekly styled, but also possess all kinds of features designed to make them ergonomically attractive.

Most successful service companies also use design in a way that confers clear strategic advantage. Everthing about McDonald's, American Express, Singapore Airlines reveals predetermined, well thought-out and usually highly creative decisions about design. The Body Shop was founded in 1976 by Anita Roddick in the United Kingdom, and now markets over 300 personal care and cosmetic products in a simply packaged, reasonably priced format. This business format franchise trades in over 40 countries and employs some 6,000 people. Its shops and products, which espouse a nature and environmentally friendly philosophy, have made clever use of a distinctive, if minimalist, design and thoughtful marketing. Indeed, the management and contribution of good design to the success of service firms are remarkably similar to that in manufacturing firms and highlight again the benefits of exploring similarities as well differences in product/services marketing.[5] Exhibit 15.1 (p. 294) illustrates how Spain has successfully branded itself as a tourist destination using as an integral part in its promotion extraordinarily well-designed and conceived print and TV advertisements celebrating the many holiday dimensions and regions of Spain. A distinctive logo incorporating the name España, devised after the Catalan painter Miró's work, provides a thematic unity to the campaign.

Understanding design activity

The companies just described exemplify a competitively advantageous harmony of design and marketing – design not just at product level, but also at the augmented product and corporate level. The products not only perform or deliver well, they also look good. A successful balance of functionality and aesthetics in design has been achieved. Such a balance is not always readily realizable. Despite the existence of fundamental principles of art and design, an industrial designer or graphic artist may be unable to bring a pleasing aesthetic to a product. This may be because some design is merely faddish or reflects a quirky personal taste. A product's technology, despite its functional excellence, may simply not facilitate other than 'putting pretty boxes round things', like the way the latterday Detroit automobile stylists shaped some of their car bodies.

The first computers had an awesome functionality for their times; they were hardly beautiful looking. In the mid-1980s Steve Jobs, founder of Apple Computers, launched his 'bicycle of the mind', the Apple Macintosh PC (after the South American Condor, a man riding a bike displays the highest muscle-to-power ratio in movement – hence Jobs' 'bicycle of the mind' appellation). It combined impressive computing power with highly pleasing physical and operational design, and balanced hardware and software, as well as symbol and language. It is not surprising that designers themselves came to be and remain loyal users of the Mac. Subsequent development of it and other Apple products continues to reflect these values (see Exhibit 21.3).

Exhibit 21.3   *Marketing in action case*

Apple's Newton MessagePad strives for the 'Ferrari' effect

When Apple Computer's Newton MessagePad was first launched, many questioned its usefulness and baulked at its $600 price-tag. Garry Trudeau, the celebrated US cartoonist, poked fun at it in his *Doonesbury* strip. But its design credentials were never in doubt. It had subtly curved lines, a rich deep colour, a tailored feel and all one would expect from Apple in user-friendliness.

It won the gold medal in the business and industrial products category in the 1994 Industrial Design Excellence Awards (IDEA), juried by the Industrial Designers Society of America. Says IDEA judge, James Shook: 'Newton broke new ground ... It took the computer off the desk and put it into your hand.' He points out that people were sceptical when the Macintosh first came out.

Even if Newton, a 'personal digital assistant' that is part-communicator and part-computer, takes time to match the Mac's commercial appeal, it has set a standard for how such a truly personal computer should look and feel. It has what Apple

Design Director Robert Brunner calls the 'Ferrari' effect – sleek sculpting that says high performance.

In the autumn of 1991, the six-person design team was given only eight weeks to come up with the Newton's design. They needed to create something entirely new, the company's first hand-held product. They did not want it to resemble a personal computer, but a notepad – hence no keyboard and a vertical rather than horizontal design. At the same time, they needed to retain design elements that buyers associate with Apple like rounded edges, complex surfaces and an emphasis on symmetry and icons.

John Sculley, then Apple's CEO, loved the first Newton on sight. But when he tried to slip it into his pocket, it would not fit. He ordered the team back to the drawing board. It had to lose 4 mm – no problem, except the components could not get any smaller. So the team shaved a bit from the sides and went back to the CEO. No go. 'We couldn't figure it out,' Brunner says. 'It fit in our pockets. We were so frustrated, we considered sneaking in and snipping his pocket seams.' Instead, the team gave up some curves and shaved a little off the stylus holder. *Voilà*. Sculley was happy. It went into production, though Brunner feels the product will probably need a few more iterations and changes before it achieves Mac-like acceptance.[6]

Design activity may seen to have four essential characteristics.[7] These might be described as the four Cs of design:

1 *Creativity*: design requires the creation of something that has not existed before (ranging from a variation on an existing design to a completely new concept).
2 *Complexity*: design involves decisions on large numbers of parameters and variables (ranging from overall configuration and performance to components, materials, appearance, method of manufacture and delivery, and media).
3 *Compromise*: design requires balancing multiple and sometimes conflicting requirements (such as performance and cost; appearance and ease of use; materials and durability, form and function).
4 *Choice*: design requires making choices between many possible solutions to a problem at all levels from basic concept to the smallest detail of colour or form in a marketing communication.

There is a common pattern to design activity across a broad spectrum of industries and types of product/service. In parallel with the NPD process, design involves repeated activities of problem exploration, solution generation and selection that transform the brief via many possible solutions to a particular design specified in sufficient detail to enable it to be manufactured and marketed. In parallel with marketing there is the need for creative origination, disciplined processes of management and an ultimately satisfied consumer. Further, this process must also be continuous. Design cannot stand still; it must evolve over time as the product itself evolves over its lifecycle.

The bicycle provides an interesting example of design lifecycle – a cycle analogous to our understanding of the lifecycle in marketing. Exhibit 21.4 charts the evolution of bicycle design from invention, through a divergent, innovative phase at the early stages of the industry, towards convergence on a single dominant design. A second divergent phase can then be observed as the mature industry attempts to innovate and differentiate its products to avoid declining demand. There is the advent of the small-wheel 'shopper', based on Moulton's radical design, the various fun bikes for children and the mountain bike. The National Panasonic Bicycle in Japan saw bike design move into a new phase in the 1990s with its fully customized product offering. NPB's use of electronic technology in a highly sophisticated order generation, fulfilment and service process enables a customer to order and receive within two weeks a bike tailored to his or her own personal requirements – to the tune of over 11 million variations! (See Exhibit 3.1, p. 45.)

The dynamic for such movement in design and creative innovation, whether evolutionary, revolutionary or re-inventive, lies in many forces for change and growth in a society: technology, economic development, physical resource endowment, population growth, political upheaval, government regulation, culture, education, climate, and so on. To explain why Finland enjoys a reputation for furniture design, Germany for mechanical engineering design, Italy for fashion design, or Switzerland for watch design involves a consideration of a number of these factors taken in their particular cultural and historical context.

Yet different eras have produced movements in design which have greatly enriched the quality and appearance of industrial products. The Arts and Crafts Movement of late nineteenth-century Britain set out to restore dignity to work in the new machine age. The *Deutscher Werkbund* was conceived by the Prussian government in 1907 to develop a 'new aesthetic' for machines. One of its main tenets was that there was such a thing as an absolute standard of 'good design'. In 1919 it spawned the Bauhaus, an organization whose impact was to reverberate for many decades. The Bauhaus developed a set of challenging theories about the relationship of aesthetics to functionalism, emphasized the importance of geometry, precision, simplicity and economy in design, and provided the intellectual underpinning for more than a half century of architectural practice, urban and environmental planning, and industrial design, under the banner of the 'modern movement'.

Exhibit 21.4

Lifecycle of bicycle design

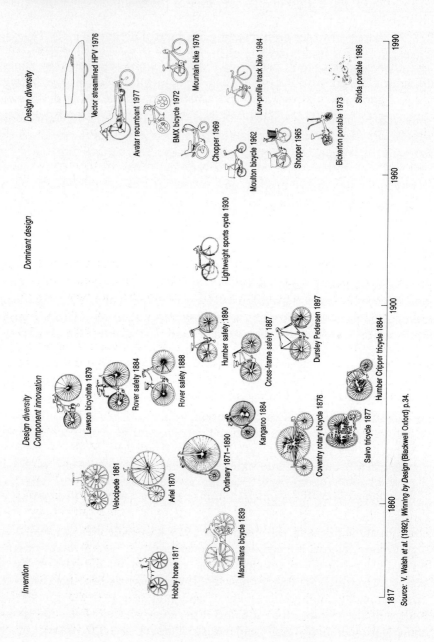

Source: V. Walsh et al. (1992), *Winning by Design* (Blackwell Oxford) p.34.

Our trepidatory approach towards the twenty-first century has witnessed a rise in so-called postmodernism. Postmodernism questions many of the precepts of the modern movement such as its belief in rationality and universality, and its optimism about scientific discovery and technological innovation. It has had an impact on many domains of intellectual endeavour, from psychology to media studies, and from anthropology to organization studies. Its impact on marketing is also to be observed.[8] Equally, it has influenced design. An interesting example is so-called retro design, where product and industrial designers are reinventing and re-using designs of earlier eras, such as the Japanese cars which replicate 1950s' design, kitchen toasters similar to those of the 1930s and furniture in Art Deco mode. Similarly, retrographics are eschewing clear, precise lines in printed media design and advertising in favour of more quirky, mannered, even eccentric presentation. Print advertisements for Swatch watches in the mid-1990s reflect this.

Organizing for design

If marketing and design are to achieve the necessary symbiotic relationship, the process suggested in Figure 21.1 requires active management and coordination. Marketing has a crucial input at the basic product level and is the dominant decision-maker at the augmented product and corporate levels. At the basic product level, design becomes a sub-process or stream of the NPD process itself. Its organization will likely involve a multidisciplinary, team-based approach. The team leader must appreciate the strategic role of design. This view of the world must also be fully endorsed at the top of the organization. The prescient chief executive views design as a new and intimate partner, not the distant cousin of old. In its heyday, the product designers at Olivetti were right at the apex of the firm and were celebrated as the doyens of its progress. They were process integrators as well as product designers. Further, their 'studios' also undertook design work for other firms. This permitted an openness and cross-fertilization of ideas.

Companies like Olivetti, Apple and Lego in a sense institutionalize a design ethic in their organizations. How other companies can achieve this may, like design itself, require some creative thinking; parts of the design process itself may have to be re-engineered. Parties outside the firm, but with which the firm has established a longer-term relationship, may become crucial in design activity. Sub-suppliers, design consultants and advertising agencies all become part of a consciously managed process to assure both continuity and fresh thinking in the strategic management of design and the creation of a lasting brand franchise. In this context many large advertising agencies would point out the pivotal role they have had in ensuring the long-term integrity of many FMCG brands against a background of high turnover of product/brand managers in their client companies.

REVIEW QUESTIONS

21.1 Why has good design a strategic dimension that can confer positional advantage?
21.2 A successful brand involves the symbiosis of good design and best marketing practice. Discuss.
21.3 Elaborate on the argument that one way of understanding design from a marketing manager's perspective is to see it operating at three interrelated levels.
21.4 What are the four Cs of design? Give practical examples.
21.5 Compare and contrast the role of design in the success of Apple Computer and McDonald's.
21.6 How has postmodernism impacted on design and marketing communication?

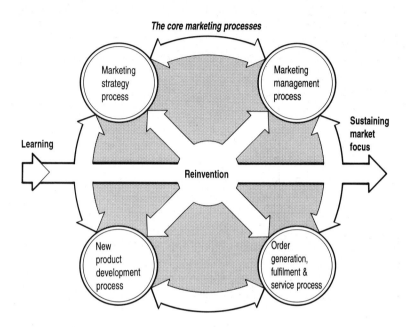

CHAPTER 22

Reinventing the business system

- It's the firm that matters
- Reinventing the business system
- Reinventing the micro business system
- The practice of business process redesign
- Redesigning the marketing processes

Marketing in action case
Re-engineering Banca di America e di Italia

ABOUT THIS CHAPTER

Sustaining market focus demands a dedication to the dual nature of focus – externally towards customer need and internally to align company capability – *and* a constant commitment to renewal in the organization and its market relationships. Ensuring that capabilities remain market-oriented and are configured to deliver maximum value at minimum cost for the targeted market need is a resource-based view of competitive advantage. The distinctive competences and vision of the company determine its destiny rather than any selective power of the competitive marketplace.

The most dramatic and entrepreneurial instances of sustaining and renewing focus are often associated with those companies that rewrite the rules of the game by recreating the business system of an industry. A rejuvenated managerial mindset allied to a deep understanding of the horizontal and vertical structure of the business system, of the opportunities therein to 'capture' added value, and of the system's dynamics are key to developing such frame-breaking strategies.

Renewal equally involves reinventing or redesigning the firm's micro business system. Best practice in business process re-engineering or redesign (BPR) is explored, and its radical mould-changing nature is highlighted. Finally, issues in redesigning the core marketing processes are examined. The OGFS and NPD processes have strong, tangible elements whereas marketing management and marketing strategy are closer to 'pure' management processes.

Focusing competence

Retaining market focus means sustaining persistent commitment to the market, its needs and competitive dynamics, and to aligning company resources to serve these needs. The company must look to markets for its revenue, its profits and its ultimate *raison d'être*. But maintaining focus also demands looking inward to the vitals of the organization in order to understand its core and distinctive competences and to bring these to bear on well-chosen parts of the marketplace.

Focus therefore has two dimensions: first, clear focusing on markets that are to be served; and second, focusing of organizational resources on these markets to do this job better than competitors. Doing this well and consistently over time is difficult. Organizations tend more readily towards stability than to change. Consequently, markets chosen as the focus at one stage in a company's history easily become fixed and immovable targets, just as resources all too readily congeal into rigid configurations of assets (people, equipment and money) and processes (the way business gets done). Such fixity is life-threatening in all but very stable market and competitive circumstances. Sustaining focus demands a dedication to the dual nature of focus (external and internal) and a constant commitment to renewal in the organization and its market relationships.

It's the firm that matters

This chapter addresses some of the demands of maintaining organizational focus – of ensuring that capabilities remain market-oriented and are configured to deliver maximum value at minimum cost for the targeted market need. This is a resource-based view of competitive advantage. It is based on the assertion that fundamentally it is the distinctive competences and vision of the company that determine its success or failure in a competitive market.

There is little point in devoting time and investment to having firms attempt to renew themselves, their industry business systems and their routes to market if ultimately it is the environment that is all-determining in dictating success or failure. Which counts for more – firms or industries – in determining performance? As discussed earlier in Chapters 2 and 9 the perspective of this book is that the firm matters and that it can shape its industry and its destiny. Put more formally, managerial choice can outweigh environmental determinism.

The popular argument about the relative importance of environment and firm in determining performance outcomes (akin to the never-ending debate about 'nature and nurture' in the human sciences) swung quite strongly in favour of environment for much of the 1980s. The acceptance of Porter's industry analysis framework based on the industrial economics assumption that industry structure determines company conduct, which then determines performance, pointed towards an explanation heavily weighted towards the industry as the critical force. The 1990s have seen a resurgence of interest in resource-based explanations, such as Hamel and Prahalad's work on core competences, strategic intent and on *Competing for the Future*.[1, 2] In addition to the popular swing towards a greater belief in the power of the firm and its managers to determine their own future, rather than being selected by the environment in a Darwinian sense, there has been an upsurge of theorizing on the subject of resource-based advantage in competition.[3, 4] New theoretical insights have argued in favour of attributing considerable importance to the actions of the individual firm, and there has been a reconsideration of some of the basic premises of the 'environment is all' school of thought.

Baden-Fuller and Stopford draw attention to the manner in which the conclusions of earlier influential work on industry and firm profitability have been subject to almost complete revision with more recent research.[5] Rumelt, for example, suggests that industry effects account for no more than about 10 per cent of a business unit's profitability, and that the right choice of strategy seems to be at least five times more important than the right choice of industry.[6] They also draw attention to the fact that economists from outside the industrial organization tradition, such as Friedman, have asserted that causality flows in the opposite direction – from firm to industry – and would claim that some industries are more profitable than others because profitable firms are unevenly distributed across industries. Industries characterized by poor profitability have a preponderance of ineffective and inefficient firms, profitable industries the opposite.

Exhibit 11.1 (p. 196) highlights how William Cook, in the UK steel castings industry, moved from being a barely profitable business with only 2 per cent share of the industry, to a highly profitable business earning an excellent return with some 30 per cent industry share in less than ten years. Cook's performance encouraged new competitors to enter the market to copy and rival it. Partly on account of all the actions of the players in the industry, industry sales stopped declining, excess capacity disappeared and the industry became more attractive. But the sequence of events was from firm action to industry improvement, not the other way around.

This latter argument – that the firms make the industry – fits well with the resource-based view of many strategy and management theorists and with the claim that frame-breaking strategies are the real key to long-term success. If an unprofitable industry is characterized by ineffectual firms, there is a high probability that they pursue similar strategies with similar organizational forms. It is, in fact, this very sameness that drives down profits, makes advantage unsustainable and results in the 'commoditization' of products and services. But sameness is a mental trap – an artefact of the mental maps that managers have of their markets, technologies, organizations and competitive options and of the risk-aversion or the failure of imagination that prevents them from seeing their industry and markets in new and different ways. It is for these reasons that a commitment to reinventing business systems is so central to renewal and improved performance.

The mould-breaking strategies of many firms are described in this book. Exhibit 3.1 (p. 45) outlines National Panasonic's customized bicycle with its 11 million custom combinations and its unique ordering/delivery system which effectively reinvented the bicycle business system; its success dramatically reversed the company's fortunes. Exhibit 8.2 (p. 145) illustrates how Bill Gates, founder of Microsoft, is rewriting the rules of the game in art education, publishing and museum management by assembling a digitized inventory of the world's greatest works of art.

Chapter 8 also profiles the Cott Corporation, a global manufacturer of own-label cola, which quickly capitalized on the decade's growth in retailer power and distributor own brands (DOBs), and changed deeply the business system of the cola industry right through from concentrate manufacture to final purchase, and dealt a striking blow to the two players who dominated the cola industry, Coca-Cola and Pepsi Cola. ISPG is a small aquaculture firm which has successfully re-engineered its industry's value chain – primarily downstream distribution practice – to its advantage; it has done so from a peripheral Atlantic coast location while serving markets in continental Europe (see Exhibit 18.2, p. 373). Each of these examples instances the primary challenge of marketing, to decommoditize the firm's goods and services by creatively differentiating its offerings and imaginatively adding value for the customer.

Reinventing the business system

The most dramatic and entrepreneurial instances of sustaining and renewing focus are often associated with companies that rewrite the rules of the game by recreating the business system of an industry. It is therefore important to realize that renewal may take two paths:

1 recreation of the industry business system in a manner that only the firm which has precipitated the change can initially understand; and
2 recreation of the way in which competition is conducted within a given business system.

The first of these is the most powerful source of market advantage as it gives the firm a double advantage – it recreates the business system through its innovation and makes it the only competitor which initially understands the new critical success factors for competing. Followers have two problems to overcome – understanding the new business system *and* understanding how to rebuild their individual competitive strategies.

There would appear to be several important steps involved in reinventing a business system. A first consideration has to do with reinvigorating the mindset and attitude of a management group. It is impossible to rethink the business system in a management team that is not only steeped in the conventional wisdom of how things have always been done, but is unwilling to give serious and extensive thought to different ways of doing business. The reasons for such inertia are many, but include fear of departing from long-established practice, past success which reinforces a belief that the company has found the one and only formula for success, 'group think', where a management team with similar experience and backgrounds has little capacity to contest its own assumptions and decisions, or fear of upsetting predictable relationships with suppliers, trade members, channels and customers. A further requirement for reinventing the business system is the development of insight into the structure of the existing system and the factors which drive its performance, and then being able to consider restructuring the system. These considerations are now explored in more depth.

Reinvigorating the managerial mindset

The companies that reinvent business systems are often more likely to be industry newcomers rather than traditional competitors – one has only to think of Benetton's impact on fashion clothing, IKEA's impact on furniture or the Body Shop's effect on toiletries and cosmetics. Their great advantage was the absence of deeply entrenched views of the conventional ways of bringing a product or service to market. But there are only fixed, unchallenged assumptions and organizational inertia standing in the way of mature companies bringing the same radicalism to their industries.

Hamel and Prahalad argue that if companies are to compete successfully in the future they must abandon improving the competitive positions in which they find themselves and devote their energies to creating new strategies and industry contexts – they must vote in favour of being different rather than cheaper or better:

> When performance declines the first assumption is that the company has gotten fat, so investment and headcount are attacked. If this fails

to bring about a lasting improvement in performance, as is usually the case, senior managers may conclude that the company has also gotten lazy, and that core processes are rife with needless bureaucracy and 'make-work'. A reengineering program is adopted with the objective of shaping up sloppy processes. But as we have argued, restructuring and reengineering may ultimately be too little, too late if a company's industry is changing in a profound way and if the company has fallen far behind that change curve .... . To get ahead of the industry change curve, top management must recognize that the company may be blind as well as fat and lazy. It must attack the strategy regeneration and industry reinvention agenda in concert with, or better yet, in anticipation of, the restructuring and reengineering agenda.[7]

In the language of this book, Hamel and Prahalad argue for the redesign of industry or macro business systems and of company micro business systems. Their emphasis is on reinterpreting market needs and wants, redrawing market boundaries, reconfiguring industry and company busines systems to deliver customer value in new ways, not just in improved old ways. This is the route to entrepreneurial strategy and therefore to renewal. They suggest that self-imposed limits on a company's way of doing business may be probed by asking the following questions about the basic premisses of any current strategy:

▶ *The served market:* What customers and needs are we *not* serving?
▶ *Revenue and margin structure:* Could profits be extracted at a *different point* in the value chain?
▶ *Configuration of skills and assets:* Might customers' needs be better served by an *alternative configuration* of skills and assets?
▶ *Flexibility and adaptiveness:* What is our *vulnerability* to new rules of the game?[8]

They propose from their research that foresight about the feasible future shape of an industry comes from an ability to:

▶ escape the myopia of the current concept of the served market,
▶ escape the myopia of the current product concept,
▶ challenge current price–performance assumptions,
▶ speculate with child-like curiosity,
▶ develop an endless curiosity,
▶ be humble enough to speculate,
▶ value eclecticism,
▶ use metaphor and analogy,
▶ be contrarian,
▶ move beyond being 'customer-led',

▶ empathize with human needs.

We can view their laundry list approach to ways of challenging conventional wisdom about an industry and its business system as having three main components:

1   Avoiding a 'market-led' approach to business in favour of one that we have called market focus – a relationship in which the customer's needs are understood and addressed creatively by the carefully focused and unique resources of the firm, and in which the marketer, when appropriate, takes the initiative to bring a creative solution to the customer that the customer could never have envisaged. This is a fundamental challenge to pedestrian, ineffective, marketing practice which so often cloaks inexpertness with the excuse of being devoted to 'doing what the customer tells us to do'.

2   Contesting current strategy parameters and assumptions whether they concern the company's served market, product concept, price–performance tradeoffs or any other aspect of the conventional competitive formula. In other words, setting up contestability as one of the essential criteria for effective decision-making in marketing and strategy.

3   Supporting creative insights through the kinds of technique and discipline that those who counsel on creativity have always advised – using metaphor and analogy, being child-like in inquiry, being speculative, curious and open to many different viewpoints.

Rethinking business system structure

To rethink and redesign the structure of the business system it is generally helpful to:

1   Understand the vertical and horizontal structure of the system with a view to reconsidering governance options and the configuration of activities.

2   Understand the value-added structure with a view to reconsidering the opportunities for 'value capture'.

3   Understand the driving forces behind the system's dynamics with a view to controlling these forces.

Horizontal and vertical structure

The horizontal structure, as described in Chapter 3, reflects the chain of linked activities which are undertaken to bring the final product or service to market and the manner in which all the participants in the system have decided to deal with the matter of ownership of the links – the governance of the transactions – involved. The latter may range at one extreme from complete system integration under unified ownership, such as is seen in petrochemicals where, for example, Royal Dutch Shell owns activities from seismology research and field exploration to petrol retailing on the high street, to completely separate ownership of each link. In between these two extremes of governance, hybrid forms may be found, such as alliances, partnerships and networks.

The vertical structure represents the various 'vertical' inputs to the horizontal chain, such as equipment supplies, specialized service inputs and consumables. Take, for example the women's fashion clothing business system. Its core, materials-based, horizontal chain starts with design and moves on through yarn manufacture, to textile manufacture to textile distribution, to clothing manufacture (cut, make and trim), to clothing wholesaling, to retailing and customer service. The vertical structure includes the subsidiary (derived demand) business systems that provide dyes to the yarn-maker, textile-making equipment to the textile manufacturer, information technology for inventory management to the textile wholesaler, sewing machines and trim items (buttons, braids, buckles) to the clothing manufacturer, just-in-time delivery scheduling software to the clothing wholesaler and display and merchandising fittings to the retailer (see Figure 22.1).

It is worthwhile to point out that understanding an industry or industry sector in terms of an identifiable dominant set of horizontal value-adding activities, with linking vertical inputs, represents a substantive difference to the conventional economist's definition of an industry in terms of substitutable goods and services. This latter perspective leads to a limited examination of just a few points of transformation or value-adding steps in the industry. A business system perspective, however, involves a much broader and deeper systemic understanding of where a firm 'fits in' in its industry, and allows the imaginative firm the possibility to identify frame-breaking strategies which restructure the chain of activities to its advantage.

Most industries, after the initial turmoil of the embryonic and early growth stages of their lifecycle, settle down with an industry standard which applies not only to the dominant technology but also to the *dominant business system structure*. A dominant structure allows specialization of roles around the various horizontal and vertical linkages, which in turn normally drives cost down and quality up. But as this happens, specialization generates ever more specific assets associated with the different links. Specialized assets – whether physical or intangible – reduce the flexibility of the structure. It becomes more and more difficult to change the system without destroying the value of the idiosyncratic assets that are in place.

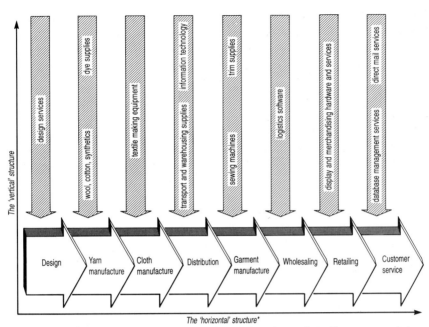

Figure 22.1 Horizontal and vertical business system structure; women's clothing industry

The more specialized and costly these assets the more likely it is that the business system will move towards a pattern of governance that stresses integration, because this protects the owners of the assets from many of the risks and uncertainties of governance by market transaction. Long-term contracting, supply partnerships, internal administration of supply and demand help to provide greater certainty about the future flow of earnings needed to cover investment in one-of-a-kind and non-redeployable assets.

The forces of specialization leading to less general purpose and less redeployable assets are therefore two-edged. They stabilize the industry, its technology, knowledge base and managerial practice and through this allow lower cost and higher quality products and services to be produced. But they simultaneously, through the creation of ever more specific assets, bind industry members to doing business in the now conventional manner. Once the dominant form of a business system emerges significant barriers to change are in place. Specialized physical assets demand stability in order to generate a return. Specialized knowledge assets may be rendered obsolete by a new structure and may not be redeployable through the labour market and will in consequence fear and resent change.

So it is not surprising that it is newcomers who are so often the ones to reinvent business systems – they have little to lose, while the existing competitors have a great deal to lose. The dilemma for the existing competitors is considerable. Should they be ruled by the drive to exploit an existing specialized asset base while running the risk of being destroyed by an innovator who renders that investment largely irrelevant? Or should they be driven to reinvent the business system and, in the course of doing so, leave the old asset base obsolete but dominate the exploitation of the new asset base in a redefined industry? The Phoenicians perhaps had this dilemma in mind when they told the story of the phoenix, the mythical bird that lived for centuries in the deserts of Arabia and then burnt itself on a funeral pyre only to rise from the ashes with renewed youth to live through another cycle. Renewal in the corporate world has the same recurring theme – destruction of the old to create the new, the act of creative destruction, as Schumpeter called it.

Restructuring the horizontal and vertical chain of activities in the business system may be done in one of two ways:

1 *Alter the governance structure.* This involves reconsidering and moving between the options of make-buy-or-partner. Moving to or from open market transactions, complete system integration under unified ownership, and hybrid forms of partnering and alliance may allow cost to be reduced and/or customer value to be increased. The key consideration is whether a change in the governance structure of the chain of transactions will bring transaction cost savings or improve quality and performance without a cost penalty. The almost universal move towards out-sourcing of non-core activities is an example of how business system governance was restructured radically from the mid-1980s to the mid-1990s. This process typically starts with the out-sourcing of vertical elements of the business system in order to lower costs and increase flexibility. Because many vertical elements of a business system have limited power to affect the performance of the horizontal system this could be done with little threat to underlying power and control patterns in an industry. Horizontal disintegration along the business system has been less common because where it exists for good reason, it is usually tied to features of asset specificity which will not cease until there is a significant change in core technologies.

2 *Alter the activity chain by rendering established links obsolete, resequencing them and/or introducing new links.* For example, IKEA reinvented the furniture busines system by out-sourcing manufacturing and by giving two links in the traditional chain to the customer – assembly (normally

done in a factory) and final delivery (normally done by the retailer's small trucks in congested urban areas). By getting rid of these activities IKEA radically reduced the fixed overheads and variable costs of the system while not diminishing customer value and increasing it through instant delivery by the customer. The customer value-for-money trade-off was altered by sharing some of the cost savings from the restructured system with the customer in return for using his or her time to undertake the assembly task.

When agro-chemical companies move from traditional chemistry technologies to biology-based technologies they radically alter their business systems too. A traditional fungicide is delivered through a long business system chain to the farmer for application to his field crops at the time of likely fungal attack – a system that carries high costs in terms of logistics, storage, information tracking, customer advice and increasing problems arising from the environmental impact of surplus and non-absorbed residue which enters the soil and water system. Biologically-based technology offers the possibility of altering the genetic character of a plant through the application of recombinant DNA techniques in the laboratory so that a strain of cereal, for example, becomes inherently resistant to certain kinds of fungal attack. As it begins to exploit genetic engineering technology, the plant health company has to reconstruct the traditional chemical technology-based business system. It now has to focus on R&D, laboratory genetics and the production of seed. Once the fungus resistant seed is 'produced' it is shipped to the farmer and sown. There is no need for stocks of chemicals to be held throughout the channel and sold to the farmer at the appropriate season, and no need to conceive of ways to minimize residue in the soil and water.

Value-added structure

The value-added structure of the business system deserves attention because different links in the chain will generate greater or lesser value-added. More importantly, the distribution of value-added will change through time, typically moving downstream as the industry matures – that is, more of the value created by the system will come from marketing and services as opposed to research and manufacturing as time passes, the technology standardizes and best manufacturing practice diffuses. Early movers in precipitating these shifts in the location of value-added will often reap high rewards, especially if competitors remain wedded to their existing fixed and specialized investment in upstream activities and cannot find ways to reduce radically their costs as value-added and associated margins tumble. The computer industry is an interesting example of how value-added has progressively moved from hardware manufacture to software manufacture to customer service and support. These changes left IBM and Digital, for instance, with their specialized asset base still firmly fixed upstream and without having yet made the transition to being either low-cost producers in order to sustain low upstream margins or to downstream operators with the specialized assets capable of competing for customer support and service in a world of networks and distributed computing power.

Restructuring the firm to chase value-added in the dynamic economic structure of a business system presents difficulties other than the mobility of the firm's asset base and its ability to recreate that asset base. Value-added must also be *captured* to be worth chasing. If the greater proportion of value-added in the computer industry moves downstream to customer service and support activities, there is no guarantee that it will be easily captured. In fact, much of the current turmoil of the industry reflects difficulties in capturing downstream value. Support and service are generally required at a very local level and in highly responsive form. Problems with running networks are usually best dealt with by smaller, flexible service and support organizations run independently or as offshoots of distributor/reseller companies. This makes for a competitive structure that has few barriers to entry and many reasonably capable entrants. The result is a fragmented and intensely competitive supply situation serving increasingly knowledgeable, experienced and impatient customers. There is a great deal of the industry's value-added in these downstream links, but it is very difficult for any company to 'capture' it. This is, of course, also an entrepreneurial signal – the existence of significant value-added but no 'formula' for capturing it in a sustainable manner by the innovating firm. Cracking this business system puzzle will perhaps lead to new companies the size of a Microsoft. Microsoft cracked the formula for capturing the value-added in the PC software operating system and associated application programs in the software production link in the same industry chain.

System dynamics

Finally, it was noted that the third approach to reinventing the business system was to understand the driving forces behind the system's dynamics with a view to influencing and controlling these forces. The steps that are necessary in taking this approach are first, to understand the anatomy and physiology, the structure and process of the existing business system. Second, one must then identify what forces are critical to determining change in both structure and process – Does the substitution of biological science for chemical science drive the underlying structure and process of the plant health business system? To what extent is it driven by smaller numbers of farmers working more and more on commercial grounds? Or is environmentalism shaping the nature and cost of products and their application? Or is it the impact of the reform of the European Common Agricultural Policy that will determine quantities and types of crops that will be grown? Or is it a persistent trend towards larger, more concentrated and more powerful farm distributors and retailers that will really call the shots in the future? Or is it in the complex interaction of these major forces that change will be born?

Only individual and open-minded analysis of individual business systems can lead to effective answers to these kinds of questions. The challenge of renewal is to respond to the answers with well-developed strategies for restructuring the business system pre-emptively and capturing the sources of value-added. Understanding the dynamics of a business system, therefore, presents the possibility of renewal by providing the company with the opportunity to dominate and channel the driving forces (for example, by being early to dominate a new technology or to develop ways of working with regulators as in pharmaceuticals), or at a less entrepreneurial level by being a fast and well-prepared reactor to changes that have been anticipated.

Reinventing the micro business system

Discussion so far has concentrated on renewal by reinventing the industry business system, a route that suits the more entrepreneurial and often the more risk-seeking firm or the firm in an apparently end-game situation in an industry that shows no possibility of adequate returns unless it is restructured. If a company succeeds in reinventing the business system, it must also reinvent its own micro business system. If a company can see no worthwhile reason or opportunity to reinvent the industry business system, it still faces the necessity to consider the renewal of its micro business system. Firm-level renewal is therefore necessary whether the motivation is to do things differently or do things better – whether inventing or improving.

If the micro business system is well aligned with the industry system and its structure and process, then the focus of renewal is most often on continuous improvement within that framework. The prime tool in widespread use in the early 1990s has been called business process re-engineering or redesign (BPR). While BPR may be applied to the task of system reinvention, its discipline and the overwhelming majority of its practical applications are to continuous improvement. The caveat that must be entered is, of course, that applying BPR to an ineffective or inappropriate system does no more than encourage the system to fail in a more efficient manner.

Hammer and Champey's work is often seen as the standard-bearer for the BPR movement. Their central themes are consistent with those of this book – a process orientation, a willingness to consider radical change and a focus on performance. They define re-engineering as 'the fundamental rethinking and radical redesign of business processes to achieve dramatic improvements in critical, contemporary measures of performance, such as cost, quality, service, speed' and emphasize that the key words in the definition are fundamental, radical, dramatic and processes.[9] Of particular concern for marketing is their emphasis on understanding and specifying the outcomes of all processes which inevitably leads to a central concern with customer satisfaction. Designing and redesigning processes that are driven by an objective of customer satisfaction along with other outcome requirements are central to re-engineering efforts. Marketing's input to re-engineering is vital to both the specifically marketing processes and to the successful design of all of a company's core processes. Much of the effort in re-engineering has been invested in processes that have quite tangible materials flows, especially in manufacturing and in the paper trails of service activities. Marketing processes have many features that are based on human interfacing, communication and decision-making, and have perhaps for this reason been less exposed to redesign and re-engineering efforts. Davenport notes that what he calls the 'customer facing processes' are less structured than many others, with the exception of the general management function. None the less, he also notes that they are perhaps the most critical to an organization's success and that 'opportunities for innovation in marketing and sales management, order management, and service processes, are manifold'.[10]

The practice of business process redesign

What do we know about the practice of redesign and re-engineering of business and marketing processes? In general, current practice in approaching redesign appears to follow a broadly agreed pattern involving:

1 *Selection of the process(es) to be redesigned:* This is seen as critical to success as it is all too easy to redesign processes that may appear at first sight to be important but turn out to have very limited impact on the firm's overall performance. The identification of processes that yield substantial impact on performance must reflect the factors that strategic reflection has marked out as the underlying levers on cost and value creation and that are therefore essential to the organization's competitive advantage.

2 *Definition of the performance requirements:* The performance requirements for the selected processes must be defined, working from the

imperatives, the key success factors, of the business and marketing strategy. Performance requirements are likely to be defined in terms of operational measures such as service level, response time, quality, on-time delivery, new product success or total cost. They will be driven by forces such as customer requirements, by competitive necessity, by resource capability and by financial necessities.

3 *Developing an understanding of the current process(es):* This is the diagnostic phase, which requires that analysis be broadly rather than narrowly based if the current process of cost and value creation is to be properly understood. For this reason it is best not to limit the diagnosis to current inputs and outputs and to the transformational activities between. The most appropriate methodology is to begin at the customer end of the process by devoting time and detailed analysis to understanding what the process customer (whether an 'internal' or 'market' customer) wants. The next step is then to understand what the current process gives the process customer (the process output). The diagnosis may then proceed to developing a general understanding of the current process itself, with a primary focus on the what and why rather than the how of the process as the aim is redesign, not adjustment. Finally, the diagnosis must turn to learning and understanding what is critical to process performance – to identifying what are the drivers of performance or the levers on performance.

4 *Redesign of the process(es):* The objective of this phase is not to 'fix' old processes, not to look for marginal improvements, but to create so-called step-change or order-of-magnitude benefits that result from redesign as distinct from design improvement. This phase may be helped by using benchmarking techniques in order to learn from other organizations that manage the process to exceptionally successful performance standards. The use of benchmarking must, however, avoid any danger of becoming trapped in a redesign exercise that is limited to a catch-up objective. If a process is redesigned on a purely catch-up basis it is almost certain that the company from which the benchmarked methods and standards were taken will already be ahead again by the time the redesign is complete. If benchmarking is used, it is probably best to benchmark against the best in the world for the particular process or class of process and not against the best in the industry.

5 *Preparing for change and roll-out:* The redesign phase will produce a programme of action and organizational change which must be viewed in the light of the likely barriers to change and the necessity to structure and sequence implementation activities. Teamwork and

extensive consultation will help to anticipate the organizational and individual barriers to change and a good redesign will already have taken such learning into account. None the less, it is important for the redesign team explicitly to review the challenges involved in introducing change and to prepare appropriate communication, training, reskilling and other necessary organizational initiatives. An important feature in the planning of the roll-out of the redesigned process is often to plan for some obvious and short-term 'quick-hits' – successes that have a very high probability of occurrence and that will be very visible and rewarding to all those involved in the process of change. Such quick-hits provide early positive reinforcement for the new behaviours and practices and encourage all concerned to proceed and deal with some of the more difficult and/or longer-term changes that the redesign demands.

6 *Continuous improvement of the process:* Once the implementation of the redesign is complete, the process team must incorporate continuous improvement into their routine management of activities in order to exploit learning and to gain experience effects through repeated execution of the process task.

7 *Use of teams to conduct the redesign and continuous improvement work:* It is clear from all work in the area of redesign that teams are the essential vehicle for the work of redesign and then for continuous improvement. This is the case because virtually all processes are multidisciplinary in nature and require simultaneous input from persons with those different disciplinary skills and because the teams that redesign work are ideally the teams that should implement and manage the redesigned work.

The effectiveness of process redesign

In terms of the effectiveness of redesign programmes, Hall, Rosenthall and Wade's study of over 100 companies that undertook re-engineering projects suggests several important conclusions.[11] They suggest that the breadth and depth of re-engineering projects are important determinants of long-term benefits. If the process being redesigned is not broadly defined in terms of cost and/or customer value, performance across a business is unlikely to be improved. If the redesign does not extend deeply into the company's core – involving change in roles and responsibilities, measurements and incentives, organizational structure, information technology, shared values and skills – then they suggest that it is unlikely to enhance long-term performance. They define *breadth* on a spectrum running from the redesign of a single activity in a single function at one end, to the redesign of the entire business system for a business unit at the other. Their research points to increasing cost savings for the total business unit as the redesign effort moves from narrow to broad. By *depth* they mean the extent of use of six mechanisms for influencing behaviour that they consider important to the successful implementation of a redesign project. These six mechanisms, or levers, as Hall, Rosenthall and Wade call them, are:

1 roles and responsibilities,
2 measurements and incentives,
3 organizational structure,
4 information technology,
5 shared values,
6 skills.

In their research they divided the cases observed into quartiles based on how many of the depth levers were changed in the redesign. They found that the more levers that were changed, the greater the reduction in cost of the individual processes being redesigned. Overall, their conclusions are that greater breadth in redesign results in business unit cost savings, while greater depth results in greater process cost savings. Exhibit 22.1 provides an interesting example of effective process redesign in the financial services sector.

| Exhibit 22.1 | *Marketing in action case* |

Re-engineering Banca di America e di Italia

Banca di America e di Italia is a medium-sized Italian bank owned by Deutsche Bank. In 1993 a customer could walk into a branch of BAI and experience the following level of service provision:

▶ Customer fills out a deposit slip for the five cheques she wishes to deposit to her account.
▶ Goes to the closest of three tellers in the open plan branch office.
▶ Teller types in her account number, amount of deposit, passes cheques through a scanner.
▶ IT system takes 2–3 seconds to record cheques and notify correspondent banks electronically.
▶ Cheques are debited and credited to the appropriate accounts.
▶ While this is happening teller requests the customer's profile from the customer database and sees that she is a potential customer for a certificate of deposit product.
▶ Teller now has a printed receipt for the five cheques and asks if she is interested in a certificate of deposit product.
▶ A 'help screen' assists the teller in presenting the benefits of the certificate of deposit product and in dealing with typical customer queries.

▶ Teller hands the receipt to the customer and some promotional material on certificates of deposit.
▶ All this has happened in 30 seconds.
▶ At the end of the day the teller will total all cheques deposited during the day and reconcile this number with that displayed on the computer.

All this is undertaken without the presence of a 'back office' and back room staff at the branch – the information technology system has taken that work from the branch to a central 'IT factory' location. The chief executive and chief information officer of BAI set out to recreate a bank and customer service levels based on just-in-time principles. They focused their redesign of the bank's branch system on improving customer service levels and the branch's efficiency and effectiveness. Starting in late 1988, two teams diagnosed and then redesigned the main branch banking processes. The organization team defined ten classes of retail banking transactions: payments, deposits, withdrawals, money orders, bills, consumer credit, foreign exchange, credit cards, sourcing and end-of-day branch processes. They then documented the process activities and flows involved in any one process and next redesigned the process. The cheque deposit transaction originally involved 64 activities, 9 forms and 14 accounts. After redesign it took 25 activities, 2 forms and 2 accounts to complete the same process. The technology team then took on the task of designing and providing the IT support and infrastructure for the new process design.

With 300 processes in redesigned form, the organization team turned to preparing the organization for change and identifying the organizational mechanisms (e.g. staff characteristics, new skills, branch layout) that would determine success. In parallel the technology team began to operationalize their IT redesign, working with branch staff to ensure useable screen presentation of data and early cooperation of the system users. Beginning 15 months after commencement of the project (February 1990), the new software became available for each of the ten families of transaction in sequence.

By 1993, BAI had recorded some important achievements:
▶ It had expanded its branch network by 50 new branches without any increase in personnel and with minimal investment in systems development.
▶ Average staff per branch had dropped from 7–9 to 3–4.
▶ Time taken for cashier closing at the end of each day had dropped from over 2 hours to 10 minutes.
▶ Revenue had doubled between 1987 and 1992, with 24 per cent of that increase being attributed to the redesign programme.[12]

Michael Hammer, when asked by *The Economist* magazine to defend the record of re-engineering, noted that it must not be equated with downsizing and cost-reduction exercises and that it cannot be dismissed as a tactical palliative. In relation to the former point he argues that re-engineering is 'the radical redesign of a company's business processes, reinventing the way business operates in order to meet the demands of a modern economy. It is about rethinking work, not eliminating jobs, and it does indeed succeed, as demonstrated at companies as diverse as AT&T, American Express, Sun Life Assurance, Ford and Procter & Gamble'.[13] In response to the latter point, he argues that re-engineering creates and cultivates innovative strategies and offers as an example the following illustration from Texas Instruments:

> in the early 1990s the semiconductor group of Texas Instruments (TI), a chip and computer maker, decided that its future lay in the rapidly growing 'application-specific integrated circuits' business, which focused on custom-designed chips rather than generic ones. However, the company quickly discovered that it was unable to put this strategy into practice, since it took about 180 days to turn a customer's order into a shipped product.
>
> It would be suicidal to build up stocks of custom products without any assurance that the customer would actually order them, and it would be ruinously expensive to expedite all orders through such a glacially slow fulfilment process. TI used reengineering to help it implement its strategy. By rethinking the order fulfilment process from beginning to end, the company has managed to cut process cycle time by well over 50% (and is well on its way to an ultimate goal of a two-week cycle time).

Redesigning the marketing processes

The methodology of redesign, as described above, is of course general and is just as applicable to marketing processes as to any others. The major lessons gleaned from practice to date suggest that greater success follows for the business as a whole if the redesign is undertaken on a broad scale and if it is conducted in depth, taking into consideration the organizational factors and mechanisms that are essential to the implementation of any change process. Redesign initiatives in the marketing area must be very self-conscious of this advice and must especially beware of defining projects in too 'local' a manner.

Earlier chapters of this book deal with the processes involved in marketing strategy, marketing management, OGFS and new product development. Redesign efforts must start with identifying the boundaries of these processes in the individual organization, diagnosing their customer outcomes and outputs and the critical levers on process performance, on cost and value creation and on the competitive advantage of the business. The challenge at the redesign phase is always to find step-change solutions to the process task rather than just incremental improvements. As marketing processes are so bound up with other areas of expertise and functional authority in the typical business, the necessity for cross-functional, inter-departmental and interdisciplinary teamwork has a particularly high priority in preparing for change and in maintaining the momentum of the redesign through continuous improvement teams.

The challenges facing redesign teams in marketing are different for the four core processes. The OGFS process, despite being long, complex and crossing many traditional organizational boundaries, has a very physical manifestation in the trail of paper and physical flows that it creates. This tangibility will typically assist in identifying, describing and considering the reconfiguration of the process and in communicating the redesign goals and plans. The new product development process has many of these character-istics too as strategy is converted into research activity, into design, into prototyping/pilot manufacture, into market testing, into production plan-ning, into launch planning, and so on. The great challenge in approaching redesign in this area is normally that of reconciling traditionally independ-ent functional fiefdoms to the necessity for bowing to an overriding cross-functional process imperative. The interfunctional team is therefore particularly critical, as are well-tuned political skills within the team and unwavering top management support. The depth factors, to use Hall, Rosenthall and Wade's language, are always critical to success.

The other two core marketing processes are somewhat different in being closer to 'pure' management processes with few physical traces and flows to provide concrete evidence of process activities and consequences. Daven-port notes that 'of all the processes in an organization, management processes are the most poorly defined, and least likely to be viewed in process terms'.[14] In this book we have tried to deal with both marketing strategy and marketing management in a manner and in terms that allow both to be viewed in process terms. Particular challenges in viewing these managerial processes in a redesign context relate to:

▶ Identifying boundaries and process customers, where it is clear that marketing activity does not fit neatly within a functional 'box' and where management process customers range from shareholders, other external stakeholders and top management to those charged with the practical operation of the core marketing processes on a day-to-day basis – whether sales assistant, order entry clerk or technical service engineer.

▶ Identifying, describing and giving a concrete reality to what are, in many instances, process activities that are based on discussion, debate, implicit assumptions and expectations, real-time adaptation, formal documentation that leaves much unsaid and represents an historical record of thinking at the time of formal planning exercises, all overlaid with the subtleties of organizational politics.

▶ Identifying operational performance measures for management processes – such as speed in decision-making, success in learning from experience, acting on fact and analysis as well as intuition – all outcomes of managerial activity that should 'add value' to the organization's work, and even more important, that should add more value than the management processes of competing firms.

▶ Developing robust process frameworks (such as the market choice matrix in the case of the marketing strategy process) that facilitate the 'production' of good management decision-making, action-taking and learning.

▶ Forming, and managing, marketing and senior management inter-functional teams to redesign and take ownership of continuously improving these processes.

REVIEW QUESTIONS

22.1 What is meant by a resource-based view of competitive advantage?

22.2 What steps and conditions are necessary for a firm to go about reinventing the macro business system?

22.3 Give examples of frame-breaking strategies which have effectively changed the rules of the game in an industry.

22.4 The central themes of the business process redesign (BPR) movement are consistent with those in this book – a process orientation, a willingness to consider radical change and a focus on performance. Consider this comment.

22.5 What advice would you have for the manager considering redesigning the core marketing processes?

22.6 Each marketing process ultimately is what Davenport calls a 'customer facing process'. What is the significance of this?

CHAPTER 23

Renewal and shared values

▶ Organization renewal
▶ Losing focus: pathways to decline
▶ Networks, relationships and cooperation
▶ The 'green' challenge
▶ People, shared values and the learning organization

Marketing in action cases
ASEA and Brown Boveri create a new global company
The Rolling Stones' Voodoo Lounge *tour is a virtual corporation*

ABOUT THIS CHAPTER

There are many organizational and human factors involved in sustaining performance in the marketplace. Even 'excellent' companies can go into decline – the so-called Icarus paradox. Any organization and any good manager must be both entrepreneurial (effective) and administratively wise (efficient). In strategic terms, the roots of these two dimensions of behaviour lie in innovation and cost competitiveness. The challenge of renewal is one of achieving balance.

Between the extremes of open market transaction and full vertical integration lies an increasing array of hybrid forms of market organization, from relationships to alliances to networks and 'spiders' webs' to 'virtual corporations'. These demand of the marketing manager a new understanding of negotiation and relational skills as well as an ability to calculate more frequently the relative gains from different ways of organizing the market relationship.

The 'green' revolution offers the marketer the opportunity to build new sources of positional superiority. However, sustaining performance is ultimately achieved by people in the organization. Shared values are key, as is the process of learning. In many respects, learning is the axial principle of the market-focused firm.

Balancing efficiency and effectiveness

The twin tasks of achieving efficiency and effectiveness in any organization must receive constant attention. Over-emphasis on one will inevitably damage the other. Too much attention to efficiency will usually breed rigidity within fixed strategic and organizational parameters: a company will prefer doing what it does well in a repeated manner to doing new things or doing things differently. Under such circumstances great short-term success may lead managers to ignore or to dismiss the need to reinvent some of the company's activities. Yet the latter may well be essential to secure viability in a changed marketplace of the future.

Equally, unbalanced emphasis on effectiveness and the long term can lead to inattention to the vital daily detail of managing well. All too many new ventures die in the short term while promising their investors and customers pay-off in the long term. Similarly, all too many large successful companies can run close to bankruptcy while planning a glorious strategic future. In the early 1990s, Philips, one of Europe's proudest electrical and electronics companies, found itself facing competitive and financial disaster despite a huge apparatus dedicated to long-term planning.

Organizational renewal

To remain successful, organizations must balance being simultaneously efficient and effective. Efficiency underpins the short-term operational health of the company – how it transacts its business at appropriate cost levels and gets its services and products to the market in a timely manner at acceptable quality levels. Efficiency, therefore, pays today's bills. Effectiveness underpins the organization's long-term health. This involves, from a marketing perspective:

▶ choosing markets well and allocating the company's scarce resources to or across these markets for greatest long-term pay-off;
▶ positioning the company and its market offerings in these markets in a manner that ensures and protects profits by serving customer needs and outperforming competitors;
▶ integrating market-focused activity with the other strategic concerns of the company and helping to build the kinds of structures, processes, competences and value systems that make it possible to implement the chosen strategy with regard to market position.

The challenge of renewal is therefore one of achieving balance. Any organization and any good manager must be both entrepreneurial (effective) and administratively wise (efficient). In strategic terms, the roots of these two dimensions of behaviour lie in *innovation* and *cost-competitiveness*.

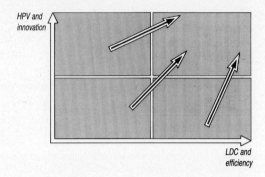

Figure 23.1 Renewal through balancing innovation and efficiency

Innovation in turn is reflected in the market in what has been previously referred to as 'high perceived value', while cost-competitiveness may be found in a market appreciation of 'low delivered cost'. The relationship between these ideas is seen in the elements of Figure 23.1. The companies that prove to be true and consistent winners are those that move towards the north-east corner of the final illustration, that are simultaneously innovative and efficient by providing goods and services that yield superior customer value at low delivered cost.

Achieving this balance between innovation and efficiency in order to serve the market with a customer and competitive strategy of both value and cost typically demands unique organizational arrangements. Lawrence and Dyer, in their study of the renewal phenomenon, suggested that the required organizational form consists of high degrees of organizational differentiation and integration, balanced power structures and balanced human resource practices.[1]

Differentiation and integration

Companies capable of self-renewal are likely to be both differentiated and integrated in structure. A differentiated structure is one that contains variety and subdivision so as to allow different units to respond differently to varied aspects of the environment. A differentiated form will normally entail allowing decision-making discretion at decentralized levels and the empowerment of the members of the organization to analyze their situation and take action. Integration by contrast implies centralization and unified control of the company's activities. The prescription for renewal is to have both of these apparently contradictory features combined. This is the feature of excellent companies to which Peters and Waterman drew attention when they spoke of companies that were simultaneously 'loose and tight'.[2]

Their observations of very successful companies suggested that they all were 'loose' in the manner in which they allowed managers to be entrepreneurial throughout the organization in order to ensure close and responsive relationships with customers and rapid response to competitive forces. Project teams abound in such circumstances and entrepreneurial groups may often remove themselves from the mainstream of the company to 'skunk works' or 'garden shed' environments. At the same time they observed that these same companies had a significant degree of 'tightness' in the form of a unified strategy towards markets and competition; shared values that managers, no matter how entrepreneurial or idiosyncratic, all subscribed to; and systems of assigning responsibility and authority that made clear measurement of performance and explicit controls possible.

Why should organizational differentiation and integration be associated with self-renewal? The answer is clearly that differentiation (the 'looseness' factor) supports innovative and entrepreneurial behaviour. And our contention is that organizational differentiation is the foundation stone on which companies build an ability to deliver high perceived value to customers. Integration (the 'tightness' factor), on the other hand, supports efficiency through the unification and coordination of action and through clear measurement and control. Efficiency, as has been noted, is the root of corporate ability to provide services and products at low delivered cost to customers. The combined strategy of value and cost therefore reasonably leads to a need for a combined organizational form. One of the reasons why so few companies succeed in being both high in perceived value and low in delivered cost is that few have the managerial capability to create and operate a structure that is simultaneously loose and tight. The barrier to imitation is high if one seeks to copy the self-renewing firm and this invaluable barrier inheres in managerial competence rather than in any financial or physical asset.

Power

Self-renewing organizations are ones that are characterized by an appropriate balance of power both vertically and horizontally. Ensuring vertical balance demands that power be spread among organizational levels – neither too centralized at the top nor too decentralized at the bottom. Spreading power vertically results in what is often referred to as empowerment – people throughout the organization have, and act on, the freedom to make decisions proper to their jobs. In structuring decision-making, good vertical balance of power makes it possible to drive corporate and marketing planning in both a top-down and a bottom-up manner, ensuring the involvement of all who can contribute to the process and ensuring support for execution.

Achieving a balance of power horizontally entails ensuring that no one area of expertise dominates decision-making and action-taking. This implies that marketing, finance, human resource management, operations management, R&D should each find themselves with the power to advance their perspectives on the business and to ensure that their concerns and requirements for success are not dismissed summarily. This has an important implication for those employed in marketing. Market success based on market focus can only be achieved through the coordinated efforts of all parts of an organization. The solution to achieving and sustaining market focus in a company is not to give the marketing function undue power or precedence. It is rather to provide it with sufficient power to manage among equals representing other functional specializations. The more shared and group-based the decision-making the more likely one is to find outcomes that reflect balance among all the important aspects of company action. It is only through such balance that customers are properly served and competitors outperformed.

The recent history of ABB, the result of a merging of two major European firms – ASEA of Sweden and Brown Boveri of Switzerland – provides an interesting illustration of a determined struggle to strike a balance between differentiation and integration, and to craft the balance of vertical power, as shown in Exhibit 23.1.

Exhibit 23.1   *Marketing in action case*

ASEA and Brown Boveri create a new global company

Between 1988 and 1992, Percy Barnevik, a thin, bearded Swede, brought two long-established European companies, ASEA of Sweden and Brown Boveri of Switzerland, together in one of the most successful international mergers since Royal Dutch Petroleum merged with Britain's Shell in 1907. He added, through acquisition, 70 more European and US companies and created ABB, a new kind of global company that competes in markets for electrical power generation and transmission equipment, high speed trains, automation and robotics, and environmental control systems.

In doing this he wanted a market-responsive, flexible, cost-effective and innovative company. To fashion these qualities he cut more than 20 per cent of jobs, closed many factories, eliminated most head office staff and moved businesses from one country to another. He now manages 210,000 employees led by 250 senior managers, and in 1994 earned the accolade of Europe's most admired boss – at least among the senior executives of Europe's top 500 companies! His advice for fashioning the global corporation is:

▶ *Marry in haste, retrench just as fast.* Merge and acquire quickly and deal with all the related issues and problems fast. As well as closing and off-loading companies, Barnevic has been involved in over 70 acquisitions.

▶ *Cut headquarters staff and decentralize.* ASEA and Brown Boveri had total head office staff numbers of 6,000 in Vasteras, Sweden and Baden, Switzerland. In 1992 ABB had 150 HQ staff opposite the train station in Zurich. Traditional head office tasks are now managed by line managers with remaining staffers acting as coaches for line managers around the world.

▶ *Live locally, source globally.* ABB is developing a network of suppliers for each of its businesses by picking the best world-wide including Eastern Europe and Russia. By working closely with these suppliers, costs are reduced and cycle times are cut: 'Any idiot can reduce price by 10 per cent to become more competitive ... but if you can offer an electric power transmission cable under the Baltic one year earlier than your competitor can, that is of tremendous value to your customer, and your competitor can't touch you.'

▶ *Two bosses for everyone.* Everyone has a country manager and a business sector manager. About 100 locals run the country businesses locally. About 65 global managers run eight business sectors. Businesses compete effectively locally, but share technology, innovation, products and learn globally.

▶ *Increase spending on R&D and globalize it.* 'Be in command of your future in your core technology, gain competitive edge from unifying it and applying it across all businesses and out-innovate your competitors,' says Barnevic.

And what kind of managers does this practitioner of corporate reengineering look for? 'Managers with patience, good language ability, stamina, work experience in a least two or three countries, and, most important, humility.'[3]

In the domain of international business and marketing, Bartlett and Ghoshal also urge a balance between integration and differentiation and a symmetry in vertical power.[4] As described in Chapter 13, their concern is how large international firms develop the organizational capability to implement complex global strategies. Differentiation, in an international context, takes on a broadened meaning to include flexibility and the ability to respond to local or national circumstances. Drawing on their research with Unilever they map the varying degree to which different businesses, functions and tasks may have to be managed in a centrally coordinated or locally decentralized manner (see Figure 10.1, p. 180). For instance, the detergent business occupies an intermediate position among Unilever's activities, requiring less coordination by corporate managers than the chemicals business, but more than personal products. Within the detergents business itself, research is controlled by headquarters, while marketing decisions are significantly influenced by local managers. Among marketing tasks, HQ is likely to be involved in product policy, while local promotion decisions are left to the discretion of subsidiary managers.

Human resource practices

Lawrence and Dyer suggest that human resource practices fall into three categories: bureaucratic, market and clan-based. Furthermore, they claim that the self-renewing company uses all three sets of practices in a balanced manner.

Bureaucratic human resource practices rely on rules and established procedures to guide and reward behaviour in the firm. Various aspects of any successful market-focused organization will have bureaucratic process. In managing customer service one of the first simple rules that many companies establish is that all telephones must be answered before the third 'ring', or that all enquiries must be answered within 12 hours. These are examples of simple rules that establish and control performance. If you run an automotive parts production company in Denmark and supply a Peugeot assembly plant in the France, bureaucratic rules and processes are vital to guaranteeing timely delivery of exactly what is needed. Bureaucratic is a word often used in a popular sense to deride organizations and their behaviour. It is important to appreciate that bureaucratic process, properly designed and managed, is essential to much of success in any business and especially to its ability to perform efficiently and to deliver at low cost and with speed. Cost and speed are two vital competitive advantages.

Market-based human resource practices assume that behaviour may be traded in a marketplace – crudely, that desired behaviour can be bought. This view leads to an emphasis on payment for performance. This is very clearly seen in the manner in which most salesforces are paid. Typically, sales personnel will be paid a basic salary and a performance-related commission or bonus which varies with their sales success. The assumption is that if people work harder and more effectively, they will achieve higher sales and be rewarded through proportionately higher payment. The same philosophy has been applied to executive pay where performance-related bonuses have become common, but in this instance the performance is that of the whole company. As before, the assumption is that if a manager's pay is tied directly to the company's profitability, he or she will work harder. In all such practices it must be noted that the basic assumption is that behaviour in an organization is a tradeable commodity. Brought to extremes this can rebound disastrously if members of an organization begin to use this as the only rule governing behaviour. Under such circumstances organizational life degenerates into continuous bargaining about the 'price' of every work practice or task or change in behaviour.

Clan-based human resource practices are rooted in an assumption that those in an organization do or can have a sense of belonging to the organizational group – a sense of being in the 'clan' or being part of an extended family. If this is the case, then one might expect certain aspects of behaviour to be driven by this sense of belonging – by loyalty, by adherence to shared values governing behaviour in the group, by pride in membership and by an emotional solidarity in the face of competitive threat. Human resource practices based on a clan approach therefore appeal strongly to emotional rewards. Many young people embarking on a career in marketing will opt for this kind of reward when they join a company known for its excellent professional practice – becoming a member of the family is seen by the marketer and by others as a mark of distinction. The feelings associated with being part of a group that is acknowledged as highly competent and successful are powerful motivators. It must be remembered that pride in a job and the extra effort that comes with it cannot be bought through market mechanisms any more than it can be evoked by a rule or regulation. New and growing ventures often provide excellent examples of clan mechanisms working at their most powerful. Many such ventures live on the extraordinary commitment and investment of energy, enthusiasm and creativity engendered by the feeling of belonging to something vibrant, growing and intimate in scale. Such practices are, in fact, essential to the success of most new market-focused ventures since their newness and lack of adequate resources usually mean that they cannot afford to pay for all the energy being expended and they cannot risk being too rule-based while their entrepreneurial success depends primarily on innovative activity.

The prescription for renewal is not that one of these approaches to managing human resources is better, but that all are needed in an appropriate balance in a successful company. The overall message about managing a self-renewing organization is therefore one of seeking balance in structure – between differentiation and integration; balance in power – vertically and horizontally; and balance in human resource practice – between bureaucratic, market and clan mechanisms. Achieving balance of this nature helps the company to avoid the development of a monoculture – a fixed approach to all its concerns. In contrast it promotes an organization full of variety and constructive tension between different approaches to doing business and sustaining market focus. Because the task demands significant managerial skill, companies of this form erect high barriers to imitation and can therefore succeed and earn high levels of profitability even in industries where there are low barriers to entry – competitors can enter readily but they cannot copy!

Losing focus: pathways to decline

Studying how organizations lose focus can also tell us a great deal about what has to be done to sustain healthy focus. It is salutary to reflect that of

Peters and Waterman's 43 excellent companies, only 14 were excellent five years later and only 6 eight years on. In fact, many of the companies had disappeared completely. In the United Kingdom, the management publication, *Management Today*, each year identifies Britain's best companies. Of the eleven top companies identified between 1978 and 1989, only five survived to 1990. Of these five survivors, only one could still be described as a high flyer. The majority had either collapsed or been sold in distress.[5] The lack of staying power in these 'excellent' companies dramatizes the transient nature of much commercial success.

Based on many years of research into the strategic histories of companies Miller has suggested that decline in excellent companies is typically a result of the excesses to which their success leads them. He calls this the Icarus paradox. The power of Icarus's wings led to the excess which killed him by flying too close to the sun – his greatest asset became his downfall and 'that same paradox applies to many outstanding companies today: their victories and their strengths often seduce them into the excesses that cause their downfall. Success leads to specialisation and exaggeration, to confidence and complacency, to dogma and ritual.'[6] Miller's research suggests four pathways or trajectories in the riches-to-rags experience of failing companies which are described below.

From craftsman to tinkerer

A craftsman company builds its success on a strategy of quality leadership, usually based on the technical excellence of its founding team and embodied in a relatively narrow market focus which it sustains through primarily bureaucratic controls. Such companies face the threat of losing their market focus through narrowing their market scope and becoming ever more stable in behaviour. They can become rigid in their control mechanisms and detail-obsessed in their tinkering with the original formula for success. The craftsman becomes a tinkerer by self-indulgence, by searching for technical perfection without reference to market perceptions of value, and by becoming rigid and technocratic in organization. Market focus degenerates into self-absorption.

From builder to imperialist

Here we find companies that grow successfully through acquisition and diversification, pushed along by a strong entrepreneurial acquisitive culture and run in a financially dominated manner, that become greedy and imperialist in character. The imperialist behaviour leads to over-expansion especially into markets about which management knows little. However, the over-confidence of the emerging 'imperialist' culture suggests that management can manage anything and everything and just like imperialist countries the realization of having over-reached their abilities usually comes too late for corrective action to be possible. In this trajectory, focus which usually inheres in the initial acquisition path is lost in helter-skelter growth and dealsmanship such as characterized the late 1980s in Europe and North America.

From pioneer to escapist

Pioneers build successful companies based on high innovative ability often rooted in their R&D capability and developed through an organic, creative organization form. Their goal of technical progress and their strength in technology can, however, readily lead to escapist, utopian pursuit of invention. Technology-obsessed managers lose their focus on real markets and solutions to real problems and chase imagined markets of the future that are attractive to unrestrained invention.

From salesman to drifter

Organizations with exceptional sales and marketing skills that carry well-known brand names to their markets sometimes lose internal focus and begin to believe that focusing on customers and competitors to the exclusion of their internal resources is the key to long-term success. Brought to its extreme this trajectory leads to the triumph of image over substance. In such circumstances excessive reliance on communication with the customer and promotional 'hype' surrounding products and brands temporarily obscures lack of investment and indeed interest in product design, development and delivery systems. Ultimately, the market sees the difference between promise and reality, but by then the company may have lost its vital internal competences and its competitive position to competitors who focus well-managed resources on well-chosen markets.

What is common across all these observed pathways to decline is the general pattern of success leading to excess. Companies develop a form of focus based on a combination of strategy, structure and market choice but then, encouraged to believe in their own invincibility, begin to become rigid and over-reaching in their pursuit of what has become a 'success formula'. This momentum can then become a headlong and headstrong rush to self-destruction. The lesson for the company seeking to sustain a healthy form of market focus is to remember that it is essentially dynamic. Being focused demands constant attention to change in the marketplace in terms of customer needs and competitors' strategies and to change within the company in the form of growth and development in competences. Achieving focus demands clever management of the organization and its strategy in the manner suggested by Lawrence and Dyer when they discuss the required balance in structure, power and human resource practice. Indeed, one can now see the essential role which balance plays in avoiding rigidity and excessive pursuit of a 'one-best-way' approach to management.

Networks, relationships and cooperation

In Chapters 1 and 2 we noted a need to reappraise the past concentration of marketing literature on short-term and single market transactions and to deal additionally with the management of multiple transactions in relationships that involve more than market contracts – that involve commitment to longer-term exchange arrangements capable of lowering transaction costs and enhancing value. Such relationships were seen to be bounded at the extreme by full system integration; the transactions are taken under common ownership and administered fully within the firm – sometimes referred to as vertical integration.

But there are many other relationship forms along the spectrum from market transaction to vertical integration. Strategic alliances and joint ventures are often a feature of new product development. In Chapter 17 relationship marketing and the nature of relationships are explored, in particular where the possibility of genuine mutuality exists. Relational marketing is most likely to be successful where both firm and customer perceive that the purchasing stakes are rising, where purchase decisions require more buyer involvement, and order generation, fulfilment and service process requires greater investment on the part of the firm. With well-managed relationships, both parties can lower their search, communication and evaluation costs by having preferred supplier or priority customer commitments.

Network organizations have always existed in many industries for two purposes. A network is ideal when the market need is for a complex one-off, one of a kind, as opposed to a recurring, product or service. The construction of a dam or an airport is a good example. For such needs, the main contractors for building projects have for long practised the art of creating, mobilizing, managing and then disbanding very complex networks of firms whose products and services are all needed and in a very finely coordinated and scheduled manner in order to complete the project. The same applies to the delivery of a house, an office building, a roadway or a nuclear power plant. The second common purpose of networks flows from the need for work to be completed in a stable, longer-term managerial context in order to maximize communication and mutual adaptation and lessen uncertainty. Certain business systems have this character where the participants judge it to be more beneficial to their interests to manage the linkages in the business system chain by administrative agreement rather than market contract. Clothing districts in most major cities have traditionally provided a physical representation of this approach. Working together in a tightly drawn city area, cloth suppliers and wholesalers have relationships with cut-make-and-trim companies who have preferred relationships with clothing wholesalers and jobbers who in turn have specialized relationships with retailers.

It is interesting to observe how this well-established model of organizing has been retitled by some 'the virtual corporation',[7] especially in the instance of the temporary network organization. Quinn speculates about the rise of the 'spider's web' organization:

> When creatively harnessed, these smaller, highly independent, flexible structures can generate significantly increased returns on lower investments. Formal consortia now seem to work most effectively when targeted toward a single goal, like developing an oilfield, a book, a gold mine, a new biological entity, or a complex new electronics system. But increasingly, these organization forms are becoming strategic models for companies seeking to leverage limited investments – but very high talent levels – at their centre through significant outsourcing to other specialists. High-fashion, high-technology, and knowledge enterprises have led the way to date – for good reasons. All live in a world dominated by fast response times, high value added, and significant risk, making it essential and less costly to harness the parallel capabilities of multiple suppliers rather than make all investments and take all risks internally. As more companies realize they too must live in these worlds, the trend will grow apace.[8]

In a survey of the virtual corporation, *Business Week* magazine claimed that it is a form of organization in which companies 'can share costs, skills, and access to global markets, with each partner contributing what it's best at'.[9] Furthermore, it suggested that such a corporate form: (1) has its technology base in information networking, (2) exploits only the core competence of each 'member', to create a 'best of everything' company, (3) is temporary, informal and opportunistic, (4) requires considerable mutual trust and interdependency among members, and (5) will blur the boundaries around and between organizations. Exhibit 23.2 suggests how a rock band's tour may be seen as an example of a virtual corporation.

Exhibit 23.2   *Marketing in action case*

The Rolling Stones' *Voodoo Lounge* tour is a virtual corporation

It is 9:30 am, prime sleeping time for rock 'n' rollers, but Michael Cohl is wide awake and well into his first pack of cigarettes. The Canadian concert promoter is padding around his Philadelphia hotel suite shoeless – scanning faxes, taking phone calls and sweating the details of his latest venture: the Rolling Stones' 1994–95 world tour, *Voodoo Lounge*. Mick Jagger and the other Stones will open the first of two shows at the Veterans' Stadium in 12 hours. And in the meantime Cohl has a business to run: 'In our minds, we try to approximate your ordinary go-to-the-office kind of company,' he explains.

Only the most callow of rock fans would be surprised to learn that the current Stones tour – like the band itself – is fundamentally a business. What's surprising about the *Voodoo Lounge* tour, though, is just how sophisticated an enterprise Cohl and the Stones have assembled. With 250 full-time employees and potential worldwide revenues of $300 million, the tour operates like a full-size corporation. But because its staff will disband after it ends in late 1995, *Voodoo Lounge* is less a company than a virtual corporation.

Start with the definition of a virtual corporation: a temporary network of companies assembled to exploit a specific opportunity. No hierarchy, no central office, no organization chart. Cohl, who once owned a strip club in Ottawa before his Toronto-based Concert Productions International, seems only vaguely familiar with the term 'virtual corporation'. But he has created a perfect one.

Consider his office. Though he is fronting as much as $140 million to finance *Voodoo Lounge*, Cohl runs the tour with enviable 'lean' values. He travels with just a crate of files, a laptop computer and a fax machine, which spits out updates on labour costs, travel schedules and ticket sales.

Here-today, gone-tomorrow organizations are nothing new in the concert business. But *Voodoo Lounge*'s sheer size and complexity set it apart. The stage requires 56 trucks to haul from city to city. Because the set takes four days to build, three stages leapfrog each other around the US. Overseas, the stage will be ferried in two 747 cargo jets and a Russian military cargo plane.

True to 'virtual' form, Cohl lets his partners handle much of the logistics. To supply the stage, lighting, sound, and other elements of the show, the Stones have contracted with RZO Productions, a company owned by their longtime business manager, Joseph F. Rascoff. (Rascoff and Cohl both answer to Prince Rupert Loewenstein, the band's financial adviser in London.) Rascoff, who is a Wharton graduate, employs a team of 200 stagehands, and lighting and sound technicians, plus scores of labourers hired for the individual venues. With labour costs of up to $300,000 per city, Rascoff uses a network of portable computers and fax machines to track costs: 'We have as sophisticated a budget operation as any company,' he says.

As in any virtual corporation the partners succeed individually by succeeding together. Cohl guarantees the band an estimated $85 million, both to cover expenses and as base salary. But after the tour breaks even, he and the Stones stand to make even more money. Perhaps that's why the Stones, particularly

Jagger, immerse themselves in the business of *Voodoo Lounge*. Cohl and Rascoff both consult them on issues such as merchandise and concert dates. The Stones also act as brand managers: 'They understand better than anyone what it means to be a Rolling Stone,' says Cohl, 'and how that name should be used and treated.'[10]

What are the implications for marketing of the apparent increase in hybrid forms of organization ranging from relationships to alliances to networks and spiders' webs to virtual corporations? Clearly, marketing is increasingly a matter of managing the networks and relationships that encompass supplier partnerships, deep customer linkages and cooperative alliances with other companies in an industry. An individual implication, which redefines the task and required expertise of the marketing manager, is that working in networks demands an increased understanding of negotiation processes and skills in forming and maintaining alliances. At a 'design' level, these trends imply that the marketing manager will have to deal more frequently with calculating the relative gains from different ways of organizing the market relationship. The manager will also have to face the risk that miscalculation can carry very heavy costs where competitors, with a more entrepreneurial mindset, design their delivery systems in novel and surprising ways that provide lower cost and/or higher value to customers.

The old dilemma of make-or-buy – do I do it myself through integration or do I get someone else to do it for me? – is being recast as make-buy-or-partner. The latter is a much more complex question that now recurs with increasing frequency. The logic of transaction costs is one of the best design guides for the marketing manager in assessing the available options – through which mechanism are the costs of conducting the transaction minimized and how do these costs change through time? Williamson has suggested that an organization is a 'nexus of contracts'. How the necessary contracting is to be organized is a question that must occupy a great deal of the attention of the marketer interested in sustaining market focus and promoting effective renewal.[11]

The 'green' challenge

One of the central challenges to firms for the late 1990s and one of the sources of real market opportunity is to respond to the demands for environmental protection – the 'green' challenge. Business systems are being driven to become either partial loops or complete closed loops which deal with the waste and after-effects of the activities of the industry. The paper industry has already adjusted to recovering and recycling much of its used or waste product. As a result the demand on timber resources is reduced and the problem of disposing of discarded paper and paper products is lessened. In 1991 BMW launched a new range of cars with an advertising theme that stressed that 80 per cent of the car was recyclable and that the company was committed to raising this proportion to 90 per cent. Products and services that may be recycled and that do not damage the environment are among the commercial winners of the decade and the criterion of environmental friendliness has become an important one for an increasing number of consumers as they make purchasing decisions. Similarly, in business-to-business marketing, firms increasingly insist on supplier adherence to codes of practice that are environmentally friendly. In most instances this is becoming less a matter of choice and more one of necessity as national and international laws and regulations demand environmentally safe services, products and processes.

The opportunities that arise from this change in markets are many. Companies that respond early and well to market demand can clearly establish significant competitive advantage over their slower-moving competitors. Those who treat environmental protection as a market in itself also face real opportunities to create new businessess and products and services. Services such as environmental engineering consultancy are growing. Products and technologies that treat harmful waste and allow it to be neutralized and/or recycled are in demand. Businesses that demanufacture and recycle used products face growing demand.

Exhibit 21.2 describes 'design for disassembly' – simplifying parts and materials and making them easy and inexpensive to snap apart, sort, and recycle – in car manufacturing at BMW using recyclable thermoplastic supplied by GE Plastics, a division of General Motors. GE Plastics, in fact, already has buy-back deals for thermoplastic with a number of car and computer companies. It reprocesses the material and sells it back to the manufacturer, competing with Dow Chemical, Du Pont, Hoechst Celanese, and other suppliers of virgin plastics.

One surprise coming from the BMW experience is the rediscovery of repairability. In a throwback to the Tin Lizzies of the 1930s, when cars and everything else were built to be repaired, design for disassembly allows cars to be worked on faster and easier. Put in a wider context, the throwaway society is having a rethink about itself. The green revolution is therefore a very special and exciting challenge and presents marketers everywhere with the opportunity to build new sources of competitive advantage and to develop new kinds of services, products and technologies. The interface between marketing and design becomes ever more important in this context.

People, shared values and the learning organization

It is only because of people that market focus is achieved and sustained. The choice of markets, competitive strategy and resource management required is done by and through people. Since this is true at the level of the obvious, it should equally be a truism to state that the creation and management of the human resource base of the company are the ultimate key to market focus. But somehow this assertion is less likely to be viewed as a truism – as long as one is in debate with Western managers. To a typical Japanese manager the assertion is likely to be viewed as self-evident.

If people, or human resources in technical jargon, are viewed as the central resource then our attitudes as managers to recruitment, selection, enculturation, development, appraisal, communication and decision-making are likely to have a fundamental impact on doing business successfully. In order to achieve and sustain market focus an organization needs people from top to bottom who share a commitment to the essential ideas of focus and who are empowered to carry out their individual tasks in a manner that is consistent with the goal of focus. This lies at the heart of the notion of internal marketing. It is best achieved through people who are well suited to the tasks they are assigned and whose behaviour is influenced not just by the necessary bureaucratic rules of procedure and good practice and whose motivation is sought not just through market mechanisms of payment for performance but also through those clan mechanisms which draw on shared values concerning the company and its customers. Shared values built around a dynamic notion of focus are probably the best guarantee of long-run competitiveness as well as the best proof against success turning to excess.

Waterman, Peters and Phillips note that shared values 'are the fundamental ideas around which a business is built. They are its main values. But they are more as well. They are the broad notions of future direction that the top management team wants to infuse throughout the organisation. They are the way in which the team wants to express itself, to leave its own mark.'[12]

The merit of shared values is that while they provide a sense of overarching direction and commitment, they are also open to reasonable interpretation and reinterpretation by the members of an organization. This is what distinguishes them from rules or goals. And this openness gives them the loose–tight property discussed earlier in this chapter. Values are loose in so far as people in a company can discover novel ways of pursuing valued ends. They are tight in so far as they dictate what is unacceptable. Values are essential to all aspects of the self-renewing organization – the loose–tight or differentiated–integrated structure as well as the distribution of power and the mix of human resource practices. An organization of this form is necessarily infused with values that lead to strategies of both innovation and efficiency, high perceived value and low delivered cost.

The people in an organization of this self-renewing character are committed to learning (to be innovative) and to striving (to be efficient) and develop a strong, satisfying and motivating sense of group membership in pursuing these ends. In an era in which the limitations of hierarchy have been brought into sharp focus, we find ourselves designing and working in companies that emphasize horizontal processes and flatter structures. The traditional emphasis on function is being counterbalanced by a renewed emphasis on process. These new forms have radical implications. It means that learning becomes the axial principle of organizations and replaces control as a fundamental job of management.[13]

The people in 'post-hierarchical' companies are empowered to learn and to take action about their work in ways that might be inconceivable in a traditional setting. As one of the advocates of business re-engineering notes, 'In the future executive positions will not be defined in terms of collections of people, like head of the sales department, but in terms of process, like senior-VP-of-getting-stuff-to-customers, which is sales, shipping, billing. You'll no longer have a box on an organization chart. You'll own part of a process map.'[14] However, the learning adaptive organization is no new creation. There are many long-established companies that have already 'written the book' on learning and adaptation – it is one of the great tragedies of management studies that their histories are so little read. The Bata Shoe Organization was founded over one hundred years ago in the Moravian village of Zlin in today's Czech Republic. This company is a world leader in shoe production with operations in over 75 countries which has lived through the break-up of the Austro-Hungarian Empire, World War II, communist takeover, nationalization and subsequent privatization of companies in Africa, Asia and Latin America and numerous civil wars. But through this staggering record of turmoil it has preserved its integrity and its ability to survive and prosper in the most extraordinary way thanks to leadership, important shared values and evolving structural arrangements.[15]

The market-focused firm

The new emphases on process as well as function, on heterarchy as well as hierarchy, on learning and reinvention, on cooperating and negotiating, on redesigning and re-engineering business systems and on empowerment and shared values give a deep underlying rationale to the business system view of marketing that has been central to this book. Business systems, whether macro or micro, are process-based views of industries, markets and competing companies, and encourage managers to think laterally, to redesign, to search for alliances and to empower those who perform the interdependent activities in any micro business system.

The market-focused company views the management of the four marketing processes as an on-going looped activity. The central idea of market focus involves persistent attention to the dynamics of the macro business system – its suppliers, customers, rivals, technologies – so that the company may focus and refocus its particular micro business system, align its resources and capitalize on the ensuing opportunity so as continually to deliver a valued product or service at acceptable cost. It relentlessly scrutinizes and understands the dynamics of the macro business system, in order to configure in turn its own micro business system – and, if it is lucky and imaginative enough, to reinvent the macro business system to its advantage. Commitment to this as an underlying approach to business is at the heart of managing marketing. It results in creatively matching arenas of market need with unique company competences through durable profitable relationships.

REVIEW QUESTIONS

23.1 Consider how each of the four marketing processes contributes to efficiency and effectiveness in a firm.
23.2 What is meant by balancing integration and differentiation as well as vertical power structure in an organization? How might this balance vary in the case of a firm marketing multinationally?
23.3 Why do some companies lose impetus in their performance and surrender to competitive decline?
23.4 Describe some newly evolving 'hybrid' forms of market organization and how these are affecting the work and skills of the marketing manager.
23.5 What opportunities are offered by the 'green' revolution?
23.6 Shared values are key as is the process of learning in an organization. Discuss.

Notes

Chapter 1 **Market focus**

1 E.J. McCarthy and W.D. Perreault (1990), *Basic Marketing: A managerial approach*, 10th edn (Irwin, Boston) p. 5.
2 Peter Drucker (1983), *Managing for Results* (Heinemann, London).
3 M. Hammer and J. Champey (1993), *Reengineering the Corporation: A manifesto for business revolution* (Brealey, London).
4 P. Kotler and G. Armstrong (1991), *The Principles of Marketing*, 5th edn (Prentice Hall, Englewood Cliffs, NJ), p. 20.
5 P. Kotler and G. Armstrong (1991), *The Principles of Marketing*, 5th edn (Prentice Hall, Englewood Cliffs, NJ), p. 5.
6 Derek Abell (1980), *Defining the Business: The starting point of strategic planning* (Prentice Hall, Englewood Cliffs, NJ).
7 George Day (1984), *Strategic Market Planning* (West Publishing Company, St Paul).
8 George Day (1986), *Analysis for Strategic Market Decisions* (West Publishing Company, St Paul).
9 David Aaker (1992), *Strategic Market Planning*, 3rd edn (Wiley, New York).
10 G. Hamel and C.K. Prahalad (1990), 'The core competence of the corporation', *Harvard Business Review*, May–June.
11 G. Hamel and C.K. Prahalad (1994), *Competing for the Future* (Harvard Business School Press, Cambridge, Mass.).
12 P. Kotler (1991), 'From transactions to relationships to networks', paper to the trustees of the Marketing Science Institute, Boston, November.
13 Tom Peters (1987), *Thriving on Chaos* (Macmillan, Basingstoke), p. 91.
14 J.A. Murray and A. O'Driscoll (1993), *Managing Marketing: Concepts and Irish cases* (Gill & Macmillan, Dublin), pp. 16–17.

Chapter 2 **Marketing contexts**

1 O.E. Williamson (1975), *Markets and Hierarchies: Analysis and antitrust implications* (The Free Press, New York).

2 O.E. Williamson (1985), *The Economic Institutions of Capitalism* (The Free Press, New York).

3 M. Hammer and J. Champey (1993), *Reengineering the Corporation: A manifesto for business revolution* (Brealey, London), p. 4.

4 *Ibid.*, p. 28.

5 Thomas Stewart (1992), 'The search for the organisation of tomorrow', *Fortune*, 18 May.

6 J. Weiner (1994), *The Beak of the Finch* (Cape, London).

7 L. Hrebiniak and W.F. Joyce (1985), 'Organisational adaptation: strategy choice and environmental determinism', *Administrative Science Quarterly*, vol. 30, pp. 336–49.

8 Michael Porter (1980), *Competitive Strategy: Techniques for analyzing industries and competitors* (The Free Press, New York).

9 G. Hamel and C.K. Prahalad (1994), *Competing for the Future* (Harvard Business School Press, Cambridge, Mass.).

10 P. Doyle (1994), *Marketing Management and Strategy* (Prentice Hall, Hemel Hempstead), p. 38.

11 E.J. McCarthy and W.D. Perreault (1990), *Basic Marketing: A managerial approach*, 10th edn (Irwin, Boston), p. 10.

Chapter 3 **The business system**

1 O.E. Williamson (1985), *The Economic Institutions of Capitalism* (The Free Press, New York).

2 B.J. Pine, B. Victor and A.C. Boynton (1993), 'Making mass customisation work', *Harvard Business Review*, September–October, pp. 108–19.

3 R. Westbrook and P. Williamson (1993), 'Mass customisation: Japan's new frontier', *European Management Journal*, vol. 11, no. 1, pp. 38–45.

4 Michael Porter (1985), *Competitive Advantage* (The Free Press, New York), ch. 2.

5 T.H. Davenport (1993), *Process Innovation* (Harvard Business School Press, Cambridge, Mass.), p. 5.

6 B.P. Shapiro, J.J. Sviokla and V.K. Rangan (1991), 'Manage orders, satisfy customers, make money', working paper no. 9–591–098 (Harvard Business School, Boston).

7 J.F. Rockart and J.E. Short (1988), 'Information technology and the new organisation', Working Paper CISR 180, MIT Sloan School of Management, Centre for Information Systems Research, September.

8 Davenport (1993), *op cit.*, p. 28.

9 R.B. Kaplan and L. Murdock (1991), 'Core process redesign', *The McKinsey Quarterly*, no. 2.

10 Davenport (1993), *op cit.*, pp. 243–50.

Chapter 4 **Strategy and process**

1 Michael Porter (1980), *Competitive Strategies; Techniques for analyzing industries and competitors* (The Free Press, New York).

2 X. Gilbert and P.J. Strebel (1989), 'From innovation to outpacing', *Business Quarterly*, Summer.

3 X. Gilbert and P.J. Strebel (1989), 'Taking advantage of industry shifts', *European Management Journal*, December.

4 S. Vandermerwe and M. Trishoff (1991), 'SKF Bearings: market orientation through services', IMD, Switzerland, Case No. M–383.

5 R.D. Buzzell and B.T. Gale (1987), *The PIMS Principles* (Free Press, New York).

6 George S. Day (1977), 'Diagnosing the product portfolio', *Journal of Marketing*, vol. 41, no. 2, pp. 29–38.

7 Henry Mintzberg (1987), 'Crafting strategy', *Harvard Business Review*, July–August.

8 L.K. Wright (1995), 'Avoiding services marketing myopia', in J. Barnes and L. Glynn (eds.), *Understanding Services Management* (Oaktree Press, Dublin).

9 T.S. Kuhn (1970), *The Structure of Scientific Revolutions* (University of Chicago Press, Chicago).

10 R.B. Chase and D. Garvin (1989), 'The service factory', *Harvard Business Review*, July–August, pp. 61–76.

Chapter 5 **The job of the marketing manager**

1 R.B. Kaplan and L. Murdock (1991), 'Core process redesign', *The McKinsey Quarterly*, no. 2, pp. 32–5.

2 J.A. Murray and A. O'Driscoll (1993), *Managing Marketing: Concepts and Irish cases* (Gill & Macmillan, Dublin), pp. 42–3.

3 F.A. Maljers (1992), 'Inside Unilever: the evolving transnational company', *Harvard Business Review*, Sept.–Oct., p. 49.

Chapter 6 **Understanding the customer**

1 F.M. Nicosia (1966), *Consumer Decision Processes* (Prentice Hall, Englewood Cliffs, NJ).

2 J.F. Engel, R.D. Blackwell and P.W. Miniard (1990), *Consumer Behavior*, 6th edn (Dryden Press, Chicago) (1st edn published 1968).

3 J.A. Howard and J.N. Sheth (1969), *The Theory of Buyer Behavior* (Wiley, New York).

4 F. Webster and Y. Wind (1972), *Organizational Buyer Behavior* (Prentice Hall, Englewood Cliffs, NJ).

5 J.N. Sheth (1973), 'A model of industrial buyer behaviour', *Journal of Marketing*, vol. 37, no. 4.

6 H. Hakansson (ed.) (1982), *International Marketing and Purchasing of Industrial Goods* (Wiley, New York).

7 *Market Focus Review* (1993), 'ICI plc', May, pp. 4–5.

8 Darach Turley (1994), 'The senior market: opportunity or oxymoron', *Irish Marketing Review*, vol. 7, pp. 16–30.

9 J.-P. Jeannet and H.D. Hennessey (1995), *Global Marketing Strategies*, 3rd edn, (Houghton Mifflin, Boston), p. 810.

Chapter 7 **Measuring the market**

1 R.D. Buzzell and B.T. Gale (1987), *The PIMS Principles* (Free Press, New York).
2 D.J. Ravenscraft (1983), 'Structure–profit relationships at the line-of-business and industry level', *Review of Economics and Statistics*, February, pp. 22–31.
3 P. Kotler (1991), *Marketing Management: Analysis, planning implementation and control*, 7th. edn, (Prentice Hall, Englewood Cliffs, NJ), chs 4 and 9.
4 T.S. Tull and D.I. Hawkins (1990), *Marketing Research: Measurement and methods*, 3rd edn (Macmillan, New York).
5 *Business Week* (1994), 'Database marketing: a potent new tool for selling', 5 September.

Chapter 8 **Analyzing competition and industry structure**

1 G. Hamel and C.K. Prahalad, 'Corporate imagination and expeditionary marketing', *Harvard Business Review*, July–August 1991, pp. 81–92.
2 Michael Porter (1980), *Competitive Strategy: Techniques for analyzing industries and competitors* (The Free Press, New York), ch. 9.
3 *Ibid.*, ch. 1.
4 *The Irish Times* (1995), 'Old masters on the Internet', 18 January.

Chapter 9 **Assessing company capability**

1 G. Hamel and C.K. Prahalad (1990), 'The core competence of the corporation', *Harvard Business Review*, May–June, pp. 74–93.
2 Theodore Levitt (1975), 'Marketing myopia', *Harvard Business Review*, Sept.–Oct.
3 G. Hamel and C.K. Prahalad (1989), 'Strategic intent', *Harvard Business Review*, May–June, pp. 63–76.
4 G. Hamel and C.K. Prahalad (1994), *Competing for the Future* (Harvard Business School Press, Cambridge, Mass.).
5 R. Grant (1991), 'The resource-based theory of the firm', *California Management Review*, vol. 33, no. 3, pp. 114–34.
6 J.B. Barney (1991), 'Firm resources and sustained competitive advantage', *Journal of Management*, vol. 17, no. 1, pp. 99–120.
7 M. Peteraf (1993), 'The cornerstones of competitive advantage: a resource-based view', *Strategic Management Journal*, vol. 14, no. 3, pp. 179–92.
8 R. Rumelt (1991), 'How much does industry matter?', *Strategic Management Journal*, vol. 12, no. 3, March, pp. 168–82.
9 C. Baden-Fuller and J.M. Stopford (1992), *Rejuvenating the Mature Business: The competitive challenge* (Routledge, London), ch. 2.
10 Charles Baden-Fuller and John M. Stopford (1992), *Rejuvenating the Mature Business: The competitive challenge* (Routledge, London), pp. 31–4.

Chapter 10 **Convergence, divergence and pan-Europeanism**

1 E.G. Friberg (1989), '1992: moves Europeans are making', *Harvard Business Review*, vol. 67, May–June, pp. 85–9.

2 D. Aron (1990), 'Where are the Americans?', *Industry Week*, vol. 239, 19 February, pp. 67–9.

3 JETRO (1992), *Handy Facts on EC–Japan Economic Relations*, Tokyo.

4 R. Abravanel and D. Ernst (1992), 'Alliance and acquisition strategies for European national champions', *McKinsey Quarterly*, vol. 2, pp. 44–62.

5 Harvard Business School (1991), *Citibank (A): European Strategy*, 9–392–021 (Boston, Mass.).

6 J.A. Quelch, R.D. Buzzell and E.R. Salama (1990), *The Marketing Challenge of 1992* (Addison-Wesley, Reading, Mass.).

7 J. Fahy (1992), 'Competition in the New Europe: perspectives from the structural analysis of industries', Association for Global Business, Annual Proceedings, pp. 236–44.

8 *Ibid.*

9 C.W.F. Baden-Fuller and J. Stopford (1991), 'Globalisation frustrated: the case of white goods', *Strategic Management Journal*, vol. 12, pp. 493–507.

10 W. Echikson (1993), 'Learning how to sell in Europe', *Fortune*, vol. 128, no. 6, 20 September, pp. 44–5.

11 IMD (1993), *The World Paint Industry* (IMD, Lausanne, Switzerland).

12 G. Guido (1992), 'What US marketers should consider in planning a pan-European approach', *Journal of Consumer Marketing*, vol. 9, no. 2, pp. 29–33.

13 S. Vandermerwe and M.A. L'Huillier (1989), 'Euro-consumers in 1992', *Business Horizons*, vol. 32, no. 1, pp. 34–40.

14 IMD (1993), *op. cit.*

15 *Financial Times* (1994), 'Washing whiter proves a murky business', 21 December, p. 8.

16 T. Levitt (1983), 'The globalization of markets', *Harvard Business Review*, vol. 61, May–June, pp. 92–102.

17 K. Kashani (1992), *Managing Global Marketing* (PWS-Kent, Boston, Mass.).

18 *Euromonitor* (1992), *European Marketing Data & Statistics*.

19 *Ibid.*

20 R. Abravanel and D. Ernst (1992), 'Alliance and acquisition strategies for European national champions', *McKinsey Quarterly*, vol. 2, pp. 44–62.

21 R.Z. Sorenson and U.E. Weichmann (1975), 'How multinationals view marketing mix standardisation', *Harvard Business Review*, vol. 53, May–June, pp. 38–56.

22 J.M. Whitelock (1987), 'Global marketing and the case for international product standardisation', *European Journal of Marketing*, vol. 21, no. 9, pp. 32–44.

23 J. Reichel (1989), 'How can marketing be successfully standardised for the European Market?', *European Journal of Marketing*, vol. 23, no. 7, pp. 60–7.

24 H. Reisenbeck and A. Freeling (1991), 'How global are global brands?', *McKinsey Quarterly*, vol. 4, pp. 3–18.
25 S. Daser and D.P. Hylton (1991), 'European Community Single Market of 1992: European executives discuss trends for global marketing', *International Marketing Review*, vol. 8, no. 5, pp. 44–8.
26 C.A. Bartlett and S. Ghoshal (1989), *Managing Across Borders: The transnational solution* (Harvard Business School Press, Boston, Mass.).

Chapter 11 **Strategic market choice**

1 D.F. Abell (1980), *Defining the Business: The starting point of strategic planning* (Prentice Hall, Englewood Cliffs, NJ).
2 George Day (1990), *Market Driven Strategy: Processes for creating value* (Free Press, New York).
3 AGB Home Audit (1988).
4 Charles Baden-Fuller and John M. Stopford (1992), *Rejuvenating the Mature Business: The competitive challenge* (Routledge, London), pp. 19–22.
5 Michael Porter (1980), *Competitive Strategy: Techniques for analyzing industries and competitors* (Free Press, New York).
6 G.S. Yip (1982), *Barriers to Entry: A corporate strategy perspective* (Lexington Books, Lexington, Mass.).
7 R.D. Buzzell and B.T. Gale (1987), *The PIMS Principles* (Free Press, New York).
8 W.T. Robinson and C. Fornell (1985), 'The sources of market pioneer advantages in consumer goods industries', *Journal of Marketing Research*, vol. 22, no. 3, pp. 305–17.
9 M. Lambkin (1989), 'Timing market entry: a key to competitive success', *Irish Marketing Review*, vol. 4, no. 2, pp. 42–53.
10 K. Ohmae (1992), *The Mind of the Strategist: The art of Japanese business* (McGraw-Hill, New York), ch. 11.

Chapter 12 **Managing strategy**

1 H. Mintzberg (1990), 'The design school: reconsidering the basic premises of strategic management', *Strategic Management Journal*, March, pp. 171–95.
2 H.I. Ansoff (1991), 'Critique of Henry Mintzberg's "The design school: reconsidering the basic premises of strategic management"', *Strategic Management Journal*, September, pp. 449–61.
3 H. Mintzberg (1991), 'Learning 1, planning 0: reply to Igor Ansoff', *Strategic Management Journal*, September, pp. 463–6.
4 K.R. Andrews (1987), *The Concept of Corporate Strategy*, 3rd edn (Irwin, Homewood, Ill.).
5 B.S. Chakravarthy and P. Lorange (1991), *Managing the Strategy Process: A framework for the multibusiness firm* (Prentice Hall, Englewood Cliffs, NJ).
6 H. Mintzberg (1994) *The Rise and Fall of Strategic Planning* (Prentice Hall, Hemel Hempstead).

7 P.M. Senge (1990), *The Fifth Discipline: the art and practice of the learning organisation* (Century Business, London), p. 299.
8 R.T. Pascale (1984), 'Perspectives on strategy: the real story behind Honda's success', *California Management Review*, Spring, pp. 47–72.
9 Senge (1990), *op. cit.*, pp. 293–4.
10 G.S. Day (1990), *Market Driven Strategy: Processes for creating value* (Free Press, New York).
11 *The Economist* (1994), 'Furnishing the world', 19 November, pp. 83–4.

Chapter 13 **Organizing and integrating**

1 Alfred D. Chandler, Jr (1962), *Strategy and Structure* (The MIT Press, Cambridge, Mass.).
2 T. Burns and G.M. Stalker (1961), *The Management of Innovation* (Tavistock Publications, London).
3 *The Economist* (1994), 'Death of the brand manager', 9 April, pp. 71–2.
4 McKinsey & Company (1994), *Marketers' Metamorphosis* (McKinsey & Co., New York).
5 M. George, A. Freeling and D. Court (1994), 'Reinventing the marketing organisation', *The McKinsey Quarterly*, no. 4, pp. 43–62.
6 J.R. Katzenbach and D.K. Smith (1993), *The Wisdom of Teams* (Harvard Business School Press, Cambridge, Mass.).
7 James G. Barnes (1989), 'The role of internal marketing: if the staff won't buy it, why should the customer?', *Irish Marketing Review*, vol. 4, no. 2.
8 Nigel Piercy and Neil Morgan (1990), 'Internal marketing: the missing half of the marketing programme', *Long Range Planning*, vol. 24, no. 2, pp. 82–93.
9 J.-P. Jeannet and H.D. Hennessey (1995), *Global Marketing Strategies*, 3rd edn (Houghton Mifflin, Boston), ch. 9.
10 C.A. Bartlett and S. Ghoshal (1989), *Managing Across Borders: The transnational solution* (Harvard Business School Press, Cambridge, Mass.).

Chapter 14 **Competitive positioning**

1 D. Aaker and G. Day (1990), *Marketing Research*, 4th edn (Wiley, Chichester).
2 Redmond O'Donoghue (1994), 'Marquis by Waterford: creating a new international brand', *Irish Marketing Review*, vol. 7, pp. 31–7.
3 A. Brown (1994), 'Better suited for good business', *International Management*, September, pp. 34–7.

Chapter 15 **Product choice**

1 E.J. McCarthy and W.D. Perreault (1990), *Basic Marketing: A managerial approach*, 10th edn (Irwin, Boston).
2 Y. Wind (1982), *Product Policy: Concepts, methods and strategy* (Addison-Wesley, Reading, Mass.).

3 B.D. Gardner and S.J. Levy (1955), 'The product and the brand', *Harvard Business Review*, March–April, pp. 33–9.
4 S. Parkinson *et al.* (1994), 'España: an international tourist brand', *Irish Marketing Review*, vol. 7, pp. 54–64.
5 J. Fanning (1995), 'Branding: regaining the initiative', *Irish Marketing Review*, vol. 8, pp. 21–31.
6 D. Aaker (1992), *Managing Brand Equity* (Macmillan, Toronto).
7 C. Macrae, S. Parkinson and J. Sheerman (1995), 'Managing marketing's DNA: the role of branding', *Irish Marketing Review*, vol. 8, pp. 13–20.

Chapter 16 **Pricing**

1 *The Economist* (1991), 'What price glory?', 24 August.
2 M.V. Marn and R.L. Rosiello (1992), 'Managing price, gaining profit', *Harvard Business Review*, Sept.–Oct.
3 A.E. Serwer (1994), 'How to escape a price war', *Fortune*, 13 June, pp. 47–51.
4 R.A. Garda and M.V. Marn (1993), 'Price wars', *The McKinsey Quarterly*, no. 3, pp. 87–100.
5 J. Sasseen (1993), 'Tyre makers on the rack', *International Management*, March, pp. 40–3.

Chapter 17 **Communication and selling**

1 Robert D. Buzzell, John A. Quelch and Walter J. Salmon (1990), 'The costly bargain of trade promotion', *Harvard Business Review*, March–April, pp. 141–9.
2 Tony Meenaghan and Caolan Mannion (1994), 'The changing face of marketing communications', in M. Lambkin and T. Meenaghan (eds), *Perspectives on Marketing Management in Ireland* (Oaktree Press, Dublin).
3 *The Irish Times* (1991), 3 December.
4 M. Christopher, A. Payne, and D. Ballantyne (1991), *Relationship Marketing* (Butterworth-Heinemann, Oxford).
5 Tom Peters (1987), *Thriving on Chaos* (Macmillan, Basingstoke), p. 91.
6 F.F. Reichheld (1993), 'Loyalty-based management', *Harvard Business Review*, March–April, pp. 64–73.
7 F.F. Reichheld and W.E. Sasser (1990), 'Zero defections: quality comes to services', *Harvard Business Review*, Sept.–Oct., pp. 105–11.
8 James G. Barnes (1995), 'Establishing relationships – getting closer to the customer may be more difficult than you think', *Irish Marketing Review*, vol. 8, pp. 107–16.

Chapter 18 **Distribution**

1 C. Lovelock (1994), *Product Plus: How Product + Service = Competitive Advantage* (McGraw-Hill, New York), ch. 6.

2 S. Garvey and S. Torres (1993), 'Winning success in aquaculture marketing', *Irish Marketing Review*, vol. 6, pp. 5–12.
3 Alan West (1989), *Managing Distribution and Change – The total distribution concept* (Wiley, Chichester).
4 Martin Christopher (1992), *Distribution and Supply Chain Logistics* (Pitman, London).

Chapter 19 **Managing performance**

1 R.S. Kaplan and D.P. Norton (1992), 'The balanced scorecard – measures that drive performance', *Harvard Business Review*, Jan.–Feb., pp. 71–9.
2 R.S. Kaplan and D.P. Norton (1993), 'Putting the balanced scorecard to work', *Harvard Business Review*, Sept.–Oct., p. 134.
3 F.F. Reichheld and W.E. Sasser (1990), 'Zero defections: quality comes to services', *Harvard Business Review*, Sept.–Oct., pp. 105–11.
4 P.F. Drucker (1994), 'The theory of the business', *Harvard Business Review*, Sept.–Oct., pp. 95–104.
5 B.P. Shapiro, V.K. Rangan and J.J. Sviokla (1992), 'Staple yourself to an order', *Harvard Business Review*, July–August, pp. 113–22.
6 B.S. Chakravarthy and P. Lorange (1991), *Managing the Strategy Process: A framework for the multibusiness firm* (Prentice Hall, Englewood Cliffs, NJ).
7 J. Maximov and H. Gottschlich (1993), 'Time–cost–quality leadership: New ways to gain a sustainable competitive advantage in retailing', *International Journal of Retail and Distribution Management*, vol. 21, no, 4, pp. 3–13.

Chapter 20 **New product development**

1 C. Merle Crawford (1987), *New Product Management*, 2nd edn (Irwin, Homewood, Ill.), p. 21.
2 Booze, Allen and Hamilton (1982), *New Product Management for the 1980s* (Booze, Allen and Hamilton, New York).
3 R.T. Hise, A. Parasuraman and R. Viswanathan (1984), 'Product elimination: a neglected managerial responsibility', *Journal of Business Strategy*, Spring.
4 R. Duke (1991), 'Winning and losing in product innovation: a case history', *Irish Marketing Review*, vol. 5, no. 1, pp. 11–19.
5 C. Lorenz (1987), 'Scrum and scrabble – the Japanese style', *Financial Times*, 19 June, p. 19.
6 Peugeot case, in G. Johnson and K. Scholes (1994), *Exploring Corporate Strategy* (Prentice Hall, Hemel Hempstead).
7 Peugeot case in Johnson and Scholes (1994), *ibid.*
8 K.B. Clark and T. Fujimoto (1991), *Product Development Performance* (Harvard Business School Press, Cambridge, Mass.).
9 *Financial Times* (1992), 'From design studio to new car showroom', 11 May, p. 15.
10 P. Kotler (1991), *Marketing Management: Analysis, planning, implementation, and control*, 7th edn (Prentice Hall, Englewood Cliffs, NJ), pp. 297–301.

11 *Business Week* (1993), 'Flops – why too many new products fail', 16 August, pp. 33–40.
12 Mark Watson (1993), 'Quick response as a competitive tool: Thermo King Europe's SMX', *Irish Marketing Review*, vol. 6, pp. 38–44.
13 G. Hamel and C.K. Prahalad (1991), 'Corporate imagination and expeditionary marketing', *Harvard Business Review*, July–August, pp. 81–92.
14 *Aviation Week & Space Technology* (1994), 'Europeans to unite aeronautics efforts', 7 November, pp. 24–5.

Chapter 21 **Design as strategy**

1 P. Kotler and G.A. Rath (1984), 'Design: A powerful but neglected strategic tool', *Journal of Business Strategy*, vol. 5, no. 2.
2 W. Olins (1989), *Corporate Identity*, (Thames and Hudson, London).
3 *Business Week* (1990), 'Design for disassembly', 17 September, pp. 26–9.
4 C. Lorenz (1990), *The Design Dimension* (Blackwell, Oxford).
5 G. Hollins and B. Hollins (1991), *Total Design: Managing the design process in the service sector* (Pitman Publishing, London).
6 *Business Week* (1994), 'Winners: The best American designs of the year', 6 June, pp. 39–52.
7 V. Walsh, *et al.* (1992), *Winning by Design* (Blackwell, Oxford).
8 S. Brown (1995) *Postmodern Marketing* (Routledge, London).

Chapter 22 **Reinventing the business system**

1 G. Hamel and C.K. Prahalad (1989), 'Strategic intent', *Harvard Business Review*, May–June, pp. 63–76.
2 G. Hamel and C.K. Prahalad (1994), *Competing for the Future* (Harvard Business School Press, Cambridge, Mass.).
3 R. Grant (1991), 'The resource based theory of the firm', *California Management Review*, vol. 33, no. 3, pp. 114–34.
4 M. Peteraf (1993), 'The cornerstones of competitive advantage: A resource based view', *Strategic Management Journal*, vol. 14, no. 3, pp. 179–92.
5 C. Baden-Fuller and J.M. Stopford (1992), *Rejuvenating the Mature Business: The competitive challenge* (Routledge, London), ch. 2.
6 R. Rumelt (1991), 'How much does industry matter?', *Strategic Management Journal*, vol. 12, no. 3, March, pp. 168–86.
7 Hamel and Prahalad (1994), *op. cit.*, pp. 21–2.
8 *Ibid.*, p. 64.
9 M. Hammer and J. Champey (1993), *Reengineering the Corporation: A manifesto for business revolution* (Brealey, London), p. 32.
10 T.H. Davenport (1993), *Process Innovation* (Harvard Business School Press, Cambridge, Mass.) pp. 270–1.
11 G. Hall, J. Rosenthall and J. Wade (1993), 'How to make reengineering *really* work', *Harvard Business Review*, Nov.–Dec., pp. 119–33.

12 *Ibid.*, pp. 124–6.
13 *The Economist* (1994), 'Hammer defends reengineering', 5 November, p. 96.
14 T.H. Davenport (1993), *Process Innovation* (Harvard Business School Press, Cambridge, Mass.), p. 275.

Chapter 23 **Renewal and shared values**

1 P.E. Lawrence and D. Dyer (1983), *Renewing American Industry* (Free Press, New York).
2 Thomas J. Peters and Robert H. Waterman (1982), *In Search of Excellence: Lessons from America's best-run companies* (Harper & Row, New York).
3 A. Brown (1994), 'Top of the bosses', *International Management*, April, pp. 26–9.
4 C.A. Bartlett and S. Ghoshal (1989), *Managing Across Borders: The transnational solution* (Harvard Business School Press, Cambridge, Mass.).
5 Peter Doyle (1992), 'What are the excellent companies?', *Journal of Marketing Management*, vol. 8, no. 2.
6 D. Miller (1990), *The Icarus Paradox: How exceptional companies bring about their own downfall* (Harper, New York), p. 3 and *passim*.
7 C. Handy (1994), *The Age of Paradox* (Harvard Business School Press, Cambridge, Mass.), p. 35.
8 J.B. Quinn (1992), *Intelligent Enterprise* (The Free Press, New York), p. 128.
9 *Business Week* (1993), 'The virtual corporation', 8 February, pp. 36–41.
10 *Business Week* (1994), 'It's only rock 'n' roll', 10 October, pp. 42–3.
11 O.E. Williamson (1985), *The Economic Institutions of Capitalism* (Free Press, New York).
12 R. Waterman, T. Peters and S. Phillips (1990), 'Structure is not organisation', *Business Horizons*, June.
13 F. Ostroff and D. Smith (1992), 'The horizontal organisation', *McKinsey Quarterly*, vol. 1.
14 *Fortune* (1992), 'The search for the organisation of tomorrow', 18 May.
15 B. Schofield (1994), 'Building – and rebuilding – a global company', *McKinsey Quarterly*, no. 2, pp. 37–45.

Index